Connectionism and the Mind

D1043920

Connectionism and the Mind

An Introduction to Parallel Processing in Networks

William Bechtel and
Adele Abrahamsen

Basil Blackwell

Copyright © William Bechtel and Adele Abrahamsen 1991

First published 1991

Basil Blackwell, Inc.
3 Cambridge Center
Cambridge, Massachusetts 02142, USA

Basil Blackwell Ltd
108 Cowley Road, Oxford, OX4 1JF, UK

All rights reserved. Except for the quotation of short passages for the purposes of criticism and review, no part of this publication may be reproduced, stored in a retrieval system, or transmitted, in any form or by any means, electronic, mechanical, photocopying, recording or otherwise, without the prior permission of the publisher.

Except in the United States of America, this book is sold subject to the condition that it shall not, by way of trade or otherwise, be lent, re-sold, hired out, or otherwise circulated without the publisher's prior consent in any form of binding or cover other than that in which it is published and without a similar condition including this condition being imposed on the subsequent purchaser.

Library of Congress Cataloging in Publication Data

Bechtel, William.
  Connectionism and the mind: an introduction to parallel
processing in networks/William Bechtel and Adele Abrahamsen.
        p. cm.
  Includes bibliographical references.
  ISBN 0-631-16576-2—ISBN 0-631-16577-0 (pbk.)
  1. Parallel processing (Electronic computers). 2. Computer
      networks.   I. Abrahamsen, Adele A.   II. Title.

QA 76.5.B365 1991   89-18536
004.6—dc20   CIP

British Library Cataloguing in Publication Data
A CIP catalogue record for this book is available from the British Library.

Typeset in 10 on 12 pt Imprint
by Graphicraft Typesetters Ltd, Hong Kong
Printed in Great Britain by T.J. Press Ltd, Padstow, Cornwall

QA
76.5
.B3365
1991

This volume is dedicated to the memory of

Yoda

WITHDRAWN

KELLY LIBRARY
Emory & Henry College
Emory, VA 24327

WITHDRAWN

Contents

Preface

Cognitive science is an interdisciplinary research cluster which emerged from the cognitive revolution that began in the 1960s and matured in the 1970s. Its constituent disciplines, which include artificial intelligence, cognitive psychology, linguistics, and parts of neuroscience, philosophy, and anthropology, have managed an uneasy unity amid diversity, because they have shared certain core assumptions of the symbolic approach to cognition. Cognitive science is still rather young, but already this modicum of unity has been challenged by an alternative theoretical approach that rejects those assumptions.

The new approach is variously referred to using the terms *connectionism*, *parallel distributed processing*, or *neural networks*. (We shall employ the term *connectionism* as it seems most generic.) In keeping with its varied designations, connectionism has a number of central theorists who draw upon widely varying disciplinary backgrounds and advocate somewhat different conceptions of their common cause. Among the major investigators who have stirred interest in connectionism are David Rumelhart, James McClelland, Geoffrey Hinton, James Anderson, Gerald Edelman, Stephen Grossberg, John Hopfield, Teuvo Kohonen, Jerome Feldman and Terrence Sejnowksi.

Our own presentation emphasizes the work of the first three investigators, to whom we owe a considerable debt. One of us (Abrahamsen) was Dave Rumelhart's graduate student at the University of California, San Diego, during the period when he worked with semantic networks rather than connectionist networks. Not everyone has the opportunity to follow the work of their dissertation advisor through not just one, but two, revolutions in their discipline. She is grateful to have benefited from his talents as an advisor, and for the example he has set as a student of cognition. His deep curiosity, innovative approach to theory, and careful but flexible use of research tactics are more than worthy of emulation. Jay McClelland's role in her initiation into connectionism is more limited but nevertheless appreciated: he graciously allowed her to sit in on his research meetings when she was an intermittent visitor at Carnegie Mellon University during the fall of 1987. His energy and creativity, and that of his students as well, made for a very stimulating group. (She is also grateful to David Klahr for making an office and other resources available to her at CMU.) The other of us (Bechtel) co-directed a workshop on connectionist models with Ulric Neisser at Emory University in the summer of 1988. Geoff Hinton gave a first-rate series of lectures during this workshop, and we both benefited immensely from his deep understanding of networks and from his adept handling of the astounding ideas which he comes by so naturally. Dick Neisser did his usual superb job of holding gems of ideas up to the light and examining them for their flaws and unexpected angles. In this workshop he played the role of interested observer, rather than convert to connectionism; however, we see a fit between his own neo-ecological psychology and the future development of networks (as we discuss in chapter 8). There are many other contexts in which we have benefited from his wit and wisdom since we all came to Atlanta in 1983, and we take this opportunity to express our appreciation. Finally, we issue the standard disclaimer: None of these individuals is responsible for any errors that we may have made in presenting their work or ideas in this book; also, our interpretations of connectionist systems and their implications are our own except where we have specifically attributed a position to a particular individual.

This book is intended to provide a wide range of readers with a basic understanding of connectionist networks, and with some appreciation for the conceptual issues that networks raise with respect to our theorizing about the mind. For those with little or no previous exposure to connectionist networks, chapters 2 and 3 are intended as a primer, which can provide sufficient understanding to appreciate new proposals and ongoing arguments about connectionism. (Appendix B offers a glossary which should also be helpful for reference.) Subsequent chapters focus on conceptual issues and implications of connectionism. In particular, chapters 4 and 5 examine pattern recognition and nonpropositional representations of knowledge, respectively, as tasks that are (a) more broadly relevant than is generally acknowledged, and (b) particularly suitable for connectionist modeling. Chapter 6 then presents two connectionist simulations that were designed to model higher mental capabilities in the domains of language (development of past-tense formation) and reasoning (making inferences about kinship relations). Some representatives of the symbolic tradition have made vigorous arguments against the viability of connectionist modeling. In chapter 7 we review two well-known papers in this genre, and then consider three avenues of response on the part of connectionists. Finally, in chapter 8 we explore the implications of connectionism for the various disciplines that compose the cognitive science research cluster.

Connectionist networks are dynamical systems that are described by mathematical equations. To make the mathematics as accessible as possible, we have used a mnemonic notational system and have minimized the amount of detail presented. To provide concrete experience with the functioning of connectionist networks, we have provided a step-by-step guided tour of several running simulations. These simulations have all been run using the software provided with McClelland and Rumelhart's *Explorations in Parallel Distributed Processing: A handbook of models, programs, and exercises* (1988). Versions of the software are available for both the IBM-PC (or compatibles) and the Macintosh. Readers who are attracted to connectionist modeling are advised to explore this software. There is no better way to begin to appreciate the character of connectionist systems than to run some simple simulations, and this software makes it quite easy to do so.

Because we refer so frequently to the three PDP books by David Rumelhart and James McClelland, we use a special set of abbreviations for these books. The two 1986 volumes entitled *Parallel Distributed Processing: Explorations in the Microstructure of Cognition* are composed of 26 chapters, each of which was written by some combination of Rumelhart, McClelland, and the members of the PDP Research Group at UCSD. We refer to these chapters by their authors, date of publication (1986), and by chapter number. For example, chapter 14 (which happens to be in volume 2) is referred to as Rumelhart, Smolensky, McClelland, and Hinton (1986, in *PDP:14*). The third volume, which is the 1988 book described in the preceding paragraph, is referred to as the *Handbook*. The PDP books use more than one notation, and it is somewhat different from ours. Appendix A compares our notation to that of *PDP:2* and *PDP:8*, and also shows schematically at what point in processing each equation is applied.

There are a number of people to whom we are specifically indebted for their help with this project. Four people read the initial draft of the entire manuscript and offered us detailed constructive advice: Lawrence W. Barsalou, Robert N. McCauley, Robert C. Richardson, and Paul R. Thagard. James Garson read and commented on chapters 5, 7, and 8. Each of these individuals offered copious good suggestions, many of which we have incorporated into the publication version of the book. They also provided ideas and interpretations, which we gave up trying to credit individually because they were so numerous. Also, Larry

Barsalou wrote sufficient rude remarks on his copy of the manuscript that we responded by giving increased attention to non-traditional symbolic models in the publication version. We express our deep thanks to these four individuals for their contributions. In addition, much of the material in this book was presented informally to the Cognitive Science Group at Georgia State University, which included James L. Pate, Richard Thompson Putney, Paul Allopenna, David Washburn, Robert Mankoff, and Quinton Gooden. Also, a study group at the University of Cincinnati, consisting of Christopher Gauker, Kelly Hite, Melinda Hogan, William E. Morris, and Robert Richardson, read the manuscript during the fall of 1989. We appreciate the comments made by the members of these groups, which helped to improve the manuscript. We have benefited more generally from discussion of issues explored in this book with a number of individuals, including Richard Billington, Dorrit Billman, and Suge-Yuki Kuroda. Henri Madigan and Britten Poulson provided valuable assistance in collecting bibliographical materials that were used in preparing the text. We also wish to acknowledge a Georgia State University Research Grant which provided computer resources for the simulations presented in this book. Finally, during fall 1989, one of us (Abrahamsen) was a visiting scholar at Skidmore College, and is grateful for the college's support and stimulating discussions with a number of its faculty.

1

Networks versus Symbol Systems: Two Approaches to Modeling Cognition

A Revolution in the Making?

The rise of cognitivism in psychology, which, by the 1970s, had successfully established itself as a successor to behaviorism, has been characterized as a Kuhnian revolution (Baars, 1986). Using Kuhn's (1962/1970) term, the emerging cognitivism offered its own *paradigm*, that is, its way of construing psychological phenomena and its research strategies, both of which clearly distinguished it from behaviorism (for overviews, see Neisser, 1967; Lindsay and Norman, 1972). This change was part of a broader cognitive revolution that not only transformed a number of disciplines such as cognitive and developmental psychology, artificial intelligence, linguistics, and parts of anthropology, philosophy, and neuroscience; it also led to an active cross-disciplinary research cluster known as *cognitive science*. As the cognitive paradigm developed, the idea that cognition involved the manipulation of symbols became increasingly central. These symbols could refer to external phenomena and so have a semantics. They were enduring entities which could be stored in and retrieved from memory and transformed according to rules. The rules that specified how symbols could be composed (syntax) and how they could be transformed were taken to govern cognitive performance. Given the centrality of symbols in this approach, we shall refer to it as the *symbolic paradigm*.

In the 1980s, however, an alternative framework for understanding cognition has emerged in cognitive science, and a case can be made that it is a new Kuhnian (Schneider, 1987). (We shall be using the term *cognition* very broadly to cover a range of mental processing, including not just activities involving reasoning and memory, but also language, perception, and motor control.) This new class of models are variously known as *connectionist, parallel distributed processing* (*PDP*), or *neural network* models. The "bible" of the connectionist enterprise, Rumelhart and McClelland's two volumes entitled *Parallel Distributed Processing* (1986), sold out its first printing prior to publication and sold 30,000 copies in its first year. Clearly connectionism has become the focus of a great deal of attention.

Connectionism can be distinguished from the traditional symbolic paradigm by the fact that it does not construe cognition as involving symbol manipulation. It offers a radically different conception of the basic processing system of the mind–brain. This conception is inspired by our knowledge of the nervous system. The basic idea is that there is a network of elementary *units* or nodes, each of which has some degree of *activation*. These units are *connected* to each other so that active units excite or inhibit other units. The network is a *dynamical system* which, once supplied with initial input, spreads excitations and inhibitions among its units. In some types of network, this process does not stop until a *stable state* is achieved. To understand a connectionist system as performing a cognitive task, it is necessary to supply an interpretation. This is typically done by viewing the initial activations supplied to the system as specifying a problem, and the stable configuration produced at the end of processing as the system's solution to the problem.

Both connectionist and symbolic systems can be viewed as computational systems. But they advance quite different conceptions of what computation involves. In the symbolic approach, computation involves the transformation of symbols according to rules. This is the way we teach computation in arithmetic: we teach rules for performing operations specified by particular symbols (e.g., $+$, $\div$) on other symbols which refer to numbers. When we treat a traditional computer as a symbolic device, we view it as performing symbolic manipulations specified by rules which typically are written in a special data-structure called the *program*. The connectionist view of computation is quite different. It focuses on causal processes by which units excite and inhibit each other and does not provide either for stored symbols or rules that govern their manipulations.

While connectionism has achieved widespread attention only in the 1980s, it is not a newcomer. Network models, which were predecessors of contemporary connectionist models, were developed and widely discussed during the early years of the cognitive revolution in the 1960s. The establishment of the symbolic paradigm as virtually synonymous with cognitive science only occurred at the end of the 1960s, when the symbolic approach promised great success in accounting for cognition and the predecessors of connectionism seemed inadequate to the task. A brief recounting of this early history of network models will provide an introduction to the connectionist approach and to the difficulties which it is thought to encounter. The issues that figured in this early controversy still loom large in contemporary discussions of connectionism and will be discussed extensively in subsequent chapters. (For additional detail see Cowan and Sharp (1988) from which we have largely drawn our historical account, and Anderson and Rosenfeld (1988) which gathers together many of the seminal papers and offers illuminating commentary.)

Forerunners of Connectionism: Pandemonium and Perceptrons

The initial impetus for developing network models of cognitive performance was the recognition that the brain is a network. Obviously, given the complexity of the brain and the limited knowledge available then or now of actual brain functioning, the goal was not to model brain activity in complete detail. Rather, the goal was to model cognitive phenomena in systems that exhibited some of the same basic properties as the network of neurons in the brain. The foundation was laid by Warren McCulloch and Walter Pitts in a paper published in 1943. They proposed a simple model of neuron-like computational units and then demonstrated how these units could perform logical computations. Their "formal neurons" were binary units (i.e., they could either be on or off). Each unit would receive excitatory and inhibitory inputs from certain other units. If a unit received just one inhibitory input, it was forced into the *off* position. If there were no inhibitory inputs, the unit would turn *on* if the sum of the excitatory inputs exceeded its threshold. McCulloch and Pitts showed how configurations of these units could perform the logical operations of AND, OR, and NOT. McCulloch and Pitts further demonstrated that any process that could be performed with a finite number of these logical operations could be performed by a network of such units, and that, if provided with indefinitely large memory capacity, such networks would have the same power as a Universal Turing machine.

The idea captured by Pitts–McCulloch "neurons" was elaborated in a variety of research endeavors in succeeding decades. John von Neumann (1956) showed how such networks could be made more reliable by significantly increasing the number of inputs to each particular unit and determining each unit's activation from the statistical pattern of activations over its input units (e.g., by having a unit turn on if more than half of its inputs were active). In von Neumann's networks each individual unit could be unreliable without sacrificing the reliability of the overall system. Building such redundancy into a network seems to require vastly increasing the number or units, but Winograd and Cowan (1963) developed a procedure whereby a given unit would contribute to the activation decision of several units as well as being affected by several units. This constitutes an early version of what is now referred to as "distributed representation" (see chaper 2).

In addition to formal characterizations of the behavior of these networks, research was also directed to the potential applications of these networks for performing cognitive functions. McCulloch and Pitts' first paper was devoted to determining the logical power of networks, but a subsequent paper (Pitts and McCulloch, 1947) explored how a network could perform pattern-recognition tasks. They were intrigued by the ability of animals and humans to recognize different versions of the same entity even though they might appear quite different. They construed this task as requiring multiple transformations of the input image until a canonical representation was produced, and they proposed two networks that could perform some of the required transformations. Each network received as input a pattern of activation on some of its units. The first network was designed to identify invariant properties of a pattern (properties possessed by a pattern no matter how it was presented), while the second transformed a variant into a standard representation. Because their inspiration came from knowledge of the brain, they presented evidence that the first type of network captured properties of the auditory and visual cortex, while the second captured properties of the superior colliculus in controlling eye movements.

Frank Rosenblatt was one of the major researchers to pursue the problem of pattern recognition in networks. Like Pitts and McCulloch, he worked principally with binary units in layered networks, that is, networks in which one set of units receives inputs from outside and sends excitations and inhibitions to another set of units, which may then send inputs to yet a third group. He also explored networks in which later layers of units might send excitations or inhibitions back to earlier layers. Rosenblatt referred to such systems as *perceptrons* (see figure 1.1). He supplemented McCulloch and Pitts' networks by making the strengths (commonly referred to as the *weights*) of the connections between units continuous rather than binary, and by introducing procedures for changing these weights, enabling the networks to be trained to change their responses. For networks with two layers and connections running only from units in the first layer to

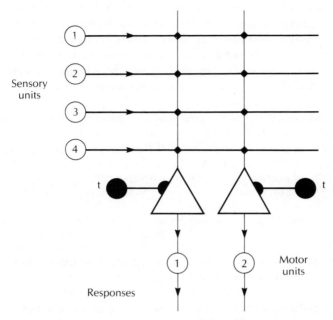

Figure 1.1 An elementary perceptron, as investigated by Rosenblatt (1958). Inputs are supplied on the four sensory units on the left and outputs are produced on the two motor units at the bottom. The horizontal and vertical lines represent connections; the diamonds at their intersections represent synapses whose weights can be modified if incorrect outputs are generated. From J. D. Cowan and D. H. Sharp (1988) Neural nets and artificial intelligence, *Daedalus*, 117, p. 90, Reprinted with permission.

those in the second, Rosenblatt's procedure was to have the network generate, using existing weights, an output for a given input pattern. The weights on connections feeding into any unit that gave what was judged to be an *incorrect* response were changed (those feeding into units giving the correct response were left unaltered). If the unit was off when it should have been on, an increase was made to all weights on connections that had carried any activation to it (i.e., came from units that had been active). Conversely, if the unit was on when it should have been off, these weights were reduced. Rosenblatt demonstrated the important Perceptron Convergence Theorem with respect to this training procedure. The theorem holds that if a set of weights existed that would produce the correct responses to a set of patterns, then through a finite number of repetitions of this training procedure the network would in fact learn to respond correctly (Rosenblatt, 1961; see also Block, 1962).

Rosenblatt emphasized how the perceptron differed from a symbolic processing system. Like von Neumann, he focused on statistical patterns over multiple units (e.g., the proportion of units activated by an input), and viewed noise and variation as essential. He contended that by building a system on statistical rather than logical (Boolean) principles, he had achieved a new type of information processing system:

> It seems clear that the class C' perceptron introduces a new kind of information processing automaton: For the first time, we have a machine which is capable of having original ideas. As an analogue of the biological brain, the perceptron, more precisely, the theory of statistical separability, seems to come closer to meeting the requirements of a functional explanation of the nervous system than any system previously proposed. . . . As a concept, it would seem that the perceptron has established, beyond doubt, the feasibility and principle of non-human systems which may embody human cognitive functions at a level far beyond that which can be achieved through present day automatons. The future of information processing devices which operate on statistical, rather than logical principles seems to be clearly indicated. (Rosenblatt, 1958, p. 449, quoted in Rumelhart and Zipser, 1986, in *PDP:5*, pp. 56–7)

Oliver Selfridge (1959) was another of the early investigators of the pattern recognition capabilities of network models. Unlike Rosenblatt, he assigned a particular interpretation to each of the units in his network. One of the pattern-recognition tasks he explored was recognition of letters, a task that is made difficult by the fact that different people write their letters differently. He called his model *pandemonium*, capturing the fact that his model was composed of *cognitive demons* that performed computations in parallel without attention to one another, and each "shouted out" its judgement of what letter had been presented (see figure 1.2). These cognitive demons each specialized in gathering evidence for one particular letter; the greater the evidence the louder they shouted. The decision demon then made the identification of the letter on the basis of which unit shouted the loudest. The evidence gathered by each cognitive demon was supplied by a lower layer of feature demons. Each feature demon responded if its feature (e.g., a horizontal bar) was present in the image. The feature demon was connected to just those cognitive demons whose letters contained its feature. Thus, a cognitive demon would respond most loudly if all of its features were present in the image, and less loudly if some but not all of its features were present. One of the virtues of this type of network is that it would still make a correct or plausible judgement about a letter even if some of its features were missing or atypical (see Selfridge, 1959; Selfridge and Neisser, 1960).

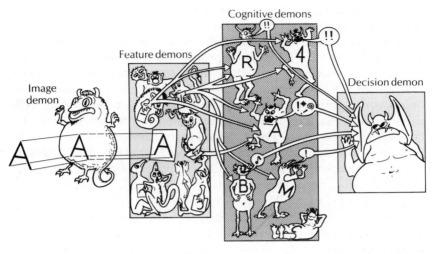

Figure 1.2 Selfridge's pandemonium model. The *demons* at each level beyond the image demon (which merely records the incoming image) extract information from the demons at the preceding level. Thus, a given feature demon responds positively when it detects evidence of its feature in the image, and a cognitive demon responds to the degree that the appropriate feature demons for its letter are active. Finally, the decision demon selects the letter whose cognitive demon is most active. From P. Lindsay and D. A. Norman (1972) *Human Information Processing*, San Francisco: Freeman, p. 116. Reprinted with permission.

Early researchers recognized that, in addition to modeling pattern recognition, networks might be useful as models of how memories were established. In particular, researchers were attracted to the problem of how networks might store associations between different patterns. An extremely influential proposal was developed by Donald Hebb (1949), who suggested that when two neurons in the brain were jointly active, the strength of the connection might be increased. This idea was further developed by Wilfrid Taylor (1956), who explored networks of analog units that took activations within a continuous range (e.g., -1 to $+1$). In the network he proposed, a single set of motor units was connected to two different sets of sensory units (which we shall call the base units and the learning units). The network was set up such that each pattern on the base units was associated with a pattern on the motor units. A different set of patterns was defined for the learning units. No associations to the motor units were specified, but each learning unit pattern was assigned an association with one base unit pattern. When the network was run, the associated sensory patterns were activated at the same time. The eventual outcome was that the learning units acquired the ability to generate the same motor patterns as the base units with which they were associated.

Another researcher who pursued this type of associative memory network was David Marr (1969), who proposed that the cerebellum is such a network which can be trained by the cerebrum to control voluntary movements. The cerebellum consists of five different kinds of cell or unit, with the modifiable connections lying between the granule cells and Purkinje cells. The other cell types serve to set the firing thresholds on these two cell types. The development of connections between the granule cells and Purkinje cells, he proposed, underlay the learning of sequences of voluntary movements in activities like playing the piano. Marr subsequently proposed similar models for the operation of the hippocampus (Marr, 1971) and the neocortex (Marr, 1970).

The early history of network models we have summarized in this section indicates that there was an active research program devoted to exploring the *cognitive* significance of such networks. It is important to emphasize that while some of this research was explicitly directed at modeling the brain, for Rosenblatt and some other researchers the goal was to understand cognitive performance more generally. The relative prominence of research devoted to network models diminished in the late 1960s and early 1970s, as the alternative approach of symbolic modeling became dominant. (Semantic networks, hybrid models that place symbols in network structures, also arose and thrived in the 1970s; as discussed in chapter 4.) In the next two sections we shall examine what made the symbolic approach so attractive to cognitive researchers, and how network research (in the original tradition pioneered by Rosenblatt) declined until rejuvenated in the 1980s. Finally, we shall sketch the relation between the network and symbolic models of the 1980s.

The Allure of Symbol Manipulation

The symbol manipulation view of cognition has several roots. One of these lies in philosophy, in the study of logic. A logical system consists of procedures for manipulating symbols. In propositional logic the symbols are taken to represent propositions or sentences and connectives such as AND and OR. Generally, there is a clear goal in such manipulation. For example, in *deductive logic* we seek a set of rules that will enable us to generate only true propositions as long as we start with true propositions. A system of such rules is spoken of as *truth preserving*. The simple inference rule *modus ponens* is an example of a truth-preserving rule. From one proposition of the form "If p, then q" and another of the form "p," we can infer a proposition of the form "q" (where p and q are placeholders for specific propositions).

We have actually adopted two perspectives in the previous paragraph, and it is the relation between them that makes logic, and systems designed to implement logic, so powerful. From one perspective, we treat the symbols for propositions as representational devices. For example, we conceive of a proposition as depicting a state of affairs that might or might not hold in the world. From this perspective, we speak of a proposition as either *true* (if the proposition corresponds to the way the world is) or *false* (if it does not correspond). This perspective is generally known in logic as a *model theoretic* perspective. We think of a model as a set of entities and identify those propositions as *true* whose ascriptions correspond to the properties that the entities in the model actually possess. Within this framework we can evaluate whether a pattern of inference is such that for any model in which the premises are true, the conclusion will also be true. The second perspective, known as the *proof theoretic* perspective, focuses not on the relations between the propositions and the objects they represent, but simply on the relations among the propositions themselves, construed as formal entities. When we specify inference rules in a logical system, we focus only on the syntax of the symbols and disregard what they refer to. What gives logic its power is, in part, the possibility of integrating these two perspectives, of designing proof procedures that are complete, that is, that will enable us to derive any proposition that will be true in all models in which the premises are true.

The relation between proof theory and model theory gives rise to a very powerful idea. If intelligence depended only upon logical reasoning, for which the goal was truth preservation, then it would be possible to set up formal proof procedures, which will achieve intelligent performance. However, intelligence does not depend solely on being able to make truth-preserving inferences. Sometimes we need to make judgements as to what is likely to be true. This is the domain of inductive logic. The goal of inductive logic is to establish formal rules, analogous to the proof theoretic procedures of deductive logic, that lead from propositions that are true to those that are likely to be true. If such rules can be identified, then we may still be able to set up formal inference procedures that produce intelligent performance.

The crucial assumption in both deductive and inductive logic is that in order to process a symbol, we only need to consider its formal properties. We can disregard its representational function, that is, whether it is true or not, and if true, what state of affairs it describes. Thus, with a formal system, it is often possible to reinterpret the symbols that are used (i.e., assign them a new representational role) without affecting how the symbol processing system itself operates.

The idea that intelligent cognitive processes are essentially processes of logical reasoning has a long history, captured in the long-held view that the rules of logic constitute rules of thought. It is found in authors such as Hobbes, who treated reasoning as itself comparable to mathematical computation and suggested that thinking was simply a process of formal computation:

When a man *reasoneth*, he does nothing else but conceive a sum total, from *addition* of parcels; or conceive a remainder, from *subtraction* of one sum from another; which, if it be done by words, is conceiving of the consequence of the names of all the parts, to the name of the whole; or from the names of the whole and one part, to the name of the other part. . . . These operations are not incident to numbers only, but to all manner of things that can be added together, and taken from one out of another. For as arithmeticians teach to add and subtract in *numbers*; so the geometricians teach the same in *lines, figures*, solid and superficial, *angles, proportions, times*, degrees of *swiftness, force, power*, and the like; the logicians teach the same in *consequences of words*; adding together two *names* to make an *affirmation*, and two *affirmations* to make a *syllogism*; and *many syllogisms* to make a *demonstration*; and from the *sum* or *conclusion* of a syllogism, they subtract one *proposition* to find the other. (Hobbes [1651], 1962, p. 41)

The idea of thinking as logical manipulation of symbols was further developed in the works of rationalists such as Descartes and Leibniz and empiricists such Locke and Hume, all of whom conceived of the symbols as ideas, and formulated rules for properly putting together or taking apart ideas.

With the development of automata theory and physical computers in the mid-twentieth century, there was a burgeoning of more subtle and varied views of symbols and symbol manipulation. From one perspective (well characterized in Haugeland, 1981), the digital computer is simply a device for implementing formal logical systems. Symbols are stored in memory registers (these symbols may simply be sequences of 1's and 0's, implemented by *on* and *off* settings of switches). The basic operations of the computer allow recalling the symbols from memory and executing changes in the symbols according to rules. In the earliest computers, the rules for transforming symbols had to be specially wired into the machine, but one of the major breakthroughs in early computer science was the development of the stored program. The stored program is simply a sequence of symbols that directly determines what operations the computer will perform on other symbols. The relation between the stored program and those other symbols is much like the relation between the formally written rule *modus ponens* and the symbol strings to which it can be applied. Like the formal rules of logic, the rules in the computer program do not consider the semantics of the symbols being manipulated, but only their form. This perspective has been given a variety of renderings by such symbolic theorists as Dennett (1978), Fodor (1980), and Pylyshyn (1984).

An alternative way to construe the semantics of computational systems was offered by Newell and Simon (1981). For them, a computer is a *physical symbol system* consisting of symbols (physical patterns), expressions (symbol structures obtained by placing symbol tokens in a physical relation such as adjacency), and processes that operate on expressions. They point out that there is a semantics (designation and interpretation) within the system itself; specifically, expressions in stored list-processing programs designate locations in computer memory, and these expressions can be interpreted by accessing those locations. They regard this internal semantics as a major advance over formal symbol systems such as those of logic, and argue that intelligence cannot be attained without it:

The Physical Symbol System Hypothesis. A physical symbol system has the necessary and sufficient means for general intelligent action.

By "necessary" we mean that any system that exhibits general intelligence will prove upon analysis to be a physical symbol system. By "sufficient" we mean that any physical symbol system of sufficient size can be organized further to exhibit general intelligence. (Newell and Simon, 1981, p. 41)

Hence, with respect to the question of the autonomy of syntax from semantics, some cognitive scientists have emphasized the continuity between computers and formal logical systems, whereas others (such as Newell and Simon) have viewed computers as enabling advances beyond formal systems. A similar difference in perspective arises with respect to what work the computer is regarded as carrying out. From a continuity perspective, computers are powerful devices for implementing logical operations; one can write programs that will serve the same function as inference rules in a logical system. From an alternative perspective (Simon, 1967), it took work in artificial intelligence to show us that *heuristics* (procedures that *might* obtain the desired result, often by means of an intelligent shortcut such as pruning unpromising search paths) are often more useful than *algorithms* (procedures that are guaranteed to succeed in a finite number of steps but may be inefficient in a large system).

Hence, work in artificial intelligence is rooted in formal logic, but has achieved distinctive perspectives by pursuing the idea that computers are devices for symbol manipulation more generally. AI programs have replaced formal logic as the closest external approximation to human cognition; programs exist, for example, not only for proving logical theorems or performing logical inference, but also for playing chess at a master's level and diagnosing diseases. The (partial) success of these programs has suggested to many researchers that human cognitive performance also consists in symbol manipulation; indeed, this analogy provided, until recently, a locus of unity among cognitive scientists.

Yet another root of the symbolic approach is found in Noam Chomsky's program in linguistics. In his review of B. F. Skinner's *Verbal Behavior*, Chomsky (1959) argued that a behavioristic account was inadequate to account for the ability of humans to learn and use languages. Part of his argument focused on the "creativity" of language; Chomsky contended that any natural language has an infinite number of syntactically well-formed sentences, and that its speakers can understand and produce sentences that they had not previously encountered (Chomsky, 1957, 1968). This ability did not seem explicable in terms of learned associations between environmental stimuli and linguistic responses, even if these were augmented by such processes as generalization and analogy. In Chomsky's view, Skinner had not succeeded in adapting the constructs of behaviorism to the precise requirements of a linguistic account, and a quite different approach was needed.

In particular, Chomsky developed the notion of *generative grammar* as an approach to linguistic theory: to write a grammar was to specify an automaton that could generate infinite sets of sentences (this was easily assured by including at least one recursive rule). To evaluate such a grammar, the linguist must determine whether it generates all of the well-formed sentences of the target language, and only those sentences. Chomsky described and evaluated several different classes of generative grammars with respect to natural languages. Of particular importance, he argued that finite state grammars (those most consistent with a behaviorist account), were too weak even when they included recursive rules. They could generate an infinite set of sentences, but not the *correct* set. Specifically, they were unable to handle dependencies across indefinitely long strings (e.g., the dependency between *if* and *then* in sentences of the form "if A, then B" where A is indefinitely long).

To handle such dependencies, at least a phrase structure grammar (and preferably a transformational grammar) was required. These grammars produce constituent structures by applying a succession of rewrite rules (rules which expand one symbol into a string of subordinate symbols); indefinitely long constituents can be embedded within a phrase structure tree without affecting the surrounding dependencies. Transformational rules (rules that modify one phrase structure tree to obtain a related, or transformed, tree) provide additional power, but the most important and enduring part of Chomsky's argument is the rejection of finite state grammars.

Chomsky viewed generative grammar as a model of linguistic *competence*; that is, a model of the knowledge of their language that speakers actually possess in their minds. Although he pioneered the use of (abstract) automata for specifying grammars, he did not intend to model linguistic *performance* (the expression of competence in specific, real-time acts such as the production and comprehension of utterances), nor did he implement his grammars on physical computers. Hence, his version of cognitivism is somewhat more abstract than that of information-processing psychology. Nevertheless, many psychologists were influenced by Chomsky as they moved from behaviorism to information processing, because his grammars suggested ways to model human knowledge using linguistic-style rules (that is, formally specified operations on strings of symbols).

Although Chomsky focused on linguistic competence, he did make some general, controversial claims about linguistic performance. One of these claims, that a process of hypothesis testing is involved in language acquisition, bore implications that were fruitfully developed by Jerry Fodor (1975). Before we can test a hypothesis, such as that the word *dog* refers to dogs, we must be able to state it. Fodor reasoned that this requires a language-like medium, which he called the *language of thought*. Further, since there is no way for a child to learn this language, it must be innate. Thus, Fodor contended that procedures for formal symbol manipulation must be part of our native cognitive apparatus. Fodor's argument represents a minority position within psychology, but virtually all researchers in the majority tradition of information processing assume some weaker version of a symbolic approach to cogniton.

We have briefly reviewed two strands of the symbolic approach: a strand leading from formal logic to artificial intelligence, in which computers came to be viewed as symbol manipulation devices, and a strand leading from linguistics to psychology, in which human cognition came to be viewed likewise as consisting in symbol manipulation.

In cognitive science, these two strands are often brought together in a cooperative enterprise: the design of computer programs to serve as models or simulations of human cognition. This raises a number of interesting issues that we can only briefly mention here (a number of penetrating discussions are available, e.g., Haugeland, 1985). Does a successful computer simulation closely approximate mental symbol processing at some appropriate level of abstraction, so that both the human and the computer are properly construed as symbol processors? Or should true symbol manipulation be attributed to only one of the two types of system; and if so, to the human or the computer? On one view, the human is the true symbol manipulator (because, for example, the human's symbols have causal relations to external referents), and the computer is merely a large calculator or scratchpad that can facilitate the process of deriving predictions from models of human performance (similar to the meteorologist's use of computers to calculate equations that describe the fluid dynamics of the atmosphere, for example). A contrasting view holds that the computer is the true symbol manipulator, and that human cognition is carried out quite differently (in less brittle fashion, as might be modeled in a network, for example). These issues, which have been troublesome for some time, have gained increased salience with the re-emergence of network models in the 1980s. We turn now to a brief history of networks as an alternative to the symbolic tradition.

The Disappearance and Re-emergence of Network Models

By the 1960s substantial progress had been made with both network and symbolic approaches to machine intelligence. But this parity was soon lost. Seymour Papert has provided a whimsical account:

Once upon a time two daughter sciences were born to the new science of cybernetics. One sister was natural, with features inherited from the study of the brain, from the way nature does things. The other was artificial, related from the beginning to the use of computers. Each of the sister sciences tried to build models of intelligence, but from very different materials. The natural sister built models (called neural networks) out of mathematically purified neurones. The artificial sister built her models out of computer programs.

In their first bloom of youth the two were equally successful and equally pursued by suitors from other fields of knowledge. They got on very well together. Their relationship changed in the early sixties when a new monarch appeared, one with the largest coffers ever seen in the kingdom of the sciences: Lord DARPA, the Defense Department's Advanced Research Projects Agency. The artificial sister grew jealous and was determined to keep for herself the access to Lord DARPA's research funds. The natural sister would have to be slain.

The bloody work was attempted by two staunch followers of the artificial sister, Marvin Minsky and Seymour Papert, cast in the role of the huntsman sent to slay Snow White and bring back her heart as proof of the deed. Their weapon was not the dagger but the mightier pen, from which came a book – *Perceptrons* ... (1988, p. 3)

Clearly the publication of *Perceptrons* in 1969 represented a watershed. Research on network models, such as perceptrons and pandemonium, no longer progressed apace with work on symbolic models. Some researchers did continue to pursue and develop network models and in fact established some important principles governing network systems (see J. A. Anderson, 1972; Kohonen, 1972; Grossberg, 1976). Their work, however, attracted only limited attention and funding. What is less clear is whether Minsky and Papert's book precipitated the demise, or whether it was only a symptom.

Minsky and Papert's objective in *Perceptrons* was to study both the potential and limitations of network models. They used the tool of mathematics to analyze what kinds of computation could or could not be performed with a two-layer perceptron. The centerpiece of their criticism was their demonstration that there are functions, such as determining whether a figure is connected or whether the number of active units is odd or even, which cannot be evaluated by such a network. An example is the logical operation of *exclusive or* (XOR). The statement A XOR B is defined as true if A is true and B is not, or B is true and A is not. In order for a network to compute XOR, it is necessary to include an additional layer of units (now referred to as *hidden* units) between the input units and output units (see chapter 3). While Minsky and Papert recognized that XOR could be computed by such a multi-layered network, they raised an additional problem: there were no training procedures for multi-layered networks that could be shown to converge on a solution. As we shall discuss in chapter 3, an adaption of Rosenblatt's training procedure for two-layer networks has now been developed for multi-layered networks. But Minsky and Papert raised further doubts about the usefulness of network models. Even if the problem were overcome, would it be possible to increase the size of networks to handle larger problems? In more technical terms, this is a question as to whether networks will *scale* well. Minsky and Papert offered the intuitive judgement that research on multi-layered networks would be "sterile."

The inability of networks to solve particular problems was, for many investigators, only symptomatic of a more general problem. For them, the fundamental problem was that the only kind of cognitive processes of which networks seemed capable were those involving associations. Within limits, a network could be trained to produce a desired output from a given input, but that merely meant that it had developed procedures for associating that input with the desired output. Associationism was exactly what many of the founders of modern cognitivism were crusading against. Chomsky contended, for example, that finite automata or simple associationistic mechanisms were inadequate to generate all the well-formed sentences of the language. One needed a more powerful automaton capable of performing recursive operations. The identification of network models with associationism thus undercut their credibility and supported the pursuit of symbolic programs as the major research strategy in cognitive science. As we shall see in chapter 7, many advocates of the symbolic tradition continue to fault modern connectionism on precisely this ground.

In the early 1980s the type of network research pioneered by Rosenblatt began once again to attract attention. Papers that employed networks to model various cognitive performances began to appear in cognitive journals. Geoffrey Hinton and James A. Anderson's (1981) *Parallel Models of Associative Memory* offered an accessible presentation of the re-emerging network research. At the 1984 meeting of the Cognitive Science Society, two symposia presented the network approach and debated its role in cognitive science. One, entitled "Connectionism versus Rules: The Nature of Theory on Cognitive Science," featured David Rumelhart and Geoffrey Hinton advocating network modeling (connectionism) and Zenon Pylyshyn and Kurt VanLehn arguing that networks were inadequate devices for achieving cognitive performance. Debate at that session and others during the conference occasionally became acrimonious as the connectionists began to press their alternative and challenged the supremacy of the symbolic approach.

Connectionist research has increased dramatically in the 1980s. While opposition continues, a growing number of cognitive scientists have either "converted" to connectionism or have added connectionist modeling techniques to their repertoire as tools they will employ for at least some purposes. An intriguing question is why connectionism should have re-emerged so strongly in the 1980s. While we do not offer a comprehensive answer to this question, there are a number of factors that seem relevant.

First, powerful new approaches to network modeling were developed, including new architectures, new techniques for training multilayered networks, and advances in the mathematical description of the behavior of nonlinear systems. Many of these innovations can be directly applied to the task of modeling cognitive processes. Second, the credibility of some of the researchers attracted to network research has played a role. For example, in chapters 2 and 3 we discuss an important mathematical insight into network behavior that was proposed by John Hopfield, a distinguished physicist. Anderson and Rosenfeld comment:

John Hopfield is a distinguished physicist. When he talks, people listen. Theory in his hands becomes respectable. Neural networks became instantly legitimate, whereas before, most developments in networks had been in the province of somewhat suspect psychologists and neurobiologists, or by those removed from the hot centers of scientific activity. (1988, p. 457)

Third, cognitive science had remained, either intentionally or unintentionally, rather isolated from neuroscience through the 1970s. In large part this was because there was no clear framework to suggest how work in the neurosciences might bear on cognitive models. But by the 1980s cognitive scientists' interest in the neurosciences had increased, and network models were attractive because they provided a neural-like architecture for cognitive modeling. Fourth, the interest in neuroscience was one reflection of a more general interest in finding a fundamental explanation for the character of cognition. Rule systems, as they became more adequate, also became more complex, diverse, and *ad hoc*. The desire for parsimony, which earlier had characterized behaviorism, re-emerged. Fifth, a number of investigators began to confront the limitations of symbolic models. While initially the task of writing rule systems capable of accounting for human behavior seemed tractable, intense pursuit of the endeavor raised doubts. Rule systems were hampered by their "brittleness," inflexibility, difficulty, learning from experience, inadequate generalization, domain specificity, and inefficiencies due to serial search through large systems. Human cognition, which the rule systems were supposed to be modeling, seemed to be relatively free of such limitations.

These and other factors operated together to make networks models attractive to some cognitive scientists, beginning with a few pioneers in the early 1980s and reaching substantial proportions by the end of the decade. During the same period, however, other cognitive scientists were also concerned about the limitations of traditional symbolic models; no one who models performance wants a brittle system, for example. These investigators focused only on the fifth factor above, rather than all five factors, and adopted the conservative strategy of modifying the existing approach rather than initiating a new, relatively untried approach. Hence, if the symbolic approach is a target of criticism on the part of network modelers, it is a moving target and therefore harder to hit.

Most of the modifications incorporated in the most recent symbolic models have narrowed the gap between symbolic and network models. (It could even be argued that the real revolution is the development of a variety of ways to overcome the limitations of earlier models, including but not limited to connectionist modeling.) First, a large number of rules at a fine grain of analysis (microrules) can capture more of the subtleties of behavior than a smaller number of rules at a larger grain of analysis. Second, rule selection, and perhaps rule application as well, can be made to operate in parallel. Third, the ability to satisfy soft constraints can be gained by adding a strength parameter to each rule and incorporating procedures that use those values in selecting rules. Fourth, resilience to damage can be gained by building redundancy into the rule system (e.g., making multiple copies of each rule). Fifth, increased attention can be given to learning algorithms (such as the genetic algorithm), knowlege compilation and "chunking" of rules into larger units, and ways of applying old knowledge to new problems (such as analogy).

The most comprehensive and successful nontraditional rule systems, such as J. R. Anderson's (1983) ACT* and Newell's (1988) SOAR, incorporate some of these design features (and Anderson makes explicit use of networks in addition to rules). Some differences with networks remain, but their importance and consequences are not as obvious as those involving traditional symbolic models. One of the remaining differences is that nontraditional symbolic models retain the use of ordered symbol strings whereas connectionist networks have no intrinsic ordering of their elements. In the most common architecture, the *production system*, these strings are rules of the form "If A, then B" where A is a Boolean combination of conditions, and B is a set of actions to be carried out when the conditions are met. Another difference is that sequenced operations and nonlocal control are inherent capabilities of symbolic models but not of networks. There presently is no adequate research base for determining what differences in empirical adequacy might result from these differences, but the differences are likely to be small enough that empirical adequacy will not be the primary determinant of the fate of symbolic versus connectionist models. Within either tradition, if a particular inadequacy is found, design innovations that find some way around the failure are likely to be forthcoming. Personal taste, general assumptions about cognition, the sociology of science, and a variety of other factors can be expected to govern the individual choices that together will determine what approaches to cognitive modeling will gain dominance.

Given this state of affairs, in this book we shall draw our primary contrasts between traditional symbolic models and connectionist models. In this way we can convey, to some extent, why connectionists decided to abandon the traditional symbolic approach as a medium for modeling. In chapter 8 we shall present an argument that there are important tasks, other than modeling the cognitive mechanism, for which traditional symbolic theories are the theories of choice. In our view, connectionist and traditional symbolic inquiries should be carried out as distinctive enterprises, each of which can make contributions to the other; the availability of both approaches can strengthen cognitive science by providing multiple perspectives. The key to successful cooperation is that each approach be used for the tasks most suitable to it, rather than fighting for the same turf. For example, linguistic theories will always have a distinctive role to play, and presumably will remain symbolic. These theories efficiently describe the domain in which a connectionist (or other mechanistic model) must perform.

Within this framework, nontraditional symbolic theories do not have the same role to play as traditional ones: they are indeed fighting for the same turf as connectionism (that is, fine-grained modeling of the workings of the cognitive mechanism). However, the degree of polarization is not as great as it may seem, and the future could bring a pluralistic approach to mechanistic modeling within which connectionist themes and techniques are more distributed than is currently the case. Recent history provides some support for this scenario. Connectionist networks, in their incarnation as cognitive models, have origins in the symbolic tradition of the 1970s as well as in the neural network tradition. Schema theory and story grammars (Rumelhart, 1975), probabilistic feature models (Smith and Medin, 1981), prototype theory (Rosch, 1975), and scripts (Schank and Abelson, 1977) all emerged from the symbolic tradition but do not fully reside in either the symbolic or connectionist camp. All can be given a connectionist implementation, and these arguably are superior implementations. For example, schemata should be flexible and easy to modify, but this is much harder to achieve in a symbolic than in a connectionist implementation (Rumelhart, Smolensky, McClelland, and Hinton, 1986, in *PDP:14*). Furthermore, semantic networks with spreading activation (J. R. Anderson, 1983) are hybrid models that place symbols in network structures that dynamically change their activations; they can be regarded as a predecessor of connectionist models of cognition.

We shall point out where nontraditional and hybrid models are relevant at various points in the discussion. There is such a variety of models, however, that we cannot provide a full treatment or make detailed comparisons within a book of this scope. Also, although we are favorably inclined to connectionist models, we decline to predict the outcome of the competition between connectionist and nontraditional symbolic models. The degree to which accommodation will be found, as in hybrid models or pluralism, simply is not known at this time. It is clear, however, that the cognitive science of the year 2000 will be a quite different cognitive science than would have emerged in the absence of the new connectionism.

2

Connectionist Architectures

Connectionist networks are intricate systems of simple units which dynamically adapt to their environments. Some have thousands of units, but even those with only a few units can behave with surprising complexity and subtlety. This is because processing is occurring in parallel and interactively, in marked contrast with the serial processing to which we are accustomed. To appreciate the character of these networks it is necessary to observe them in operation. Thus, in the first section of this chapter we shall describe a simple network that illustrates several features of connectionist processing. In the second section we shall examine in some detail the various design principles that are employed in developing networks. In the final section we shall discuss several appealing properties of networks that have rekindled interest in using them for cognitive modeling: their neural plausibility, satisfaction of "soft constraints," graceful degradation, content-addressable memory, and capacity to learn from experience. Connectionists maintain that the investment in a new architecture is amply rewarded by these gains.

The Flavor of Connectionist Processing:
A Simulation of Memory Retrieval

We shall begin by describing a connectionist model which was designed by McClelland (1981) in order to illustrate how a network can function as a content-addressable memory system. Its architecture is atypical in some respects, but it conveys the flavor of connectionist processing in an intuitive manner. The information to be encoded concerns the members of two hypothetical gangs, the Jets and the Sharks, and some of their demographic characteristics (figure 2.1). Figure 2.2 shows how this information is represented in a network, focusing on just five of the

The Jets and the Sharks

Name	Gang	Age	Education	Marital status	Occupation
Art	Jets	40's	J.H.	Sing.	Pusher
Al	Jets	30's	J.H.	Mar.	Burglar
Sam	Jets	20's	COL.	Sing.	Bookie
Clyde	Jets	40's	J.H.	Sing.	Bookie
Mike	Jets	30's	J.H.	Sing.	Bookie
Jim	Jets	20's	J.H.	Div.	Bulglar
Greg	Jets	20's	H.S.	Mar.	Pusher
John	Jets	20's	J.H.	Mar.	Burglar
Doug	Jets	30's	H.S.	Sing.	Bookie
Lance	Jets	20's	J.H.	Mar.	Burglar
George	Jets	20's	J.H.	Div.	Burglar
Pete	Jets	20's	H.S.	Sing.	Bookie
Fred	Jets	20's	H.S.	Sing.	Pusher
Gene	Jets	20's	COL.	Sing.	Pusher
Ralph	Jets	30's	J.H.	Sing.	Pusher
Phil	Sharks	30's	COL.	Mar.	Pusher
Ike	Sharks	30's	J.H.	Sing.	Bookie
Nick	Sharks	30's	H.S.	Sing.	Pusher
Don	Sharks	30's	COL.	Mar.	Burglar
Ned	Sharks	30's	COL.	Mar.	Bookie
Karl	Sharks	40's	H.S.	Mar.	Bookie
Ken	Sharks	20's	H.S.	Sing.	Burglar
Earl	Sharks	40's	H.S.	Mar.	Burglar
Rick	Sharks	30's	H.S.	Div.	Burglar
Ol	Sharks	30's	COL.	Mar.	Pusher
Neal	Sharks	30's	H.S.	Sing.	Bookie
Dave	Sharks	30's	H.S.	Div.	Pusher

Figure 2.1   Information about individual members of two gangs, which is encoded in McClelland's (1981) Jets and Sharks network. From J. L. McClelland (1981) Retrieving general and specific knowledge from stored knowledge of specifics, *Proceedings of the Third Annual Conference of the Cognitive Science Society*. Copyright 1981 by J. L. McClelland. Reprinted by permission of author.

27 gang members for readability. These figures are reproduced from McClelland and Rumelhart's *Handbook* (1988, pp. 39, 41), which uses the gang database for several exercises; there is related discussion by Rumelhart, Hinton, and McClelland (1986) in *PDP:2* (pp. 25–31). In this section we present the results of several different runs which we performed on the Jets and Sharks network using the **iac** (interactive activation and competition) program in chapter 2 of the *Handbook*.

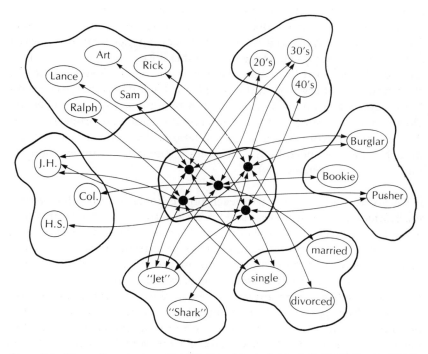

Figure 2.2 The units and connections for five of the individuals in McClelland's (1981) Jets and Sharks network. From J. L. McClelland (1981) Retrieving general and specific knowledge from stored knowledge of specifics, *Proceedings of the Third Annual Conference of the Cognitive Science Society*. Copyright 1981 by J. L. McClelland. Reprinted with corrections by permission of author.

Components of the Model

The most salient components of a connectionist architecture are: (a) simple elements called *units*; (b) equations that determine an *activation* value for each unit at each point in time; (c) weighted *connections* between units which permit the activity of one unit to influence the activity of other units; and (d) *learning rules* which change the network's behavior by changing the weights of its connections. The Jets and Sharks model exhibits components (a)–(c); we defer the important topic of learning until later.

(a) *The units*   There are 68 units in the complete model: a unit for each gang member (27 units); a unit for each gang member's name (27 units); and a unit for each of the properties members can exhibit (14 units). The units are grouped into seven clusters (the "clouds" in figure

2.2); within each cluster the units are mutually exclusive.[1] In addition
to two clusters for the members and their names, there are five clusters
for properties that distinguish the members (age, occupation, marital
status, educational level, and gang membership). Note that the names
are regarded as a special kind of property; the name cluster is just one
cluster among others around the periphery. Each individual gang member is represented, not by his name, but by a person unit in the center
cluster that is connected to the appropriate name and property units.
As a notational convention in the equations that follow, any of these
units can be referenced by the variables u (the *unit* of interest) and i (a
unit that provides *input* to u).

(b) *Activations*   Associated with each unit is an activation value, *activa-
tion$_u$*. Initially each unit is set at a "resting activation" of -0.10. When
a simulation is run, the activations vary dynamically between the values
-0.20 and $+1.00$, reflecting the effects of external input, the propagation of activation from other units in the system, and decay over
time. External input is the activation of certain units by the environment (in practice, the investigator, who wishes to observe the effects).
It is only the property and name units, however, that can receive external input; for this reason they are referred to as the *visible* units. The
person units cannot be directly accessed from outside the network, and
are therefore referred to as *invisible* or *hidden* units. Their only source
of change in activation, besides decay, is the propagation of activation
from other units to which they are connected.

(c) *Weighted connections*   In this particular network, all connections
are bidirectional and are assigned a binary weight. Whereever there is
a connection from unit i to unit u with *weight$_{ui}$*, there is a converse
connection from unit u to unit i with *weight$_{iu}$* of the same value.
(Conventionally, the order of subscripts is the reverse of the direction
of propagation of activation.) Specifically, for each person unit there is
a two-way excitatory connection (weight $+1$) with that person's name
and with each of his properties (one property unit per cluster). Hence, a
person unit propagates activation to all of its property units, and a
property unit propagates activation to all of the units for persons who
exhibit that property. Weights of -1 are used to form inhibitory
connections among units within a cluster; hence, activation of one
property tends to suppress the activity of other properties in its cluster.

---

1   Usually the word "cluster" is used for sets of items that are similar in some way,
whereas here the items in each cluster form a contrast set.

(However, we deleted the inhibitory connections between name units to obtain certain generalizations across names.) For example, if the property **divorced** is activated, the immediate effects are that the property units **single** and **married** will become less active (due to their inhibitory connections with **divorced**) at the same time that the person units **JIM**, **GEORGE**, **RICK**, and **DAVE** will become more active (due to their excitatory connections with **divorced**). Note that person units (which are hidden units) are indicated by upper case.

Dynamics of the Model

The Jets and Sharks model exhibits a variety of interesting behaviors when it performs memory retrieval tasks. To understand the dynamics, it is important to work through the equations that govern the propagation of activation through the network. In this section we introduce the general task of memory retrieval and then describe the equations that are involved in carrying it out. In the final section, we illustrate the operation of the network by tracking its performance across several specific memory retrieval tasks.

Memory retrieval in the Jets and Sharks network   To simulate a memory retrieval task, we supply an external input to one or more of the visible units and observe the effects. For example, to simulate using Art's name to retrieve his properties, we can increase the input into "**Art**" (Art's name unit). The excitatory connections in the network will propagate this activation first to the person unit **ART**, and from there to the units for Art's properties. This is only the beginning, however; the increased activation will continue to reverberate through the network across numerous cycles of processing, during which Art's property units will become increasingly active (in addition to other, less direct effects). At the same time, each active unit will send inhibitions to other units in its cluster. Every change in activation produces additional changes in other units, and the process of dynamically changing activation values can be repeated many times. For tractability, it is useful to set up discrete processing cycles; once per cycle, the fixed amount of external input is again supplied, and each unit sends and receives excitations and inhibitions and updates its own activation. After a number of cycles, the system will stabilize so that the input to each unit will be precisely that which enables it to retain its current activation. At this point, only a subset of the units will have high activation values. In our "**Art**" example, the units that would stabilize at high activations include **ART**, **Jets**, **single**, **pusher**, **40's**, and **junior high**. Thus, by querying the network with a name, we recovered the person's other properties.

The equations   To explain how these effects are produced, we shall present some of the relevant equations. We have made every effort to make this material accessible even to those with some degree of math anxiety. To enhance readability, we use English-like labels for variables and constants; most are similar to those in McClelland and Rumelhart's (1988) *Handbook*. The subscripts that we use to index units are mnemonic (and therefore idiosyncratic). It is fairly straightforward to translate our equations into the *Handbook's* relatively accessible notation. To aid with tranfer to the somewhat less accessible notation in Rumelhart and McClelland's (1986) *PDP* volumes, we provide translations of important equations in Appendix A. Notation varies widely in connectionist modeling, and we leave it as an exercise for the reader to carry out any additional translations when reading primary sources.

Most of the equations can be viewed as focusing on a particular unit, for example, a unit whose activation is being calculated. We refer to this unit as u. (Actually, in its usual use as a subscript, u is an index that ranges over all of the units to which the equation will be applied.) Often the equation refers as well to another unit (or units) that is feeding into u; we refer to such a unit as i. (This notation is not particularly mnemonic here, but it will be later when we discuss feedforward networks.) To propagate activation, each unit i sends an excitatory or inhibitory *output* to every unit u to which it is connected. In the simplest case, the output sent by a unit would be identical to its *activation*. In practice, a variety of output functions have been explored. For the Jets and Sharks model as implemented in the *Handbook*, the output is identical to the activation if it is above a threshold of zero, and is set at zero otherwise. That is:

$$output_i = activation_i \text{ if } activation_i > 0 \text{ and } output_i = 0 \text{ otherwise.}   (1)$$

When i's output value is multiplied by the *weight* of its connection with u, the resulting value serves as an *input* to u:

$$input_{ui} = weight_{ui}\, output_i   (2)$$

For the Jets and Sharks network, in which weights are either $+1$ or -1, the weight simply determines the sign of the input (whether it is excitatory or inhibitory). In most models, the weight varies within a continuous range, such as $+1$ to -1, and therefore affects the magnitude of the input as well.

Next, the concept of *net input* is needed. Unit u receives input from all of the units to which it is connected. Usually these inputs are simply added together, and the total multiplied by a strength parameter, to obtain the net input to u. (The strength parameter is simply a number that is selected to scale down the input to a desired degree; the lower its value, the more gradual are the changes in activation values.) However, if u is in contact with the environment (as are the property and name units in Jets and Sharks), it might also receive an external input. In this model any external input is supplied at a value determined by the modeler, which is then scaled by its own strength parameter. The two strength parameters allow for adjusting the relative influence of internal input versus external input; we have used the *Handbook's* default values of 0.1 (internal) and 0.4 (external). (There is an option of setting different internal strength parameters for excitatory versus inhibitory inputs; for simplicity we omit that distinction here.) Therefore, for the options we have taken, the equation for calculating the net input is:

$$netinput_u = 0.1 \sum_i weight_{ui} \, output_i + 0.4 \, extinput_u \qquad (3)$$

The term in this equation that begins with a summation sign (Σ) with an index i tells us that the input to u from each unit i is calculated as in equation (2) above, and that the inputs from all of the i units are then added together for inclusion in the *netinput*. On the basis of the net input, the unit will now either increase or decrease its activation according to a fairly simple activation rule, as shown in equations (4) and (5) below. We shall use a_u to represent the current *activation$_u$*, and Δa_u to represent the net change to be made to *activation$_u$*. There are two terms in the equation. The first calculates the change that is due to the net input (an increase for positive net input, a decrease for negative net input). The second term is a decay term that decreases activation, even in the absence of net input. (One effect of this is that external input has its greatest effect when it is first presented to a unit.) Because the first term depends on the sign of the input, there are two versions of the equation. If the net input is positive (greater than 0), then the change in the activation is given by:

$$\Delta a_u = (max - a_u)(netinput_u) - (decayrate)(a_u - rest) \qquad (4)$$

Here *max* represents the maximum activation value that a unit can take (1 in this case). Hence, the first term says that if we have a positive net input, we scale it by a multiplier that depends upon how far the current activation is from the maximum activation, and then increase the activation by that amount. Thus, the greater the net input and the lower the current activation, the more we increase the activation. The decay term, which is subtracted from that amount, is determined by the decay rate (which is set at 0.1) and the difference between the current activation and the unit's resting activation (which is set at -0.1). Thus, the lower the current activation, the less we adjust for decay.

If the net input is less than or equal to 0, the change in activation is given by:

$$\Delta a_u = (a_u - min)\,(netinput_u) - (decayrate)\,(a_u - rest) \qquad (5)$$

The decay term is the same as above. If the net input is 0, the unit will simply decay by that amount. When the net input is negative, on the other hand, we shall determine how much further to decrease the activation by multiplying the net input by the difference between the current activation and the minimum activation (which is set here at -0.2). Hence, the greater the current activation, the greater is the effect of negative input in decreasing that activation.

Illustrations of the Dynamics of the Model

With the basic machinery in place, we now can work though what happens in the network when it performs memory retrieval tasks. By varying the queries that we present to the Jets and Sharks network, we can observe it perform several different tasks: retrieving properties from a name, retrieving a name from properties, categorization, prototype formation, and utilizing regularities.

Retrieving properties from a name   This is the task that we briefly described above. The investigator activates the "**Art**" unit (by supplying it with external input), and consequently Art's properties become activated. On cycle 1, every unit's current activation is equal to the resting activation of -0.10. Equation (1) specifies that any unit with an activation below the threshold of zero (0.0) produces an output of 0.0; since this is the case for all units, their net inputs to other units are also 0.0 The name unit "**Art**" is supplied with an external input of 1.00, with the result that it is the only unit with a non-zero net input. By equation (3):

$$netinput_{\text{"Art"}} = (0.10)\,(0.0) + (0.40)\,(1.00) = 0.40$$

This strong net input causes the activation of "**Art**" to increase. By equation (4):

$$\Delta a \,_{\text{"Art"}} = (1.00 - (-0.10))\,(0.40) - (0.10)\,(-0.10 - (-0.10))$$
$$= (1.00 + 0.10)\,(0.40) - (0.10)\,(0.00) = 0.44 - 0.0 = 0.44$$

While all other units, including the hidden (person) units, remain unchanged at the resting activation value:

$$\Delta a = (-0.10 - (-0.10))\,(0.0) - (0.10)\,(-0.10 - (-.10))$$
$$= 0.0. - 0.0 = 0.0.$$

Because the current activation of "**Art**" for cycle 1 is -0.10, adding 0.44 yields a new activation of 0.34. For all other units, adding 0.0 to -0.10 yields a new activation that is the same as the current activation, -0.10. These new activations are used as the current activations for cycle 2.

Beginning on cycle 2 the activation of "**Art**," which now is positive, sends excitatory (positive) input to **ART**, the person unit for Art. By cycle 4, **ART** has climbed to a positive activation. At the same time "**Art**" continues to grow in activation. This is partly due to the continued presentation of external input on each cycle, and partly (beginning in cycle 4) from the input it begins to receive from **ART**. After **ART** becomes positively activated, it begins to send excitatory inputs to the units for Art's properties. Thus, on cycle 5 the units **Jets**, **40's**, etc., start to become less negative and eventually become positive (on cycle 12). Once Art's properties become positive, the competing properties in their clusters, such as **Sharks**, **20's**, and **30's**, become slightly more negative. The reason is that the units for **Jets** and **40's** send inhibitory inputs to their competitors, thus driving them below the resting activation. These changes in activation are illustrated for the age property cluster in figure 2.3.

Hence, the person unit **ART** becomes active during the early cycles of processing, and by propagating activity to the property units to which it is connected, enables the retrieval of Art's properties. Beginning with cycle 18, though, some other activities begin to appear in the network. The person units **CLYDE** (and also **RALPH**, not shown), and subsequently **MIKE** (and also **FRED** and **GENE**, not shown) become less negative, and on cycle 25 **CLYDE** becomes positive. The reason for this is that the units for Art's properties begin to send positive activations to the units for persons who share properties with Art. Clyde, in fact, shares all of Art's properties except for profession (he is

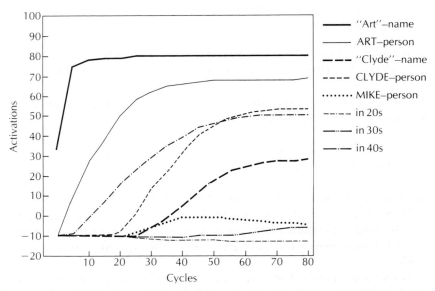

Figure 2.3 The activation values across cycles of some of the units in the Jets and Sharks network after the unit for Art's name is activated by an external input.

a bookie whereas Art is a pusher). Mike shares three of five properties with Art, and so his person unit too begins to rise in value, but not sufficiently to achieve a positive activation.[2] Eventually the activation on **CLYDE** becomes high enough that it sends a positive input to the name unit "**Clyde**," and it too becomes active. The result is that by accessing the system through Art, we not only get back Art's properties, but also the names of people similar to Art. One way to interpret this process intuitively is to note that thinking about a person's properties may tend to remind us of people who are very similar to that person.

Retrieving a name from other properties   The network is even more versatile than this, however. Suppose we access it by supplying external inputs simultaneously to several units, namely, the units for Art's demographic properties (40's, junior high, single, pusher). These will activate **ART**, which will activate "**Art**," and in this way Art's name will pop out. This is the clearest illustration of what is meant by a *con-*

2   In fact, as processing continues, Mike's activation begins to drop again. The reason is that as the units for Art and those individuals most similar to Art grow in activation, they send even more strongly inhibitory inputs to **MIKE**, thus pushing down the activation of his person unit.

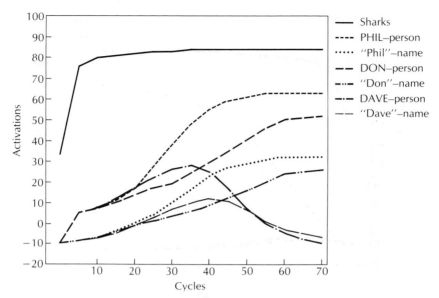

Figure 2.4 The activation values across cycles for name and person units of various members of the Sharks after the property unit for Shark is activated by an external input. The name units become less active than the person units since the name units receive activation only via the person units.

tent-addressable memory: the name is retrieved by supplying contents (see discussion of content-addressable memory below). Generalization comes free along with this capability; that is, names of persons with similar properties will pop out also at a lower degree of activation.

Categorization and prototype formation   The same memory retrieval processes can produce less obvious phenomena, which have been observed in human categorization performance. First, the network can recover category instances. If we supply external input to **Sharks**, for example, that unit will activate the person units for the individual Sharks. Second, as processing continues these individuals become graded according to how well they exemplify the category (analogous to the human ability to judge the relative typicality of various category members; see Rosch, 1975). Figure 2.4 shows the activation across cycles for three of the person units and three of the name units after we activated **Sharks**. Some names clearly acquire more activation than others. For example, after 70 cycles of processing, "**Phil**" is most active, "**Don**" is less active, and "**Dave**," after being initially activated, has dropped almost to its resting level. What causes this emergence of

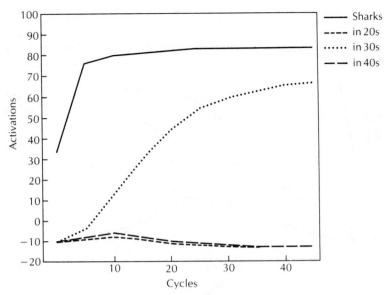

Figure 2.5 The activation values across cycles for the three age units after the property unit for Shark is activated by an external input.

grading by typicality? The third capability, the extraction of proto-types, provides a key part of the mechanism (and is exhibited by humans as well; see Posner and Keele, 1968). Activating **Sharks** results in the activation of the person units for the Sharks, which results in the activation of the property units to which they are connected. The most widely shared properties become the most active. Thus, in figure 2.5 we see that the **30's** unit becomes quite active, while the **20's** and **40's** units never rise much above their resting level. This is due to the fact that nine of the twelve Sharks are in their 30's. These activations are then forwarded to those person units that exhibit the most frequent proper-ties, thus creating a positive feedback loop which further sharpens the prototype. The name units are too individual to regard them as part of the prototype, but they change by the same process as the other proper-ties, and their activations come to reflect the extent to which each indi-vidual displays the prototypical properties (hence displaying the second capability mentioned just above).

An interesting twist can be observed for the profession properties in figure 2.6. Initially the units for all three professions rise in activation. This is because the gang members are equally distributed in their chosen careers. Nevertheless, subsequently the unit for **pusher** con-

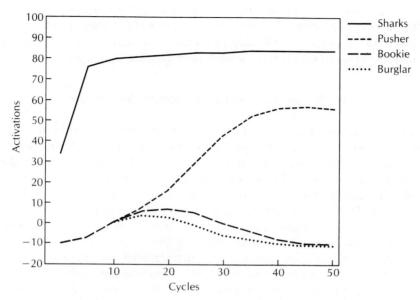

Figure 2.6   The activation values across cycles for the three profession units when the property unit for Shark is activated by an external input.

tinues to grow in activation, while those for **burglar** and **bookie** drop back below zero. This is due to the fact that those individuals who provide the best match on those properties that are not equally distributed grow in their activations, and so provide increased activation to **pusher**, and it, in turn, inhibits both of the other profession units.

Utilizing regularities   As a final example of the variety of ways in which the memory can be queried, we can activate two properties, such as **20's** and **pusher**, and discover which individuals are most likely to fit that scenario. The network will initially produce higher activations in the person units for all individuals who possess any one of these properties, with those sharing both properties (**GREG**, **FRED**, and **GENE**) getting the highest activations. As person units become active, they not only activate name units, but also other property units. The units for the most widely shared properties (**Jet**, **single**, and **high school**) also became more active than other units in their cluster. This leads to Pete's person and name units receiving significant activation even though Pete did not fit the original description, since he is a bookie, not a pusher. Thus, the network not only identified which individuals shared the initial pair of properties, but what their other properties were likely to be, and who amongst those not possessing the initial pair show the best fit with those who did satisfy the initial pair of properties. Making inferences from known properties to other properties is a kind of behavior that is familiar to social psychologists working in attribution theory.

The Design Features of a Connectionist Architecture

In the Jets and Sharks simulation we have presented one particular network architecture that has some very nice characteristics for modeling recall of information from memory and for illustrating some of the capabilities of connectionist networks. However, this design is not suitable for most purposes, and work has proceeded using a variety of other designs. In fact, connectionism as a research paradigm is still in its infancy, and investigators are still in the process of exploring different kinds of connectionist systems. Many of the design features are rather complex, and require considerable mathematics to characterize. In order to provide a general overview of the various types of systems, we shall bypass material that is foundational but complex. (For example, we make no direct use of vector notation[3] or matrix algebra.) Also, we limit ourselves to those architectures that are emphasized in Rumelhart and McClelland's (1986) *PDP* volumes, which can be consulted for a more technical treatment. For other technical treatments of these or other architectures see, in particular, Grossberg (1982, 1988), Kohonen (1988), and Wasserman (1989). We can characterize the distinctions between different connectionist architectures by considering four issues: (a) how the units are connected to one another; (b) how the activations of individual units are determined; (c) the nature of the learning procedures which change the connections between units; and (d) the ways in which such systems are interpreted semantically. We use a mnemonic notation in these sections; see Appendix A for a translation into two different notations used by Rumelhart and McClelland in the *PDP* volumes.

Patterns of Connectivity

The first decision in setting up a connectionist network is to determine which units are connected to one another, that is, the pattern of connectivity. There are two major classes of patterns. (a) *Feedforward networks* have unidirectional connections. Inputs are fed into the bottom layer,

---

3   The activation pattern across a layer of *n* units can be treated as a *vector* (directed line segment) in an *n*-dimensional space.

and outputs are generated at the top layer as a result of the forward propagation of activation. (b) *Interactive networks* have bidirectional connections. The Jets and Sharks exercises illustrate how interactive networks change state gradually over a large number of processing cycles, as dynamically changing activations are passed back and forth over the two-way connections. We shall discuss each of these classes in turn.

Feedforward networks   In feedforward networks, units are organized into separate layers, with units in one layer feeding their activations forward to the units in the next layer until the final layer is reached. The simplest such configuration consists of only two layers of units: *input units* and *output units*. There is a weighted connection from each input unit to each output unit. When the weights (connection strengths) are properly set, this type of network can respond to each of a variety of input patterns with its own distinctive output pattern; therefore, it is sometimes referred to as a *pattern associator*.

For example, consider a network with eight input units ($i_1 - i_8$), each of which is connected unidirectionally to each of eight output units ($u_1 - u_8$), with output activations allowed to range over a continuous domain (figure 2.7). Several input patterns are constructed, each of which consists of a series of eight binary values ($+1$ and -1). When a pattern is presented to the input layer, each of its binary values is the external input to one input unit, which takes that value as its activation. In presenting the input pattern $+1-1+1-1+1+1+1+1$, for example, an external input of -1 is supplied to the second input unit, (i_2), so its activation becomes -1. The activations of the input units are then propagated to the output units by an activation rule that can supply a different weighted sum of the various input activations to each output unit. Therefore, each output unit achieves an activation value that reflects the activity of some input units more than others (see the following section for details). The activation patterns across the input and output units are, technically, eight valued vectors. We shall refer to them using the more familiar term "patterns."

It is informative to compare figure 2.7 with figure 1.1 in the previous chapter. These figures illustrate the two approaches that are taken to diagramming two-layer networks. In figure 1.1, the sensory layer is drawn vertically and the motor layer horizontally. As a result, each connection must be drawn with a change of direction from horizontal to vertical, and its weight (not shown) can be placed at the junction. The advantage is that the layout of the nodes for the weights is the same as in a weight matrix (cf. the matrix for Case A below). In figure 2.7, the

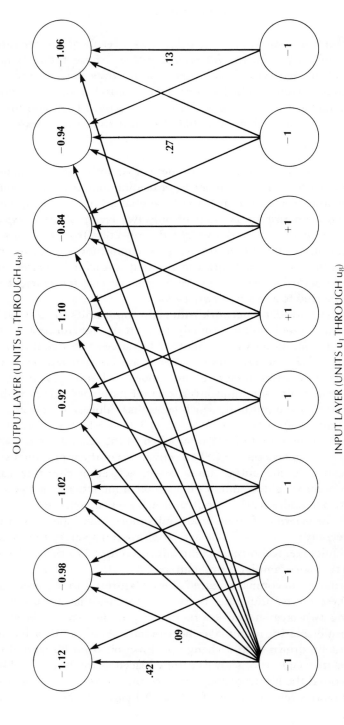

OUTPUT LAYER (UNITS u₁ THROUGH u₈)

INPUT LAYER (UNITS u₁ THROUGH u₈)

Figure 2.7 Pattern recognition network with two layers of units. Activations for the input layer are all set at + 1 or − 1; they are multiplied by the weights on the connections and summed to obtain the activations for the output layer. Only some of the connections are shown; for four of them, the weights are also shown.

layers are parallel and the connections are indicated by straight lines; a few of the weights are shown for illustration but it would be unwieldy to include all of them. This latter format has the advantage, though, that it can be adapted to more complex networks (see below).

The paradigmatic task for a pattern associator is paired-associate learning in which the input–output pairings are arbitrary (e.g., supplying names for objects). However, with appropriate weights it could instead be used to reproduce each input pattern on the output layer, in which case it would be a type of *auto associator*. Or, the output layer could be used to represent a small number of categories into which a larger number of input patterns would be sorted or classified. We shall often use the term *pattern associator* generically for these varieties of two-layer networks.

Pattern associators have many useful applications, and we discuss several simulations that make use of them in subsequent chapters. There are, however, problems for which a two-layer network is inadequate, as we shall discuss in chapter 3. A well-known example is the Boolean function of *exclusive or* (XOR), which is a special case of parity detection. To overcome the limitations of two-layer networks, it is necessary to add *hidden units* to the system. These are units which serve neither as input nor output units, but facilitate the processing of information through the system. We have already encountered hidden units in the Jets and Sharks network (in that network, however, there was no distinction between input and output units; all nonhidden units could serve both functions). In chapter 3 we illustrate how the XOR problem can be solved by a network with two input units, two hidden units, and one output unit. Most tasks for which multi-layered networks are used, however, require considerably more units in each layer. For examples, see the discussion of NETtalk in chapter 3, the logic network in chapter 5, and the kinship network in chapter 6.

As a point of terminology, note that investigators frequently refer to a network that has three layers of units as a two-layer network; in that case, it is the number of layers of *connections* that is being referenced. In this book we reference the number of layers of *units*, but reserve the term *multi-layered network* for networks with hidden units (i.e., three or more layers of units).

There is a number of variations that can be made on two-layer and multi-layered architectures. One variation is to allow units in the same layer to send inhibitions and excitations to each other as well as to units in the next layer. A more interesting variation is the *recurrent network*, which can receive input sequentially and alter its response appropriately depending upon what information was received at previous steps in the sequence. It does this by feeding a pattern achieved on a higher layer back into a lower layer, where it functions as a type of input (Elman, 1988; see also the sequential networks of Jordan, 1986). We shall discuss such a network in chapter 7 below. Finally, Rumelhart, Hinton, and McClelland (1986, *PDP:2*) discuss the interesting idea that multi-layer feedforward networks could be used for top-down rather than bottom-up processing, by reversing the direction of the connections without changing the units and patterns at each level. All of these variations soften the design constraint that activations be propagated exclusively in one forward pass. In the next section, we discuss a type of network that departs more dramatically from the basic feedforward design.

Interactive networks   For interactive networks, at least some connections are bidirectional and the processing of any single input occurs dynamically across a large number of cycles. Such networks may or may not be organized into layers; when they are, processing occurs backwards as well as forward. A major exemplar of an interactive network is the *Hopfield net*, developed by the physicist John Hopfield (1982) by analogy with a physical system known as a *spin glass*. In their review, Cowan and Sharp (1988) characterize a spin glass as consisting of a matrix of atoms which may be spinning either pointing up or pointing down. Each atom, moreover, exerts a force on its neighbor, leading it to spin in the same or in the opposite direction. A spin glass is actually an instantiation of a matrix or lattice system which is capable of storing a variety of different spin patterns. In the analogous network that Hopfield proposed, the atoms are represented by units and the spin is represented by binary activation values that units might exhibit (0 or 1). The influence of units on their neighbors is represented by means of bidirectional connections; any unit can be (but need not be) connected to any other unit (except itself). As with any interactive network, activations are updated across multiple cycles of processing in accord with an activation rule (see below).

Hopfield (1984) has also experimented with networks taking continuous activation values. Other examples of interactive networks include *Boltzmann machines* (Hinton and Sejnowski, 1986, in *PDP:7*) and *harmony theory* (Smolensky, 1986, in *PDP:6*). As in the original Hopfield nets, the units take binary activation values. We shall not discuss harmony theory further, but it uses a probabilistic activation rule and a *simulated annealing* technique very similar to those of the Boltzmann machine (see below).

Activation Rules for Units

Networks differ not only in their pattern of connectivity, but also in the activation rules that determine the activation values of their units after processing. We have already encountered the major classes of possible activation values. (a) Discrete activations are typically binary, taking values of 0 and 1 (as in Boltzmann machines and harmony theory) or -1 and $+1$. (b) Continuous activations can be unbounded or bounded. As examples of bounded ranges, -0.2 to $+1.0$ was stipulated for the Jets and Sharks network, and a range of -1 to $+1$ is a common choice. In figure 2.7, we used binary input activations and continuous unbounded output activations.

Even greater variation is found in activation rules, which specify how to calculate the level of activation for each unit at a given time. In the following sections we present some of these rules, first for feedforward networks and then for interactive networks. Often the rules for the two types of networks are quite similar, and we will find a rule used in the interactive Jets and Sharks network useful as a framework for introducing our first feedforward activation rule.

Feedforward networks   Recall that for the Jets and Sharks network, the activation rule for unit u made use of the net input to that unit:

$$netinput_u = 0.1 \sum_i weight_{ui} \, output_i + 0.4 \, extinput_u \qquad (3)$$

Note that the net input has two components: the effects of activity in other units to which u is connected, and the effects of external input.[4] In a pattern associator (a two-layer feedforward network), the functions served by these two components are divided between specialized sets of units. As shown in figure 2.7 above, units in the input layer (i) are specialized to receive external input, and take the values of the input patterns as their activations. The input unit's activation depends only on the external input, and therefore does not need to be determined by an activation rule. Based on that activation, the input unit then sends an output along each of its connections. In the simplest case, $output_i = activation_i$, but other functions are possible.

Units in the output layer (u) are specialized to receive activation from other units in the network (rather than receiving external input). The

4   The hidden units did not receive external input, so that term would always have a zero value for those units.

terminology now gets a bit confusing, because "input" and "output" are used to refer to the transmission of values as well as to types of units. Each input unit (i) sends output towards each output unit (u). To convert the input unit's output into the output unit's input, $output_i$ is multiplied by the weight of the connection: $input_{ui} = weight_{ui}\ output_i$. Adding these together for every unit i in the input layer yields the net input to u ($netinput_u$). The equation describing this is one component of the preceding equation (3) that was used for the Jets and Sharks network:

$$netinput_u = \sum_i weight_{ui}\ output_i \qquad (6)$$

Optionally, a term $bias_u$ can be added to equation (6) in order to adjust the responsiveness of each output unit individually; it can be thought of as a fixed input supplied by a special unit that is not affected by what is happening in the rest of the system. If the value of the bias is low or negative, the output unit will respond conservatively to activation sent from the input units; if it is high, the output unit will behave "impulsively." We consider this version of equation (6) in chapter 3.

Finally, an activation rule is applied which makes use of the net input to determine the activation of each unit u. We shall refer to $activation_u$ simply as a_u. In the simplest case, the *linear activation rule*, $a_u = netinput_u$ (producing a straight-line, or linear, function). This rule is very useful when two-layer networks are provided with patterns that meet certain constraints (see chapter 3). The additional power needed to violate those constraints can be obtained by adding one or more layers of hidden units, but only if the activation rule is also changed to a nonlinear function. Typically the function chosen is a continuous, monotonically increasing (or at least nondecreasing) function of the input for which a derivative exists. In particular, the *logistic function* has been widely used (in two-layer as well as multi-layer networks):

$$a_u = \frac{1}{1 + e^{-(netinput_u - \theta_u)/T}} \qquad (7)$$

This function is sigmoidal in form (as figure 2.8 illustrates for the stochastic version of this function in the section on Boltzmann machines below). Within the exponent, θ_u is a threshold that is subtracted from the net input; it has the same effect on the activation value as adding a bias to the net input equation (6) if $\theta_u = -bias_u$. (In their 1988 *Handbook* McClelland and Rumelhart uniformly used a bias term, whereas in their 1986 *PDP* volumes they usually subtracted a threshold from net input instead.) *T* is a parameter which determines how flat the curve is across the range of net input values. (When the number of input units that feed into each output unit is large, the range of net input values also tends to be large. A higher value of *T* stretches the function so that it will cover this range.)

Each of these activation rules can be adapted to obtain discrete rather than continuous activation values, typically for use in networks in which both input and output units are binary (on or off). For the linear activation rule, the adaptation is to compare the net input to a threshold value. If net input exceeds the threshold, the output unit's activation is set to 1 (on); otherwise it is set to 0 (off). With a zero threshold, for example, positive net input turns the output unit on and negative net input turns it off. A unit that uses a threshold in this way is called a *linear threshold unit*. A network with an output layer of linear threshold units and an input layer of binary units is an elementary *perceptron* (Rosenblatt, 1959). Linear threshold units can also be used in the hidden and output layers of multi-layered feedforward networks and in interactive networks.

For the logistic activation rule, discrete activations can be achieved by using a stochastic version of equation (7); this is presented as equation (9) in the discussion of Boltzmann machines in the next section. When equation (9) is used in a feedforward network of binary units, presenting the same input pattern on different trials will not always have the same effect on a given output unit; that is, the relation between its net input and its activation becomes probabilistic. The equation determines the relative frequency with which the unit will turn on versus turn off. An example of a feedforward network with a stochastic activation function is discussed in chapter 6 (Rumelhart and McClelland's (1986) past tense model).

Interactive networks   The equations that govern the propagation of activation in feedforward networks can be used in interactive networks as well. A parameter *t* for time (or in some notations, *n* for cycle number) must be included, however, because activations are updated many times on the same unit as the system works towards settling into a solution to a particular input. (For readability, we show *t* in our equations only when it is necessary to distinguish it from *t* + 1.) Interactive networks may use a *synchronous update* procedure, in which every unit's activation is updated once per timing cycle, or an *asynchronous update* procedure, in which there is no common sequence of cycles, but rather a random determination of the times at which each unit separately is updated. Each update requires a separate application of the activation rule. (In contrast, in a feedforward network there is just one forward sweep of activation changes; the activation rule is applied just once to each unit.)

In the original Hopfield nets (Hopfield, 1982), each unit is a linear threshold unit. That is, the activation rule is the same as that of Rosenblatt's perceptron (but it is applied many times to each unit). On each update, if a unit receives net input that is above its threshold, it acquires an activation of 1. Otherwise, its activation is 0. (Alternatively, values of $+1$ and -1 can be used if the threshold is adjusted appropriately.) Hopfield employed an *asynchronous* update procedure in which each unit at its own randomly determined times would update its activation depending upon the net input it received at that time. (This helps to prevent the network from falling into unstable oscillations.) Processing is initiated in a Hopfield net by providing an initial input pattern to a subset of units (i.e., each unit receives an activation value of 1 or 0). Then, all units will randomly update their activations until a state is achieved in which no unit will receive a net input that would lead it to change its activation. If that occurs, the network is then said to have *stabilized* or reached a state of *equilibrium*. The particular stable configuration into which the network settles constitutes the system's identification of the initial input. (Some networks, however, never stabilize; rather: they behave as chaotic systems that oscillate between different configurations.)

Hopfield's analogy between this sort of network and a physical system paid an important dividend when he showed that one could calculate a very useful measure of the overall state of the network (*energy*, or E)[5] that was equivalent to the measure of energy in a physical system (Hopfield, 1982). A Hopfield net tends to move towards a state of equilibrium that is mathematically equivalent to a state of lowest energy in a thermodynamic system. Using the update rule described in the previous paragraph, each change in activation of any unit will result in an overall lower (or same) energy state for the system. In our notation, the global energy measure E is given by:

$$E = -\sum_{u<i} weight_{ui}\, a_u\, a_i + \sum_u \theta_u\, a_u \tag{8}$$

To see how the update rule lowers the value of E, consider one example that focuses on just two units in a network of binary units taking

5 Hopfield's E should not be confused with the measure of mean squared error that is used in deriving the delta rule. In Boxes 1 and 2 of chapter 3 we call this measure *Error*, but it is often called E.

activations of 0 and 1. If at the outset $a_u = 0$, $a_i = 1$, *weight$_{ui}$*
$= 1$ and $\theta_u = 0.5$, then the contribution to E of these two units is:
$-(1 \times 0 \times 1) + (0.5 \times 0) = 0$. Now assume that unit u has been
randomly selected to have its activation updated. The input to unit u
from unit i equals *weight$_{ui}$* $a_i = 1 \times 1 = 1$. Since this exceeds the
threshold of 0.5, unit u changes its activation from 0 to 1. We now
evaluate E for this part of the network as: $-(1 \times 1 \times 1) + (0.5 \times 1) =$
-0.5. Therefore, the network has moved to a state with a lower value
for E. (Note that in actual practice, we must apply the update rule by
considering all inputs to a_u not just that from a single a_i. This insures
that we would change a_u only if it would contribute to an overall lower
value for E.) Rumelhart, Smolensky, McClelland, and Hinton (1986,
PDP:14) emphasized that E indicates how well the network satisfies the
constraints that are implicit in the pattern of weights and the input to
the network. They therefore adapted Hopfield's energy measure to obtain G, a measure of the *goodness of fit* of the state achieved by the network to the constraints. G is the negative of E and may also include a
separate term for input if the input is continuously supplied during
processing (a procedure that is referred to as *clamping* the relevant
subset of units to a constant activation value).

Hopfield nets are useful for solving a variety of optimization problems. The connections literally constrain the possible stable configurations into which the network can settle. If we regard the initial
pattern of activation supplied to such a network as specifying a problem
and the stable state as a solution, then the connections will represent
conceptual constraints on the solution and the stable state should be the
state of the network that best satisfies these constraints. The travelling
salesperson problem is one type of constraint satisfaction problem
which has traditionally been used as a challenging case for developing
optimization procedures. The salesperson needs to visit a number of
cities and desires to travel the shortest distance. Hopfield and Tank
(1985; for a more recent model, see Durbin and Willshaw, 1987) developed a modified Hopfield net which offers quite good solutions to this
problem. Although it does not find the absolutely shortest route, its
performance is comparable to that of a (nonnetwork) computational
procedure for constrained optimization problems developed by Lin and
Kernighan (1973).

One of the difficulties confronted by the Hopfield net is that it can
settle into local minima, in particular, situations in which there would
not be sufficient net input to any given unit to get it to change its value,
but in which the system would still not have reached the optimal overall solution given the constraints imposed by the weights in the network. That is, the stable state is not the state that would yield the

lowest possible value of E (the global energy minimum). This may result when different parts of the network have settled into incompatible solution patterns, each part of which is stable and unable to be altered by the other partial solutions. The Boltzmann machine is an adaptation of the Hopfield net that reduces this tendency.

The Boltzmann machine was proposed by Hinton and Sejnowski (1983, 1986; see also Ackley, Hinton, and Sejnowski, 1985). Like the Hopfield net, it updates its binary units by means of an asynchronous update procedure. However, it employs a *stochastic activation function* rather than a deterministic one. Specifically, it is a probabilistic version of the logistic function in equation (7). On each update of a particular unit u, the probability that it becomes active is a function of its net input:

$$probability\ (a_u = 1) = \frac{1}{1 + e^{-(netinput_u - \theta_u)/T}} \tag{9}$$

The effect of T is to alter the slope of the probability curve, as illustrated in figure 2.8 (with $\theta = 0$). When T is close to zero, the curve approaches a discontinuous step function that jumps from 0 to 1 when $netinput_u$ crosses the value 0.0 (i.e., it approximates a linear threshold unit). When T becomes very large, the curve flattens, so there is more variability in the unit's response to a given net input value across updates. At high values of T the network will jump quickly into a solution to a new input (that is, it will require relatively few updates) but the solution is unlikely to be optimal.[6]

Equation (9) works best when a procedure called *simulated annealing* is used to vary the temperature parameter during the processing of a single input pattern. The procedure is based on an analogy from physics. Something comparable to local minima occurs in formation of crystals when incompatible sets of bonds begin to form in different parts of the crystal. If these bonds become fixed, the crystal will have a fault in it. The common way to avoid such faults is referred to as *annealing*. In this process, a material is heated, thereby weakening the bonds and allowing the atoms to reorient, and then cooled very slowly so that there is a maximal chance that as the bonds reform the atoms will orient appropriately with each other. If the cooling is carried out slowly enough around certain critical temperatures, the alignment

---

6   When equation (9) is applied to a feedforward network, temperature does not affect the time to reach a solution (because each output unit's activation is calculated just one time). If a learning rule is also being applied, however, high variability of response across different presentations of the same input will make learning slower (which often is desirable).

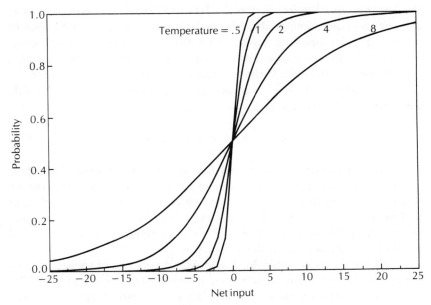

Figure 2.8 Probability that a unit takes an activation value of one as a function of net input at five different values of T (temperature). Note that θ (threshold) is zero. From D. E. Rumelhart, G. E., Hinton, and J. L. McClelland (1986) A general framework for parallel distributed processing, in D. E. Rumelhart, J. L. McClelland, and the PDP Research Group (1986) *Parallel Distributed Processing: Explorations in the microstructure of cognition.* Volume 1: *Foundations*, Cambridge, MA: MIT Press/Bradford Books, p. 69. Reprinted with permission.

emerging in one part of the structure has the greatest opportunity to affect that emerging elsewhere in the structure so as to develop one cohesive structure. The idea is carried over to networks by treating the patterns of activation in different parts of the network as comparable to the alignment of atoms. Raising the temperature value T has the effect of increasing the probability that activations of units in the network will shift. Reducing T very slowly at critical junctures allows time for patterns of activation developing in one part of the network to affect the patterns developing elsewhere so that one coherent pattern emerges as the network settles into a solution.

Note that the equations just presented make no reference to the prior state of activation of the unit. In contrast, the Jets and Sharks network computed a change in activation (Δa_u) which was added to u's current activation ($a_{u,t}$) to obtain u's new activation($a_{u,t+1}$):

$$a_{u,t+1} = a_{u,t} + \Delta a_u \tag{10}$$

We left this equation implicit in the Jets and Sharks discussion, but did present two equations for Δa_u . In that case, the change in activation of a unit depended upon its current activation $a_{u,t}$ (relative to the discrepancy with its maximum or minimum activation), its net input, and the rate of decay with time. If the net input was sufficient to overcome the decay, the activation increased; otherwise it decreased. A simpler rule for capturing the same idea is:

$$\Delta a_u = k\ netinput_u - decay \tag{11}$$

where k is a constant determined by the network designer, $netinput_u$ represents the net input to the unit of interest, and *decay* represents a function that specifies an amount by which the activation of each unit will be decremented on each processing cycle. Note that this simple linear rule will not keep activations within a bounded range unless special care is taken in crafting the decay function.

Finally, J. R. Anderson's ACT and ACT* versions of spreading activation in (nondistributed) semantic networks (Anderson 1976, 1983) utilize activation functions that are similar in many respects to some of those used by researchers who work within the PDP tradition. Anderson's functions achieve nonlinearity by incorporating a negative exponential function of current activation, they utilize a decay function, and processing is interactive (vs. feedforward). Anderson's models can account for a variety of empirical findings, in particular, fact retrieval (Anderson, 1974) and priming effects (e.g., McKoon and Ratcliff, 1979; but see Ratcliff and McKoon, 1988, for an alternative account of priming). An important difference, however, is that Anderson's network is used in the service of a production system; it enables a degree of parallel processing within the production system architecture by making a number of productions simultaneously active so as to compete with one another, and allows a partially matching production to fire if there is no stronger competitor (see also Thibadeau, Just, and Carpenter, 1982). This is similar to the notion of *soft constraints* that is discussed later in this chapter.

Hence, the parallel propagation of activation is an idea that has been used to good effect immediately prior to and during the current era of connectionist research, by J. R. Anderson and other spreading activation modelers. At least three differences distinguish spreading activation from connectionist models, however. First, Anderson retains a control structure (by means of a production system that utilizes his network), whereas connectionists are committed to trying to model cognition with no control other than the network's own highly decentralized local control. The control becomes relevant in Anderson's model in a process of pattern-matching, in which the more active nodes in the network are considered as matches to the conditions on productions and one production is ultimately selected and executed. For example, in a categorization task the production would be one that chooses the particular category that best fits the activation of features in the network. Second, the most radical version of connectionism, PDP, emphasizes the use of distinctive types of distributed representation such as coarse coding (discussed in the section on semantic interpretation which follows). Third, there are differences in the equations that govern the propagation of activation.

As this sketch makes clear, there is a variety of options network designers can use in determining both the types of activation a unit might take and how that activation is determined. The common element to all of these functions is that the new activation of a unit will be dependent in some degree on the net input a unit receives from other units. This net input is determined in part by the weights on the connections. These can be hand-tailored, but much of the interest in connectionist networks arises from their ability to modify their own weights adaptively, that is, to learn. In the next section we consider the basic idea of learning in such networks and introduce one quite simple learning procedure. Active research in this area has generated a large number of different learning procedures, however, and we shall devote chapter 3 to a more detailed discussion.

Learning Principles

For a connectionist system, learning is accomplished not by adding or modifying propositions, but rather by changing the connection weights between the simple units. Since the weights of these connections partly determine the state a network reaches as a result of its processing, these changes in weights result in changing the overall characteristics of the system. The basic goal is to provide a way of changing weights that increases the ability of the network to achieve a desired output in the future. The challenge is to have the network figure out the appropriate changes in weights without the aid of an external programmer or an internal executive in the network. Thus, the control over weight change should be entirely *local*. The information that is generally available locally to any weight is the current value of that weight and the activations of the units to which it is connected. If other information is to be employed, it must be provided to the units involved so that it is just as available as the current activations of the units.

One of the simplest such learning procedures for two-layer networks draws upon an idea proposed by Donald Hebb, who suggested that learning might occur in the nervous system by strengthening the connections between two neurons whenever they fired at the same time. Expanding on this idea for connectionist networks, the strength of the connection between two units (the weight) can be increased or decreased in proportion to the product of their activations. What is now referred to as the *Hebbian learning rule* specifies this function:

$$\Delta weight_{ui} = lrate\ a_u\ a_i \qquad (12)$$

where *lrate* is a constant specifying the rate of learning, a_u is the activation of the output unit, and a_i is the activation of the input unit. Thus, whenever both units have the *same* sign (positive or negative), the connection between them is *increased* proportionally to the product of the two activations. But when the activations of the two units have *different* signs, the weight of the connection is *decreased* proportionally to the product of their activations.

To see how the Hebbian procedure can enable a network to learn, let us consider a two-layer network that is using the Hebbian rule. Assume that the activations of the output units *u* are determined by the simplest linear rule; that is, the output of each input unit *i* is identical to its activation, the activation of each output unit *u* is identical to its net input, and the net input to a given output unit *u* can therefore be obtained by simply summing the products of each *i* unit's activation by the weight of its connection to *u*:

$$a_u = \sum_i weight_{ui}\ a_i \qquad (13)$$

To train the weights using the Hebbian learning rule, we supply the network with the paired input and output patterns that it is supposed to learn (we shall refer to each such pair as a *case*). If the learning rate (*lrate*) is set to $1/n$, where *n* is the number of input units, the system will exhibit "one trial learning." That is, if it is presented with the same input again on the next trial, its weights will already be adequate to generate the appropriate output. To illustrate, suppose that a simple network with four input and four output units is presented with Case A, that is, input pattern A $(1\ 1\ -1\ -1)$ paired with output pattern A $(1\ -1\ -1\ 1)$. If it is allowed to set its own weights according to the Hebbian principle, it will create the following matrix of 16 weights:

CASE A

Input unit	Input activation	Output unit			
		e	f	g	h
a	1	0.25	−0.25	−0.25	0.25
b	1	0.25	−0.25	−0.25	0.25
c	−1	−0.25	0.25	0.25	−0.25
d	−1	−0.25	0.25	0.25	−0.25
Desired output activation		1.00	−1.00	−1.00	1.00

For example, the value of the upper left cell in the matrix was obtained by multiplying the learning rate ($1/4 = 0.25$) by the input value for unit **a** (1) and the output value for unit **e** (1), yielding 0.25. We can readily see that this weight matrix will enable the network to reproduce the same output pattern if we now test it with the same input pattern. To obtain the value 1 on unit **e**, for example, the input values on **a** and **b** are each multiplied by 0.25, the input values on **c** and **d** are each multiplied by −0.25, and the four resulting values are added together. (Note that when we train the network, the input and output activations are fixed and the weights are calculated. When we then test the network, the input activations and weights are fixed, and the output activations are calculated. Case A, above, is illustrated in training mode; the label "desired output activation" indicates that this is a fixed output pattern supplied to the network.

This same network can in fact learn to produce specified output patterns for several different inputs without decreasing its performance on those it has already learned. It can do this as long as the new inputs are not correlated with those it has already learned. (Unfortunately, this is a highly constraining assumption that is difficult to satisfy.) Consider input pattern B: (1 −1 −1 1). We can verify that input pattern B is uncorrelated with input pattern A by calculating that, with the current weights, presenting input pattern B would cause the network to produce the output (0 0 0 0). This tells us that we could now *train* it to produce some designated output pattern B; let us specify (1 1 −1 −1). This training would result in the following modified weight matrix:

CASE B

Input unit	Input activation	Output unit e	f	g	h
a	1	0.50	0.00	−0.50	0.00
b	−1	0.00	−0.50	0.00	0.50
c	−1	−0.50	0.00	0.50	0.00
d	1	0.00	0.50	0.00	−0.50
Desired output activation		1.00	1.00	−1.00	−1.00

With these weights, the network will still respond correctly if presented with Case A again (because the new weights are an alternate solution to that problem), but now it also will respond correctly to Case B.

While the Hebbian rule produces impressive results, we shall see that there are serious limits to what it can accomplish. Thus, in the next chapter we shall explore a variety of different learning procedures that are now employed in connectionist networks. The idea that links all of them, though, is that learning involves changing weights in a network and that this is to be accomplished using only information that is available locally, that is at the units linked by the connection on which the weight is placed.

Semantic Interpretation of Connectionist Systems

In designing a connectionist network to function as a model of human performance in a particular domain, attention must be given to the question of how the concepts relevant to that domain will be represented in the network. There are two approaches: in *localist* networks each concept is assigned to one unit; in *distributed* networks the representation of each concept is distributed across multiple units. (The use of the term *local* here should not be confused with that in the preceding paragraph.)

Localist networks The Jets and Sharks network exemplifies the localist approach. Each concept (being a burglar, having the name "Art," etc.) is represented by one individual unit of the network. The semantic networks of the 1970s were also clearly localist, and when these have been augmented by equations that specify *spreading activation*, the resulting models (particularly the network portion of J. R. Anderson's

(1983) ACT* theory) have been similar in many respects to localist connectionist networks. Localist networks, from whatever research tradition, share the advantage that units can be labeled in the investigator's own language to facilitate keeping tabs on what the network is doing. This carries a danger: it is easy to forget that the label conveys meaning to the investigator, but not to the network itself. The correspondence between unit and concept relies on an external process of semantic interpretation, which must be performed with care. When the network is being used as a model of a particular domain, its success will be limited by the designer's intuitions of what concepts in that domain should be encoded (i.e., associated with a unit in the network) and by his or her skill in setting up connections appropriate to that encoding.

Despite these demands on the designer, it is generally even more difficult to set up a distributed network. Therefore, a localist network may be preferred when the task does not require the distinct advantages of distributed encoding (which are discussed below). The task of *multiple constraint satisfaction*, for example, can be adequately performed by an interactive localist network. Units represent concepts, and positive or negative connections between pairs of units represent constraints between those concepts. A positive connection between two units puts a constraint on the entire network to favor states (overall activation patterns) in which the two units have the same activation (e.g., both *on* or both *off*); a negative connection favors states in which the two units have opposite activity. To run this procedure, each unit is given a baseline activation value (often zero), and each connection weight is fixed as positive or negative. External input is optional, and acts as an additional source of constraint. The network then runs interactively until it settles into a stable state (pattern of activation values); if a global energy minimum is attained, that state will be the state that best satisfies the constraints. One of the important features of this procedure is that these are *soft* constraints. Even if there is a negative constraint between two units, if other constraints involving those units favor their having the same state, the most stable solution may have both units *on* or both units *off* (violating that one particular constraint but satisfying a number of other constraints).

Distributed networks   In a distributed network, each concept is represented by a pattern of activation across an ensemble or set of units; by design, no single unit can convey that concept on its own. To convert the Jets' and Sharks' three occupations to distributed representations, for example, we might continue to use three units, but arbitrarily associate each occupation with a different pattern of activation values across those units as follows:

$$1 \ 1 \ 1 \ = \ \text{Burglar} \qquad -1 \ -1 \ 1 \ = \ \text{Bookie} \qquad 1 \ -1 \ -1 \ = \ \text{Pusher}$$

In this example individual units do not have a semantic interpretation. Rather, each semantic interpretation is distributed over three units (rather than assigned to one localist unit), and each unit is involved in three different semantic interpretations.

An alternative way to achieve a distributed representation of a concept is to carry out a featural analysis of the concept, and encode that analysis across an appropriate number of units. Featural representation is widely used in the psychological literature on concepts and categories, for example in exemplar models (see chapter 4). What is new here is to situate the featural representation in a network architecture.[7] The idea that this constitutes a distributed representation is often difficult to grasp, because the features themselves are typically encoded on individual units. That is, there is a localist representation of the features (one unit per feature), and a distributed representation of the target concept. In illustration, suppose that a large number of professions are the objects to be represented. The network designer might craft a set of 50 units in which each unit is interpreted as corresponding to some feature that is salient to professions, and represent each profession as a pattern across those units. Those professions chosen by the Jets and Sharks would all share the feature *illegal*, for example, but only the pusher profession (like the pharmacist profession) would have the feature *involves drugs*.

How does one obtain a featural analysis of a domain in order to build these representations? One method is to let an existing theory guide this work; for example, a particular linguistic account might be used as a basis for representing words as patterns over phonemic units. In the connectionist research program the interest lies, not so much in the particular features and assignments, but rather in how the system makes use of its distributed representation once it has been built. We might, for example, explore generalization or associative learning under the conditions offered by such a representation. A second method is to let

---

7 This kind of representation has also been used by J. R. Anderson (1983) in ACT* networks. For example (pp. 137–9), he has implemented McClelland and Rumelhart's (1981) featural decomposition of letters in his activation-based pattern matcher for recognition of four-letter words. Both Anderson and Rumelhart and McClelland also had a localist encoding of the letters themselves in a higher layer of units, however; exclusively distributed encodings would lack this hierarchical structure.

the system perform its own analysis of the domain. When a multi-layered network is run in a learning paradigm (as described in chapter 3), the network designer specifies the interpretations only of the input and output units; the input–output cases used for training are selected with respect to this interpretation. The designer does not know what aspects of the input–output cases each hidden unit will become sensitive to; the learning process is in part a process of feature extraction, and observing this is one of the most intriguing aspects of connectionist research. Usually the hidden units do not arrive at a simple, localist representation of the most obvious regularities (features) in the input. Rather, each hidden unit is sensitive to complex, often subtle, regularities that connectionists call *microfeatures*. Each layer of hidden units can be regarded as providing a particular distributed encoding of the input pattern (that is, an encoding in terms of a pattern of microfeatures).

One virtue of distributed representation is that part of the representation can be missing without substantially hurting performance. Using the arbitrary distributed representations of three occupations displayed at the beginning of this section, for example, we might specify an input only for the first two units and leave the third questionable (1 1 ?). Nevertheless, the network will treat this pattern similarly to a complete *burglar* input (1 1 1), since this is the pattern to which the partial input is most similar. The point is even clearer in networks with more units. Consider, for example, a pattern associator network with two layers of 16 units each. Each of the units in the input will be connected to all of the units in the output layer, and depending upon the size of the weights, will contribute either a little or a lot of the information needed to determine the value of the output unit. Each output unit will be receiving inputs from 16 different input units. If there is no input from a given input unit, or the wrong input, the activity on the other input lines generally will compensate. The point here is that once we distribute information as a pattern across units, we also distribute the resources used to process it. Thus, a distributed system becomes more resilient to damage. Beyond this, we make it possible for the system to learn new information without sacrificing existing information. For example, without adding new units, we can teach the network to respond to a new input that is different from any it has learned so far. It often is sufficient to make slight changes to a variety of weights, which do not significantly alter the way the network responds to existing patterns. (There are limits to this capacity, however; in some circumstances teaching a new input disrupts previous learning to an unacceptable degree. For a demonstration of "catastrophic" interference, see McCloskey and Cohen, in press; for a connectionist response, see Hetherington and Seidenberg, 1989.)

see McCloskey and Cohen, in press; for a connectionist response, see Hetherington and Seidenberg, 1989.)

For a final virtue of distributed networks, consider a distributed network that has encoded a structured domain of knowledge, in which there are regularities in the input–output pairings. If the network is presented with a new input pattern, a reasonable response should appear on the output units. Humans often exhibit a similar capacity when provided with only partial information about a new entity. Generally, we infer some of the other properties the entity might have, based on its similarity to entities we already know. In their discussion of distributed representations, Hinton, McClelland, and Rumelhart (1986, *PDP:3*) provide the following example: if we are told that chimpanzees like onions, we shall probably revise our expectations about whether gorillas like onions as well. This reflects a general tendency of organisms to make *generalizations* (and specifically exemplifies what Shipley (1988) calls an *over-hypothesis*). Distributed representations are well suited to producing and investigating generalization.

There is one additional approach to achieving distributed representations that is counterintuitive in many respects, but is ingenious and exhibits some very useful properties. This is a technique known as *coarse coding*. The basic idea is that, rather than deploying units so that each unit represents information as precisely as possible, we design each individual unit (called a *receptor* in this context) to be sensitive to many different inputs (which constitute its *receptive field*). Each unit is sensitive to (activated by) a different set of inputs, and each input has a number of units that are sensitive to it. In this architecture, the fact that a particular unit is active is not very informative; but if a high percentage of the units that are sensitive to a particular input are active, the presence of that input can be inferred with high confidence.

To consider a concrete example, coarse coding was used by Touretzky and Hinton (1988) in a connectionist system that they constructed to implement a production system. One of their purposes was to show that connectionist systems can indeed represent and use explicit rules; for discussion of that aspect of their paper, see chapter 7. Their other purpose was to illustrate certain advantages of coarse coding. The production system that they implemented was designed to follow rules involving meaningless triples composed from a 25-letter vocabulary. The triples themselves were not directly encoded in the network; rather, each coarse-coded triple was presented by turning on all of the units (28 on average) that were designated as its receptors in the "working memory" network that was one component of the system. Each such unit was a receptor for a large number of different triples. For example, one of the units that was a receptor for the triple (F A B) was also a receptor for any other triple that could be formed from the following receptive field by selecting one letter from each column in the order shown:

Position 1	Position 2	Position 3
C	A	B
F	E	D
M	H	J
Q	K	M
S	T	P
W	Y	R

Hence that particular receptor unit was turned on (became active) if (F A B) was to be presented; but the same unit would be turned on if (C A B) or (S H M) or any one of 216 (6^3) different triples was to be presented. The particular sets of letters were determined randomly and were different for each unit. For example, another of the receptor units for (F A B) might have had the following receptive field:

Position 1	Position 2	Position 3
F	A	B
I	C	D
K	H	E
P	K	J
S	R	M
V	W	U

From the perspective of the triple itself, those two receptor units and their distinctive receptive fields were only two of the approximately 28 different units that would be activated as the means of presenting (F A B) to the working memory network. From the perspective of a single receptor unit, it might have been turned on as a means of presenting any one of the 216 different triples in its receptive field. To know which triple was actually being presented, one would need to know the particular combination of 28 activated units and to consult the external listing of their receptive fields (which would reveal that they had in common only that F was one of the six letters in position 1, A was one of the six letters in position 2, and B was one of the six letters in position 3).

This may seem like a very strange way to design a memory, but Touretzky and Hinton pointed out several advantageous or human-like properties gained from coarse coding. First, the number of units

needed to store all possible triples is minimized. There are 15,625 possible triples, about half a dozen of which are present in working memory
at any given time. But the working memory is composed of only about
2,000 different units. Second, the memory is tolerant of noise (i.e., a
few units can be in the wrong state without materially affecting performance). Third, the memory does not have a rigid, fixed capacity;
rather, its ability to distinguish triples will gradually decline as the
number of stored items increases. Fourth, active triples will gradually
decay as new triples are stored. Fifth, a degree of generalization is
exhibited: if two of the triples that have been presented to the memory
network both happen to have F as their initial letter, more than the
usual number of receptors will be active for other F-initial triples.

Course coding is one of the most distinctive, nonobvious techniques
made possible by the use of distributed (rather than localist) representations. Hinton, McClelland, and Rumelhart (1986, *PDP:3*) provide
further discussion of coarse coding, including design considerations
that must be attended to (e.g., a tradeoff between resolution and accuracy in setting the size of the receptive fields). They also make the following intriguing suggestion, with which we shall close this section:

Units that respond to complex features in retinotopic maps in visual cortex
often have fairly large receptive fields. This is often interpreted as the first step
on the way to a translation invariant representation. However, it may be that
the function of the large fields is not to achieve translation invariance but to
pinpoint accurately where the feature is! (1986, *PDP:3*, p. 92)

The Allure of the Connectionist Approach

One reason many people are attracted to network models of cognition is
that they seem to exhibit many properties found in human cognition
that are not generally found in symbolic models. In this section we shall
review, without much critical discussion, some of the properties that
have been cited.

Neural Plausibility

Certainly one of the major features that has attracted researchers to network models is that they seem more compatible than symbolic models
with what we know of the nervous system. This is not surprising: Network models are *neurally inspired*. Pitts and McCulloch, for example,
built their models using a simplified conception of how neurons work.

Hence, the state of activation of a unit (especially of units that only acquire discrete activations, 0 and 1) was intended to correspond to a neuron either resting or firing. The connections between units were conceived on the model of the axons and dendrites of neurons. Thus, the propagation of activation within a network is, at least on this very general level, similar to the kinds of processing that we observe in the nervous system.

Of course, connectionist networks do not capture all features of neural architecture and processing in the brain. For example, little attention is paid to trying to model the particular pattern of connectivity of neurons in the brain. Nor is there any attempt to simulate the differences between various neurotransmitters, or the very intricate way in which excitations to neurons are compounded to determine whether the neuron will actually fire. Thus, networks only capture aspects of the coarse architecture of the brain. Conversely, there are aspects of connectionist networks that do not clearly map onto what is known about the nervous system; the back-propagation procedure for learning (chapter 3) is a particularly important example.

These differences present no difficulty, and in fact may be desirable, if one focuses on connectionist models as cognitive (rather than biological) models. Some investigators, however, prefer to push the neural analogy as far as possible. For example, it is known that neural systems carry out basic processing (e.g., recognizing a word) very quickly, that is, within a few hundred milliseconds. Since it takes each neuron several milliseconds to fire, it has been argued that basic cognitive tasks cannot require more than a hundred steps of sequential processing (Feldman and Ballard, 1982). This, it is claimed, poses a serious problem for traditional symbolic architectures, since to model even simple tasks often requires programs embodying several thousand instructions. But since network processing relies on performing many different operations in parallel, it seems much easier for networks to satisfy the 100 step constraint. For example, the network described at the beginning of this chapter could identify a gang member on the basis of some of his properties and then determine the remainder of those properties, well within 100 processing steps (assuming it were implemented on appropriate, parallel hardware).

Neural plausibility is most obviously advantageous if one is concerned with the interface between psychology and neuroscience, and least advantageous if "mere implementation" is regarded as outside the domain of concern for psychologists (see chapter 7). A middle position is to view the neural metaphor as a source of ideas that may or may not pan out, with its biological underpinnings favoring but not determining that it will succeed. Other useful metaphors might come from such remote areas as physics (e.g., the hologram theory of memory). On this view the neural metaphor is superior to the extent that it inspires models that deal nicely with particular problems or phenomena, such as generalization. The further idea that the models work well *because* they use neurally-inspired concepts (i.e., that there is a causal relation) is speculative, but points the way to a potentially attractive bonus that is not shared by most other metaphors, including the currently dominant von Neumann computer metaphor.

Satisfaction of "Soft Constraints"

The existence of a connection between two units in a network constitutes a constraint on the processing of that network. If that connection is excitatory (has a positive weight), then, if the first unit is active, the second unit is constrained to be active as well. Rules in a symbolic system likewise serve as a constraint. If the antecedent of a production system rule is satisfied so that the rule fires, then the consequent action is constrained to occur. In this sense connections serve the same function as rules: they determine the future action of the system. But there is an important difference. Rules are deterministic so that if a rule fires, its action is certain to occur. In a network, on the other hand, a given unit receives input from many other units. If one unit delivers an excitatory constraint while two others deliver inhibitory constraints of greater total magnitude, the overall effect will be inhibitory (using the simplest activation function). The unit finds the best overall solution to the multiple constraints, and that solution may not be compatible with all of the individual constraints. Thus, the constraints imposed by the connections are often spoken of as *soft constraints*.

Note that this is not an absolute distinction; there are degrees of softness in constraints. Some rule systems allow for competition between rules whose antecedents are equally satisfied, and even allow the resolution of this competition to be probabilistic (MacWhinney and Bates, 1989). These systems exhibit some, but not all, of the advantages of networks. As for networks, it is possible to design networks that (like rules) exhibit relatively hard constraints; the trained XOR network in chapter 3 provides an example. Hence, although connectionist networks offer a particularly natural way to achieve soft constraints, the association is not exclusive or inevitable.

There are many tasks or domains in which cognition seems to be better modeled by soft constraints than by hard constraints. For example, in decision-making a person is often confronted with conflicting desiderata and must choose among them. The most realistic preconnectionist decision-making models have been mathematical rather than purely propositional. They have been limited, however, by their reliance on linear functions. A localist interactive network, in contrast, can be designed as a nonlinear dynamic system. Each possible desideratum may be modeled as a soft constraint between one of the units representing different aspects of the situation and one of the units representing possible actions. When a new situation is presented, we can allow the network to settle into a stable state which represents the best satisfaction of these constraints. Not all desiderata will be satisfied, but the network will have efficiently identified the best outcome. The use of soft constraints enables connectionist systems to account for the competition between competing desiderata without having to specify rules that arbitrate the competition, and without the limitations of linear models.

Soft constraints are also beneficial in designing systems to deal with new situations that have not been envisaged in advance. If a new input is provided to a connectionist network, for example, it will respond with no special effort using the connections it has already developed. If the situation is like one on which the network had previously been trained, it will generate a similar response. If the new situation shows weaker similarities to a variety of old situations, the network will use the connections developed in the old cases to construct a plausible new response. Designers of rule systems have also shown increased interest in developing strategies for flexible response to new situations; the next few years should bring some vigorous discussion of the relative merits of different approaches.

The naturalness with which connectionist networks implement soft constraints is part of what enables connectionist networks to overcome a common problem that confronts researchers in the symbolic tradition. The problem is that rules tend to have exceptions. This is seen particularly clearly in attempts to formalize principles of language, where in fact we see two different kinds of exception. First, there are the exceptions to generally applicable rules that nevertheless are recognized as proper uses of the language. For example, many irregular verbs violate the general rules for forming the past tense, but these irregular forms are the correct forms for those verbs. To handle these cases, symbolic theorists may write more complex sets of rules in which the exceptions themselves are specified by rules of limited application. The more exceptions there are, the less satisfactory is this approach. (See Lakoff (1970) for a consideration of the problems posed by exceptions.) Second, there are the mistakes people make in actually speaking the language, which result in sentences that are more or less ungrammatical. Chomsky's *competence/performance* distinction has frequently been invoked as a way of construing these cases. A speaker is assumed to have a system of rules, which constitutes his or her linguistic competence. Additional factors become involved when this competence is expressed in specific linguistic acts, all of which create variations (e.g., in the timing of pauses in sentence production) among which are grammatical errors. Preferably, the errors would be accounted for within the same mechanistic explanation that accounts for how we produce sentences at all.

Connectionists, in fact, have some hope of accounting for both rule-like and exceptional behavior by means of a single mechanism. In each case, it is the set of connections in the network that determine the response of the system. The particular set of constraints found in a network may enable it to perform consistently with a general rule in some contexts, but to select the appropriate exceptional response in other contexts. Sometimes when we analyze a network we can find connections that can be interpreted as serving the same function that a rule might serve in a symbolic system. But even when we find such an interpretable connection, it is only a soft constraint that the system as a whole might override. Hence, connectionism attempts to avoid some of the problems posed by exceptions to rules by using a system of *soft* constraints rather than *hard* rules. The goal is to account for exceptions as well as regularities within the same system. (See chapter 7 for opposing views of the success of one such attempt.)

Graceful Degradation

One of the notable features of the human brain is that it seems to be an extremely reliable device. Like any mechanism, though, it has its limits. It can be overloaded with too many demands or too much information, or it can be impaired by physical damage. But when its limits are exceeded, generally it does not crash. It simply begins to perform sub-optimally. When confronting a task that makes too many demands, it begins to ignore some of the demands or some of the information. The more it is overloaded, or the more it is impaired, the less well it functions. The same gradation of effect is found when some components are destroyed. In a very few situations, a clearly delineated behavioral deficit will arise. For example, the classical work on aphasia correlated particular lesions (e.g., in Broca's area) with particular behavioral deficits (inability to produce articulate speech). But in general the brain is rather resilient in the face of damage. Nerve cells die everyday, but generally this does not leave a trace in terms of specific impairment of performance. Loss of even large numbers of neurons may lead not to specific losses but to a nonspecific gradual impairment of function. For example, we do not forget how to divide 12 by 2 and yet remember the rest of the division tables; rather, we gradually become more limited in our numeric abilities. This characteristic of gradually failing performance is generally referred to as *graceful degradation*.

A traditional symbolic system does not exhibit graceful degradation. If any of its elements are lost, the information they encode is no longer available to the system. This is particularly clear if we consider what happens if a rule is eliminated. The system is simply not able to respond to any of the situations in which that rule was needed. It is possible to develop implementations of symbolic systems that are more resistant to damage, for example, by storing information at redundant locations or using error-checking techniques to recover from damage. Such an implementation still may fail to exhibit the more subtle phenomenon of graceful degradation.

A connectionist network, on the other hand, does exhibit graceful degradation. Destruction of a few connections or even of a few units (except in networks which only have a few units to begin with) generally does not significantly impair the activity of the system. In a localist system, destroying a unit will destroy a particular piece of that system's information, with possibly serious consequences, but destroying connections instead will result in graceful degradation. For example, using the Jets and Sharks network which employs a localist encoding, we destroyed at random 53 of the 1,062 connections in the network (5 percent of the total) and then explored its performance on the same tasks that we discussed at the beginning of this chapter. On two of the tasks its performance was qualitatively the same: it still correctly identified Art's properties and it still correctly identified the individuals that met the specification of being in their twenties and being pushers. It did perform differently when queried about Sharks. It still responded by activating particular Sharks, but it offered different judgements as to who were the most prototypical Sharks (Nick, Neal, and Dave). The reason the network was still able to identify Art's properties was that none of the connections between Art's person unit and his properties happened to be broken. But as an additional experiment we broke one of these connections (between **ART** and **junior high** education). The network now answered incorrectly that Art had a high school education. What is interesting is how it arrived at this answer: those individuals who were most similar to Art in other respects tended to activate the unit for **high school** education. Thus, even when disabled, the network still offered plausible judgements. It did not crash.

In systems using distributed representation, we can eliminate a number of units in the system and the system will still behave in only a slightly distorted fashion. For example, if an input normally consisted of a distributed representation over eight units, and one of these was disabled, the system will still respond normally to most input patterns. With more damage, the system will increasingly make errors; however, even these will not be random, but rather be associated with closely related patterns to which the distorted input is now more similar. Hence, a connectionist cognitive system inherently displays graceful degradation as a consequence of its own architecture. It will display that property whether it is implemented in a nervous system, on a parallel machine, or even on a serial computer.

Content-addressable Memory

The human ability to remember information is quite remarkable. Frequently information that we need comes to mind spontaneously. We identify a book that we need, and we remember that we loaned it to a student. Sometimes, though, we need to work at recalling information: we remember we loaned the book to a student, but now have to work at trying to recall who the student was. This may involve retrieving cues that will help us identify the person. Typically, we can retrieve the same piece of information from a variety of different cues that constitute part of the contents of the memory itself. Since such memory is accessed through its content, it is generally termed *content addressable memory*. Designing this type of memory access into a symbolic system is a challenge, and requires maneuvering around the architecture of the system rather than taking advantage of it.

A common model for a symbolic memory is a filing system: we store information on paper, place the paper in a file folder, and position the folder in a cabinet sorted according to some procedure we take to be reasonable. If each folder is positioned by an arbitrary index, or by the serial order of its creation, there is no content addressability in the filing system. More frequently, each folder will be positioned in accord with one or at most two aspects of its content. For example, suppose that we keep track of students in our classes by placing information about them in file folders arranged alphabetically. Sometimes this works very well. If we want information on a particular student, we can rapidly access the file with that student's name. If, however, we seek to recover the information by taking a different route, the task is more difficult. Suppose that the information we want to access about a student is her name, and the cues we start with are what class she took and what grade she got. Now we face a serious problem: since the information is not organized in this manner, the only way to retrieve the student's name is to go through each folder until we find a student who took the class in question and received the specified grade. If we had known in advance that there might be different ways in which we would want to access the information in our filing cabinet, we could have developed an indexing system that would have told us where information satisfying certain descriptions would be found. For example, we might have constructed an index identifying by name the students in each class. But then it is necessary to identify in advance all the ways we might want to access the file. Furthermore, if we make errors in recalling the contents that are indexed (e.g., confusing our course on research methods with our course on statistics), the index is of little or no use.

The disadvantages of the filing cabinet system are exhibited in a variety of memory systems. In computer systems, for example, information is stored at register locations, and the only way to access information directly is by means of the address of the location. Symbolic systems that are implemented on such computers often (although not necessarily) make some of the same assumptions about storage and retrieval. Serial search through separate items therefore figures prominently in memory retrieval. Some such systems attain superior performance by means of intelligent search procedures that mitigate this difficulty.

Connectionist networks offer a relatively natural alternative means of achieving content addressable, fault tolerant memory. The Jets and Sharks network provides a simple illustration. Properties could be retrieved from names, names from properties, and so forth. We might even make a mistake on one property and still retrieve the right person. For example, we gave the network the task of remembering George's name and we described him as a Jet, in his thirties, junior high educated, and divorced. As an experiment, we deliberately made a mistake about one of George's properties (he is in fact still in his twenties). No one, in fact, precisely fits this description. But, since the connections only constitute soft constraints, the network proceeds to find the best match. The units for Jim and George become most active (0.31 after 70 cycles), while Al is slightly less active (0.30). Jim and George actually have identical properties and match on three out of four cued properties, while Al has different properties, but also matches on three out of four. Thus, even with erroneous cues, the network has recalled the persons who best match what cues were given.

The advantages of content-addressable memory are particularly evident in systems employing distributed representations; in such systems it is often possible, given part of a pattern, to reconstruct the whole pattern. A question arises, however, as to how we should characterize this sort of memory. Within symbolic systems remembering is a process of retrieving a symbol that has been stored away. But in connectionist networks, remembering is carried out by the same means as making inferences; the system fills in missing pieces of information. As far as the system's processing is concerned, there is no difference between reconstructing a previous state, and constructing a totally new state (confabulating):

One way of thinking about distributed memories is in terms of a very large set of plausible inference rules. Each active unit represents a "microfeature" of an item, and the connection strengths stand for plausible "microinferences" between microfeatures. Any particular pattern of activity of the units will satisfy some of the microinferences and violate others. A stable pattern of activity is one that violates the plausible microinferences less than any of the neighboring patterns. A new stable pattern can be created by changing the inference rules so that the new pattern violates them less than its neighbors. This view of memory makes it clear that there is no sharp distinction between genuine memory and plausible reconstruction. A genuine memory is a pattern that is stable because the inference rules were modified when it occurred before. A "confabulation" is a pattern that is stable because of the way the inference rules have been modified to store several different previous patterns. So far as the subject is concerned, this may be indistinguishable from the real thing. (Hinton, McClelland, and Rumelhart, 1986, *PDP:3*, pp. 80–1)

Capacity to Learn from Experience

A final feature of networks that makes them attractive is their capacity to learn from experience by changing the weights of connections. In the next chapter we shall examine connectionist learning in greater depth, so we shall make just one comment here.

The comment is that not all learning has the gradual character that we have been emphasizing. At least in the case of human beings, some information can be learned rapidly in one or two encounters. Also, some information is encoded in relative isolation rather than as part of a highly connected system. In illustration of both of these points, suppose that I am told verbally, "To make this thing work, push a candy bar through the slot in the center." I am highly likely to remember that rather bizarre instruction. It is this kind of learning that symbolic models are best equipped to handle, and for which the relevance of connectionist modeling is unclear at this point. In contrast, learning a language or learning to do arithmetic is awkward to model symbolically, but is natural (although challenging) to model using networks. One would hope that a unified account will eventually be attained; but at present it is not obvious how connectionism might handle some of the most distinctively human capabilities for dealing with information.

Summary

In this chapter we have presented a simple connectionist network (the Jets and Sharks network), and examined some of the basic architectural features that can be employed in connectionist networks more generally. We have also examined some of the features of connectionist systems that have served to attract interest in them. In the next chapter we shall examine in more detail the ability of connectionist systems to learn before turning to a cognitive task, pattern recognition, for which connectionist networks appear particularly adept.

3

Learning

One of the features of connectionist systems that has been most attractive to researchers is the capacity of these systems to learn. In this chapter we first discuss alternative approaches to learning that were developed earlier than, and compete with, connectionism. Second, we describe and illustrate some of the principal learning strategies that have been developed for connectionist networks. Third, we discuss two essentially philosophical issues that are raised by connectionist learning strategies.

Traditional and Contemporary Approaches to Learning

Treatments of learning generally divide along a major philosophical distinction, that between empiricism and rationalism. Empiricism and rationalism represent two major intellectual traditions that can be traced back at least to Plato and Aristotle. They were developed most systematically in the wake of the Scientific Revolution in the seventeenth century, which overthrew the then current Aristotelian theories of the natural world (according to which objects behaved in accord with their natural forms or essences) and of the human capacity for knowledge (which involved internalizing the forms of objects). The distinctive claims of these two traditions have continued to divide contemporary disciplines such as psychology and linguistics.

Empiricism The tradition of philosophical empiricism emerged in Britain and is associated with such theorists as Bacon, Locke, Berkeley, and Hume. The empiricists faulted the Aristotelian tradition for excessive dependence on established principles of reasoning and for insufficient attention to our sensory experience of the world. For the empiricists, such sensory experience provided the only authority that we could employ if we sought truth. The empiricists' primary concern was thus epistemological: knowledge must be grounded in sensory experience. Also incorporated within their framework, however, was an account of psychological processes that became known as *associationism*. In this account, sensory experience gave rise to simple ideas (e.g., *red*, *round*), which then became composed into more complex ideas (e.g., *apple*). In this example, it is spatial contiguity that produces the association. For Hume and others, temporal contiguity was also important, because it was viewed as giving rise to our idea of causation. Once associated, the idea of a cause could elicit the idea of its effect. Similarity was an additional principle governing the formation of associations in most treatments. The associationist approach was further developed by psychological theorists such as David Hartley in the eighteenth century and James Mill, John Stuart Mill, Alexander Bain, and Herbert Spencer in the nineteenth century. J. R. Anderson and Bower (1973) offered a useful review that suggests four defining features of associationism: the notion that mental elements become associated through experience; that complex ideas can be reduced to a set of simple ideas; that the simple ideas are sensations; and that simple additive rules are sufficient to predict properties of complex ideas from simple ideas.

A kind of associationism found expression in the behaviorist models of classical and operant conditioning, which were developed in the United States in the twentieth century. Here, the strategy was to limit the entities involved in the posited associations to what could be observed by an investigator: environmental events (stimuli, reinforcements) and the behavioral responses of the organism. During the era when behaviorism dominated psychology, learning was the central topic of concern. Researchers actively investigated the efficacy of different ways of arranging the environment (by varying the timing and degree of reinforcement, punishment, contiguity, and the like). Some used the tool of mathematical modeling to develop general theories of learning. Learning was operationally defined as changes in the frequency of a particular response. The major limitation of this work was the lack of an adequate means of modeling what occurred *inside* the system as it learned. In fact, this limitation was regarded as a virtue: learning theorists preferred to regard the organism as a black box. Some investigators developed notions of mediated learning that referred to internal stimuli and responses, but had no way of actually building models of the internal events. They were intrigued, for example, by the ability of older children (but not younger children or animals) quickly to reverse the responses made to two kinds of stimuli when the experimenter suddenly reversed the contingencies. "Reversal learning" was regarded as a phenomenon that presented a challenge for learning theory. Although no solution was directly forthcoming, the limitations of behaviorism made some of its practitioners receptive to the information processing approach that emerged in the 1960s. Hence, behaviorism has lost its pre-eminence but endures as a research tradition within psychology.

Rationalism   The other major intellectual tradition that the cognitive sciences have inherited is rationalism, represented by philosophers on the European continent such as Descartes, Spinoza, and Liebniz. Rationalism rejected empiricism's strong reliance on sensory experience and offered a different diagnosis of the problems with Aristotelianism (in particular, the fact that it had not achieved true knowledge). Rationalists did not seek to restrict ideas to those grounded in experience. Ideas, for the rationalist, were innate; what was critical in arriving at true beliefs was the way we reasoned using these ideas. Rationalists did not reject reliance on sensory experience altogether. They proposed that it could tell us which of several possible coherent arrangements of ideas were actually instantiated in this world. But they insisted that far more basic than experience was careful reasoning using our native ideas.

The rationalist tradition has had its major contemporary impact in the discipline of linguistics. Rejecting the behaviorist foundations of structural linguistics, Noam Chomsky (1957, 1968) embraced mentalism and claimed that grammars are essentially cognitive theories. For Chomsky grammars are models of human linguistic *competence*, and the crucial core of that competence, Universal Grammar, is innate. Chomsky took a distinctly rationalist position with respect to learning. In his well-known review of B. F. Skinner's *Verbal Behavior*, Chomsky (1959) objected to Skinner's claim that a behaviorist theory could account for language learning, and he further developed his position in *Language and Mind* (Chomsky, 1968). One of Chomsky's main arguments, known as the *poverty of the stimulus* argument, contended that the amount of data a child receives in his or her early years is not sufficient to determine uniquely the rules of the child's grammar.

In fact, two issues are combined in Chomsky's attack on behaviorist models of language acquisition. First, what role is played by innate knowledge in language acquisition? Second, for those aspects of a language that must be learned (e.g., particulars of the inflectional system), by what process does that learning occur? Language acquisition researchers within the Chomskian tradition initially put forward the "little linguist" model: that the child formulates hypotheses and tests them against data (typically not consciously). With changes in linguistic theory that have occurred since then, Chomskian students of language acquisition now are more likely to talk about the child using the incoming data to set parameters. On this view, the child is born with a set of unmarked (default) parameters that can be reset on the basis of experience. For example, *pro drop* specifies that subject pronouns can be omitted, and is assumed unless the child encounters disconfirming evidence (as in English; see Hyams, 1986). There has been an ongoing tension in developmental psychology between those adopting the Chomskian approach, and those preferring an empiricist framework. Neither group has been able to offer a detailed model of the mechanisms involved in language acquisition.

Contemporary cognitive science   Chomskian linguists have continued into the 1980s as the contemporary representatives of a rationalist view of learning. Cognitive psychologists and artificial intelligence researchers, in contrast, tended to ignore learning until recently. In formulating an alternative to behaviorism, they addressed questions on which immediate progress could be made using rule-based symbolic models: how information is represented in the mind, what kinds of memory systems are involved, and what processes operate on mental representations. Several factors have resulted in increased attention to learning in the 1980s; prominent among these is the rise of connectionist approaches to learning. Some symbolic-tradition researchers have also exhibited a new interest in learning, but have expressed that interest by designing rule-based systems that can learn. For instance, by the 1980s there was new work on such approaches as learning by analogy and by other inductive procedures (e.g., J. R. Anderson, 1981; Holland, Holyoak, Nisbett, and Thagard, 1986).

Within artificial intelligence, an active research area known as *machine learning* has emerged, which pursues strategies for getting machines to learn from experience. Since rules are the major determinant of behavior in symbolic systems, the strategies focus on modifying or adding rules. One of the factors that makes this work challenging is that altering rules can have fairly global effects on behavior; hence, a rule modification designed to deal with one circumstance may inadvertently result in new, incorrect behavior in certain other circumstances. A more general problem is that modifying or adding rules can be too crude a techniques to capture the gradualness and subtlety of learning. As research has proceeded, techniques have emerged to make much finer adjustments to rule systems that overcome these difficulties and result in performance that is more human-like (see, for example, Holland et al., 1986). Hence, a researcher interested in learning in the 1990s has a choice of approaches. The empiricist branch of the symbolic approach (e.g., cognitive psychology and AI) offers increasingly sophisticated methods for modifying rules and symbolic representations. The rationalist branch of the symbolic approach (e.g., linguistics and Chomskian language-acquisition research) offers new interpretations of how adjustments are made to an innate grammar in order to acquire a specific language. And connectionism offers new, powerful learning algorithms that have revived interest in subsymbolic network architectures as a vehicle for an essentially empiricist program. We turn now to a more detailed consideration of how connectionist networks learn.

Connectionist Models of Learning

In the previous chapter we have already provided an introduction to learning in connectionist systems. Learning consists in changing the weights of connections between units, so as to alter the way in which the network will process inputs on subsequent occasions. When a network is run in training mode, both activations and weights change on each learning trial; after training, the network can be tested by presenting inputs and observing their effect on the activations alone. It is important to understand that although both weights and activations can change in response to inputs, their roles are distinct. Activation values are the vehicle for temporary state changes in a network that should tell us which one of a set of possible input patterns has just been processed. Weights are the vehicle for more enduring changes in a network that make it capable of processing all of the various input patterns on which it has been trained. In fact, some training procedures make the weight changes only after the entire batch of input patterns has been processed rather than on every trial; in the end, the results are very similar. In contrast, it would not make any sense to change activations less frequently than every trial (that is, every presentation of an input pattern).

One similarity between activations and weights is that their changes are determined *locally*; that is, they are based solely on information that is directly available to a particular unit or connection. In the case of a weight change, the outputs (which are often simply the activations) of each of the two units between which the connection is being adjusted count as local. Any units other than those indexed in the weight's subscripts are remote, not local. In a multilayer or interactive network these remote units can affect the activation of the local units by means of unit-to-unit (local) propagation of activity through the network; hence they can affect the changes in weights as well. However, the effects must come only via the series of local changes; it is somewhat like playing a game of rumor (A whispers to B, B whispers to C) rather than A simply talking to everyone at once.

A variety of learning procedures is now employed in connectionist networks. The precise procedure chosen depends in part upon the architecture of the network that is to learn. In this chapter we shall describe some of the most commonly used learning procedures. In order to make clear the basic principles, we have chosen to provide a detailed treatment of representative examples of learning in one class of networks (feedforward networks). Recall that in such networks, a pattern of activation is provided across the units of the input layer, and the network is supposed to produce an appropriate pattern of activation across the units of the output layer. We shall begin with learning procedures for two-layer feedforward networks (pattern associators) and then move on to multi-layered feedforward networks. We must be briefer in our treatment of other learning procedures, including those for the Boltzmann machine (as an exemplar of interactive networks), competitive learning, and reinforcement learning. Note that learning procedures are often classified as exemplifying *supervised learning* versus *unsupervised learning*. In supervised learning, the network is explicitly told what output was desired for a particular input (and must compare that to its actual output). In unsupervised learning, the network classifies a set of inputs without feedback. This distinction seems clear enough, but considerable controversy has emerged regarding the proper application of these terms; we shall refer to it only for the clearest cases.

Learning Procedures for Two-layer, Feedforward Networks

The goal of the learning procedure is to develop weights that enable a network to respond appropriately to a set of cases. Each case is composed of a pattern of activations across the units of the input layer (the *input pattern*) and a pattern of activations across the units of the output layer (the *output pattern*). These patterns technically can be treated as *n*-dimensional *vectors*, where *n* is the number of units; however, we shall simply refer to them as *patterns*. Typically, the network's ability to learn is determined by running it in two different modes: a training mode, in which entire cases are presented (input patterns with their associated output patterns) and a test mode, in which only the input patterns are presented. During training, the weights increasingly accommodate the constraints in the set of cases. Minimally, every case would be presented once in the training mode (so that the number of training trials would equal the number of cases); this is referred to as one *epoch* of training. Depending upon the learning procedure used and the difficulty of the set of cases, a large number of epochs may be required to achieve satisfactory performance. If the training has been sufficient, when the network is tested with the input patterns, it will respond with the appropriate output pattern on its own.[1]

We shall consider two different learning rules that are variations on this general scheme: the *Hebbian rule* (which we have already introduced) and a more powerful variation known as the *delta rule*.

The Hebbian rule   When a two-layer feedforward network incorporates a linear activation rule, and applies the Hebbian rule to a set of input–output cases, the result is a learning device called a *linear associator*. In training mode, as described in chapter 2, a linear associator is presented with each input pattern together with its associated output pattern. (Since the Hebbian rule treats them identically, however, the input–output distinction is not really relevant until test mode.) The Hebbian rule tells the network how to change the weight of each of its connections after each such presentation:

$$\Delta weight_{ui} = lrate \, a_u \, a_i \qquad (1)$$

That is, the weight change is obtained by multiplying the activations of the two connected units along with a constant (the learning rate). If the two units have similar activations (e.g., both positive or both negative), the current weight will be incremented by the amount given by equation (1). If the activations are dissimilar (e.g., one positive and one negative), the value of equation (1) will be negative and the current weight will be reduced. The efficacy of the weight change can be evaluated by running the revised network in test mode (that is, presenting the input pattern alone and observing what output is obtained).

The Hebbian rule works well as long as all the input patterns are uncorrelated.[2] However, it fails if we try to use it to teach patterns that

1   If the weights are updated every trial, on a given trial both the activations and the weights would be changed. Alternatively, weights may be updated at the end of each epoch. During testing, only the activations change in order to evaluate the weights; on each trial the weights are applied to the input pattern to obtain an actual output pattern.
2   A simple way to determine if two patterns are correlated is to compare the two patterns position by position, and score +1 every time the two patterns have the same

are correlated. Consider what happens if we try to train the network described on p. 48 above using an additional case C, after it had already
learned to respond to cases A and B. Case C's input pattern is (1 1 −1
1) and desired output pattern is (1 1 1 −1). Because its input pattern is
positively correlated with the input patterns in cases A (1 1 −1 −1)
and B (1 −1 −1 1), learning case C disrupts the ability of the network
to respond properly to cases A and B. For example, after one learning
epoch in which the three patterns were presented in the order A–B–C,
the weight matrix would look like this:

CASE C

Input unit	Input activation	Output unit e	f	g	h
a	1	0.75	0.25	−0.25	−0.25
b	1	0.25	−0.25	0.25	0.25
c	−1	−0.75	−0.25	0.25	0.25
d	1	0.25	0.75	0.25	−0.75
Desired output activation		1.00	1.00	1.00	−1.00

To evaluate the success of these weights, we can run the network in test
mode. On input pattern C, it will produce the erroneous output pattern
(2 1 0 −1). Moreover, its performance on inputs A and B is also
diminished. For A it will now produce output pattern (1.5 −0.5 −0.5
0.5) instead of (1 −1 −1 1), and for B it will now produce (1.5 1.5
−0.5 −1.5) instead of (1 1 −1 −1). Furthermore, additional training
on the three patterns will not improve matters; the added trials will
only increase the size of the weights and hence the size of the output
values, without increasing accuracy.

The requirement that all input patterns be uncorrelated with one
another, in fact, imposes a serious limitation on what can be taught to
a linear associator. There are sets of cases (with correlated inputs) for
which a two-layer network can *produce* the correct responses on a test, if
the weights have been manually set (or have been determined by means
of a more powerful procedure than the Hebbian rule). However, when
the Hebbian rule is applied to make the two-layer network a linear

value in a position, and −1 every time they differ. If the total score after comparing all
positions is 0, the patterns are uncorrelated (orthogonal); if not, the patterns are
correlated (nonorthogonal). In the example which follows, there are four positions. The
score for case A versus B is 0 (the sum of +1, −1, +1, −1 obtained by comparing the
four positions), but the score for case A versus C is 2 (the sum of +1, +1, +1, −1).

associator (a learning device), there is no guarantee that it can *learn* to respond to the same sets of cases.

The delta rule   A far more powerful learning rule is the least mean squares (LMS) or Widrow–Hoff rule (see Widrow and Hoff, 1960). Rumelhart and McClelland (1986), who call this the *delta rule*, regard it as a variant of the Hebbian rule, because it maintains the basic intuition that each change in weight should depend upon what is happening at the relevant input unit and at the relevant output unit. The delta rule is more powerful than the simple Hebbian rule, however, because it directly utilizes the discrepancy between the *desired output pattern* and an *actual output pattern* to improve its weights during the training phase. Specifically, the network receives an input pattern, generates an actual output pattern using the existing weights (a step that is omitted in Hebbian learning), compares that to the desired output pattern, and changes each weight based upon the difference at each output unit (referred to as the unit's *error* or *discrepancy*). Thus, this procedure is an *error correction procedure*, and it is regarded as a prototypical example of supervised learning.

The error for the entire output pattern is referred to as *pss* (*pattern sum of squares*) in McClelland and Rumelhart's (1988) *Handbook*. It is computed as follows: for each output unit u, compute the difference (discrepancy) between the desired output of u (d_u) and the actual output of u (a_u); square each of the differences; and add together the squared differences over all of the output units:

$$pss = \sum_u (d_u - a_u)^2 \qquad (2)$$

By summing the *pss* values across all of the input–output cases being learned by the system, we can obtain the value of *tss* (*total sum of squares*). This is a useful indicator of how much room for improvement remains to achieve perfect performance on the entire set of input–output cases.

Five points should be noted. First, it is the use of the *differences* ($d_u - a_u$) that motivates calling this the *delta* rule (Rumelhart, Hinton and McClelland, 1986, in *PDP:2*, p. 53). Second, both d_u and a_u are activation values (a desired and actual activation on output unit u, respectively). Third, chapter 2 made a different distinction that we shall be able to ignore here: the *output* of a unit was sometimes, but not always, identical to its *activation*. In the learning procedures reviewed here, the identity function $output_u = activation_u$ always holds; we can therefore simplify matters by referring directly to activations. Fourth, most presentations use an error measure, $Error_p$, which is the same as pss except that the sum of squares is divided by 2. Using $Error_p$ simplifies the derivation of the delta rule (see below); for all other purposes in this chapter we find pss more convenient. Fifth, a more careful rendering of most of the equations in this chapter would include a subscript p on most variables, indicating that the equation applies to each output pattern (or input–output case). For the sake of readability, we omit this index here and in the equations that follow.

The delta rule requires that each weight in the network be changed according to the following equation:

$$\Delta weight_{ui} = lrate\,(d_u - a_u)\,a_i \qquad (3)$$

The underlying strategy is to change each weight in the network so as to reduce the total error (as revealed in a test or during the next epoch of training). If a particular unit produced the desired output, then $(d_u - a_u)$ equals 0 and so none of the weights feeding in to it is changed. If there is an error on the output unit, we still do not change the weight if the input unit for that connection had 0 activation, since that weight could not have been contributing to the error. When there is an error and the input was not zero, this equation causes a change in the weight in the direction that would reduce the error.

A deeper understanding of this informal characterization can be obtained by working through a derivation of the delta rule. Rumelhart and McClelland (1986) note that there is a variety of ways of deriving the delta rule. They select one that shows that the delta rule (which changes weights) indeed achieves this minimization of total squared discrepancies (which is the error measure). They do this by showing that the derivative of the error measure with respect to each weight is (negatively) proportional to the amount of change in the weights that results from applying the delta rule. (They further interpret this as an implementation of *gradient descent* in *weight space*, which can be visualized as seeking the lowest point on a landscape of error values across possible weights.) We recapitulate their derivation in Box 1, translated into our notation and with some differences in exposition. (We have placed this in a box to indicate that it is relatively technical material that can be bypassed without loss of continuity.)

The increased power obtained by using the delta rule can be illustrated empirically by returning to the problem of learning input–output cases A, B, and C. Recall that all three could not be learned by a linear associator, which uses a simple Hebbian rule, because input pattern C

BOX 1
Derivation of the Delta Rule

The general strategy underlying the delta rule is to start with a measure of *Error* in the output

$$Error = \tfrac{1}{2}\sum_u (d_u - a_u)^2$$

and then to modify the weights in a way that decreases error. An initial difficulty we face is that the error measure is calculated for the whole pattern so that information about it is not available locally at each weight. What we actually need in order to know how to change the weights, however, is not the *Error* itself, but the partial derivative of *Error* with respect to the activation of each output unit so that we can determine how *Error* will change with change in that activation. This partial derivative can be evaluated locally. In fact, it is simply the difference between the desired and actual output activations (with appropriate sign):

$$\frac{\partial Error}{\partial a_u} = -(d_u - a_u)$$

This tells us how much the activation of each output unit must change in order to reduce to zero that unit's contribution to *Error*. Now we work backwards, because the relevant way to change the output unit's activation is to change the weight of each of its connections with an input unit. (The irrelevant way would be to change the input activations.) Therefore, the problem has become one of specifying how to change the connection weights so as to reduce *Error*. This requires that we determine the partial derivative of *Error* with respect to the weights. Here we appeal to the chain rule:

$$\frac{\partial Error}{\partial weight_{ui}} = \frac{\partial Error}{\partial a_u} \frac{\partial a_u}{\partial weight_{ui}}$$

We need now to evaluate the partial derivative of the activation with respect to the weight. If we are using the linear activation function,

$$a_u = \sum_i weight_{ui}\, a_i$$

then this partial derivative is simply the activation of the input unit:

$$\frac{\partial a_u}{\partial weight_{ui}} = a_i$$

Hence, the partial derivative of the error with respect to each weight (with negative sign) can be computed by simply multiplying the discrepancy by the activation of the input unit:

$$\frac{\partial Error}{\partial weight_{ui}} = -(d_u - a_u)\, a_i$$

The delta rule now multiplies the negative of this derivative by the learning rate to determine the change in the weight between units i and u:

$$\Delta\, weight_{ui} = lrate\, (d_u - a_u)\, a_i$$

If weights are changed after the presentation of each case c, error is calculated separately for each case. Alternatively, error can be summed across cases to obtain an overall measure of error, on the basis of which weights can be changed just once per epoch:

$$weight_{ui} = \sum_c lrate\, (d_{cu} - a_{cu})\, a_{ci}$$

The latter method achieves true gradient descent with respect to the overall error measure; however, weight changes made after each case yield a very similar result if $lrate$ is sufficiently small.

is correlated with input patterns A and B. To see how the delta rule overcomes this limitation, let the network begin with all weights = 0 and $lrate = 0.25$. Case A specifies that input pattern (1 1 −1 −1) should elicit the desired output pattern (1 −1 −1 1). When input pattern A is first presented to the network, since all weights are 0, all four output units will take activation values of 0. (See chapter 2 to review how each input activation is multiplied by each weight, with the four resulting quantities for each output unit summed at the bottom of the column.) Hence, the actual output pattern will be (0 0 0 0). The error (discrepancy) for output unit e is obtained by taking $1-0 = 1$; for unit f, the error is obtained by taking $-1 -0 = -1$; and so forth, resulting in errors on the four output units of $(1 -1 -1 1)$. The squared errors are therefore $(1\ 1\ 1\ 1)$; summing these would yield a *pss* of 4 for Case A.

CASE A, Training Trial 1

Input unit	Input activation	e	f	g	h
a	1	0.00	0.00	0.00	0.00
b	1	0.00	0.00	0.00	0.00
c	−1	0.00	0.00	0.00	0.00
d	−1	0.00	0.00	0.00	0.00
Desired output activation		1.00	−1.00	−1.00	1.00
Actual output activation		0.00	0.00	0.00	0.00
Error (discrepancy)		1.00	−1.00	−1.00	1.00

The delta rule is now applied to each of the 16 weights. To see how this is done, consider just the upper left cell (the weight for the connection between input unit a and output unit e). The change in the weight is obtained from equation (3), that is, by multiplying the learning rate (0.25) by e's error (1) by a's activation (1):

$$\Delta weight_{ui} = lrate\ (d_u - a_u)\ a_i, \text{ so } \Delta weight_{ea} = (0.25)\ (1 - 0)\ (1) = 0.25$$

This weight change ($\Delta weight_{ea} = 0.25$) is added to the current weight (0) to obtain the new weight (0.25). By applying the delta rule to each of the 16 weights in the matrix, a new weight matrix is obtained. Although a test mode trial would not ordinarily be inserted at this point, we do so in order to observe the consequences of these new weights:

CASE A, Test Trial 1

Input unit	Input activation	e	f	g	h
a	1	0.25	−0.25	−0.25	0.25
b	1	0.25	−0.25	−0.25	0.25
c	−1	−0.25	0.25	0.25	−0.25
d	−1	−0.25	0.25	0.25	−0.25
Desired output activation		1.00	−1.00	−1.00	1.00
Actual output activation		1.00	−1.00	−1.00	1.00
Error (discrepancy)		0.00	0.00	0.00	0.00

This new weight matrix, and therefore the output activations, are the same as those produced by the linear associator with its simple Hebbian rule (although by a different computational path; see chapter 2). Furthermore, the network will behave the same as the linear associator did when we now present input–output case B in training mode. Specifically, the network will again produce 0 on all output units (and would do the same for any input pattern that was uncorrelated with input pattern A):

CASE B, Training Trial 1

Input unit	Input activation	Output unit e	f	g	h
a	1	0.25	−0.25	−0.25	0.25
b	−1	0.25	−0.25	−0.25	0.25
c	−1	−0.25	0.25	0.25	−0.25
d	1	−0.25	0.25	0.25	−0.25
Desired output activation		1.00	1.00	−1.00	−1.00
Actual output activation		0.00	0.00	0.00	0.00
Error (discrepancy)		1.00	1.00	−1.00	−1.00

Applying the delta rule to obtain new weights that will work well for case B (while not losing the ability to handle case A), we again obtain the same new weight matrix as we did previously using the Hebbian rule. Again inserting a test trial we exhibit the new weights and their consequences:

CASE B, Test Trial 1

Input unit	Input activation	Output unit e	f	g	h
a	1	0.50	0.00	−0.50	0.00
b	−1	0.00	−0.50	0.00	0.50
c	−1	−0.50	0.00	0.50	0.00
d	1	0.00	0.50	0.00	−0.50
Desired output activation		1.00	1.00	−1.00	−1.00
Actual output activation		1.00	1.00	−1.00	−1.00
Error (discrepancy)		0.00	0.00	0.00	0.00

The difference in power between the two learning rules becomes apparent only when we present input–ouput case C to the network:

CASE C, Training Trial 1

Input unit	Input activation	Output unit e	f	g	h
a	1	0.50	0.00	−0.50	0.00
b	1	0.00	−0.50	0.00	0.50
c	−1	−0.50	0.00	0.50	0.00
d	1	0.00	0.50	0.00	−0.50
Desired output activation		1.00	1.00	1.00	−1.00
Actual output activation		1.00	0.00	−1.00	0.00
Error (discrepancy)		0.00	1.00	2.00	−1.00

Again applying the delta rule and running a test trial on the new weights, we obtain the following:

CASE C, Test Trial 1

Input unit	Input activation	Output unit e	f	g	h
a	1	0.50	0.25	0.00	−0.25
b	1	0.00	−0.25	0.50	0.25
c	−1	−0.50	−0.25	0.00	0.25
d	1	0.00	0.75	0.50	−0.75
Desired output activation		1.00	1.00	1.00	−1.00
Actual output activation		1.00	1.00	1.00	−1.00
Error (discrepancy)		0.00	0.00	0.00	0.00

For the first time, the weights are different from those obtained using the Hebbian rule. Those feeding into output unit *e* are unchanged from the preceding weights (after Case B), because there is no discrepancy between the actual activation of *e* and the desired activation; the Hebbian rule, working only with the desired output activations, produced a quite different set of weights for this unit. The weights feeding into output unit *g* do reflect changes to the previous weights, but the changes are different from those produced by the Hebbian rule. Finally, the weights feeding into output units *f* and *h* happen to be the same as those produced by the Hebbian rule at this point in training. Over all 16 weights, therefore, half are the same and half are different from those produced by the Hebbian rule.

Table 3.1 Two learning rules contrasted

Epoch	Output Pattern A				Output Pattern B				Output Pattern C			
				Desired pattern								
NA	1.00	−1.00	−1.00	1.00	1.00	1.00	−1.00	−1.00	1.00	1.00	1.00	−1.00
				Learning with the Hebbian rule								
1	0.00	0.00	0.00	0.00	0.00	0.00	0.00	0.00	1.00	0.00	−1.00	0.00
2	1.00	−0.50	−0.50	0.50	1.50	1.50	−0.50	−0.50	3.00	1.00	−1.00	−1.00
3	3.00	−1.00	−1.00	1.00	3.00	3.00	−1.00	−3.00	5.00	2.00	−1.00	−2.00
4	4.50	−1.50	−1.50	1.50	4.50	4.50	−1.50	−4.50	7.00	3.00	−1.00	−3.00
				Learning with the delta rule								
1	0.00	0.00	0.00	0.00	0.00	0.00	0.00	0.00	1.00	0.00	−1.00	0.00
2	1.00	−0.50	0.00	0.50	1.00	1.50	0.00	−1.50	1.00	0.50	0.00	−0.50
3	1.00	−0.75	−0.50	0.75	1.00	1.25	−0.50	−1.25	1.00	0.75	0.50	−0.75
4	1.00	−0.87	−0.75	0.87	1.00	1.12	−0.75	−1.12	1.00	0.87	0.75	−0.87
5	1.00	−0.93	−0.87	0.93	1.00	1.06	−0.87	−1.06	1.00	0.93	0.87	−0.93
6	1.00	−0.96	−0.93	0.96	1.00	1.03	−0.93	−1.03	1.00	0.96	0.93	−0.96
7	1.00	−0.98	−0.96	0.98	1.00	1.01	−0.96	−1.01	1.00	0.98	0.96	−0.98
8	1.00	−0.99	−0.98	0.99	1.00	1.00	−0.98	−1.00	1.00	0.99	0.98	−0.99
9	1.00	−0.99	−0.99	0.99	1.00	1.00	−0.99	−1.00	1.00	0.99	0.99	−0.99

As for the pattern of activations on the output units, the 16 weights produced by the delta rule have generated the correct output for case C, an outcome not achieved by the Hebbian rule. As with the Hebbian rule, however, trying to learn case C has disrupted the ability of the network to generate the correct output for cases A and B. Running these cases once again in test mode, the actual output patterns are now (1.0 −0.5 0.0 0.5) instead of (1 −1 −1 1) for A and (1.0 1.5 1.0 −1.5) instead of (1 1 −1 −1) for B. Fortunately, the discrepancies are not as serious as those produced by the Hebbian rule, and additional training epochs will gradually bring further improvement in the ability of the network to respond to all three patterns. Table 3.1 contrasts the course of learning across epochs for the Hebbian rule (which shows no improvement) and the delta rule (which learns the patterns virtually perfectly by epoch 9; this extended run was carried out using the **pa** (pattern associator) program in McClelland and Rumelhart's (1988) *Handbook*, chapter 4). Hence, our exploration of cases A, B, and C illustrates that the delta rule, unlike the simple Hebbian rule, need not be restricted to sets of input patterns that are uncorrelated (orthogonal).

Having observed these differences in performance between the Hebbian and delta rules, it is worth considering how the rules themselves compare. The two rules have in common that they use only information that is locally available at each connection as a basis for changing the weight of the connection. Hence, there is no need to posit an executive; learning is under local control. Also, both rules make use of desired pairings of input and output patterns that are determined by the trainer. With the Hebbian training procedure, however, the desired output patterns are imposed on the output units. The network is not free to generate its own actual output, and therefore cannot use the discrepancy between desired and actual outputs to guide its learning. In test mode we can observe the network generating an actual output, and as observers we can note how discrepant it is from the desired output, but we have no way of telling the network about this discrepancy. The innovation in the delta rule is that it offers a way for the network to compute and utilize the discrepancies. The discrepancy can be regarded as a transformation of the desired output pattern (obtained by subtracting from it the actual output pattern) that is more informative than the desired output pattern itself. The delta rule is identical to the Hebbian rule except that this transformation is carried out before multiplying the output value by the input value. Hence, the delta rule can use the discrepancies to improve its weights, whereas in Hebbian learning the discrepancies can be obtained only while in test mode and are used to evaluate, but not change, the weights.

Exactly how powerful is a two-layer network that is using the delta rule? That is, how weak are the constraints that limit the sets of cases that it can learn? The network is guaranteed to converge on a weight matrix that is capable of producing the desired outputs as long as such a weight matrix exists. The weight matrix will exist, however, only under certain conditions. First, if you want the network to learn an arbitrary output for each input pattern, you will have to construct the input patterns in such a way that they form a *linearly independent* set. That is, none of the input patterns can be derived as a linear combination of the other patterns (e.g., by adding patterns together; see McClelland and Rumelhart's (1988) *Handbook*, pp. 95–6). For example, suppose that you have a network with just two input units. If you choose 1 0 as one input pattern, then you can also use the pattern 0 1 since neither pattern can be derived from the other. But now you cannot introduce the pattern 1 1 and teach an arbitrary output, since this input pattern is the sum of the other two. Furthermore, the number of patterns you desire to teach places a constraint on the size of the network that is required. (In general, encoding *n* linearly-independent patterns requires *n* units; see Jordan (1986), in *PDP:9*, pp. 370–3).

What if you ignore the first constraint, and design a set of input–output cases for which the input patterns are *not* linearly independent? Whether the network can learn the proper output patterns will then depend upon whether the input–output pairs are *linearly separable*. To

meet that requirement, there must exist at least one set of weights such
that the same weights can be used to generate the desired output pattern for every input pattern. If such a set exists, the delta rule will find
it. (This is automatic when the inputs are linearly independent, but
must be determined when they are not.) For a simple example, suppose
we try to teach the following function to a network with two input units
and one output unit:

Pattern	Input unit 1	Input unit 2	Desired output
a	0	0	0
b	0	1	1
c	1	0	1
d	1	1	1

This is the logic function of *inclusive or* (OR). If the network has sufficiently high positive weights on the connections, and the activation
function for the output unit is a threshold function, it can compute this
function perfectly. Even though pattern d is a linear combination of
patterns b and c, the weights that generate the desired output for b and c
happen to generate the desired output for d as well. But consider what
would happen if we changed the desired output for d; that is, suppose
we sought to teach the following function:

Pattern	Input unit 1	Input unit 2	Desired output
a	0	0	0
b	0	1	1
c	1	0	1
d$'$	1	1	0

This is the logic function of *exclusive or* (XOR), which exemplifies the
more general problem of parity detection that was one focus of Minsky
and Papert's (1969) argument against perceptrons. This sort of problem cannot be solved by a network with two inputs and one output, because the input–output pairs are not linearly separable.[3] Just as for the
OR function, to handle patterns b and c we need positive weights on
both connections between the input units and the output units. But that
means there is no way to obtain a zero output when the inputs are both

---

3   A two-layer network can compute the XOR function if the input patterns are recoded
across an enlarged input layer so as to yield linearly separable inputs. The problem itself
has then been altered, however; the relation between the two sets of values is no longer an
XOR relation.

1, as required for pattern d'. A graphical interpretation is provided below. The output value for each combination of input values is placed at their intersection. In the first diagram a straight diagonal line can be drawn which will separate the three output values of 1 from the single output value of 0. But in the second diagram no straight line can be drawn to separate the 1's from the 0's.

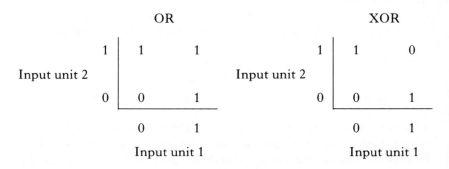

What happens if we persist in teaching a set of input–output patterns which are not linearly separable? In this case there will be no set of weights that can generate the correct outputs, and so the delta rule cannot solve the problem exactly. But, unlike the simple Hebbian rule, the delta rule will do the best job possible: it will converge on a set of weights that minimizes total squared error (*tss*). Furthermore, its sensitivity to dependencies (regularities) in the patterns can be useful. In real life, patterns tend to cluster together, and similar input patterns tend to be associated with similar output patterns. If presented with cases that show this kind of structure, rather than cases exhibiting linear independence and arbitrary association, the delta rule will do a good job of learning the cases and will (as a free bonus) generalize to new input patterns on the basis of their similarities to the training patterns. You are not guaranteed that every input pattern will elicit exactly the correct output pattern, but typically, output patterns will be similar (if not identical) to the correct pattern. As Rumelhart, Hinton, and Williams (1986a) point out in *PDP:8* (p. 318), this kind of learning is a task for which two-layer networks are well suited. For illustrations, see our discussion in chapter 6 of two simulations from Rumelhart and McClelland (1986) in *PDP:18* (the rule of 78 and English past-tense acquisition).

Even in the 1960s it was known that adding one or more layers of hidden units was a means of overcoming the constraint of linear separability. Unfortunately, there was no known learning algorithm for setting the weights in these more complex networks. It was left to researchers in the 1980s to devise procedures for training hidden units, and by any reckoning the discovery of these procedures was a major advance for connectionism. One of the most widely-used procedures, *back-propagation*, makes use of a more powerful generalization of the delta rule. It was independently discovered by Rumelhart, Hinton, and Williams (1986a, 1986b), who call it the *generalized delta rule*, by Le Cun (1986), and by Parker (1985).

The Back-propagation Learning Procedure for Multi-layered Networks

In the previous section we noted that two-layer networks cannot be guaranteed to learn sets of input–output cases when neither of the following constraints is met: (1) linear independence of the input patterns; (2) linear separability of the input–output assignments. We have already cited XOR as one problem that violates these constraints, and other violations are ubiquitous in the tasks that organisms must carry out daily. Hinton (1989) makes this point nicely with respect to the task of viewing an object (encoded in an intensity array, as on a monochromatic television screen) and producing its name as the desired output:

Consider, for example, the task of identifying an object when the input vector is an intensity array and the output vector has a separate component for each possible name. If a given type of object can be either black or white, the intensity of an individual pixel (which is what an input unit encodes) cannot provide any direct evidence for the presence or absence of an object of that type. So the object cannot be identified by using weights on direct connections from input to output units. Obviously it is necessary to explicitly extract relationships among intensity values (such as edges) before trying to identify the object. Actually, extracting edges is just a small part of the problem. If recognition is to have the generative capacity to handle novel images of familiar objects the network must somehow encode the systematic effects of variations in lighting and viewpoint, partial occlusion by other objects, and deformations of the object itself. There is a tremendous gap between these complex regularities and the regularities that can be captured by an associative net that lacks hidden units. (Hinton, 1989, pp. 5–6)

In order to solve problems like this, it is necessary to insert hidden units between the input and output units that can preprocess the information to obtain the pieces that are needed for the final solution of the overall problem. This produces a more complex flow of information in which intermediate results (such as the identification of an edge) are obtained by combining input activations in certain ways; it is then the final set of intermediate results that is used by the output units.

The introduction of hidden units raises several questions that the network designer must answer. First, how many hidden units should be used, and in how many layers should they be arranged? There is no easy recipe to follow to assure optimal performance. Second, should connections be made only between adjacent layers, or should additional connections be allowed (e.g., connect all hidden units to the output layer as well as to the next hidden layer)? Third, what activation rule should be used? Multi-layered networks are more powerful than two-layer networks only if a nonlinear activation rule is used.[4] The logistic activation function is a common choice, and is assumed throughout the remainder of this chapter. In its simplest form it is:

$$a_u = \frac{1}{1 + e^{-netinput_u}} \tag{4}$$

The final, and most interesting, challenge is to devise a learning procedure that can be applied to hidden units. The original delta rule is inappropriate, for example, because it can be applied only to connections that feed directly into output units for which an error measure can be calculated. The *generalized delta rule* bypasses this limitation by propagating the error measure that is calculated at the output units back through the network (i.e., by *back-propagation*). Hence, on a given training trial, activations propagate forward from the input units through the hidden units to the output units, and then error and the resulting adjustments to the weights propagate in the reverse direction back through the hidden units to the input units. This must be done in a way that solves the credit assignment problem. That is, for each lower layer it must be determined how each of its units contributed to error on the output layer, and the weights must be adjusted accordingly.

The equations used to change the weights are more complex in the back-propagation rule than in the delta rule; this is due to the use of a different activation function and to the addition of hidden layers. For purposes of exposition, we shall assume a network with just one hidden layer, and use *i, h,* and *u* to refer to units in the input, hidden, and output layers respectively. (For networks with additional layers, the mnemonic value of our subscripts breaks down, and a more general no-

---

4   If a linear rule is used for both hidden and output layers, then one can construct from the sets of weights used in the multi-layered network a set that will work for a two-layer network. Thus, a multi-layered network with linear activations cannot overcome the limitations of a two-layer network.

tation referring to arbitrary layers would be needed.) The equation for changing weights that feed into the output units is the simplest one, since that is the layer at which error is computed. First, $delta_u$ is computed by multiplying the error $(d_u - a_u)$ by the derivative of the logistic activation function (see Box 2):

$$delta_u = (d_u - a_u)\, a_u\, (1 - a_u) \tag{5a}$$

This more complex *delta* value is then inserted in the otherwise familiar equation for changing weights (here, the weight on the connection from hidden unit h to output unit u):

$$\Delta\, weight_{uh} = lrate\; delta_u\; a_h \tag{6a}$$

Multiplying by a_h has the effect of changing the weight on a particular connection only to the degree that the hidden unit on that connection is active; thus the weights are changed most on those connections that contribute most to the error.

Additional machinery is needed to change the weights that lie deeper in the network; in the case of our three-layer network those are simply the weights that feed from the input units to the hidden units. We do this by first apportioning to each hidden unit its contribution to the overall error, yielding the value of a new function, $delta_h$:

$$delta_h = a_h\, (1 - a_h) \sum_u delta_u\; weight_{uh} \tag{5b}$$

Once $delta_h$ is obtained, the hard work has been done; we insert it into the familiar equation for changing weights, this time for $weight_{hi}$:

$$\Delta\, weight_{hi} = lrate\; delta_h\; a_i \tag{6b}$$

It should be clear that values of *delta* can be computed recursively for networks of any depth. For a derivation of the *generalized delta rule*, which is adapted from the derivation in Rumelhart, Hinton, and Williams (1986a) in *PDP:8*, see Box 2.

An illustration   It is useful to work through an example of how a multi-layered network learns by means of back-propagation. Most such networks are too large to follow the learning events in detail. However, McClelland and Rumelhart's (1988) *Handbook* (pp. 145–52) presents an exercise on learning the XOR function by means of back-propagation.

BOX 2
Derivation of the Back-propagation Learning Rule

The strategy underlying the back-propagation learning rule is much the same as that for the delta rule. We begin with the same error measure:

$$Error = \tfrac{1}{2} \sum_u (d_u - a_u)^2$$

Our goal is to determine the partial derivatives with respect both to weights feeding into the output units and with respect to those feeding into the hidden units and to adjust each set of weights accordingly. We shall determine each of these separately.

Changing weights feeding into output units

We begin by taking the partial derivative of the error measure with respect to the activation of the output unit:

$$\frac{\partial Error}{\partial a_u} = -(d_u - a_u)$$

The next step is to determine $\partial a_u/\partial weight_{uh}$, so that we can then use the chain rule to determine the $\partial Error/\partial weight_{uh}$. But this is a more complex task than in the case of the delta rule since we are employing a nonlinear activation function (the logistic function):

$$a_u = \frac{1}{1 + e^{-netinput_u}}$$

Since the logistic activation function is specified in terms of net input to u, we shall work in stages. Let us first determine:

$$\frac{\partial a_u}{\partial netinput_u} = a_u(1 - a_u)$$

From this we can now use the chain rule to evaluate $\partial Error/\partial netinput_u$ the negative of which is often referred to as $delta_u$:

$$\frac{\partial Error}{\partial netinput_u} = -delta_u = \frac{\partial Error}{\partial a_u} \frac{\partial a_u}{\partial netinput_u} = -(d_u - a_u)\, a_u\, (1 - a_u)$$

We now need to determine $\partial netinput_u/\partial weight_{uh}$, for then we shall be able to employ the chain rule to determine $\partial Error/\partial weight_{uh}$. Since we are employing the logistic activation function:

$$netinput_u = \sum_h weight_{uh}\, a_h,$$

then:

$$\frac{\partial netinput_u}{\partial weight_{uh}} = a_h$$

Now we employ the chain rule once again:

$$\frac{\partial Error}{\partial weight_{ui}} = -delta_u \frac{\partial netinput_u}{\partial weight_{ui}} = -(d_u - a_u)\, a_u\, (1 - a_u)\, a_h$$

As with the delta rule, we shall now change weights leading to output units proportionately to the negative of this partial derivative:

$$\Delta weight_{uh} = lrate\ delta_u\, a_h = -lrate\, (d_u - a_u)\, a_u\, (1 - a_u)\, a_h$$

Changing weights deeper in the network

The major challenge at this point is to allocate Error among the units in the system. For this we need to employ a recursive procedure. For expository purposes, however, we shall assume that we are dealing with a three-layer network and shall use the subscript h to refer to hidden units and i to refer to input units; the same procedure could be iterated if there were additional layers of hidden units (with h now referring to the previous i, and i to the next layer down). What we need first is to determine the derivative of Error with respect to the activation of units in the hidden layer. We shall do this by distributing the $delta_u$ that we have already calculated. Let us focus on a particular unit h and its connection to a particular output unit u. We now determine what portion of the Error assigned to u to allocate to h. We again use the chain rule:

$$\frac{\partial Error}{\partial a_h} = -delta_u \frac{\partial netinput_u}{\partial a_h}$$

Since

$$netinput_u = \sum_h weight_{uh}\, a_h,$$

then

$$\frac{\partial netinput_u}{\partial a_h} = weight_{uh}$$

Thus, the part of $\partial Error/\partial a_h$ contributed by $weight_{uh}$ is simply $(- delta_u\ weight_{uh})$. We now sum over all the connections from h to the output level to determine

$$\frac{\partial Error}{\partial a_h} = \sum_u - delta_u\ weight_{uh}$$

With the value for $\partial Error/\partial a_h$ in hand, we now proceed as before to determine $-delta_h$, which equals the partial derivative of the error with respect to the netinput to h:

$$- delta_h = \frac{\partial Error}{\partial netinput_h} = \frac{\partial Error}{\partial a_h}\ \frac{\partial a_h}{\partial netinput_h}$$
$$= a_h\ (1 - a_h) \sum_u - delta_u weight_{uh}$$

The partial derivative of the error with respect to $weight_{hi}$ is now readily determined:

$$\frac{\partial Error}{\partial weight_{hi}} = - delta_h\ \frac{\partial netinput_h}{\partial weight_{hi}} = - delta_h\ a_i$$

and the weight of the connection from i to h is changed in proportion to this derivative:

$$\Delta weight_{hi} = lrate\ delta_h a_i$$
$$= lrate\ a_h (1 - a_h) \sum_u (- delta_u\ weight_{uh})\ a_i$$

If we needed to apply this procedure to yet another layer, we would start with $delta_h$ and distribute the error to the units in our current i level. Thus, we have a recursive procedure for figuring the delta value for units at each layer in the network and we can use this to determine the change of all connections coming into these units.

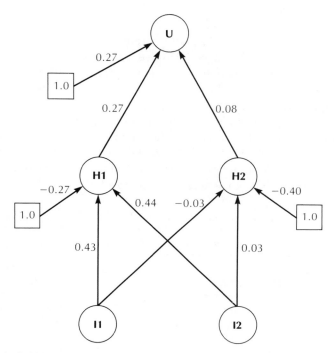

Figure 3.1 Initial state of the network that learns to compute the XOR function. Each of the three layers has one or two units (circles). Except for the input layer, each unit has a bias which is shown here as the weight on the connection from an additional unit with a fixed activation of 1 (squares).

The simulation used a very compact three-layer network (figure 3.1). It requires just two input units (I1 and I2), two hidden units (H1 and H2), and a single output unit (U), and has a total of six weights to be adjusted as the four input–output cases are repeatedly encountered across training epochs. We ran this exercise using their **bp** (back-propagation) program, and report it here in order to illustrate this learning procedure.

Included in the net input to each of the hidden units and the output unit is an additional source of incoming activation known as *bias*. Each unit has its own bias, which has the effect of increasing or decreasing the activation value that is computed on each trial. As noted in chapter 2, it plays essentially the same role as a threshold; together with the logistic activation function, it introduces nonlinearity into the system. For purposes of computation, it may help to think of the bias as coming in from an extra unit that is connected only to the unit that it biases (and therefore not directly influenced by input patterns). The hypothetical extra unit (rectangular in figure 3.1) is assumed to have a constant activation of 1. (Sometimes this is referred to as *clamping* the extra unit, because the activation is "clamped on" rather than fluctuating.) The weight on the connection from the hypothetical unit can, however, be adjusted by learning; when we speak of the bias on the unit, we are referring to that weight.

The simulation begins by initializing the weights with a random set of weight assignments,[5] which is shown in figure 3.1. We specify a learning rate of 0.50. Table 3.2 shows the activations that result when we send each of the four input patterns through the network as a test prior to training (that is, the activations at epoch 0):

Table 3.2   Results of testing the initial network with each input–output case

	Trainer-defined values			*Actual activation values*		
Case	*Input Unit I1*	*Input Unit I2*	*Desired Output*	*Hidden Unit H1*	*Hidden Unit H2*	*Output Unit*
Neither	0	0	0	0.43	0.40	0.60
Unit **I1**	1	0	1	0.53	0.39	0.61
Unit **I2**	0	1	1	0.54	0.40	0.61
Both	1	1	0	0.64	0.40	0.61

We shall calculate the activation values for the first row of this table manually to make it clear how the network operates. Since both of the input units are given the value 0, each of the hidden units receives input of 0 from these units. The net input is not 0, however, because the bias supplies an activation of -0.27 to Hidden Unit 1 (**H1**) and of -0.40 to Hidden Unit 2 (**H2**). Applying the logistic activation function (equation 4), we obtain the activations for the two hidden units that are shown in table 3.2. The activation of **H1** is now multiplied by the weight on its connection to the output unit (0.27) while the activation of **H2** is multiplied by its corresponding weight (0.08). These are summed $(0.12 + 0.03 = 0.15)$ and then are added to the bias on the output unit (0.27) to generate a net input to the output unit of 0.42. When the logis-

5   The initialization procedure utilizes a pseudo-random number generator. The particular set of initial weights used for the XOR exercise happened to be rather favorable to learning XOR. Starting with the same weights and training the network on *if and only iff* (IFF), the negation of XOR, required 540 training epochs, almost twice as many as required to teach the network XOR. This is the case even though the solutions the network generated to the two problems are essentially isomorphic.

tic activation function is applied, an output unit activation of 0.60 is obtained (rightmost column of table 3.2).

With the activations computed for the first input–output case ("Neither"), each of the weights can be altered in accord with the version of the generalized delta rule that is appropriate to its layer (or this could be done at the end of epoch 1, that is, after all four patterns have been presented). To continue with the example, we shall compute two of the weight changes now. This requires first calculating delta for certain units. For the output unit, equation (5a) yields a $delta_u$ of -0.14 ($-0.60 \times 0.60 \times 0.40 = -0.14$). The $delta_h$ values for each of the hidden units can now be calculated recursively from $delta_u$ using equation (5b): multiply $delta_u$ by the weight of the connection, and then multiply the result by the $a_h (1 - a_h)$ term for that hidden unit. This yields a $delta_h$ of -0.09 for **H1** and of -0.02 for **H2**. Next, the delta values are entered into the $\Delta weight$ equation, and $\Delta weight$ is added to the current weight to obtain the new weight of the connection. For example, for the connection from **H1** to the output unit **U**, equation (6a) specifies that the learning rate (0.50) is multiplied by the relevant delta (-0.14) and by the activation of the incoming unit (0.43) to obtain $\Delta weight_{UH1}$ (-0.03); this is added to 0.27 (obtained from figure 3.1) to yield a new weight of 0.24. For the connection from **I1** to **H1**, the calculation for $\Delta weight_{H1I1}$ from equation (6b) is $(0.50) (-0.09) (0) = 0$. Thus, the new value for $weight_{H1I1}$ is $0.43 + 0 = 0.43$. That is, there is no weight change for this connection.

The network's progress in learning the XOR problem is displayed in table 3.3 (the changes in the weights and biases) and table 3.4 (the changes in the output activation values). At first it learns very slowly. By epoch 90 it has seen each of the four input–output cases once per epoch, for a total of 90 learning trials per case. The resulting changes in the weights have not improved the network's ability to discriminate among the inputs; the output unit produces an activation of 0.50 regardless of which input is supplied. During this period most of the change is concentrated in the upper part of the network (the output unit bias and the weights between the hidden units and the output unit all *decrease* somewhat). In effect, the system is temporarily learning to ignore the input. The reason for this is that it is following a gradient descent, seeking the most efficient way to reduce its error. By simply reducing its output activation from 0.61 to 0.50 on each unit, it has indeed reduced its *tss* (total squared error across input–output cases) from 1.0507 to 1.0000. This still leaves a good deal of error, so the network must adopt a different "strategy" to continue reducing error. Specifically, it begins gradually to increase the weights from both input

Table 3.3 Weight on each connection at four points in learning

Connection	Epoch 0	Epoch 90	Epoch 210	Epoch 289
Inputs to **H1**	0.43	0.45	2.17	5.72
H1 to output	0.27	0.12	1.71	6.40
Bias of **H1**	−0.27	−0.28	0.10	−2.16
Inputs to **H2**	0.00	−0.04	0.06	3.18
H2 to output	0.08	−0.04	−0.44	−6.96
Bias of **H2**	−0.40	−0.48	−0.43	−4.82
Bias of output	0.27	−0.05	−1.17	−2.82

Table 3.4 Activation of the output unit at four points in learning

Input pattern		Epoch 0	Epoch 90	Epoch 210	Epoch 289
Neither	0 0	0.61	0.50	0.38	0.09
Unit **I1**	1 0	0.61	0.50	0.54	0.90
Unit **I2**	0 1	0.61	0.50	0.54	0.90
Both	1 1	0.61	0.50	0.57	0.10

units to **H1** (averaged in table 3.3 because these weights are very similar), and from **H1** to the output unit. Simultaneously, the bias on the
output unit becomes increasingly negative (in effect, raising its response threshold so that it will require a fairly high net input to reach a
high activation value itself). After 210 epochs of training it is clear that
H1 is becoming an OR detector: it is serving to excite the output unit
when either of the input units is active, and especially when both are active. When neither input unit is active, **H1** propagates only its own
small bias to the output unit; combined with the negative bias of the
output unit itself this results in a negative net input to the output unit.
Applying the logistic activation function has the result that any net input is scaled to a value between 0 and 1; for this particular case, the output unit's activation ends up as a somewhat low 0.38 (compared to
values above 0.50 for the other inputs).

   With **H1** moderately well established as an OR detector by epoch
210, **H2** now starts to become an AND detector. This will permit
"subtracting" the AND cases (1 1) from the OR cases (1 0), (0 1), (1 1)
at the level of the output unit, so that it can function as an XOR detec-

tor (1 0), (0 1). Specifically, the weights from the input units to **H2** become increasingly positive, while the bias on **H2** becomes so negative that it will become active only if both inputs are active. (Hence, **H2** is now an AND detector.) Meanwhile, the weight from **H2** to the output unit becomes increasingly negative (so that when **H2** detects AND, the excitation of the output unit from **H1** will be countered by inhibition from **H2**.) Hence, **H2** becomes active only when both inputs units are active, and when it does become active, it inhibits the activity of the output unit. This specialization of **H2**'s function occurs fairly rapidly once it begins around epoch 210, so that by epoch 289 the network has essentially learned the XOR function.

The learning sequence exhibited in this simple network is quite characteristic of back-propagation generally. The first stage of learning sets the weights in the network in such a way that the output units adopt the mean of the various training states. Over subsequent training epochs, the various hidden units begin to specialize; the output units receive and coordinate the hidden units' analysis of the input, and therefore can respond differentially to different input patterns. In more complex networks it is often difficult to determine precisely what information each hidden unit is responding to, but analysis often does reveal that individual units are identifying particular information in the input that is germane to solving the problem.

Back-propagation provides a powerful training technique for networks with hidden units. One particularly impressive example of a network trained by back-propagation is Sejnowski and Rosenberg's (1987) NETtalk model, a three-layer network which was trained to read English text. The text (either separate words or connected discourse) was presented letter by letter to the input layer, and a succession of phonemes was produced by the network on its output layer and submitted to a speech synthesizer. More specifically, what was supplied to the input layer was a localist encoding of the target letter, plus the three preceding and three following letters. Since spaces and punctuation were encoded by three special characters in addition to the 26 English alphabet characters, 7×29 input units were required. These units fed connections to a single layer of 80 hidden units, which then fed into 26 output units. These output units provided a localist encoding of 23 articulatory features and three features for stress and syllable boundaries. Each phoneme was represented by a distributed pattern across these 26 units.

In one simulation, the network was trained through repeated exposures to a continuous speech corpus of 1,024 words, with desired outputs determined by phonetic transcription of the speech of a child.

. After 10,000 training trials (approximately ten presentations of each word) the network's "best guess" (most active phonemic representation) was correct 80 percent of the time. After 50,000 words it achieved 95 percent accuracy. It was then tested on a 439-word continuation of the text, and achieved 78 percent accuracy (Sejnowski and Rosenberg, 1986). When the output was actually supplied to a voice synthesizer, it produced recognizable speech, albeit with a few errors. Subsequently, Sejnowski and Rosenberg (1987) analyzed the behavior of the hidden units by first determining the activation patterns across those units for each of the 79 grapheme–phoneme correspondences in English and then performing a cluster analysis. The analysis revealed that the hidden units differentiated vowels from consonants, and produced grapheme–phoneme clusterings similar to those in standard analyses of English, demonstrating that the hidden units had become sensitive to theoretically-relevant features of language. These sensitivities of the hidden units, it is important to recognize, were not directly determined by the network builder, but rather were the product of training through back-propagation and constituted the network's construal of the regularities involved in pronouncing English text.

Despite the power and versatility of the back-propagation learning procedure, there are drawbacks. First, back-propagation can be an extremely slow learning procedure. The XOR network, with only six connections to train, required 289 epochs. Learning time increases exponentially with the size of the network; NETtalk required 5,000 training epochs, consuming approximately 12 hours of CPU time on a VAX. Hinton (1989) offered the estimate that the learning time in a network simulated on a serial machine will be roughly proportional to c^3, where c is the number of connections in the network. In response, it can be noted that much of human learning occurs in domains for which the amount of input over time is massive; to model this learning we may *want* a network that requires large numbers of learning trials. Once this learning has occurred, however, humans clearly have some very efficient means of reutilizing its results in new domains or tasks (for example, learning by analogy, by verbal instruction, and by coordinating the functioning of previously independent schemata). If connectionists wish to offer a general account of human learning, they will have to learn how to incorporate these means in connectionist models. Slow adaptive learning algorithms such as back-propagation either will play no role in reutilization of already trained networks, or will operate in a way that permits very rapid convergence in the new network. A second response to this point is to agree that back-propagation as currently implemented on serial machines is too slow, but that more rapid computation will be achieved from parallel machines that are now under development. (Hinton estimated a learning time for parallel machines roughly proportional to c^2.)

A second drawback, for those whose attraction to connectionism is based on its plausibility at the biological level, is that back-propagation does not map directly onto any known biological processes. There is no evidence that information is passed backwards through the nervous system in a manner that precisely adjusts the forward performance of the system. The most straightforward response to this objection is to make a clear distinction between levels of analysis, placing back-propagation at the psychological level (i.e., at Marr's algorithmic level). On this approach, back-propagation is simply one mechanism by which multi-layered networks can achieve *gradient descent*, that is, learning by reducing the error in output. Back-propagation constituted a breakthrough for psychological modeling since it overcame the restriction of gradient descent learning to two-layer networks and so opened up the investigation of networks with hidden layers. The question of how this sort of learning is implemented at the biological level cannot easily be addressed at this time. For some suggestions, however, see McNaughton (1989).

Boltzmann Learning Procedures for Non-layered Networks

In addition to feedforward networks, there are interactive networks such as Hopfield nets and Boltzmann machines that have their own distinctive architectures. As we noted in chapter 2, one presentation of an input pattern results in multiple cycles of processing in these networks; across the cycles, the activations dynamically interact until the network settles into a stable state. These cycles should not be confused with learning epochs; they involve computation of activations, not modification of weights. They yield a response (or solution) to a single input pattern, just as a single pass through a feedforward network yields its response to an input pattern. We also noted in chapter 2 that one problem faced by interactive networks is the tendency to land in local minima, that is, states that are stable but do not represent the best solution to the constraints. We described the technique of simulated annealing, which the Boltzmann machine can employ to avoid these local minima. This involves slowly decreasing the temperature parameter (T) in the stochastic activation function:

$$probability\ (a=1) = \frac{1}{1 + e^{-(netinput_u - \theta_u)/T}} \tag{7}$$

which has the effect of reducing the probability of the network settling into a local minimum.

In *PDP:7* Hinton and Sejnowski (1986) showed that Boltzmann machines can be trained using a variation on Hebbian learning that is conceptually similar to back-propagation. Here we adapt Hinton's (1989) exposition. Each unit is designated as either an *input unit, output unit*, or *hidden unit*. In test mode, problems are posed by clamping certain input units so as to force them to maintain an activation of either 1 or 0; the network's solution is the stable pattern of activation that is reached on the output units.

In training mode, there are two stages. In stage one, each input–output case is imposed on the network by clamping both the input units and output units in the designated patterns. The units of the network are selected in random order to update their activations using the stochastic activation function in equation (7). As this processing is occurring the temperature parameter T is gradually reduced to 1. Processing stops when the network reaches a thermal equilibrium, that is, a state in which units' activations continue to change, but the probability of finding the network in a given global state (pattern of activation across units) remains constant and the most probable states are the ones that best satisfy the constraints. While at equilibrium, each input–output case is processed for a designated period of time. For each pair of connected units, the proportion of that time that both are active is measured. The proportions are averaged across cases to obtain the expected probability $<a_i\,a_j>^+$ that both units are active together under these conditions. (Note that these are non-mnemonic subscripts; the equations refer to any pairing of units, e.g., input–input, output–hidden, input–output.)

In stage two, only the input units are clamped, and the network determines its own output ("runs free," as in test mode). Except for this variation, the process used in stage one is repeated. This time the expected probability of joint activity is written as $<a_i\,a_j>^-$. The size of the discrepancy between stages one and two determines how much to change the weight of the connection:

$$\Delta weight_{ij} = lrate\,(<a_i\,a_j>^+ - <a_i\,a_j>^-) \qquad (8)$$

Ackley, Hinton, and Sejnowski (1985) showed that as long as the learning rate is set slow enough, this procedure will result in weights that minimize the error on the output units (that is, the difference in their behavior when they are clamped versus running freely).

The intuition underlying the Boltzmann procedure is similar to that of the delta rule and generalized delta rule; discrepancies between desired (clamped) and actual (free-running) outputs are used to guide changes in weights. If two connected units are jointly active more frequently when the network is running with the desired output clamped than when it is running free, the joint activity needs to be increased by increasing the weight of the connection. Conversely, if they are jointly active more frequently when running free than when the desired output is clamped, the joint activity needs to be decreased by decreasing the weight on that connection.

As Hinton points out, the Boltzmann machine faces several difficulties. Due to the time it takes the network to reach equilibrium after being presented with each pattern, learning occurs very slowly. Moreover, if not enough cases of $<a_i\,a_j>^+$ and $<a_i\,a_j>^-$ are sampled, the information used for weight change will be very noisy. For real-life applications, however, the processing speed problem may be dealt with by running the procedure on chips that are being tailored for this purpose using analog circuits. Hinton notes that these chips can speed up processing by a factor of one million over simulation on a VAX.

Competitive Learning

We now turn to a quite different learning procedure, competitive learning, in which no trainer is involved (hence, a form of unsupervised learning). In competitive learning, a network is presented with a series of input patterns and must discover regularities in those patterns that can be used to divide them into clusters of similar patterns. In the simplest case, there is one layer above the input layer, and each of its units is connected to every input unit. It is like a hidden layer in that its task is to detect regularities despite receiving no direct feedback from a trainer regarding the appropriateness of its activity. It is like an output layer in that the activity of its units constitute the response of the system to the input patterns. We shall simply call it the *detection layer* (not a standard term). The number of clusters that this network detects is determined by the network designer when the number of detector units is set. If there are three units, for example, the best way of partitioning the input patterns into three clusters will be sought (and in at least some versions, will be attained by gradient descent). The activation rule is set up to assure that on a given trial just one unit will "win:" the activation of the unit with the greatest net input will go to 1, and the other units' activations go to 0. (That is, the winning unit inhibits the others.) Learning now ensues. Each detector unit has a fixed total of incoming weights. The learning rule reallocates the weights of the winning unit, such that the weights on its connections from active input units are incremented, while those from connections with inactive input units are decremented by an amount that keeps the total of the weights constant. The connections to the losing units do not change.

The effect of this is a positive contribution to the likelihood that the same detector unit will become active the next time the same input pattern is presented. (Of course, intervening patterns will have their own effects on the rates which may themselves raise or lower that likelihood.) Furthermore, there is a negative impact on the likelihood that it will become active for input patterns significantly different from it. This increases the likelihood that different detector units will win the competition on these significantly different patterns.

Competitive learning is a clear case of unsupervised learning, because the designer has determined only the number of detector units; there are no desired patterns of activation across those units of which they are informed. (Of course, if the designer constructed the input patterns with aforethought, she or he might be aware of the optimal clustering. But the network must figure it out just by observing the input patterns.)

The designer can produce more complex behavior by including more than one set of mutually competing units in the detector layer. In particular, if these sets have different numbers of units, each set will partition the input patterns into a different number of clusters. Another option is to incorporate additional layers that can learn to detect higher-order regularities (by applying the same learning rule to the weights between each pair of layers). For variations on competitive learning, see von der Malsburg (1973), Rumelhart and Zipser (1985; reprinted in *PDP:5*), Kohonen (1982), and a variety of papers in the journal *Biological Cybernetics* (Fukushima, 1980; Grossberg, 1976; Amari, 1983).

Reinforcement Learning

One final learning paradigm, reinforcement learning, deserves at least a brief characterization. In reinforcement learning, the network is told whether or not its output pattern was close to the desired output pattern, but is not told what the desired output actually was. Thus, only global information on performance is available as a guide to changing weights. Against the context of back-propagation this withholding of information may appear unnecessarily penurious; however, it corresponds to the common-sense notion that reward and punishment are the primary means of changing behavior. This is also the basic strategy used in operant conditioning, although with considerable sophistication in the timing of reinforcement which increases its effectiveness.

Essentially, what the network does is carry out an experiment with a large number of trials. Various combinations of weights might be tried, for example, and notice taken of what global reinforcement was delivered on each attempt. On each trial, each connection will be informed of that reinforcement. Those values of weights that tend to result in greater reinforcement become favored and are tried more often on succeeding trials. Eventually, the weight matrix tends towards values that will maximize reinforcement. (For an interesting simulation that utilized reinforcement learning, see Barto and Anandan, 1985.)

Hinton (1989) points out that in one respect, reinforcement learning is much simpler than back-propagation, since it does not require computing the error derivatives for each weight. On the other hand, it can take many trials for each weight to assess the effects of its possible values on the reinforcement. This becomes especially problematic with large networks. Hinton graphically illustrates the problem: "It is as if each person in the United States tried to decide whether he or she had done a useful day's work by observing the gross national product on a day by day basis" (1989, p. 22). Nevertheless, the literature on reinforcement learning suggests points of contact between traditional learning theory and network modeling that could help to bring together typically unconnected groups of researchers. In this regard, it is interesting to note that the International Neural Network Society lists among its cooperating societies both the *Society for the Experimental Analysis of Behavior* and the *Cognitive Science Society*.

Some Issues Regarding Learning

Are Connectionist Systems Associationist?

We have now surveyed several of the best-known connectionist learning procedures, although we have not yet observed their application in large-scale models intended to simulate aspects of human cognition. It is appropriate to make a short excursion here to address one of the broad criticisms that has been raised against connectionism (Fodor and Pylyshyn, 1988). The critics object that connectionism is a return to associationism, and that to accept its construal of cognition is to give back territory that was won by diligent effort in the cognitive revolution. According to the critics, it has already been shown that an adequate model of cognition must employ the resources of a recursive system with symbols, variables, and related devices for encoding and manipulating information. Learning must therefore consist in hypothesis-testing, analogizing, or other means of manipulating symbolic representations. In chapter 7 we shall discuss a variety of limitations that these symbolic theorists impute to connectionism as a result of its eschewment of such resources. Here we shall focus just on the question of whether connectionism represents a return to associationism. Our short answer is that connectionism is an *elaboration* of associationism that has benefited from and can contribute to many of the goals of the cognitivism of the last twenty years. It is not a *return* to associationism; it is not *mere* associationism; but its most obvious ancestor is indeed associationism. (Its less obvious ancestor is cognitivism; connectionism has been informed in many ways by the computational and conceptual advances achieved within that tradition.)

Classical associationism offered a vision of how knowledge might be built up on the basis of contiguity and other principles. It offered a sketch of the form of mental representations and of learning processes that produce them (later given more specific interpretations, such as Hebbian learning as one framework for explaining classical conditioning); however, it lacked the technology and more differentiated constructs to go further. Connectionism can be regarded as the outcome of returning to the original vision of the associationists, adopting their powerful idea that contiguities breed connections, and applying that idea with an unprecedented degree of sophistication. Among the elaborations that were not even conceived of within classical associationism are: distributed representation (particularly coarse coding), hidden units (which function to encode microfeatures and enable complex computations on inputs), mathematical models of the dynamics of associationist learning, supervised learning (in which error reduction replaces simple Hebbian learning), back-propagation, and simulated annealing within a self-organizing dynamic network.

In classical associationism, the elemental units were ideas. A localist connectionist network using the Hebbian learning rule is essentially an implementation of classical associationist learning: the learning rule is increasing or decreasing the associations between ideas based on their contiguity (i.e., their pairing in the same input–output case). If the network is multi-layered, less obvious but more powerful variations on associationism can be attained. For example, hidden units can fractionate ideas into microfeatures, a degree of reduction not conceived of within associationism. Furthermore, ideas or microfeatures can achieve "contiguity" (joint activation) by means of the propagation of activity within the network, not just by occurring together in immediate experience (e.g., within the same sensory-level input pattern). This might be viewed as an implementation of the two ways that ideas can be experienced together in classical associationism (reflective thought as well as sensation).

Taken together, these elaborations provide a way to model the microstructure of rule-like systems. Within the approximationist perspective (discussed further in chapter 7), connectionist models are regarded as causal models of how rule-like behavior (as well as exceptional behavior) can be produced by a mechanism that makes no use of explicit rules. Hence, connectionism exemplifies the longstanding preference in psychology for relatively uniform mechanisms that operate at a fine grain, but it also can benefit from cognitivism's higher-level descriptions of what it is the mechanism is accomplishing. Furthermore, connectionist models of *learning* suggest a fresh approach to the question of how concepts and cognitive skills are acquired. Dealing with exceptions and with learning have been weak areas within traditional symbolic modeling. If connectionism can produce plausible, powerful learning mechanisms as well as explanatory models of rule-like behavior, it may take a prominent place in cognitive science as an integration of associationism and cognitivism that has a broader domain of applicability than either of its predecessors. (One is tempted to refer to connectionism as "associationism with an intelligent face.") Of course, the extent to which connectionism will be able to pay off all of its promissory notes remains to be seen. To the extent that connectionism succeeds, the charge of mere associationism will lose whatever force that it currently possesses.

Possible Roles for Innate Knowledge

In discussing Chomsky's criticism of Skinner's model of language learning earlier we noted that a major part of his argument, the argument from the poverty of the stimulus, was directed against the ability of the organism to learn from experience. It is now time to return to this question of nativism. There is no doubt that, historically, nativism has been more closely connected with the rationalist view of learning than with the empiricist approach. But, as many have noted, there is no reason that empiricists need be entirely opposed to nativism. In fact, if associations are to be based on similarity, empiricism requires some criterion for similarity that precedes learning. Thus, contemporary empiricists like Quine (1969a) postulate innate quality spaces as a basis for subsequent associationist learning. (Quality spaces are multi-dimensional spaces in which sensory inputs can be located so as to be able to compare them.) Since all learning theorists require some pre-existing structure within which learning is to occur, the nativism controversy should not be construed as a conflict over whether anything is innate, in the sense of being present in the organism before the organism has sensory experiences. Rather, the conflict concerns *what* is native. In the symbolic approach, since the operations performed by the system all involve manipulating symbols, it seems that at least some symbols and initial ways to manipulate symbols must be innate (and possibly compositions of symbols, such as rules, as well). For other approaches that do not rely on symbol manipulation, the capacities that are taken to be native can be specified in other ways.

It has been our general observation that most connectionists do not view the nativism issue as highly salient. To the extent that connectionism is a descendant of associationism, this represents a considerable shift in focus. Possible reasons for a reduced focus on nativism include: (1) research in genetics and developmental neurophysiology has revealed a very complex picture that does not easily reduce to empiricism or nativism in their original forms (see Wimsatt, 1986); and (2) for most connectionists, the interesting problems are computational and mathematical; many connectionists are in academic fields, such as computer science, in which nativism has not been a focal issue.

If one wished to consider the nativism issue within a connectionist framework, there are several possible approaches to incorporating native components in one's models (none of which could currently be pursued to much effect). The bottom-up approach would involve model-building that begins with the sensory transducers. If an appropriate model of sensory encoding could be achieved, this might be viewed as a constraint on the development of higher layers of the system that is at least in part innately given. A top-down approach is likewise possible: building in high-level outputs (that on this approach are viewed as innate "ideas") and trying to build a system downwards from there. A third approach is to explore the effects of design decisions that may or may not be part of our native constraints. Examples include: initial activations and weights on connections, the number of layers and units, whether or not these are malleable with experience, and so forth.

Rumelhart and McClelland (1986) devote a few pages of their discussion of general issues in *PDP:4* to the question of nativism versus empiricism. It strikes us as a very sensible discussion; they suggest that either extreme position could be implemented within a connectionist model but they focus on integrating the positions. For example, they posit an organism whose initial state is determined by genetics, but for which all connections are modifiable by experience. Two such organisms provided with similar genetics and environments would show similar trajectories through a space of possible networks as they develop.

A more extensive treatment of this question is provided by Shepard (1989). He conjectures that "in systems that have evolved through natural selection, the features of the world that are both biologically significant and absolutely invariant in the world have tended to become genetically internalized" (p. 104). That is, the species has evolved internal structures that are adapted to these features of the world, so individual members of the species need not learn them. How might such adaptations be incorporated in the initial connectivity of a network, providing a base from which learning may proceed to add its own contributions? Shepard suggests that evolution does not supply individuals with innate knowledge of which features characterize specific objects and events. Rather, it supplies knowledge of the structure of the features themselves. For example, the psychological space for colors is three-dimensional (hue, lightness, saturation) and is approximately Euclidean. Generally, psychological spaces incorporate abstract constraints that are not arbitrary but rather reflect evolutionary accommodation to the environment in which we live. For example, a rigid object moving in three-dimensional literal space has exactly six degrees of freedom of position (three of location and three of orientation); these constraints may be incorporated in the initial structure of the mental system that is responsible for recognizing objects regardless of their position in space. If so, translation invariance need not be learned.

Shepard's intriguing discussion illustrates that current connectionist modeling provides just a glimpse of what is possible within a more highly developed connectionist science. Although connectionism has roots in associationism, it is capable of incorporating a perspective as rationalist as that of Shepard. And although questions of learning have been emphasized in these early years of connectionist modeling, questions of evolution may dominate at some later time or in other quarters. The answers to either set of questions can be expected to be diverse since connectionism, just as any paradigm, provides little more than a framework within which battles can be fought in a common language.

4

Pattern Recognition:
Connectionism's Forte

The previous two chapters provided an overview of connectionist systems and their capacity to learn. We observed that networks are devices for mapping one class of patterns onto another class of patterns, and that they do so by encoding statistical regularities in weighted connections that can be modified in accord with experience. Here we turn our attention to the claim that connectionist networks are a highly suitable medium for modeling human performance. If what networks do is map patterns, then this claim would entail that (a) pattern mapping is fundamental to a variety of human capabilities; and (b) connectionist networks perform pattern mapping in a particulary advantageous manner.

Pattern mapping is actually a very broad concept, and it is useful to distinguish among types of mappings. *Pattern recognition* is the mapping of a specific pattern onto a more general pattern (that is, the identification of an individual as an exemplar of a class). *Pattern completion* is the mapping of an incomplete pattern onto a completed version of the same pattern. *Pattern transformation* is the mapping of one pattern onto a different, related pattern (for example, a verb stem such as *come* can be transformed into a past tense form such as *came*). Finally, *pattern association* is the arbitrary mapping of one pattern onto another, unrelated pattern (as in the paired-associate task that was a mainstay of the traditional psychology of learning).

We shall discuss tasks that require each of these types of mapping at appropriate points in the remainder of this book, with an emphasis on how networks can be used to model human capabilities and on philosophical implications. In this chapter we shall focus on pattern recognition. In humans, pattern recognition is most obviously involved in sensation and perception (where the initial patterns are imposed upon large arrays of sensory receptors that must operate in parallel). The outcomes of local classifications are combined to obtain more global patterns, which in turn serve as input patterns to higher-level recognition devices. Eventually, levels of abstraction are reached at which the classes have names in human languages. Researchers have given a great deal of attention to the nature and acquisition of object categories in particular (e.g., chair, furniture). Traditionally these semantically interpretable categories have been regarded as cognitive, but the same overall process of pattern recognition is involved in sensation and perception as well. In fact, the term *categorization* is generally used to refer to pattern recognition at any level. (Also, although it was once agreed that information is passed serially from level to level, many cognitive scientists now assume that processing occurs in parallel on incomplete patterns at multiple levels; see McClelland, 1979.)

Our discussion of pattern recognition is divided into four parts. First, we illustrate how connectionist networks perform this type of mapping by describing two simulations in some detail. Second, we show how the ability of networks to recognize patterns suggests an approach to accounting for the intentionality of mental states. Third, we review research in the psychology of concepts and categorization, and consider the relevance of network models. Fourth, we argue that even the capacity to reason can be viewed as a task of pattern recognition and hence amenable to network modeling.

We shall see that networks have some very useful properties as pattern recognition devices, and that pattern recognition can be viewed as fundamental to a variety of perceptual and cognitive tasks. This invites the inference that connectionist networks can be broadly useful in modeling human capabilities. Connectionist models are not the only cognitive models that emphasize pattern recognition, however, and the process of evaluating competing claims of superiority has just begun.

Networks as Pattern Recognition Devices

Pattern Recognition in Two-layer Networks

To credit a system with recognizing a pattern, it must be observed to respond in a consistent manner whenever it is presented with an instance of the pattern. This is exactly what a two-layer, feedforward network can do quite well (if the patterns meet certain constraints already discussed). Moreover, using the delta rule as a learning procedure, such a network can learn to recognize patterns for itself. To illustrate, we shall employ the network that was displayed in chapter 2 as figure 2.7. It has eight input units and eight output units, with a connection from

Table 4.1   Prototypical input patterns and desired output patterns for the
two-layer pattern-recognition network

Case	Prototypical input pattern	Desired output pattern
A	$-1\ -1\ -1\ -1\ +1\ +1\ -1\ -1$	$-1\ -1\ -1\ -1\ -1\ -1\ -1\ -1$
B	$-1\ -1\ +1\ +1\ +1\ -1\ -1\ -1$	$-1\ -1\ -1\ -1\ +1\ +1\ +1\ +1$
C	$-1\ +1\ +1\ +1\ -1\ +1\ -1\ +1$	$-1\ +1\ -1\ +1\ -1\ +1\ -1\ +1$
D	$+1\ +1\ +1\ +1\ +1\ +1\ +1\ +1$	$+1\ +1\ +1\ +1\ +1\ +1\ +1\ +1$

each input unit to each output unit. We set up this network to run
under the **pa** (pattern associator) program in the *Handbook* (Mc-
Clelland and Rumelhart, 1988, chapter 4). In specifying the program
options, we selected the delta rule with a learning rate of 0.0125 and the
linear activation rule:

$$a_u = netinput_u = \sum_i weight_{ui}\, a_i$$

For this illustration, we specified four input–output cases using
binary values of $+1$ and -1 (although the network itself will take continuous activations). For example, table 4.1 shows that the input pattern for Case A is $(-1-1-1-1\ +1\ +1-1-1)$, and the desired
output pattern is $(-1-1-1-1\ -1-1-1-1)$. (For convenience,
we shall often refer to these simply as *input A* or *output A*, or in context as the *input* and *output*.) To make the illustration concrete, we
can loosely think of the inputs as distributed representations for the
prototypical exemplars of a category (e.g., a prototypical *hat*) and the
outputs as distributed representations of conventional names that
identify the categories themselves (e.g., "*hat*").[1]

In the simplest possible simulation, we could train the network by

1 Note that a full-scale simulation of the task of naming the categories of exemplars
would use a more principled way of representing the input and output; typically, the binary values would encode features based on a systematic characterization of the domain.
For example, the input units might encode visual and other features that specify
exemplars of basic level categories, and the output units might provide a phonemic or
articulatory encoding of "*hat*." Specifying encodings of this sort presents some difficulties that we need not address; for our illustration, arbitrarily chosen strings of eight
values are adequate. Furthermore, most investigators would want separate layers or
networks for encoding the category as a mental concept and for generating a conventional
name in a language such as English. Again, we can ignore this source of added complexity
in carrying out our illustration.

presenting it with each of the four input–output cases repeatedly across a number of training epochs. On each trial the network would produce an actual output for the input, compare it to the desired output, and adjust its weights according to the delta rule. Eventually it would learn to produce the appropriate output for each input. As a bonus, by this time it would also do a good job of generalizing. That is, if we presented it with the following input that it had never seen before

$$-1 \ -1 \ -1 \ -1 \ +1 \ -1 \ -1 \ -1$$

(which differs from the standard input A in position 6), it would produce an output closely resembling output A. But this is a somewhat unrealistic model of how we learn to identify the categories to which exemplars belong. Typically, our exposure is not limited to ideal or prototypical exemplars. Rather, we confront a variety of exemplars that more or less resemble each other. Likewise, when we hear the names, they will be pronounced somewhat differently each time. We have simulated this situation by distorting both the inputs and the (desired) outputs by a randomly chosen factor ranging between 0.5 and -0.5 (generated independently for every pattern, both within and across cases). Thus, instead of the original input A (which we shall refer to as the *prototype*) we shall, on a given trial, present the network with a *distorted* input A' such as:

$$-0.76 \ -0.89 \ -1.21 \ -1.01 \ 1.33 \ 0.99 \ -0.65 \ -0.92.$$

The network's actual output will now be compared with the *distorted* output A'.

The network was trained with these distorted input–output cases across 50 epochs; during each epoch it received a distorted version of each of the four inputs and their corresponding outputs. After just a few epochs the network responded in a qualitatively correct manner: by epoch 4 the activations of all output units were on the correct side of 0 (i.e., positive or negative as appropriate). The additional training was required to refine the outputs (i.e., bring them closer to -1 or $+1$). After training, the network was tested on three different types of input for each case; these test inputs and the actual outputs that the network produced are shown in table 4.2. First, when presented with the *prototype* (which had never been seen in this simulation), the network produced an actual activation value for each output unit that was within 0.2 of the desired value. Second, when presented with a new exemplar obtained by *randomly distorting* the prototype in the way described

Table 4.2 Activation of units in the two-layer pattern-recognition network after 50 training epochs

A.   Tested with prototypes of four categories as inputs.

Units 1–8 in input or output layer

Case	Layer	1	2	3	4	5	6	7	8
A	Input	−1.00	−1.00	−1.00	−1.00	1.00	1.00	−1.00	−1.00
	Output	−1.12	−0.98	−1.02	−0.92	−1.10	−0.84	−0.94	−1.06
B	Input	−1.00	−1.00	1.00	1.00	1.00	−1.00	−1.00	−1.00
	Output	−0.99	−1.06	−0.98	−0.96	0.91	0.94	0.99	0.88
C	Input	−1.00	1.00	1.00	1.00	−1.00	1.00	−1.00	1.00
	Output	−0.91	0.96	−0.87	1.05	−0.84	1.06	−0.90	0.92
D	Input	1.00	1.00	1.00	1.00	1.00	1.00	1.00	1.00
	Output	0.99	0.94	1.05	1.07	0.93	1.03	0.92	1.15

B.   Tested with distorted instances of four categories as inputs.

Units 1–8 in input or output layer

Case	Layer	1	2	3	4	5	6	7	8
A′	Input	−0.76	−0.51	−0.82	−1.11	1.47	0.82	−0.83	−0.90
	Output	−0.81	−0.90	−0.71	−0.83	−0.77	−0.72	−0.62	−0.89
B′	Input	−1.00	−0.54	1.34	0.63	0.98	−0.59	−1.24	−0.81
	Output	−1.06	−0.81	−1.03	−0.68	0.63	1.00	0.70	0.88
C′	Input	−1.18	0.62	1.20	0.87	−1.21	1.38	−1.02	1.48
	Output	−1.07	1.11	−1.01	1.22	−1.12	1.10	−1.18	0.92
D′	Input	1.42	1.44	0.64	1.31	0.72	1.24	1.03	1.19
	Output	1.20	1.28	1.25	1.39	0.81	1.00	0.77	1.15

C.   Tested with one of the input features (italics) of a prototype replaced by a feature of reverse sign. One output response has the wrong sign (boldfaced).

Units 1–8 in input or output layer

Case	Layer	1	2	3	4	5	6	7	8
A″	Input	−1.00	−1.00	−1.00	−1.00	1.00	*−1.00*	−1.00	−1.00
	Output	−0.86	−1.39	−0.85	−1.41	−0.26	−0.78	−0.16	−0.89
B″	Input	−1.00	−1.00	*−1.00*	1.00	1.00	−1.00	−1.00	−1.00
	Output	−0.98	−1.24	−0.96	−1.22	0.30	0.06	0.39	**−0.03**
C″	Input	−1.00	*−1.00*	1.00	1.00	−1.00	1.00	−1.00	1.00
	Output	−1.20	0.38	−1.14	0.49	−0.74	0.87	−0.75	0.68
D″	Input	*−1.00*	1.00	1.00	1.00	1.00	1.00	1.00	1.00
	Output	0.13	0.75	0.21	0.85	0.38	1.18	0.41	1.15

above, the actual outputs on each unit were all within 0.5 of the desired outputs. Third, even when presented with a new exemplar obtained by *reversing the sign* of one of the prototype's input units (making the pattern in that respect closer to the prototype of a different category),[2] the network produced outputs that were usually within 0.5 of the target. All except one of these output values (boldface) were on the correct side of 0.

The fact that there is variability in the output may be disconcerting. Can we really say that the network has recognized the pattern on the basis of this kind of outcome? If this is thought to be a problem, however, it is one that is easily remedied. Instead of using a linear activation function for the output units, we could employ a threshold function that would make the value of the output unit 1 if the net input to it was greater than 0, and make it 0 otherwise. In many contexts this sort of digitalization is useful. One advantage is that the activations on the output units would have more of the character of symbolic representations (that is, a given class of output could always have the same representation; "*hat*" could always be -1 -1 -1 -1 -1 -1 -1 -1). However, for some purposes the variability produced by a continuous activation function may be preferable. For example, if a distorted input produces a distorted output, other processing components that utilize that output will be able to compute the degree of distortion. Having that information available may be useful, e.g., in suggesting a degree of uncertainty which may be due to context effects or other factors.

Even though this is a very simple network, it has done a credible job of learning to recognize several categories of input patterns. It is worth emphasizing the fact that the network can handle distorted patterns and readily classifies new patterns that are similar to the training inputs. Hence, it can deal in a natural way with some of the variability that is encountered in the real world (e.g., people identify various types of hats as "*hat*"). On the other hand, there are definite limitations to this capability for two-layer networks, as we discussed in chapter 3. Overcoming these limitations requires multi-layered networks, whose pattern recognition capacities we consider next.

Pattern Recognition in Multi-layered Networks

To recognize some patterns it is not sufficient to map input patterns directly onto output patterns. Rather, one or more intermediate layers of

---

2 This models the situation in which an instance of one category (e.g., a hat) has a feature (e.g., a strap that looks rather like a handle on a bucket) that makes the hat, in that respect, look more like a bucket than a typical hat.

units are needed to extract information that can then be passed to units in higher layers. McClelland and Rumelhart (1981) and Rumelhart and McClelland (1982) offered an interactive activation model, which illustrates how a multi-layered network can recognize visual patterns, specifically, four-letter words presented in a particular type font. They constructed an interactive network with an input layer of features (e.g., top horizontal bar), a middle layer of letters (e.g., *E*), and an output layer of four-letter words (e.g., *BOTH*). It differs from more recent multi-layered networks in that its middle layer of units is not actually a hidden layer: (a) the connection weights and interpretations of its units were specified by the designers rather than extracted by the network itself in a learning paradigm; (b) the activation patterns on that layer as well as the top layer are "visible." That is, when the network recognizes a word (top layer), it also recognizes letters (middle layer) and can report either level depending upon the task. Note that there would be little reason to report the middle layer if it were actually a hidden layer, because individual hidden units generally are interpretable only as complex microfeatures that are not easily labeled.

All of the units and connection weights in the word recognition network were hand-crafted a decade ago, before the back-propagation learning procedure was available, and is best regarded as a transitional type of multi-layered network. Nevertheless, it produces human-like responses under a variety of conditions, including low contrast (dim lighting) and missing features (as would occur if ink blots were spilled across the word). It is able to exhibit fault-tolerant processing because, like any interactive network, it operates to satisfy multiple soft constraints. (In contrast, commercial pattern-recognition systems such as those used by banks to read the special characters at the bottom of a check are *brittle*. If flexibility with respect to different fonts and scripts could be combined with fault tolerance in a pattern-recognition device, organizations such as banks and postal services could go much further than they already have in replacing human pattern-recognition systems – their line employees – with machines.)

There are some more subtle phenomena of human pattern recognition that were also addressed by McClelland and Rumelhart. In particular, they were able to simulate the *word superiority effect*. The basic effect is that very briefly displayed letters are better recognized when they are presented in the context of a word (or a pronounceable nonword). Helpful effects of context are ubiquitous in human information processing; that is, doing more often costs less effort. It might be thought that this is because context narrows the possibilities, but Reicher (1969) showed that there is more to the effect than that (see also Wheeler, 1970). Reicher constructed pairs of words that differ in just one letter position, e.g., *TOLD/COLD*. On each trial he briefly presented one word from the pair (e.g., *TOLD*); then a masking stimulus to stop visual processing; and then a test display that had the correct letter (*T*) above or below the letter from the contrasting word (*C*), with dashes placed in the positions of the three shared letters to orient the choices. Subjects' ability to choose the correct letter was better in this word context condition than in control conditions of scrambled strings of letters or isolated letters. Since either test letter would produce a word, something must occur in the course of processing that makes use of the actual word that is displayed. Exactly *what* occurs is the question that has challenged researchers; the McClelland and Rumelhart model is one promising way to answer that challenge. We shall not discuss McClelland and Rumelhart's full simulation of the word superiority effect (which involves presentation of a word, then of a mask, and then a forced choice response), but rather we shall discuss only the critical part of the model in which recognition of words affects the recognition of component letters.

As noted above, the network is built from three sets of units: one for features of letters (14 units)[3], one for letters (26 units), and one for words (1,179 units). The system is designed to deal with words of four letters, so four copies of the feature and letter sets are used (one set for the first letter of the word, one for the second letter, etc.). Each of the feature units is positively connected to units for letters that possess the feature and negatively connected to units for letters that do not. Similarly, the letter units are positively connected to units for words that contain the letter in the appropriate position, and negatively connected to words that do not. Importantly, there are also top-down connections: the word units are positively connected to the units for the letters they contain. Finally, word units and letter units are each negatively connected to all competitors within the same ensemble. Figure 4.1 shows all of the features and letters, and a few of the words and connections. Simulations can be run with this network under a variety of conditions and parameter values using the **ia** (interactive activation) program in McClelland and Rumelhart's *Handbook* (1988, chapter 7).

An input is provided to this network by activating the appropriate features in each of the four letter positions. For a word with an *E* in

---

3   Actually, for each feature there is one unit that is activated when the feature is present, and a different unit that is activated when it is absent, making a total of 28 units; absence can therefore be distinguished from lack of information. For simplicity, we do not discuss the units that encode absence.

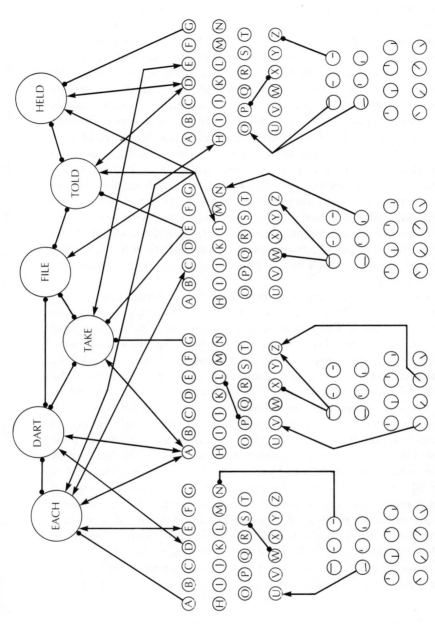

Figure 4.1 Basic architecture of McClelland and Rumelhart's (1981) word-recognition network. Connections may be excitatory (arrow) or inhibitory (filled circle). All of the feature and letter units that are used for each of the four letter positions in a four-letter word are shown; however, only a few connections and a few word units are shown.

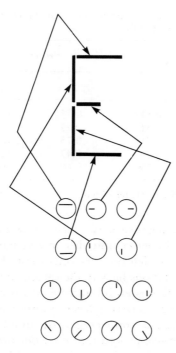

Figure 4.2 The featural encoding of the letter "E" in the Rumelhart–Siple font used by McClelland and Rumelhart's (1981) word-recognition network.

position 2, five of the units in the second ensemble of feature units will be activated. Figure 4.2 shows how an **E** is constructed in the Rumelhart–Siple font that was used in this study (Rumelhart and Siple, 1974). The features that are activated are: top horizontal bar, bottom horizontal bar, top left vertical bar, bottom left vertical bar, and leftmost center horizontal bar. (Note that the use of a fixed set of straight-line features has the result that a few letters look somewhat odd, e.g., *B* and *V*, but this is of no consequence for the simulation. Also note that sets of features can be supplied that do not correspond to actual letters, or that are incomplete and therefore ambiguous; e.g., the top and bottom horizontal bars and bottom left vertical bar alone are consistent with *C, E, G, O,* and *Q.*) Each of the active feature units then sends activation to all of the letter units in the second ensemble of letter units with which it is consistent. For example, the top horizontal bar sends activation to such letters as *C, E,* and *F*; the bottom horizontal bar sends activation to such letters as *C, E,* and *J*; and so forth. Almost every letter will receive *some* activation in this manner, but *E*

Table 4.3   Activations of output units in the word recognition network when
presented with BOTJ

| | Processing cycle | | | |
Unit	10	20	30	40
B	0.51	0.75	0.79	0.79
O	0.51	0.75	0.79	0.79
T	0.51	0.75	0.79	0.79
J	0.38	0.47	0.49	0.49
BOTH	0.29	0.60	0.66	0.67

Note: Activation for unit **H** never reached zero.

will receive the most because it is consistent with all of the activated
features. Finally, as the letter units become active, they in turn excite
those word units with which they are consistent. These word units will
then send further excitations back in the reverse direction to those same
letter units. Because this is an interactive network, the propagation of
activation will continue across a large number of processing cycles.
(Note that the backward connections are unrelated to back-propagation, which is a *learning* procedure for *feedforward* networks; here we
have an activation route in an interactive network that is not set up for
learning.) The equations used for the output from units, the net input
to units, and the change in activation are very similar to those for the
Jets and Sharks simulation discussed in chapter 2. For letter and word
units the only differences are in the values used for parameters such as
connection strength and decay (and they lack external input); feature
units, however, receive *only* external input (in the form of binary
values).

The fact that information flows both from letter units to word units
and from word units to letter units is critical in determining the
behavior of this network. The letter units receive top-down input from
the word units, and bottom-up input from the feature units. If the feature units do not correspond to an actual word, the word unit that is
most consistent with those features can override some of the featural
detail by strengthening the activations of its letters (i.e., the letters that
should be favored because they form a word). To illustrate the override
capacity, we presented McClelland and Rumelhart's **ia** network with
the input *BOTJ* instead of *BOTH*. Despite the misspelling, the word
unit **BOTH** quickly reached a high activation value (0.67 after 40
processing cycles). At the letter level, the letters **B**, **O**, and **T** quickly became more active than **J** (table 4.3). Hence, the higher-level (word) unit

Table 4.4 Activations of letter and word units when the word recognition network is presented with BOT ▓

Unit	1	2	3	4	5	6	7	8	9	10	20	30
					Processing Cycle							
Letter units in four positions (LP1–LP4)												
LP1: B	6	13	18	24	30	35	41	45	50	55	78	80
LP2: O	6	13	18	24	30	35	41	46	51	55	78	80
LP3: T	6	13	18	23	29	34	39	44	49	53	78	80
LP4: B, D					0	0	0	0	0	0	0	0
E				0	0	1	1	1	1	1	0	0
H			0	1	3	5	8	13	18	24	69	76
L				0	0	0	0	0	0	0	0	0
N, T				0	0	0	0	0	0	0	0	0
K, Y				0	0	0	1	1	1	1	0	0
Word units												
BOMB				0	0							
BOND				0	0	0						
BATH, BONE				0								
BORE, BOWL				0								
BOAT, VOTE			0	0	0	0	0					
BORN, NOTE			0	0	0	0	0	0				
BOOK			0	1	0	1	0	0	0			
BODY			0	1	1	1	1	0	0			
BOTH		0	3	6	9	13	18	23	29	35	71	75

Note: Blanks should not be confused with 0's. A blank indicates that the activation was below 0.

was able to respond and override the lower-level (letter **J**) unit in order to arrive at an actual four-letter word.

Given that the input served to activate the fourth-position **J** unit and to inhibit any other response, the top-down response from the word unit **BOTH** was not able to suppress the **J** unit completely and activate the **H** unit. But in another simulation, in which the input was simply *BOT*▓ (that is, the fourth letter position was left blank), the **H** unit became almost as active as the units for the letters that were actually presented (table 4.4). What is of particular interest is that along the way the system partially activated several other word units (e.g., **BOOK** and **BODY**). As a result, units for several letters other than **H** were brought above zero (e.g., **K** and **Y**). Note that the partially activated words agreed with the input in only two positions, whereas **BOTH** was consistent in all three of the positions that had input. Hence **BOOK** and

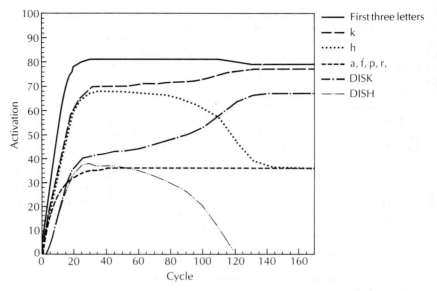

Figure 4.3 Change in activation across cycles of the most active units in McClelland and Rumelhart's (1981) word recognition network when presented with DISⱵ.

BODY were suppressed eventually by **BOTH**. This in turn had the effect of activating the fourth-position **H** unit, and interactive processing further strengthened these units: after **BOTH** activated **H**, **H** activated **BOTH**, and so it went back and forth across cycles. This reverberation effect continued until a stable state was achieved, in which both units were nearly as active as they would have been if *BOTH* had been presented to the system to begin with.

In the case just described only one four-letter word was consistent with the input in the first three positions. The behavior of the system becomes even more interesting when more than one match is available. In another experiment, we presented the system with the following input pattern:

DISⱵ

In the Rumelhart–Siple font, the partial letter in the fourth position was compatible with an A, F, H, K, P or R. Initially the units for all six letters became equally active (through cycle 5). As shown in figure 4.3, in cycle 3 the units **DISH** and **DISK** both started to become active. As these word activations increased across cycles, **H** and **K** became most active, although the other candidates for the fourth letter position continued to grow in activation at a slower rate. Through cycle 30 the units for both words grew in activation at roughly equal rates, pushing the **H** and **K** units to much higher activation levels than the other four letters. After cycle 30 **DISH** gradually lost out to **DISK** until it dropped below 0 activation after cycle 120. As a result, **H** began to lose activation after cycle 50, eventually settling back to the same level of activation as the other four letter units. The reason for this is that the word "disk" is more frequent in English than the word "dish," and so the unit **DISK** was assigned a higher resting activation than the unit **DISH**. As a result, the activation was always slightly greater for **DISK** than **DISH**, and so it was able to exert a greater inhibitory effect on its competitor, as well as a greater excitatory input to its fourth-position letter unit (**K**). Here, then, is an example in which higher-level information about which word is more likely in English serves to govern the behavior of the lower-level letter units. Clearly, this effect could be extended. For example, there could be yet a higher level that would relate words in a context. If the context were a discussion of food, that might be sufficient to override the overall frequency difference and therefore to activate **DISH** over **DISK** and **H** over **K**.

This last simulation illustrated two important characteristics of networks. In addition to *recognizing* patterns, they can also *complete* patterns by filling in what was not present in the input. This capacity is a general feature of connectionist networks. In addition, this simulation showed how higher levels of information (e.g., information about what four-letter words exist in English and their relative frequency) can affect the recognition of lower-level entities (e.g., the letters that comprise the words). It is relatively easy to see, in principle, how one might employ a model of this sort to simulate theory-laden perception (that is, the influence of perceivers' "theories," or knowledge, on how they see and identify objects). The higher-level units would encode the information that constitutes the "theory," and could influence the responsiveness of lower-level perceptual units that recognize objects. If a learning procedure were incorporated into such a network, it would be possible for the higher-level units to serve as training units, leading to the revision of weights at the lower level, and subsequently generating different recognition behavior at the lower level.

The performance of the letter-recognition network is rather impressive. The network can take in distorted sensory information and make reasonable inferences about what it is seeing. It does this without using rules, employing instead a set of weights and activation function. The simulations carried out on this network demonstrate the potential of that approach, but it is not yet a fully adequate device for carrying out pattern recognition in the real world. One limitation is that the input for each letter must be presented to the appropriate ensemble of feature units (e.g., the first letter was presented to the ensemble of units in the first position). In real life, letters and objects can appear in different parts of our visual field (and even at different orientations), and we must recognize them wherever they appear. A variety of strategies have been proposed for normalizing the input (i.e., putting the input in a canonical form) so that we could then employ a device like this network to extract the pattern. Whether these strategies will be successful, or whether more complex means will be needed, is not a matter that we can address further here.

Since McClelland and Rumelhart's word-recognition network was designed, in the early 1980s, more sophisticated multi-layered networks have been developed which can perform a variety of perceptual tasks. Most utilize a learning procedure such as back–propagation so that their intermediate layers are genuine hidden layers that learn to extract microfeatures from the input patterns that can be used for further processing. Examples of tasks for which such networks have been designed include forming compressed representations of visual scenes (Cottrell, Munro, and Zipser, 1987); sonar detection of rocks versus mines (Gorman and Sejnowski, 1988); identification of phonemes (Hampshire and Waibel, 1989); recognition of complex objects (e.g., houses) from digitalized television images (Honaver and Uhr, 1988); and recognition of hand-written characters (Skrzypek and Hoffman, 1989). Recognition of complex invariants such as shape over translations in space (Gibson, 1966) are more of a challenge and only infrequently have been addressed; but see Hinton (1987); Zemel, Mozer, and Hinton (1988); and Hummel, Biederman, Gerhardstein, and Hilton (1988). Multi-layered networks have also been used to model recognition of semantic categories, as we shall discuss later in this chapter.

Generalization and Similarity

Before leaving our general discussion of how networks perform pattern recognition and completion tasks, we need to note that one of the important characteristics of a pattern recognition network is its capacity to generalize. Once the network has been trained to classify input patterns into particular classes, if it is then given a new input pattern, it will typically respond in accordance with trained patterns to which it is similar. This, however, raises a fundamental question: what is the basis for determining similarity? Similarity poses a notorious philosophical problem. One common-sense approach is to state that object A is more similar to B than C if it shares more properties with B than with C. But this only forces us to individuate properties, and in attempting this we encounter the sorts of difficulty identified by Nelson Goodman (1955). He argued that any two objects are alike in an infinite number of respects. For example, you share with a pine tree the properties of being less that 2,000 feet tall, being approximately 93,000,000 miles from the sun, etc. This suggests that assessing similarity in terms of numbers of properties held in common is inadequate unless we can provide a plausible restriction on what counts as a property or what properties are relevant.

Despite these philosophical difficulties, we all make judgements about similarity. Moreover, there is a fairly clear sense in which connectionist networks are making similarity judgements: the similarity structure is implicit in the weight matrix. The weights are the means of treating similar inputs similarly. One question that arises is whether this approach to similarity is sufficient. Often we assume that similarity is a matter of fact, and that it has an objective basis. When we develop a network that generalizes in the way we do, we tend to be pleased and think it has found the correct solution to the task we posed. When the network is tested and generalizes in a different manner, there is a sense in which we have failed. But we might do well to remember the example of Wittgenstein (1953) in which he imagines a student who has learned, by following the teacher's example, to write a series of numbers by incrementing by two. The teacher is pleased as the student gets as far as 996, 998, 1,000, but then is puzzled to see the student write 1, 004, 1,008, 1,012. When queried, the student claims to have gone on in the same way. Wittgenstein comments:

In such a case we might say, perhaps: It comes natural to this person to understand our order with our explanations as *we* should understand the order: "Add 2 up to 1000, 4 up to 2000, 6 up to 3000 and so on."
Such a case would present similarities with one in which a person naturally reacted to the gesture of pointing with the hand by looking in the direction of the line from finger-tip to wrist, not from wrist to finger-tip. (1953, §185)

Wittgenstein's point seems to be that the only framework for evaluating the correct way to follow a rule, such as adding by twos, is the practice of a group and that someone who behaves differently is simply following a different practice. There is no independent criterion for correct performance. Likewise, the network that generalizes as we do may recognize similarity as we do, and one that does so differently may simply have a different way of determining similarity.

What is necessary to get a network to determine similarities as humans do and so generalize in the same way? In part, this may require having much the same architecture as humans. In so far as the architecture of current networks is very simple and general compared to the mind–brain, then it should not be surprising if current networks will frequently generalize in different ways from humans. But we also need to consider the fact that how a network generalizes is partly determined by the particular set of input–output cases on which it is trained, as has been demonstrated for human generalization. For example, Nelson and Bonvillian (1978) showed that children at age $2\frac{1}{2}$ years produce (and comprehend) invented names for unfamiliar objects much more successfully if they have been exposed to two or four different exemplars, rather than just one exemplar, during informal teaching sessions. Moreover, our experience does not consist simply in processing discrete pieces of information. We live in a body, interact with an environment, and play roles in various social structures. Dreyfus and Dreyfus (1986) have argued that these factors may all figure importantly in determining human cognition. This may mean that networks cannot completely share our sense of similarity and generalize as we do unless they share these other features of human existence as well.

Hence, one of the attractive characteristics of networks is that they generalize by means of the same mechanism that recognizes explicitly trained patterns; generalization comes "for free." Important questions remain, however. Exactly how well do networks generalize? How similar is their generalization to that of humans? (For example, Pavel, Gluck, and Henkle (1988) raise concerns whether the generalizations that humans find difficult are also difficult for networks.) How does network generalization compare to that of the best rule-based models, and particularly to those that implement, in a different way, such properties as satisfaction of soft constraints? Questions such as these can be expected to be a focus of concern in the 1990s.

Pattern Recognition Beyond Perception

Having demonstrated how networks carry out pattern recognition, with an emphasis on perceptual tasks, we now turn to questions concerning the broader role of pattern recognition in human cognition. Within a connectionist framework, pattern recognition plays a fundamental role at all levels of processing, from sensation through reasoning, and there is no sharp boundary between perception and cognition. Some traditional symbolic theories (e.g., Fodor, 1975), in contrast, regard symbolic processing as autonomous of sensory processing and do not characterize it in terms of pattern recognition. Certain less traditional symbolic theories are similar to connectionist accounts in their emphasis on pattern recognition at all levels of processing. In Anderson's (1983) ACT* theory, for example, an explicit process of pattern recognition within a network is the means by which production rules are selected to fire at all levels of processing. Any system that allocates a fundamental role to pattern recognition, including but not limited to connectionist systems, has the potential to account for what philosophers have sometimes construed as the distinctive feature of mental life, although they have found it extremely difficult to explain: that is, the *intentionality* of mental states. We now turn to exploring the shape that a connectionist account of intentionality might take.

Pattern Recognition and Intentionality

Intentionality is a technical term within philosophy that refers to the notion that mental states have content or meaning (cf. the ordinary use of this term, which refers to the notion that one intends to do something). Intentional states are *about* phenomena that are generally situated outside the cognitive agent. One of the central challenges in the philosophy of cognitive science has been to explain how mental states acquire their intentionality, that is, are about specific phenomena. One of the factors that makes this task difficult was identified by Brentano (1874/1973). He noted that a mental state, such as a belief, seems to involve a *relation* between the believer and an external phenomenon that is unlike ordinary relations. If Sam believes that Sarah is a neurologist, Sam's state of mind seems to stand in a relation to Sarah. Normally, for a relation to hold both relata must exist. Yet Sam could well have this belief and Sarah not exist. His mental state is still about Sarah, and not about anyone or anything else. Thus, the connection between the person in an intentional state and the object of that state cannot be handled simply in terms of relations; Brentano therefore used the term *relation-like* in order to capture this characteristic of intentional states.

Brentano's contemporary Frege worked out the basic theoretical framework that philosophers have employed for explaining what it is about states of the mind that make them be *about* specific objects. Frege (1892) differentiated two components of the meaning of a linguistic symbol: its *sense* and its *reference*. The *referent* of a symbol is the object (or class of objects) it refers to, while *sense* serves a mediating role, specifying the conditions an object must satisfy in order to be the referent of the symbol. The classic example is the term "morning star," whose referent is the object also known as Venus, but whose sense is the celestial object last seen in the morning. The term "Venus" has the same referent, but not the same sense. The sense seems to be a component of the mental state that determines reference. (Frege himself did not view senses as psychological entities. They were objective components of linguistic terms which might, however, be *grasped* by speakers of the language.) Difficulties arise when one tries to characterize how senses are supposed to *pick out* their referents (see Putnam, 1975).

The traditional symbolic approach to cognitive modeling makes the problem of intentionality particularly difficult to solve. The reason is that the representations employed in symbolic models are formal (as Fodor (1980) has emphasized). That is, they are to be operated upon by rules in virtue of their syntactic form without any consideration given to their reference. If we try to solve the intentionality problem within the confines of the formal system itself, the best we can hope to do is to give a description of the objects to which the symbols refer, which will pick out the same referents. But this does not constitute progress. The descriptions must themselves be stated using symbols, and so the problem has only been shifted; now we need an account of how *these* symbols refer to external phenomena. Symbols as merely formal objects seem to *pass over* the world in much the same way as Dreyfus and Dreyfus (1988), following Heidegger, characterized traditional philosophy as passing over the world:

According to Heidegger, traditional philosophy is defined from the start by its focusing on facts in the world while "passing over" the world as such. This means that philosophy has from the start systematically ignored or distorted the everyday context of human activity. The branch of the philosophical tradition that descends from Socrates through Plato, Descartes, Leibniz, and Kant to conventional AI takes it for granted, in addition, that understanding a domain consists in having a *theory* of that demain. A theory formulates the relationships among objective, *context-free* elements (simples, primitives, features, attributes, factors, data points, cues, etc.) in terms of abstract principles (covering laws, rules, programs, etc.). (Dreyfus and Dreyfus, 1988, pp. 24–5)

The challenge is to identify a way of relating representational states to phenomena in the world so as to explain their intentionality. Those who prefer to retain a formal (purely syntactic) symbolic account must find a way to augment that account with a separate semantic account, as in Fodor (1987). This is not an easy task, and some investigators prefer to build a new framework that does not assume the autonomy of syntax from semantics. One strategy is to appeal to the causal mechanisms that produce tokens of the symbols in us. Dretske (1981), for example, characterizes the causal relation between the object in the world and the symbol in the head in terms of the *information* that is transmitted and then tries to explain intentionality in terms of how the symbol bears information *about* the object. When a symbol is activated in the mind without being caused by its referent (e.g., when it is activated by other acts of thinking), it is still about the object which would, when perceived by the subject, normally cause activation of that symbol. This proposal has been challenged from a number of directions. In particular, it has been argued that such causal relations are inadequate to account for the possibility of error or misrepresentation (e.g., the possibility of representing nonexistent objects, which could not cause any states in us). As we have already noted, this is an important characteristic of intentional states (see Churchland and Churchland, 1983; Fodor, 1984).

In our view, the causal account does seem to be heading in the right direction in so far as it relates representational states to that which they are about. But causal analyses have generally been pursued from the perspective of *symbolic* analyses of representations, and that generates a number of the difficulties. The main problem that the causal/symbolic approach faces in explaining intentionality is that its basic symbols are treated as *atomic and arbitrary*. As a result, there is nothing about the symbol itself that determines its referent. At most, the contact with the external referent is handled by a transduction mechanism which is capable of generating tokens of the appropriate symbol in the cognizer when the relevant external referent is present. This transduction process is not involved in the mechanisms for symbol processing that figure once the token of the symbol is produced in the system. The cognitive system still seems to *pass over* the world.

There is an additional serious consequence of passing over the world in this manner. As the passage from Dreyfus noted, the symbols become *context-free*. But generally when we use representations intentionally, the particular referent that is intended varies with the context. This problem is readily seen when we consider the representational function of words in a natural language. The meaning (especially, the referents) of particular words often changes with context. It seems plausible that this will be true of mental states as well. The problem for capturing this in a traditional symbolic account is that its symbols are fixed entities; all of the tokens of a symbol are the same. In the symbolic theory, the causal relation cannot explain how on the different occasions when a symbol is used, there may be significant variation among intended referents. The most obvious ways that a purely symbolic account might countenance context are to employ a different symbol for each contextually determined referent, or to use more complex rules that include symbols that describe each context and the corresponding effect on reference. Dreyfus (1979) points to the struggles of researchers in symbolic artificial intelligence to develop context-sensitive systems as reason for pessimism regarding a symbolic solution.

More recent proposals may be more successful. For example, Barsalou (1987) has proposed that concepts are not fixed entities; rather, they are constructed on each usage by combining attribute values that are appropriate to the context. (See also Barsalou and Billman, 1989.) That raises the question of what mechanism constructs these unstable concepts. From a connectionist perspective, treating the attribute values as units in a network would be an attractive mechanism: the connectionist would call them microfeatures or subsymbols, and context sensitivity could be attained by using some of the input units to encode context. (This path from stable noncontext-sensitive symbols, to unstable context-sensitive subsymbols, to a connectionist mechanism for combining subsymbols illustrates that the difference between symbolic and connectionist approaches, while real, can be bridged.)

One of the benefits of connectionist approaches, so far as accounting for intentionality is concerned, is that the mode of processing it proposes as occurring within the system is continuous with processes occurring in the external world (see also Harnad, 1990). Connectionism does not propose a gap between symbol processing and other kinds of causal processes (such as those involved in sensation and perception). Thus it provides hope of situating cognitive processing in the world, and so begins to elucidate what Heidegger may have had in mind when he emphasized that our cognitive system exists enmeshed in the world in which we do things, where we have skills and social practices that facilitate our interaction with objects. We can begin by construing an individual as situated in a world that displays regularities at various levels of abstractness; those regularities have been captured in the individual's pattern recognition networks at various levels of abstractness, so there is a fit between the world and the system that interacts with it. The most obvious contact between the individual and the world is through the sensory receptors of the individual, but other networks quickly (and largely in parallel) recognize regularities at all levels of abstraction.

At an intermediate level of abstractness, the system will identify the objects or situations with which it is presented as exemplars of semantic categories. It thereby captures yet another aspect of intentionality: we represent an individual under a particular description (i.e., categorize it), but may fail to represent it under a different description that would also be appropriate. For example, we might recognize a person as a basketball player, but fail to recognize her as an honors student (just as we might view Venus as the evening star, but not as the morning star). This contributes to the *failure of substitutivity* (Chisholm, 1958) which is manifest in descriptions of intentional states. In non intentional sentences (e.g., "The basketball player was very tired") we can substitute one coreferential term for another without changing the truth value of the whole sentence, but not in the case of sentences describing intentional states (e.g., "I thought the basketball player was very tired"). That is, if we substitute "honors student" for "basketball player" in the latter sentence we have transformed a true sentence into a false one. This is because the nonintentional sentence is about the state of the world itself, whereas the intentional sentence is about a person's representation of that world.

Intensional logic was developed within philosophy in part to address problems like this. For example, a substitution rule can be introduced that permits the substitution of "honors student" for "basketball player" when this identity is known. To incorporate intensional logic in a mechanistic model one would need a system that could assign multiple properties or categories to the same individual. This can be accomplished in traditional symbolic artificial intelligence by means of separate propositions for each assignment, and in localist connectionist networks by means of connections leading to separate output units for each assignment (e.g., the connections from the person units to the property units in the Jets–Sharks network in chapter 2). A simple form of failure of substitutivity could be exhibited by either system, if the same individual is represented by different symbols or nodes that are provided with somewhat different sets of assignments. Further implementation of intensional logic (e.g., modeling what happens when the system is informed of the identity, or modeling second order intentionality) presents challenges to both kinds of systems. Currently we better understand how to develop such models in symbolic systems than in connectionist ones.

One important difference between the connectionist and traditional symbolic views of the interface with the world is that in the connectionist account, representations will not be arbitrary. This results from the fact that connectionist systems "decide" what representations to employ as an integral part of their learning activity in interaction with the world and the patterns it presents to the system. That is, two-layer pattern recognition networks, using a learning rule such as the delta rule, modify themselves toward weights that directly reflect environmentally-given relations between input and output patterns. Multilayered networks additionally determine what higher-order information (features or microfeatures) should be encoded in hidden units. For example, in describing how a small three-layer network learned to solve the XOR problem (in chapter 3), we noted that the two hidden units each acquired the capacity to represent distinctive information about the input. One became an OR detector, while the other became an AND detector. From the point of view of the network, these were not arbitrary decisions; these were the means that allowed the network to reduce its error in the overall task and thereby solve the problem. The role of one unit as an OR detector, as required by the input–output cases that were processed, was encoded in the pattern of connections between that unit and the input units and between it and the output unit; similarly for the AND detector. (Hinton's (1987) network for learning kinship relations, which we shall discuss in chapter 6, provides a more elaborate example of this same point.)

Most existing networks function with input representations that are chosen by the researcher, and hence the networks are not really tied to external objects in the sense needed to secure our claim that the representations are really about these objects. This limitation, however, results from the fact that each particular network is modeling only a small part of the entire cognitive system; few network designers in the modern era have chosen to interface their networks with an actual environment by including sensory and motor layers (i.e., building a robot). Gorman and Sejnowski (1988), however, trained a three-layer network which took as input the digitized outputs of a frequency analyzer into which actual sonar echoes from both rocks and mines were fed. The network learned to discriminate rocks from mines on this basis. Since the network's inputs were encodings of actual rock and mine echoes, it seems very plausible to treat its outputs as *about* rocks and mines, and to treat its hidden units as detecting features of rocks and mines.

The crucial point to be emphasized is that representations on hidden units result from the system's attempt to accommodate to its environment. They cease to be states which could have been causally connected to *any* sensory input and, hence, arbitrary as far as the operation of the system was concerned. It should be emphasized that connectionist systems in a learning paradigm are being trained to perform tasks. In more natural simulations, these tasks would involve acting in an environment in ways that would serve the needs or goals of the organism. But even in simple simulations, the learning procedure gives the network a goal: maximizing the fit of its states to those of the environment (by minimizing error in producing outputs to inputs). Thus, a teleological component is added. As a result, the representations developed in the hidden units subserve goals, and so can be thought of as representing information about things external to the system *for* the system. Hence, these representations are *about* the entities supplying the input. (The tightness of this connection is evident in the fact that in order for researchers to analyze the operation of hidden units, they must try to identify what input patterns will in fact generate the response of particular hidden units.)

As a final point, we should note that the responses the system makes to particular input states are not context-free. The system has not learned discrete responses to discrete facts, and there is no assumption that the world consists of a body of facts. Rather, the world consists of a rich body of information, some of which crosses the sensory thresholds of the organism. The information that is captured in the activation of input units in the connectionist processing system provides a broad spectrum of information about the environment in which the organism exists, some of which may be regarded as contextual, depending upon what task the organism is performing. It is up to the organism to learn to identify objects in the environment by learning responses to patterns. One advantage of this way of viewing the system's responsiveness to the environment is that the particular response of the system may be influenced by a variety of different factors, some of which we may take to be only indirectly related to the task at hand, but which are able to influence the patterns of activation arising inside of the system. For example, consider a case in which a representation becomes active due not to environmental input, but due to activity elsewhere in the network; let us say that the activity causes the network to activate a pattern much like the one that an actual ball would elicit. On one occasion this activity may result in a pattern much like that typically generated by a baseball, while on another occasion it might result in a pattern more like that typically produced by a basketball. This variation is then available to enable the system to adjust its response in a way that is sensitive to other information.

The connectionist approach to modeling cognition thus offers promise in explaining the *aboutness* or *intentionality* of mental states. Representational states, especially those of hidden units, constitute the system's own learned response to inputs. Since they constitute the system's adaptation to the input, there is a clear respect in which they would be *about* objects or events in the environment if the system were connected, via sensory-motor organs, to such an environment. They are about the situations to which they are responses in much the way that biological adaptations are adapted to situations like those figuring in the process of their selection. The fact that these representations are also sensitive to context, both external and internal to the system, enhances the plausibility of this claim that the representations are representations of particular states. The connectionist approach thus makes a start on explaining the *aboutness* of representations.

Unfortunately, there is more to be done to explain intentionality. We must also explain how mental states can represent things that do not exist. This is relatively easy to do in symbolic systems, since we could simply incorporate a symbol to stand in for the nonexistent object. Yet we could not explain why the arbitrary symbol had the referent it did. While we cannot here advance a detailed explanation of how connectionist systems could make reference to nonexisting objects, we can outline such an account. In interactive networks, activations can be brought about by activity in the network itself, and not just from external inputs. It is conceivable that activation patterns could be induced that do not correspond to anything normally caused by input patterns. These would be representations of nonexistent objects. We know they are *about* these objects, and not others, because they are the representations that would be produced if the system ever did confront such an object. Thus, if a representational pattern were created by internal processes in the system that are relevant to the featural description of a unicorn, then it would be a representation of a unicorn, not of Santa Claus. The network's response to the production of these states can be viewed as its further thinking about the nonexistent objects.

In summary, the idea that pattern recognition plays a crucial role in intentionality offers a useful new perspective on this difficult area of philosophical inquiry (for additional discussion, see Bechtel, 1989). Within cognitive psychology, the corresponding area of inquiry is research on how people form and use semantic categories. In the next section we briefly consider how a connectionist approach to categorization might be formulated and provide an overview of some empirical and theoretical contributions from cognitive psychology that must be taken into account.

Connectionist Models of Categorization

Categorization is an area in which the differences between symbolic and connectionist models are subtle rather than dramatic. Categories can be labeled by symbols, but these symbols are of little use without some sort of distributed representation across features that governs the application of those symbols to instances of the category (*exemplars*). That is, even within the symbolic tradition, categorization has had to be handled as a kind of pattern recognition in which exemplars are assigned to semantic categories on the basis of their features. Hence, much of the research that has been conducted on categorization within a symbolic framework can be incorporated into a connectionist framework as well. Within either framework, the primary difference between recognition of perceptual patterns and assignment of exemplars to categories is whether the features involved are at a low level of abstraction (e.g., "has a bottom horizontal bar" is a relevant feature of the letter "E") or at a medium level of abstraction (e.g., "has feathers" is a relevant feature of "bird"). Within the connectionist framework, but not within most symbolic theories, the distributed representation across features may be the sole way in which the category is represented; that is, there may be no separate unit or symbol corresponding to the category as a whole.

The two pattern recognition networks we discussed at the beginning of this chapter provide suggestive models of how connectionist accounts of categorization might be developed. In the two-layer network that learned to identify patterns A, B, C, and D, the specific input units were optionally thought of as specifying features that certain category exemplars possessed, such as their parts or color. A particular pattern across the input units was a distributed encoding of the exemplar in terms of these features. The output units provided a distributed encoding of the possible categories or category names; again, the network designer would determine whether or not each unit corresponds to an explicit feature, and if so, what features were involved. The weights were used to determine the assignment of exemplars to categories. Input features that were not very salient or systematic with respect to category assignments would have low weights on the connections leading out from them. When the network was presented with a specific exemplar, the activation of each input unit was propagated along each of its connections. Each output unit received a weighted sum of the activations from the input units (with a different set of weights used for each output unit). As we shall see, the use of additive combinations of weighted features is not unique to connectionist models, but rather is characteristic of a variety of categorization models.

Questions about the nature of distributed representations of categories across features, and how they are utilized, have been a major focus of psychological models of categorization. Psychologists initially presupposed the classical view of categories, which was a legacy of traditional philosophical analysis. That is, they assumed that categories identify sets, membership in which could be specified in terms of singly necessary and jointly sufficient conditions. These necessary and sufficient conditions were viewed as *defining* the category, and knowledge of a category was assumed to involve knowing those conditions. Two cognitive consequences of this view are that (a) all categories should be processed in basically the same manner, and (b) all exemplars of a category should be treated equally.

In the 1970s, psychological approaches to categorization were profoundly changed by the work of Eleanor Rosch, Edward Smith, and their students. Rosch, in particular, challenged the veracity of both cognitive consequences of the classical view in a series of important papers (for a review, see Rosch, 1978). She showed: (a) Among the different levels of categories in a class-inclusion hierarchy (e.g., desk chair, chair, furniture), one level (e.g., chair) is a *basic level* that is more easily acquired and processed. (b) Categories have a graded structure such that some exemplars of a category are recognized as more typical than others; e.g., a robin is judged to be a better exemplar of a *bird* than is a vulture (Rosch and Mervis, 1975; Rosch, 1978); see also Zadeh's (1965) notion of fuzzy sets and Posner and Keele's (1968) important demonstration that subjects exposed to dot patterns extract a prototype. Research by Rosch, Smith, and others has shown that prototypicality ratings correlate highly with a number of information-processing measures (for reviews, see Smith and Medin, 1981; Smith, 1988). For example, people categorize typical exemplars faster than atypical exemplars (Rosch, 1973) as well as more accurately (Rips, Shoben, and Smith, 1973); also, both children and adults perform better on reasoning tasks if typical exemplars are used (e.g., Carson and Abrahamsen (1976) obtained this outcome for children answering Piagetian class-inclusion questions).

Rosch and Mervis (1975) found that exemplars were judged typical of a category to the extent that they shared features. One example similar to theirs is that birds and robins have feathers, fly, are small, eat insects, and sing. A vulture, on the other hand, shares only the first two properties. Moreover, these features were often not the ones that would figure in a classical definition of the category. Also, it was not necessary for any feature to be common to all category members or for any feature to be distinctive of the category. Members of a category, they found, resembled each other much in the way that members of a family do, without possessing any defining features (this idea of family resemblance is drawn from Wittgenstein, 1953).

Subsequent research has drawn an even more complex picture. First, Armstrong, Gleitman, and Gleitman (1983) showed that typicality effects can be obtained even for categories that are most obviously classical in their definition, specifically, odd versus even numbers. From this they argued that empirical findings on typicality must involve aspects of categories other than their definitions and therefore would not bear on the correctness of the classical theory of definition. More recently, other investigators have shown that people will, when pushed, utilize certain *core* features such as *having genes* that do not seem to figure in prototypicality judgements but are definitional of categories (Carey, 1985; Keil, 1989). Hence, a complete account of categorization would include an account of the definition of categories in addition to an account of typicality effects. Even that is not sufficient, however. Armstrong, Gleitman, and Gleitman also argued that lists of features alone do not adequately capture the structure of our knowledge of categories. Some more organized, *theory-based* approach is needed (Murphy and Medin, 1985; Neisser, 1987). At the very least, theoretical considerations may influence both the saliency we give to particular features, and what we take to be features (Medin and Wattenmaker, 1987). At an extreme, featural approaches may be replaced by more elaborate kinds of knowledge structures, such as Lakoff's (1987) idealized cognitive models.

What implications do the various empirical findings and theoretical directions have for specific models of how our knowledge of categories is represented? We must limit ourselves here to just a few classes of models. Early in the cognitive era, symbolic models of semantic representation assumed the classical approach to concepts and categorization. In the notation of Raphael's (1968) declarative representations, for example, the singly necessary and jointly sufficient conditions (features) could be expressed by associating attribute-value pairs such as (*SUBPART*, FEATHER) and (*SUPERSET*, BIRD) with the concept ROBIN. Similarly, Kintsch (1974) used propositions such as (HAVE, ROBIN, FEATHERS). Much the same information was expressed in *semantic networks* by other investigators (e.g., J. R. Anderson and Bower, 1973; Norman and Rumelhart, 1975). These were extremely localist networks, in which the units (called *nodes*) encoded concepts, and the units were connected by a small number of directed relations that encoded relations between concepts. Both the units and connections were labeled by symbols. For example, the node *robin* could have a relation *haspart* connecting it to *feathers* and a relation *superset* (often called *isa*) connecting it to *bird*. Hence, propositional models and semantic networks provided two different kinds of format for organizing defining features into a symbolic knowledge structure. Within these kinds, models differed in a variety of other ways; for example, representations could be acted upon (static, declarative) or could be themselves active (dynamic, procedural).[4]

---

4 For example, within generative grammar, Katz and Fodor (1963) expressed necessary and sufficient conditions as symbols (semantic markers and distinguishers) in a tree structure which specified the lexical entry for the concept. Lexical entries like these could be incorporated in a processing model as declarative representations. The best example of a procedural representation is provided by production system rules of the form (if *condition*, then *action*). A straightforward approach is to specify the defining features in the condition (in some Boolean combination that would include the feature of having feathers), and to assign the category *robin* in the action.

These same formats can be adapted to accommodate the idea that what is mentally represented is information about a prototype, rather than necessary and sufficient conditions satisfied by all exemplars of the category. Kintsch as well as Rumelhart and Norman favorably discussed this approach in general. Within the network format, for example, one might add to the *bird* node an agent relation connected to a node *sing*, and a property relation connected to a node *small*; the same additions could be made to the *robin* node, but not to the *vulture* node.

Changes like this would be too crude, however, to account for quantitative data on typicality effects. Within the network tradition, it was necessary to move forward to a class of models that specified a process of *spreading activation* (e.g., J. R. Anderson, 1976, 1983; for early suggestions see Quillian, 1968; and Collins and Quillian, 1969). Collins and Loftus (1975) described and tested a way this process could be used to produce the typicality effects found in category judgements. They associated a weight with each connection in their network representation in order to distinguish among features on the basis of their degree of typicality or criticality for the category.[5] To determine whether a robin is a bird, activation was spread from the *robin* and *bird* nodes to the feature nodes at individual rates dependent on the number of connections and their weights. Essentially, when the number of matching features exceeded a threshold, a positive response was generated.

With the addition of weights and spreading activation, semantic networks made a major step forward, and can be regarded as forerunners to the connectionist models of the next decade. They particularly resemble localist connectionist networks. For example, both spreading activation and localist connectionist models can account for typicality and other effects by means of additive combinations of weighted features. Certain differences remain, however. (1) In a spreading activation network the connections are not used to distribute information; rather, a limited number of labeled connections are constructed such that activation along a particular path has a specific semantic interpretation. (2) The particular rules that govern the spread and use of activation differ in some respects.

A somewhat different theoretical path was taken by another group of investigators, but it led to much the same outcome (an emphasis on

---

5   Other networks that utilize numerical parameters on connections have focused on domains other than category representation, e.g., Colby's (1975) use of processing-relevant parameters for emotional states attached to beliefs (propositions), and Suppes' (1970) use of probabilistic parameters to govern the application of rules in a generative grammar. These parameters function similarly to weights in some respects.

additive combinations of weighted features). *Prototype* or *abstraction models* specify explicit means of judging the category membership of exemplars by computing their similarity to prototypes (which need not correspond exactly to any particular exemplars). Rosch (1975) assumed for convenience that categories were represented by unstructured lists of features. Rips, Shoben and Smith (1973) placed greater emphasis on the choice of representational format. Multidimensional scaling was already being used by some investigators as a way to represent concepts in terms of features that take continuously varying values; for example, various birds could be displayed as points in a space with dimensions that seemed to correspond to size and ferocity (cf. the scaling of mammals used by Henley, 1969; and by Rumelhart and Abrahamsen, 1973). The values for a robin or other basic-level bird on these dimensions would reflect characteristic (rather than defining) features of that category. Rips et al. (1973) made the intriguing suggestion that the superordinate category *bird* might be represented as a point in the same space, with Euclidean distance between the superordinate and basic-level terms predicting reaction time to verify their relation in a category judgment task. Smith, Shoben and Rips (1974) presented a more general feature comparison model in which features could be continuous or discrete and were weighted according to their importance to the category. Their general approach of computing similarity over a feature space was widely adopted, but for convenience additive computations on weighted discrete features have usually been used rather than Euclidean distance computations on continuous dimensions.

Exemplar models (e.g., Medin and Schaffer, 1978) are successors of prototype models and share their probabilistic view of category structure and their use of similarity (Medin, 1989). However, in prototype models the category is represented by the central tendency of exemplars (the prototype). In exemplar models, the category is given a much more detailed representation in terms of its exemplars. A separate featural representation of each exemplar is stored separately in memory, and a variety of computations can be made on these stored representations when needed (including the temporary extraction of a prototype). The way an exemplar model performs is highly dependent upon the processing mechanisms that utilize the information. Generally each feature is weighted, and computations of similarity may therefore involve the same additive combinations of weighted features that we encountered in network models. (In some exemplar models, however, the features are not assumed to be independent; see Medin and Schaffer, 1978.)

Medin has more recently proposed that probabilistic models in general need to be augmented by theory-based models (e.g., Murphy and Medin, 1985; Medin and Wattenmaker, 1987; Medin, 1989). Nevertheless, exemplar models are a major competitor to connectionist models of categorization, because they provide an alternative way to use distributed representations across features to retain detail while also permitting prototype extraction and generalization. Although the same kind of additive computations can be carried out within particular varieties of exemplar and connectionist models, the assumptions about storage and processing are so different that the ultimate result of computations may differ as well. In particular, connectionist models retain information about specific exemplars only in so far as processing an exemplar results in changes to the weight matrix. When the number of exemplars is small, the weights will permit a distinctive response on the output units for each exemplar; as the number of exemplars is increased, the network is forced to extract prototypes for similar sets of exemplars instead (but will retain as much individual information as possible). Feature vectors are used only to produce temporary patterns of activation on the input units. For exemplar models, in contrast, specific exemplars are stored as separate feature vectors, and prototypes are computed from multiple feature vectors when required.

Both prototype and exemplar models are able to account for the favored status of prototypes in categorization tasks, as well as effects of degree of typicality. Proponents of exemplar models claim that they can account for other effects as well (e.g., sensitivity to variability, context, and correlated attributes; see Nosofsky, 1988; and Medin, 1989). Barsalou (1990) has argued, however, that the two classes of models are empirically indistinguishable, if variations in assumptions within each class are permitted.

Prototype extraction is easily demonstrated in connectionist models (as shown for the Jets and Sharks exercise in chapter 2 and for a simple feedforward network in table 4.2). More detailed comparisons to human data have been provided by Knapp and J. A. Anderson, who taught a simple linear associator network to categorize dot patterns such as those used by Posner and Keele (1968). Knapp and Anderson (1984) obtained patterns of performance that were similar to human data in exhibiting an interaction between number of training exemplars and type of test pattern (prototypes vs. old exemplars vs. new exemplars). It is not obvious how their network could be used to model the effect that less prototypical exemplars require longer response time, because all responses were generated by a single pass through the network. The response time effect can be modeled more naturally in an interactive network, in which multiple cycles of processing are required before a stable state is obtained. McClelland and Rumelhart's word-recognition network required more cycles to achieve stable activations for some input patterns than others, for example.

Connectionist network models have clearly not been tested against human data as extensively as prototype or exemplar models, but there is no *a priori* reason to expect them to perform poorly (and if Barsalou is correct, the selection of the best model may not be empirically decidable anyway). As Knapp and Anderson pointed out, the ability of connectionist models to represent information about individual exemplars as well as prototypes within the same network may be advantageous. Also, connectionist models have a much broader range of application than categorization models (potentially, all of human perception and cognition), so they must also be evaluated on their ability to function across that range.

A further development in research on categorization suggests additional applications of connectionist systems. Category concepts are usually taken to be stable mental entities. It is in terms of them that we group objects or events together and proceed to reason and communicate about them. Even while challenging the classical view of categories, and demonstrating the role of non-defining features in categorization, Rosch defended the stability assumption. She claimed, for example, that prototypicality judgements were shared among members of a linguistic community. (Rosch (1975) reported correlations above 0.90.) That result now appears to be a statistical artifact. Using more appropriate statistical techniques, Barsalou (1987) showed not only much lower inter-subject correlations (ranging around 0.40), but also that individual subjects changed their prototypicality judgements over an interval of one month (with test–retest correlations of only about 0.80, leaving a fair amount of unexplained variability).

One way to interpret Barsalou's results is to insist that concepts are stable and to attribute the variability to different ways subjects use their concepts on different occasions. Barsalou, however, relying on these results and other indications of how context affects concepts, proposes a quite different interpretation according to which concepts are not fixed entities stored in people's memories and retrieved as needed, but are *produced* in the course of performing particular tasks. This is supported by the fact that upon demand people can readily construct new, *ad hoc* categories (such as places to go on vacation with your grandmother), and that these categories exhibit graded structures (Barsalou, 1983). By rejecting the view that concepts are fixed, Barsalou acquires the burden of explaining how they are formed. What he suggests (Barsalou, 1987) is that in long-term memory people have large amounts of "highly interrelated and 'continuous' knowledge" and that they form concepts "as temporary constructs in working memory that are tailored to current situations" (1987, p. 120; for a related view, see Kahneman and Miller, 1986).

From a traditional symbolic perspective, Barsalou's suggestions are difficult to understand. (See McCauley (1987a) for discussion of some of the difficulties.) From a less traditional symbolic perspective, there is at least one working program that handles Barsalou's findings (Peters, Shapiro, and Rapaport's (1988) semantic network processing system). However, a connectionist framework suggests an alternative interpretation of Barsalou's findings that is appealing (but has not been implemented). Concepts can be viewed as particular stable patterns of activation across an ensemble of units. These stable patterns then determine further processing. The stable patterns elicited on different occasions, however, need not be the same. Activity occurring elsewhere, or previous activity in the ensemble, could result in the production of a slightly altered pattern even without changing the weights. Intervening experience may also lead to slight changes in weights, of course, providing an additional source of variation in the patterns produced on different occasions. This pattern of weights would constitute Barsalou's "highly interrelated" and "continuous knowledge" in long-term memory which generates the patterns representing the temporary concepts.

Hence, connectionist networks can use their pattern-recognition capabilities to carry out categorization tasks, and they probably can exhibit typicality effects and task-sensitive variability. There is a variety of other criteria which networks will need to meet, however, before concluding that they can serve as accurate models of human categorization. To consider just one important example, humans find some types of category more difficult to learn than others, and realistic connectionist models should exhibit the same ordering of difficulty. Pazzani and Dyer (1987; see also Dyer, 1988) attempted to replicate a human difficulty ordering observed by Bower and Trabasso (1968). Categories defined by single attributes (e.g., squares) are easier to learn than categories that require a combination of attributes. Among combinations, conjunction (small blue circles) is easier than disjunction (small circles or large squares), which is easier than exclusive or (circles and blue objects, but not blue circles). Finally, polymorphous categories (e.g., ones that require two out of three attributes) are the hardest. Pazzani and Dyer used back-propagation to train connectionist networks and found that, contrary to prediction, conjunctive, disjunctive, and polymorphous categories were equally easy to learn. Dyer (1988) also noted that connectionist networks require more examples to learn a category than do humans. This last objection is a difficult one to judge since it is not clear how to equate human learning experiences with presentations of patterns to a network (one human encounter with an object might be comparable to several hundred cycles in a network or in several coordinated networks).

One explanation Dyer proposed for slow learning in networks is that networks do not pursue simple hypotheses first, trying more complex ones only if necessary. Rather, even for simple categories, the process of gradient descent involves considering all possible characterizations of the conditions of category membership (within the range delimited by the input units), and then through error correction, arriving at the characterization that allows it to differentiate category members from nonmembers correctly. Gluck and Bower (1988b) obtained a better approximation to a related (but not identical) complexity ordering obtained by Shepard, Hovland, and Jenkins (1961). Categories were distinguished according to whether they required attention to one, two, or three dimensions; for example, a two-dimension category was "black triangle or white square." The greater the number of relevant dimensions, the more difficult it was for humans to learn the category. Gluck and Bower attempted to teach such categories to a simple two-layer network using the delta rule. Their key innovation was to include pairs and triplets of features as well as unitary features to encode the input patterns. In this *configural-cue* approach, there were input units for the features *small, small & black,* and *small & black & triangle,* for example. Not everyone will agree that it is appropriate to load this much of the task structure onto the input layer, but it was a motivated decision for which a case can be made, and it resulted in a good fit between network and human performance. Gluck and Bower (1988a, 1988b) reported additional investigations of the category-learning capabilities of two-layer networks which yielded generally favorable evaluations of networks as a medium for modeling human categorization. Nevertheless, connectionists have a good deal more work to do if they are to produce and defend comprehensive models of human concept acquisition and categorization.

One human capability which has not yet been captured in network models is the tendency to bring existing concepts to bear in new situations. This, in fact, is what facilitates learning to extract relevant information from a single example, as in the following case presented by Dyer:

Suppose one encounters a single event in which a rich, blond-haired person is kidnapped. Immediately we know that the wealth is relevant and not the hair color. In a subsymbolic system, the importance of the wealth attribute could be represented by biasing the initial weights of the network. However, subsequent events might be about rich, blond-haired people getting skin cancer. Now it is the hair color that is relevant. What is needed is a representation that establishes separate causal relationships, between skin cancer and skin color on the one hand, and wealth with attempts at extortion on the other. (1988, p. 10)

We have already suggested that networks might incorporate theoretical knowledge of the kind Dyer describes, but how this might be done so as to enable the network to extract the relevant information when given a new input has not yet been developed. At the end of this chapter we shall discuss some ways that the connectionist account might need to be extended to account for more of the phenomena of human categorization and other capabilities. First, however, we consider how pattern recognition might be involved in some of these other capabilities.

Pattern Recognition and Higher Mental Processes

In the previous two sections of this chapter we have considered pattern recognition only in so far so it applies to relatively low-level tasks of perception, and mid-level tasks involving semantic categories. An important question is how a connectionist network uses the resulting representations to carry out higher cognitive functions. Clearly our cognitive life does not consist simply of recognizing and classifying phenomena presented to us, or even in responding appropriately to such input. We also think about phenomena without directly perceiving them, try to explain phenomena we do encounter, and plan future actions. These activities have usually been characterized in terms of logical inferences performed on symbolic representations. We need now to consider whether connectionism is at all useful in accounting for these higher cognitive activities. The proposal that we shall explore is that pattern recognition may actually underlie much of what are taken to be higher cognitive performances that require reasoning. If this is correct, then connectionists may be able to deal with these processes in much the same manner as they deal with perception and categorization.

An already developed theory which places similar emphasis on pattern recognition by satisfaction of soft constraints in networks is J. R. Anderson's (1983) ACT* theory. As we have previously mentioned, his approach differs from connectionist models in some respects, including his choice of activation rules and his interface with a production system. However, his success at implementing the idea that perception, categorization, and higher cognitive activities can be modeled in a unified manner provides some encouragement that connectionist systems might also achieve a unified account. Connectionists face the further challenge of achieving this without the used of rules such as those in Anderson's production system, however, and it is not yet known whether the architecture will be equal to the task.

How can we envisage going from recognition of individual patterns to a full accounting of mental life? One possibility is that the stable state representing one pattern could itself act as an input to the system which would initiate further pattern recognition. That is, the output units that have been activated in recognizing a pattern would themselves send activations and inhibitions to yet other units, possibly units in different networks. The idea is that higher-level cognitive performance might consist in a sequence of pattern recognition activities, so that what look to be steps of reasoning might consist ultimately in sequences of patterns that elicit one another.

The suggestion that cognition might simply consist in a sequence of pattern recognitions has been developed in a recent work by Howard Margolis (1987). In his theory, the recognition of one pattern constitutes an internal cue which, together with the external cues available from outside the system, facilitates yet another recognition. Thus, we work our way through a complex problem by recognizing something, and with the help of that result, recognizing something further. He contends that even in unfamiliar contexts we function by pattern recognition, invoking the pattern template that best matches the situation until we are able to generate a better one. Learning then involves modification of the template to accommodate the new scene better. In Margolis's account, a few species are capable not only of recognizing that something is the case, but also of *reasoning why* they have made that judgement. Reasoning why does not involve any introspection into the process of recognition, but rather is itself a process of pattern recognition – one that proceeds through smaller steps to justify the judgement. Reasoning why also facilitates a kind of critical evaluation, which can challenge the more global pattern recognition response and lead to a second kind of learning, a revision of basic pattern recognition tendencies on the basis of the critical review.

To support the view that higher-level cognition is fundamentally pattern recognition, Margolis offers two major types of evidence. First, he advances an account of some of the striking results of recent research on human reasoning that have been used to suggest that people have limited logical and statistical acumen. For example, he offers an analysis of Tversky and Kahneman's (1982) "Linda" problem (Margolis, 1987, p. 163):

Linda is 31 years old, outspoken, and very bright. She majored in philosophy. As a student, she was active in civil rights and in the environmental movement. Which is more probable:
  (a) Linda is a bank teller.
  (b) Linda is a bank teller and is active in the feminist movement?

Approximately 90 percent of subjects select (b), although according to the laws of probability, the probability of a conjunct is never greater than the probability of one of its parts. One obvious source of difficulty is that subjects may understand option (a) as "Linda is a bank teller and is not active in the feminist movement." Even when the directions are clarified to avoid this ambiguity, however, a majority still answer incorrectly. Margolis proposes that what happens is that this problem triggers the wrong scenario: people understand the word *probable* as meaning *plausible* rather than *statistically likely*. This misrecognition of the problem cues them to activate the wrong pattern and so misconstrue the problem. Hence, the difficulty, he argues, is one of pattern recognition, not of a failure of logical acumen. (Presumably, in situations that instead triggered the scenario of *statistically likely*, that acumen would be displayed.)

Margolis's other main strategy is to analyze developments in the history of science in terms of pattern recognition. In particular, he focuses on major transformations in science, such as those Kuhn termed *scientific revolutions*, and seeks to explain the difference between those practitioners of the science who succeeded in developing and using a new paradigm and those who resisted the new perspective, sometimes bitterly. Developing and learning a new paradigm involves, on Margolis's analysis, learning to recognize new patterns and guiding behavior accordingly. Those who fail to understand the new paradigm are those who do not learn the new patterns. Often this results from dependency on old pattern recognition capacities which cannot be surrendered without temporarily undergoing significant deterioration in performance.

Margolis fills this account out in part by examining the endeavors of scientists like Darwin and Copernicus, who accomplished major revolutions. In the case of Darwin, most pre-Darwinian biologists regarded each species as having its own essence, and therefore sharply distinguished from other species. Hence, they lacked the concept of gradual transition between species that was needed to grasp the notion of transmutation from one species to another. Darwin, as a result of being trained by Lyell to recognize gradual transitions in geology, was cued by his observations on the voyage of the *Beagle* to recognize gradual change in life-forms as well. This pattern was at odds, however, with biology's pattern of recognizing species as distinct. The tension between an old pattern and a new one requires the expenditure of cognitive energy. Gradual change is effected in one's pattern recognition system until the new pattern is seen as the one that clearly fits. For Darwin, this effort involved, in part, recalling the Malthusian pattern from economics and recognizing its applicability to the transmutation of species in the form of natural selection. After the new pattern recognition capacity was clearly developed, on Margolis's account, Darwin returned to the reasoning why mode. By filling in constituent steps of pattern recognition, he could build up in other individuals the ability to recognize the new overall pattern.

Margolis does not ground his view that cognition consists solely in different forms of pattern recognition on any underlying theory of how pattern recognition is accomplished, although he briefly notes that connectionism provides one possible approach. Nor does he offer a precise, verifiable account; he deliberately paints a general view of cognition with a broad brush. To see how Margolis's ideas might be actualized, one can examine certain computer-implemented models in cognitive science. We have already noted the particular relevance of J. R. Anderson's (1983) ACT* theory, and a number of other cognitive science theories can be viewed as emphasizing pattern matching as well (e.g., Schank, 1982; Holland, Holyoak, Nisbett and Thagard, 1986). However, connectionism suggests a more radical possibility: that recognizing patterns (matching current patterns to the cognitive residue of previous patterns) is not only a broadly applicable process, but is one that is carried out without the use of symbols as such. Hence, connectionism provides one avenue for empirically exploring Margolis's argument that pattern recognition is the fundamental cognitive capacity.

We need not endorse the particulars of Margolis's account to benefit from the sketch he provides of how pattern recognition capacities might be generalized to provide an account of higher-level as well as perceptual processes, and hence provide a unified explanation of how a variety of cognitive tasks might be carried out without appealing to symbol processing as such. For the most part, the details of how to develop this view are yet to be worked out. But the basic enterprise is endorsed by Smolensky in *PDP: 6* when he speaks of "an abstraction of the task of perception:"

This abstraction includes many cognitive tasks that are customarily regarded as much "higher level" than perception (e.g., intuiting answers to physics problems). . . . The abstract task I analyze captures a common part of the tasks of passing from an intensity pattern to a set of objects in three-dimensional space, from a sound pattern to a sequence of words, from a sequence of words to a semantic description, from a set of patient symptoms to a set of disease states, from a set of givens in a physics problem to a set of unknowns. Each of these processes is viewed as *completing an internal representation of a static state of an external world*. By suitably abstracting the task of interpreting a static *sensory* input, we can arrive at a theory of interpretation of static input *generally*, a theory of the *completion task* that applies to many cognitive phenomena in the gulf between perception and logical reasoning. (Smolensky, 1986, pp. 197–8)

Smolensky has also developed a more detailed model of how pattern recognition might suffice for reasoning. He used the connection weights in a *harmony network* (an interactive network that behaves in many respects like a Boltzmann machine) to encode basic laws relating voltage, resistance, and current in electrical circuits (specifically, Ohm's Law and Kirchoff's Law). He then presented problems to the network by activating units to partially specify a situation, for example, that one resistance in the circuit increases and the voltage and other resistance remain the same. The network must determine what happens to the remaining variables, in this example by specifying the current and the two voltage drops. The process is one of completing a pattern. Smolensky's simulation generated the correct answer 93 per cent of the time. Thus, he was able to demonstrate high levels of performance on physics problems when these problems were treated as pattern recognition problems in a network rather than logical reasoning problems in a symbolic system.

Nevertheless, we wish to end this section with the caveat that connectionists may find it necessary to learn how to make networks carry out other processes in addition to pattern recognition (although pattern recognition may remain as an elementary process by which more elaborate processes are carried out). To return to the example of learning natural categories in the preceding section, it should be noted that humans can make use of their knowledge in an analogous domain to help deal with a current domain. Perhaps that knowledge is copied and used as an initial sketch for the new category, so that weights need only be tuned rather than constructed from an initially random matrix. In fact, the *tabula rasa* approach to learning that is currently adopted in most connectionist models may be quite rare or even nonexistent in actual development and knowledge acquisition. (Cf. Piaget's developmental theory, in which all development germinates outward from a few initial schemes, such as sucking, and the processes of accommodation and assimilation that operate on them.) Exploring alternatives within a connectionist framework may require the incorporation of new mechanisms that go beyond the existing, basic capabilities for constraint satisfaction and generalization which currently enable simple pattern recognition. Examples include: the mechanism just mentioned of copying and adapting an existing network for new uses; mechanisms for coordinating multiple networks in a semi-modular architecture; and mechanisms by which existing relevant networks are identified, copied, combined, and expanded upon to carry out new tasks.[6]

The challenge is to figure out a way of getting a network to generate such mechanisms itself. That is, can a network that readily accomplishes pattern recognition develop emergent capabilities? Can it learn not just new patterns, but more complex procedures, as an outcome of applying its current capabilities to increasingly challenging tasks? If not, the same jumble of *ad hoc* mechanisms, which have too frequently characterized symbolic modeling, will need to be brought in. This would compromise the simplicity of the basic connectionist mechanisms of propagating activations and modifying weights; it would be so much more interesting to find that networks can truly behave adaptively instead. (For a related view, see Gluck and Bower, 1988.)

Conclusion

In this chapter we have examined one kind of cognitive performance at which connectionist networks seem to excel: pattern recognition. After demonstrating in simple simulations how networks can accomplish this task, we asked how important this ability is to human cognition. Clearly pattern recognition is relevant to perception. But is it an essential capacity that undergirds human cognition more generally? To give an affirmative answer to this question, we discussed how connectionism might be pertinent to explaining a pervasive feature of mental life: its intentionality. We also considered the applicability of connectionist models to research on concepts and categorization, although we concluded that a good deal of work remains before comprehensive connec-

---

6 Symbolic approaches have not reached this point of sophistication yet, either. For interim, partial solutions see Schank's (1982) armory of MOPS, TOPS, and other high-level devices for dealing with the complexity of cognition, J. R. Anderson and Thompson's (1989) analogy-based PUPS system (see also J. R. Anderson, 1989), and Newell's (1989) chunking in the SOAR system.

tionist models of categorization and concept learning will be available for evaluation. Finally, we discussed ways in which connectionist models might be applied to more sophisticated cognitive tasks, such as reasoning and problem-solving, in which fairly complex knowledge must be employed. This brings us to an important consideration. We often view cognition as a process of acquiring and using *knowledge*. Knowledge is most naturally represented propositionally, as in the sentences of this book. Does it make sense to think of nonpropositional connectionist systems as possessing and using knowledge? This is the topic of the next chapter.

5

Connectionism and Nonpropositional Representations of Knowledge

The idea that knowledge is represented by and can be expressed in propositions that are sentence-like seems quite natural in a highly literate culture. Knowledge is transmitted by lectures or books, which consist of sentences. Many people report that they think by means of "inner speech" (mentally constructed sentences). Thus, it seems at least plausible that knowledge is generally represented in terms of mental sentences or sentence-like propositions. This assumption has been widely accepted in the disciplines that make up cognitive science, especially cognitive psychology and artificial intelligence. In many information-processing models of cognition, language, and sometimes even perception, what is processed are propositions. Connectionism represents a clear challenge to this way of representing knowledge, because connectionist networks encode knowledge without explicitly employing propositions. In this chapter we shall explore the plausibility of this claim. We begin by briefly describing the legacy of propositional and nonpropositional representations of knowledge in cognitive science.[1]

Propositional and Nonpropositional Representations in Cognitive Science

The earliest efforts to model cognitive representations with propositions tended to employ relatively unstructured declarative representations: sets of propositions in a format adapted in one way or another from first-order predicate calculus. We briefly noted a few examples in

1 Some of the ideas discussed in this chapter have been presented separately in Bechtel and Abrahamsen (1990).

chapter 4, including Raphael's (1968) semantic information format for his artificial intelligence program, and Kintsch's (1975) propositional text base for modeling memory representations within cognitive psychology. Let us consider Kintsch's format in a little more detail to convey some of the flavor of this approach to representation. Propositions had a uniform format: one predicate followed by one or more arguments. The predicates and arguments were viewed as underlying concepts which could be variably realized in natural languages, and were capitalized to distinguish them from the words that would be used in their realization. For example (p. 18), the sentence "The subjects were 20 female students" was represented as (STUDENT, SUBJECT) & (FEMALE, STUDENT) & (NUMBER, SUBJECT, TWENTY). Connections among propositions were captured by means of a repetition rule involving recurrent concepts such as STUDENT, and by embedding. For example, (BECAUSE, α, β) is a proposition that embeds two other propositions. Kintsch and his colleagues undertook a variety of empirical studies; some provided evidence for propositional representation and others simply assumed it in the pursuit of other issues. For example, it was shown that a sentence expressing a single multi-argument proposition tended to be recalled as a unit, whereas a sentence equated for length but expressing several single-argument propositions had less stability in memory. A variety of propositional formats have been developed besides Kintsch's format; in chapter 4 we especially noted that semantic networks (not to be confused with connectionist networks) can be used as a medium for encoding propositions.

As a result of experience with propositional formats in models of language and cognition, psychologists and artificial intelligence researchers found that higher levels of structure were needed to organize propositions appropriately. The initial proposals were variously called schemata (Rumelhart, 1975, after Bartlett, 1932), frames (Minsky, 1975), and scripts (Schank and Abelson, 1977). A schema was envisioned as a structured body of information in which propositions are organized into larger units, with slots for specific components of information. When schemata were activated in the course of cognitive processing, they brought with them default values that were assumed unless explicit information was supplied to the contrary. For example, Schank and Abelson's restaurant script (one sort of schema) specifies what one knows about dining in a typical restaurant: that one is seated, obtains a menu, orders, is served, eats the meal, is presented with a bill, and finally pays for the meal. If there is a blackboard instead of menu, or payment precedes the meal, the defaults will be overwritten; otherwise the information in the script comes "for free" when the script is activated. In more recent work, Schank (1982) proposed more flexible script-like structures called *MOPs* (*memory organization packets*) and even higher-order structures called *TOPs* (*thematic organization points*). Scripts, schemata, frames, MOPs, TOPs, and other higher-order structures have in common that they provide propositional representations with some of the functions and characteristics of a pattern recognition system. A piece of knowledge is able to elicit other bits of knowledge in a systematic manner that facilitates other information-processing.

During the 1970s, the principal challenge to the dominance of the propositional approach came from investigators who argued for representing some knowledge in images. Images are generally characterized as differing from propositions in that they are modality-specific, analogue, and iconic rather than abstract, discrete, and arbitrary in form. (For an overview, see the discussion in J. R. Anderson, 1987.) It is usually visual images that are focused upon; these need not be regarded as literal pictures, but as representations that show certain isomorphisms with visual perception that give them a visual or spatial character. These distinctive properties of images led Paivio (1971) to posit a dual-code theory of memory, which holds that modality-specific representational formats are used to encode knowledge mentally. In particular, visual information is encoded in mental images, and sentential information is encoded in a verbal code that is auditory or articulatory in nature. This view contrasts sharply with the position that abstract propositional representations are adequate to encode all kinds of knowledge, including visual and spatial knowledge.

To give the flavor of the kind of data that were in dispute, we shall briefly describe a few of the early experiments. (They were followed by other, often clever studies, which ruled out certain alternative explanations but are too complex to summarize here: see Kosslyn, 1980.) Moyer (1973) asked subjects to answer questions such as: "Which is larger, moose or roach?" There was a positive linear relation between the disparity in size of the two animals and the time required to respond. Linear relationships between other analogue dimensions and reaction time have been found for tasks such as scanning a mental image of a map (Kosslyn, Ball, and Reiser, 1978) and mentally rotating letters or other patterns (Cooper and Shepard, 1973). There is even evidence to suggest a role for analogue (or at least spatially-ordered) representation in carrying out inferences. Huttenlocher and Higgins (1971) presented subjects with three-term series problems. For example: "Tom is taller than Sam. John is shorter than Sam. Who is tallest?" By varying the order and wording of the premises, they were able to obtain reaction time patterns that suggested that subjects mentally ordered the terms in a spatial array (e.g., Tom – Sam – John). Not everyone accepted this interpretation (see Clark, 1969), but the body of data from these and other studies presented a challenge to purely propositional approaches to mental representation that could not be ignored.

Given results such as these, some investigators have concluded that an alternative form of representation, which Kosslyn (1980) calls depictive or quasi-pictorial image representation, is involved in tasks with a visual or spatial character, and perhaps also in tasks that can be mapped onto visual or spatial dimensions. In one version, the long-term knowledge store itself uses different representational formats appropriate to the type of information. For example, J. R. Anderson (1983) proposes three formats including abstract propositions, temporal strings, and spatial images; the images differ from Kosslyn's in that they do not encode absolute size, and in the way structural information is incorporated. In a different version (Kosslyn, 1980), a long-term representation which is more or less propositional in format is used to generate a depictive representation (visual image) in a short-term visual buffer; the image can then be manipulated by analogue processes which produce reaction-time functions such as those summarized above. In this version, the "knowledge" itself is represented uniformly, but when that knowledge is activated there is diversity in the format of short-term representation. Very different ways of employing imagistic or spatial representations have been proposed by others (e.g., Johnson-Laird, 1983; Langacker, 1987a).

Defenders of a more traditional approach (e.g., Pylyshyn, 1981) have insisted on the primacy of propositional representations. Others have taken a more pragmatic approach. For example, prior to incorporating images in his 1983 ACT* model, J. R. Anderson (1978) described a propositional representation and associated processes which could yield a linear function for mental rotation. Given that the same kind of data could be generated by either a propositional or an imagistic model, he argued that behavioral research could not supply definitive grounds for choosing between these two forms of representation. Palmer (1978) concluded his detailed discussion of representational formats similarly, suggesting that the question was one for physiological rather than cognitive psychology. That challenge has recently been addressed: Farah (1988) reviewed an impressive array of neuropsychological data which support the view that the representations involved in imagery are the same ones that are involved in perception. However, she declined to address the issue of whether these common representations are propositional or depictive in format.

Until the re-emergence of connectionism, imagistic representations constituted the clearest alternative to propositional representations of knowledge. Typically, those advocating imagistic representations proposed them as offering an additional mode of representation to the propositional mode that were useful for specific tasks, not as an alternative that would replace propositional representations. Connectionism, however, constitutes an even more aggressive challenge to the view that knowledge should be represented propositionally. Without invoking propositionally represented knowledge at all, connectionists attempt to account for some or all of the cognitive performance that cognitive scientists have traditionally accounted for by means of propositional models. As we shall see in chapter 7, certain critics of connectionism contend that without propositional representations it is not possible to account for certain aspects of human cognitive performance. Before considering whether this contention is justified, however, we shall expand upon our characterization of connectionism by placing it within a broader theoretical perspective, We shall suggest a way in which our conception of cognitive performance itself may change rather dramatically when we depart from the propositional mode of representing knowledge. We shall begin to develop this point by employing a distinction developed by Gilbert Ryle (1949) between *knowing how* and *knowing that* and shall consider how the notion of *knowing how* may provide a context for further consideration of the nonpropositional representation of knowledge.

Knowing How and Knowing That

The distinction that Ryle develops between *knowing how* and *knowing that* is manifest in our use of language. We speak not just of people knowing certain facts (e.g., *knowing that* Sacramento is the capital of California), but also of people *knowing how* to do certain things. For example, we might say that a child *knows how* to ride a bicycle. In general, the expression *knowing that* requires completion by a proposition whereas the expression *knowing how* is completed by an infinitive (e.g., *to ride*) specifying an activity. This linguistic distinction does not, however, settle the matter as to whether there are different psychological representations involved. What we need to do is consider what is needed for an agent to possess each kind of knowledge. A person who *knows that* Sacramento is the capital of California will be able to retrieve from memory the proposition *Sacramento is the capital of California*, or to retrieve other propositions from which this one can be deduced. But the same does not seem to hold for *knowing how* to ride a bicycle. In this example, what is required is to have certain ability to control one's perceptual-motor system – a system that can plan, execute, and monitor motor activity.

When Ryle introduced this distinction he was objecting to the preoccupation of philosophers with facts and theoretical knowledge. He maintained that propositional knowledge represented only one aspect of human intelligence. Intelligence is also involved in being able to do a variety of activities, and Ryle contended that it makes sense to judge whether one performed these activities intelligently or stupidly. For example, we speak of someone driving intelligently or of someone taking a computer apart in a stupid manner. Many of Ryle's examples of *knowing how* involved physical activities such as riding a bicycle or playing tennis. Others, however, were cognitive in nature, such as making or appreciating jokes, talking grammatically, playing chess, and arguing. This begins to suggest that *knowing how* may penetrate rather extensively into the cognitive domain. Ryle suggests this very point when he comments:

Indeed even when we are concerned with their intellectual excellences and deficiencies, we are interested less in the stocks of truths that they acquire and retain than in their capacities to find out truths for themselves and their ability to organise and exploit them, when discovered. (1949, p. 28)

The radical character of Ryle's views, and of the view that we shall suggest in subsequent sections, is based in the claim that propositionally expressed theoretical knowledge (*knowing that*) is not primary, but rests on *knowing how* to perform certain activities: "Intelligent practice is not a step-child of theory. On the contrary, theorizing is one practice amongst others and is itself intelligently or stupidly conducted" (p. 26).

Ryle's approach to analyzing *knowing how* was behavioristic; he treated this knowledge as manifest in our actions and so not to be understood in terms of something hidden and internal (what he termed *the ghost in the machine*). *Knowing how* to perform an action consisted in a *disposition* to perform that action when appropriate circumstances arose.[2] For cognitivists, however, merely saying that someone has a disposition to behave in a certain way does not suffice; what is sought is an explanation of the internal mechanisms involved. One possibility is that intelligent dispositions may not be explainable in cognitive terms; it may have to do simply with the physiological conditions accruing in one's body. But in so far as we speak of *knowing* how do to these things, and of these being things we *learn* how to do, it seems plausible to attempt to give a *cognitive* account of what such knowledge consists in, that is, an account in terms of one's mental activities.

The only available means of specifying such an account, until recently, has involved rules. In cognitive theories, the knowledge required to perform an activity is often referred to as *procedural knowledge*. Such knowledge is thought to be encoded in rules, which are proposition-like in their basic format (ordered strings of symbols) but are imperative rather than declarative. That is, rule systems are dynamic (specifying actions to be taken) rather than static (specifying information). Generative grammars represent linguistic knowledge in this way (Chomsky, 1957), although the rules are intended as abstract representations of *competence* rather than as models of *performance*. Production systems, in contrast, are more often intended to model actual mental activity (e.g., Newell and Simon, 1972). Recall that each rule in a production system is a production of the form "If A then B," where A is some condition that must be met and B is an action that is then carried out. Typically when a production fires, the contents of working memory are altered, which may satisfy the condition side of yet another rule, enabling it to fire.

This strategy of explaining *knowing how* in terms of procedures that are composed of proposition-like rules gains plausibility from the fact that we often teach people how to perform new activities by providing them with verbal instructions. Thus, we seem to be providing them with the procedural knowledge which they need in order to perform the activity. For example, we may try to explain to a novice how to serve a

2 Ryle does draw an important distinction between habits, which are simply rote responses to situations, and the intelligent capacities involved in *knowing how*. The intelligent capacities of *knowing how* are far more fluid, and modified in the course of experience: "It is of the essence of merely habitual practices that one performance is a replica of its predecessors. It is of the essence of intelligent practices that one performance is modified by its predecessors. The agent is still learning." (1949, p. 42) Ryle's behaviorism prevents him from providing a model of the internal activity involved in such learning. But connectionist networks seem to offer a very constructive suggestion of how *knowing how* can involve a continued kind of learning.

tennis ball properly. Similarly, we teach people how to solve physics problems by giving them rules to follow. It must be recognized, however, that such instruction alone typically is inadequate to establish skilled performance of the activity; our interlocutor must actually practise *doing* the activity (or at least mentally rehearse doing it; see Neisser, 1983). Thus, something more than simply committing verbal rules to memory seems to be required.

What is that something more? J. R. Anderson suggests that procedural knowledge initially is encoded declaratively and is converted into actual production rules in the course of practice. Also, Newell has emphasized the importance of an ongoing process of *chunking* rules into more complex productions which, as integrated units, can be smoothly executed (see Newell, 1989; also Laird, Newell, and Rosenbloom, 1987). Rigorous implementation of proposals like this have brought production systems to a fairly mature status; they are our best-developed medium for modeling *knowing how* and it certainly would be premature to discard them at this time.

Yet production systems do not fully capture the spirit of Ryle's rejection of the intellectualistic character of theorizing about human knowledge. Instead of explicating *knowing how* in terms of fundamentally new kinds of models, production system designers have assimilated the propositional format that is already familiar from declarative knowledge representation to the task of procedural knowledge representation. To accomplish this, some accommodation has usually been made; rules do differ in some respects from declarative propositions, and the differences are not trivial.[3] Arguably though, the spirit of Ryle's analysis would be better served by a modeling medium that is not so grounded in our initial attempts to model *knowing that*.

Connectionism is an intriguing and promising contender. Unlike rule systems, connectionist networks bear little explicit resemblance to propositional formats. They are composed of units that are interconnected rather than ordered in strings, and often these units are not even symbols in the ordinary sense. When some of these units are activated, the network *knows how* to respond by propagating activation along weighted connections. Hence, *knowing how* may consist in dynamical processing in a network rather than sequential application of proposition-like rules. This raises the question, though, of what kind of

---

3   Note, however, that Norman and Rumelhart (1975) proposed a semantic network representation in which a given part of the network could function either declaratively or procedurally, depending upon whether it was needed as data or as a program. Bobrow and Winograd's (1977) KRL (Knowledge Representation Language) had a similar goal.

account is to be given of *knowing that*. If connectionism abandons symbol strings as a modeling medium, can it still account for the human
ability to assert propositions and argue for their truth? If so, *knowing
that* could be reconstrued as a special case of *knowing how*. In the last
section of this chapter we report exploratory research in which logical
inference is reconstrued in this manner. Also, in chapter 7 we consider
the adequacy of connectionist models for capturing important properties of language and language-like structures. In particular, in the
final section of that chapter we raise the possibility that symbols and
propositions are best regarded as external forms which are produced
and acted upon by a cognitive system whose own internal representations are of another kind. In the following two sections, however, we
shall limit ourselves to exploring why a clearly nonpropositional format
may be attractive at least for modeling *knowing how*.

Expert Knowledge as *Knowing How*

A great deal of research in cognitive psychology and artificial intelligence has been devoted to trying to understand skilled or expert performance. Perhaps the most celebrated of the tasks to have been studied
is chess playing, but there are many others including problem-solving
in algebra and physics, medical diagnosis, and trouble-shooting mechanical devices (for a survey, see the papers in J. R. Anderson, 1981).
The standard research strategy has been to develop rule-sets that will
generate the performance. The potential for achieving the same level of
performance as human expects has made this research not just theoretical, but also applied. In particular, in the *expert systems* approach, the
goal is to develop computer-implemented rule systems that can replicate aspects of the reasoning of humans who perform the function in an
expert fashion. The typical strategy is to interview experts to identify
the rules they seem to employ in solving particular problems. The expert system designer then tries to formulate these rules in a computer
program, which can then be used to replicate the performance of the
expert.

Many expert systems exhibit a high level of performance and hence
may offer support for the conviction that we can assimilate *knowing how*
to the propositional approach originally applied to accounts of *knowing
that*. (That is, we build an expert system by adapting the propositional
format to construct a system of rules.) Dreyfus and Dreyfus (1986),

however, have argued that expert systems are fatally flawed as models of human expertise. They based this claim on an analysis of skill acquisition and skilled performance in a variety of domains that seem to require sophisticated reasoning and problem-solving such as piloting an airplane and playing chess. On the basis of their analysis Dreyfus and Dreyfus proposed a five-step scale for the development of skills and contend that true expertise is exhibited only at the highest level. The following is a brief summary of the five stages on their scale:

1. The *novice* employs precise rules, which apply to objectively specifiable circumstances that can be recognized independently of other aspects of the situation encountered. Such a principle is: shift to second gear when you obtain a speed of 10 to 50 m.p.h. Since these rules are applicable independently of what else happens in the context, they are *context-free*.
2. The *advanced beginner* begins to recognize the role of context: in some situations the rules are to be modified. These exceptions typically are not specified in terms of additional context-free rules, but in terms of previously encountered situations. The advanced beginner learns to recognize these situations and to modify the application of the rule in similar situations.
3. The *competent performer* is distinguished by developing a set of goals that facilitate coordination of rules and known facts. Rules are no longer applied simply because they are applicable but because they will enable the performer to reach a goal. Since the competent performer sets the goals for particular situations, he or she no longer simply responds to events, but directs activity. The competent performer has become an agent responsible for his or her actions.
4. The *proficient performer* moves beyond the deliberate model of reasoning and begins to rely extensively on recalling previous events similar to the current one. This recollection is not based on specific features, but on *holistic similarity*. Once the recollection occurs, the proficient performer may proceed analytically as would a competent performer; where the proficient performer exceeds the competent performer is in the ability to bring relevant past situations to bear and use this in establishing goals and applying rules.
5. With the *expert* the whole process of responding becomes smooth and fluid (in contrast to the unevenness of the proficient performer), and the expert no longer exhibits any of the deliberativeness of competent performance. The expert sees the situation, and sees what to do. Often the expert cannot articulate the reasons behind the judgement and may confabulate if asked to explain a judgement.

The expert responds *intuitively*. When the expert is able to take time to deliberate, he or she does not revert to the sorts of deliberations characteristic of the competent performer, but recalls yet other relevant previous events and examines differences between the recalled situations and the current one to see if they suggest any modification in the response.

From the perspective of Dreyfus and Dreyfus, work in symbolic cognitive science and expert systems is directed only at the first three levels in this hierarchy. At these levels the major cognitive endeavors involve assessment of facts, determination of responses on the basis of rules, and coordination of rules so as to obtain goals; all of these lend themselves to symbolic modeling. Attempts to develop chess-playing computers provide a prime example. Typically the program consists of rules for evaluating various positions as well as rules for determining which moves are likely to be most successful in the current situation and a decision procedure for choosing between alternatives. Dreyfus and Dreyfus reject the claim that these skills are sufficient for true expertise. They deny that acquiring additional rules for reasoning, or compiling these rules into more complex rules, will suffice to make a competent performer into an expert.

The great challenge for anyone seeking to adopt the Dreyfus and Dreyfus account of expertise is to explain what it is that enables a performer to exhibit the higher levels of skill characteristic of levels 4 and 5. Clearly, Dreyfus and Dreyfus take themselves to be describing a different kind of cognitive activity, the crucial element of which seems to be what they refer to as *holistic recognition of similarity*. This crucial notion needs to be explicated, and it is worth noting how they characterize it:

With enough experience in a variety of situations, all seen from the same perspective or with the same goal in mind but requiring different tactical decisions, the mind of the proficient performer seems to group together situations sharing not only the same goal or perspective but also the same decision, action, or tactic. At this point not only is a situation, when seen as similar to a prior one, understood, but the associated decision, action, or tactic simultaneously comes to mind.

An immense library of distinguishable situations is built up on the basis of experience. A chess master, it has been estimated, can recognize roughly 50,000 types of positions, and the same can probably be said of automobile driving. We doubtless store many more typical situations in our memories than words in our vocabularies. Consequently, such situations of reference bear no names and, in fact, seem to defy complete verbal description. (Dreyfus and Dreyfus, 1986, p. 32)

What is important here is that expert knowledge involves recognizing a situation as similar to a previously encountered situation, and simultaneously recognizing the appropriate action. Dreyfus and Dreyfus frequently speak of expert practitioners of some activity as relying upon *intuition*. When they confront a situation, they do not need to calculate their response. Moreover, sometimes they are incapable of verbally explaining why they responded as they did.

In characterizing experts as relying upon intuition, Dreyfus and Dreyfus do not deny that experts may calculate and reason when time permits or the stakes are great. A chess player, for example, may double-check an intuitive judgement by examining more carefully the consequences of performing the intuited action. Dreyfus and Dreyfus point out, however, that the decrement in performance is not large if no time is allowed for checking (e.g., by allowing only 10 seconds per move).

The kind of language Dreyfus and Dreyfus used to characterize expert knowledge (e.g., relying upon *intuition*, and *holistically recognizing* what is to be done) has a mystical aura about it. What do these abilities consist in? Since we often think of *intuition* as something *nonrational*, Dreyfus and Dreyfus seem to be abandoning any attempt to explain expertise as a rational activity that can be captured in the kinds of models that are familiar to cognitive scientists. To return to the distinction made in the preceding section, it seems clear that expertise, as characterized by Dreyfus and Dreyfus, consists in *knowing how* that is quite distinct from *knowing that*. We have already seen that connectionism offers a perspective from which to understand *knowing how* while avoiding the assimilation to the propositional format of *knowing that*. It is a perspective which seems quite consistent with the notion of *holistic recognition of similarity*, and provides a means of interpreting that notion in terms of explicit models that have at least some of the right properties. For example, connectionist pattern recognition systems require a period of training, during which their weights are gradually changed and fine-tuned. A common criticism is that this learning occurs too slowly. Yet, in the context of acquiring expertise this may turn out not to be a liability, but rather a virtue of connectionist systems.

In this section we have discussed the idea that expertise involves the ability to "see" situations as similar. We now turn to the role of seeing itself, especially as it figures in scientific inquiry, and again suggest that the connectionist approach to *knowing how* provides a means to embody this idea in explicit models.

Knowing How to See

Seeing is such a basic activity that it may not seem to require knowledge in order to perform it. This has been the attitude of many philosophers. Empiricists, including the logical positivists, emphasized the role of sensation and perception – particularly visual perception – in grounding our knowledge of the world. Scientific laws and theories were evaluated in terms of whether the truth values they predicted for *observation sentences* were correct. The determination of truth values for observation sentences was viewed as unproblematic; the visual system simply recorded what there is to be seen. That is, while observation sentences provided the justification for theoretical claims, observation sentences themselves did not require justification.

However, perception is not actually so unproblematic. Two philosophers of science, Norwood Russell Hanson and Thomas Kuhn, challenged the empiricist view of the logical positivists by challenging the notion of objective observation sentences.[4] Both of these philosophers argued that perception is *theory-laden* in that what we see depends upon what we know. For example, we could not recognize something as an X-ray tube unless we knew what an X-ray tube was. Someone who was shown the same object but lacked that knowledge would not be able to see an X-ray tube; they would see something else, perhaps an apparatus made of glass. The claim that observation is theory-laden has stirred considerable controversy in philosophy of science in so far as it seems to threaten the objectivity of knowledge. For the positivists, observation sentences provided an objective and theory-neutral basis for adjudicating between different scientific theories; anyone could see the same evidence and determine whether it supported or refuted the theory. But the *theory-ladenness* objection seems to entail that a theory determines what the scientist will see, and therefore what can count as evidence, thereby introducing relativism into science. The epistemological status of science is jeopardized if it turns out that our theories determine what we see. (In practice, the epistemological concern about theory-ladenness is certainly exaggerated. Even if theories do specify the observation language, it is still up to the external world to produce

---

4 The break with the traditional analysis of perception can also be traced to Wittgenstein (1953), who probed the difference between *seeing* something and seeing it *as* something. This is just the kind of step that leads many theorists to assume that perception, or seeing something as something, requires inference. However, like Ryle, Wittgenstein raised doubts as to whether this difference could be explained in terms of differences occurring within the person, for example in terms of an act of inference or interpretation, and focused instead on the behavioral manifestations of this difference.

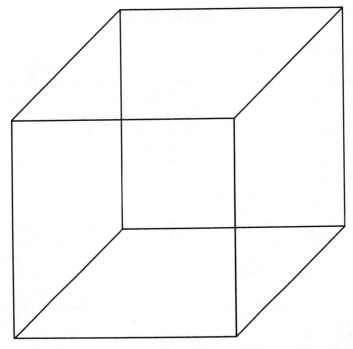

Figure 5.1 A Necker cube. It is an ambiguous figure, which can be seen in one of two ways: (1) with a front face at the lower left; (2) with a top surface at the upper right.

circumstances in which we can see the kinds of objects that the theory tells us to look for.)

The preoccupation of philosophers with the epistemological concerns raised by the notion of theory-laden perception may actually impede us from recognizing an aspect of Kuhn's and Hanson's approach that is even more radical: a perspective on perception as an activity that is *learned* and depends upon *knowledge*, but knowledge that is not represented propositionally. Hanson (1958) mounted a sustained argument against the view of perception as a simple act of recording. He did this by focusing on scientific conflicts that involved differences in perception. For example, in the late 1940s the reality of the Golgi apparatus was in dispute, with major investigators such as Albert Claude and George Palade, both later Nobel Laureates, arguing that the Golgi was an artifact. Viewing the same slide, one scientist would "see" the Golgi apparatus of the cell, whereas another would "see" an artifact due to methods of staining. As an analogy to these situations, Hanson pointed to ambiguous figures such as the Necker cube (figure 5.1), which can be seen in at least two ways. Hanson rejected the view that all people see the same thing (for example, an arrangement of lines in two dimensions), with some proceeding to see the figure first *as* a cube looked at from the front, and others first *as* a cube viewed from above. Rather, he maintained, each individual directly sees the cube from one perspective, and may then switch to the other perspective. Hanson applied this idea to the perception of objects in a scientific domain, such as the X-ray tube cited above. The physicist does not first see as the layperson sees and then make an inference, but rather directly sees the X-ray tube. Moreover, this depends upon learning: "The layman must learn physics before he can see what the physicist sees" (Hanson, 1958, p. 16). Hanson characterized this process as depending on the "knowledge, experience, and theories" (ibid., p. 18) that the physicist possesses.

When Hanson began to characterize knowledge of physics, however, he reverted to a purely propositional format. The physicist's knowledge consisted, for Hanson, in the propositions in which the laws of physics are stated. This raises a question: how does knowing these propositions facilitate perception? There must be some mechanism through which, as a result of encoding and storing these propositions in the cognitive system, the perceptual system becomes tuned to see what it would not otherwise see. Hanson did not advance a proposal as to how this occurs. It is clear, however, that the mechanism cannot, for Hanson, be an inferential process. He could not accept a bottom-up process according to which we first identify features of objects and then infer what the object is; this would undercut the very claim that he was eager to advance. Presumably, what Hanson envisaged is that learning the laws of physics alters our perceptual processes in some manner that enables us to respond directly to the object without engaging in inference.

Kuhn (1962/1970) shared much of Hanson's perspective on the role of theoretical knowledge in perception, but was not as committed as Hanson to the propositional view of knowledge. While Kuhn's notion of a *paradigm* is notoriously imprecise (Shapere, 1964; Masterman, 1970; Kuhn, 1970), it is clear that he thought that learning the paradigm of a given discipline involves more than internally encoding the propositionally-stated laws of the discipline. It involves learning how to carry out activities (e.g., design and conduct research) in the manner accepted within the discipline. (Given the analysis of *knowing how* already developed, we can see that this ability may involve the acquisition of skills more than propositions.) One of the skills that must be acquired in order to practise science, according to Kuhn, is to perceive objects and events in the manner prescribed by the discipline. This became particularly clear in Kuhn's account of the changes that occur in the course of scientific revolutions. He treated the revolution as promoting a gestalt shift such as that involved in the case of the Necker cube: "at time of revolution, when the normal-scientific tradition changes, the scientist's perception of his environment must be re-educated – in some familiar contexts he must learn to see a new gestalt" (1962/70, p. 112).

The idea that a scientist needs to learn to see the world in a particular manner suggests that a part of what a scientist knows consists in *knowing how* to see as a practitioner of that science would. Kuhn made it clear that he did not see this learning as involving a translation manual whereby one learns to translate between one's new scientific vocabulary and a pre-existing observational vocabulary. Moreover, it is an activity that takes time. Committing to memory the propositions in a textbook does not itself generate mastery of a science. Kuhn emphasized the importance of student scientists learning by replicating paradigmatic work in the science. Much of the real learning in science is accomplished by apprenticeship; a student goes into the laboratory and there learns how to deal with the world as a practitioner of the discipline. This aspect of Kuhn's account has been little developed; however, at least he alluded to an important aspect of science that has been generally neglected by other philosophers.

The joint thrust of Hanson and of Kuhn, then, is to construe the ability to perceive objects and events as resting on a kind of *knowing how* and Kuhn at least tries to resist the temptation to assimilate this *knowing how* to the concept of *knowing that*. But the task of actually describing the perceptual systems involved in *knowing how*, and how they are acquired, remains undone. Here is one place where connectionism can offer a promising advance. We have already noted that connectionist models are adept at pattern recognition. Pattern recognition is clearly fundamental to perception and is critical for recognizing objects even under appearance-altering variations. One characteristic of connectionist pattern recognition systems is that they do not require precise matches between a current pattern and an already learned pattern, and are tolerant of distortions. Also, they can learn subtle as well as obvious regularities which are used to recognize exemplars as particular types of objects.[5] This is performed within the limitations of the input encoding, which supplies an initial encoding (perhaps in terms of

5   This is not to say that connectionist networks are the only kind of system that can recognize patterns robustly and in a subtle manner; exemplar models of categorization are the most obvious competing model with these capabilities. The choice between connectionist models and their strongest competitors must be made on other grounds, for example, storage and processing requirements and ability to model additional aspects of human data.

simple features) from which the regularities are extracted. These regularities are represented in the network's weights, which may be interpreted as a nonpropositional way to encode the knowledge that is needed in order to accomplish a perceptual task.

Even the two-layer network that we described at the beginning of chapter 4 could accomplish pattern recognition in this manner. In multi-layered networks, regularities among *combinations* of input features can be captured as well, providing additional power that is sometimes needed. Typically there is no simple linguistic description for the regularities to which hidden units are sensitive. This would account for the ability of such networks to learn to recognize objects even when we find it difficult to specify how they do this. Networks with additional layers of units can also provide a vehicle for investigating Kuhn's and Hanson's contention that higher level knowledge affects how we see objects in the world. The word recognition simulation we discussed in chapter 4 can serve as a model for this. Units at different levels encoded different pieces of knowledge (specifically, knowledge about what lower-level units were consistent or inconsistent with the higher-level hypotheses). We saw how downwards connections in such a network could be used to simulate the word superiority effect, by which hypotheses about what word is being recognized affect the identification of the constituent letters. We can construe this network as *knowing how* to see letters in a theory-laden manner – that is, by incorporating top-down as well as bottom-up processing.

Hence, connectionism offers a new and very specific interpretation of the intuition that *knowing how to see* is crucial to science and other endeavors. Previously, the only interpretation specific enough for model-building has been the procedural approach, which utilizes productions or other rules as the means of modeling *knowing how*. Since rules are similar in format to declarative propositions (in that both are composed of strings of symbols), this approach distinguishes *knowing how* from *knowing that* much less clearly than does the connectionist approach. This raises a final question: How far into the cognitive system can connectionist models of *knowing how* penetrate? In the last section, we consider whether logical reasoning, a much higher level ability than visual perception and object recognition, might also be a skill that we learn to *know how* to do without relying on rules.

Knowing How to Perform Logical Inferences

From the symbolic perspective, the ability to make logical inferences must be taken to be a primitive cognitive ability. Rules for manipulating symbols have been developed by logicians, and adapted by cognitive scientists. For example, the logical inference rule of *modus ponens*,

$$\text{If } p, \text{ then } q$$
$$\underline{p}$$
$$\therefore q,$$

is the basis for the format of rules in a production system. A production (If p, then q) fires when the antecedent (p) is satisfied, with the result that the specified action (q) is carried out. If our minds are symbolic systems, then when we learn *modus ponens* in a logic class, we are learning to express a principle that our mind already has encoded within it, albeit in a different format. (Sometimes this is referred to as *explicit* versus *tacit* knowledge.) According to this account, when we learn rules our mind may not yet have encoded, such as the *alternative syllogism*:

$$p \text{ or } q$$
$$\underline{\text{Not } p}$$
$$\therefore q,$$

these rules are encoded into the symbolic reasoning system as new productions that may fire when their conditions are satisfied.

The question is whether this is a really plausible account of how we learn formal logic. One of us (Bechtel) has considerable experience teaching both informal and formal logic, and reflection on that experience is quite revealing. Consider first informal logic, where the goal is to teach students not to prove theorems, but only to evaluate and construct arguments using basic valid forms such as the sentential forms noted above. To do this we typically begin by presenting students with valid argument forms and demonstrate that these forms are indeed valid (e.g., using truth tables). We contrast these valid forms with invalid forms such as *affirming the consequent*:

$$\text{If } p, \text{ then } q$$
$$\underline{q}$$
$$\therefore p,$$

which we demonstrate to be invalid. The next step is to present students with a set of problems consisting of arguments presented either in abstract symbols (as above) or in natural language, and to ask them to identify which form is used and judge whether or not the argument is valid. Alternatively, we can present students with enthymemes (arguments in which either a premise or the conclusion is missing), and ask them to supply the missing component. As experienced instructors recognize, at this point students require practice, usually in the form of homework. At least at our large urban university, homework performed after students have simply read the material in a textbook, or heard it in lectures, usually contains numerous errors. But after these errors are pointed out, many students come to perform quite well. They seem to have learned the rules governing basic logical forms and know how to apply them.

But what have the students really learned? Have they simply entered additional rules into their inventory of rules, so that they can now employ them in various tasks? Students' patterns of learning and their performance after learning, however, suggests something else. As we noted, on initial homework exercises students typically make a large number of errors. This process of making mistakes and having them corrected seems to be critical to learning informal logic. Moreover, most students do not achieve flawless levels of performance; even on fairly straightforward tests, many students still get 25 percent of the problems wrong.

How could students perform so poorly? A symbolic approach, in which students posit mental rules to accord with the external rules, offers at least two avenues of explanation. First, some of the posited rules may have been partly incorrect. For example, the difference between *modus ponens* and *affirming the consequent* is a subtle one, and it is plausible that students had collapsed them into a more general mental rule that would later be split into two correct rules. Siegler's (1976) rule-assessment method for characterizing cognitive development in children is an elegant, well-developed example of this approach. Second, the same problem might elicit the use of different mental rules on different occasions. For example, the overly general rule that was just mentioned may still be utilized on some proportion of trials during a transition period towards replacement by the correct rules. This can be modeled by attaching quantitative parameters to the rules that determine their probability of being utilized. Examples include the fixed probabilities of Suppes (1970) and the experience-sensitive strength parameters used in Anderson's (1983) ACT* model and in models proposed by Holland (1975) and Thagard (1988). In the latter three models, learning is accomplished most simply by functions that change the strength parameters, but additional mechanisms are also explored. These include knowledge compilation and production tuning (Anderson, 1983) as well as algorithms for positing and evaluating new rules (as described in Holland, et al., 1986) and in Anderson and

Thompson (1989). Do any of these models provide the best way to understand what is happening with the logic students? Perhaps; but further observation of the students has led us to view logic learning as an appropriate domain in which to explore the connectionist alternative.

We made these further observations as we pursued the goal of enhancing students' learning rather than settling for 70 percent or 80 percent accuracy. One of our first steps was to allow students to correct their homework answers during class review, and then still collect and grade the homework (with their self-corrected answers counting for their grade) to make sure that students recognized their errors and could learn from them. We were greatly surprised to note that many students who made errors did not realize that they had done so when the correct answer was presented in class, and that sometimes students changed correct answers to incorrect ones. (Typically, these errors were between closely related forms such as *modus ponens* and *affirming the consequent*.) Clearly, these students had failed to recognize what made an answer correct when it was discussed in class. To try to draw their attention to what distinguished the various forms, we then introduced computer-aided instruction (CAI), in which students were informed immediately when they had an incorrect answer and could not proceed until they had corrected it. On a given type of problem, students continued to receive new problems until they reached a criterion such as 14 out of the last 15 correct. Also, two forms of problems were used at different times; the student was required (1) to identify the form and assess the validity of a complete argument; or (2) to complete an enthymeme.

The use of CAI did generate substantial improvement on subsequent tests, but it also provided an opportunity to observe students in the process of learning. The observations revealed that some students were quite surprised when the computer told them that their answer was incorrect after they thought they had mastered the material from reading. They now had to look more carefully to determine what was expected in a correct answer. After a short time, many of the students who were having difficulty would copy out a template for each of the forms on which they were working, and then explicitly compare the form of the questions to the templates. Even then some errors were made, but over time, performance improved and students came to rely less on their templates.

The experiences related above strongly suggested to us that students were *learning how* to perform the logic tasks, not just *learning that* certain rules hold in logic. Furthermore, it appeared that to succeed in

Table 5.1   Twelve argument forms

Name and abbreviation	Valid forms	Invalid forms
Modus ponens (MP)	If p, then q p ∴ q	If p, then q q ∴ p
Modus tollens (MT)	If p, then q not q ∴ not p	If p, then q not p ∴ not q
Alternative syllogism (AS)	p or q not p ∴ q	p or q p ∴ not q
	p or q not q ∴ p	p or q q ∴ not p
Disjunctive syllogism (DS)	Not both p and q p ∴ not q	Not both p and q not p ∴ q
	Not both p and q q ∴ not p	Not both p and q not q ∴ p

the judgement and enthymeme tasks, students needed to learn how to recognize and complete certain patterns. As we noted in chapter 4, many rule-based models have been designed in a way that incorporates pattern recognition or matching (including those of Anderson, Holland, and Thagard, cited above; Newell's (1989) SOAR system; and Schank's (1982) MOPs and other higher-order structures). Here we raise the possibility that the rules can be eliminated entirely in the modeling medium, letting networks do all the work. Specifically, we report our initial attempts to build localist connectionist networks that would learn to respond to valid and invalid logical forms as patterns to be recognized or completed.

For this exercise we developed 12 argument forms from the variables p and q and the connectives *if*, *then*, *or*, and *not both*; six of the forms were valid and six were invalid, as shown in table 5.1 (Note that we encoded arguments that affirm the consequent as invalid instances of *modus ponens* and arguments that deny the antecedent as invalid instances of *modus tollens.* This is somewhat arbitary in that these assignments could have been reversed.) Specific problems were generated by substituting any two of the atomic sentences A, B, C, and D for the variables p and q; either order could be used (e.g., $p = A$ and $q = B$, or $p = B$ and $q = A$); and each atomic sentence could be either negated or positive. Altogether, this generated a problem set of 576 different arguments. We also considered two types of problems. In what we shall refer to as *judgement problems* the network was presented with a complete argument; its task was to identify the argument form employed and to evaluate the validity of the argument. In what we refer to as *enthymeme problems* we presented arguments for which either the second premise, conclusion, or argument name and validity were missing. The task was to supply the missing information.

In developing a simulation model to solve problems such as these one of the challenges is to identify what features are employed in recognizing the various argument forms. Since we did not have a well-developed theory as to what information students were actually using to recognize argument forms, we could not engineer a network specifically to simulate student performance. Rather, we proceeded simply by constructing networks that we thought might be able to perform the task. The network that we used for judgement problems is shown in figure 5.2. It is composed of: 14 input units (which encode the two premises and the conclusion); three output units (which give the network's judgement of which argument form was used and whether or not it was valid); and two layers of ten hidden units each. (The number of units in the input and output layers was the minimum number adequate to encode the problem and the answer; the number of hidden units was determined experimentally.) By way of example, consider this invalid *modus ponens* problem:

> If A, then not C
> Not C
> _____
> ∴ A

As shown at the bottom of figure 5.2 and more specifically just below, this problem is encoded on the 14 input units as follows: the first eight units encode Premise 1 (if A, then not C); the next three units encode Premise 2 (not C); and the final three units encode the conclusion (A). Within each premise, an atomic sentence (A, B, C, or D) requires two units, the negation indicator (negated to positive) requires one unit, and the connective (Premise 1 only: *if, then; or*; or *not both*) requires two units. Hence, the input encoding for this problem is:

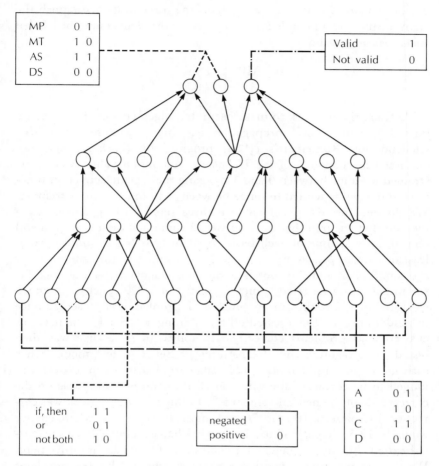

Figure 5.2 Multi-layered network for evaluating simple argument forms from sentential logic. The interpretation of each unit in the input and output layers is shown in one of the boxes. The network includes all possible connections between adjoining layers; only some of these are shown.

	Premise 1				Premise 2		Conclusion	
	((Neg1 Prop1)	Conn	(Neg2 Prop2))		(Neg3 Prop2)		(Neg4 Prop1)	
+	A	→	−	C	−	C	+	A
0	0 1	1 1	1	1 1	1	1 1	0	0 1

At the top of figure 5.2, it can be seen that the first two units of the output layer indicate which of the four argument forms is instantiated in the input pattern, and the third unit indicates whether it is the valid or invalid verson of that form; altogether, the three units distinguish the eight forms shown in table 5.1. Our example problem should be labeled *modus ponens*, invalid:

MP	INV
11	0

To teach the network to make accurate judgements of this kind, we trained it with a back-propagation learning procedure using Mc-Clelland and Rumelhart's (1988) program **bp** (back-propagation), discussed in chapter 5 of the *Handbook*. Activation values were constrained to range between 0 and 1 by using the logistic activation function, and weights tended to range between -10 to $+10$ after training. We divided the 576 problems into three sets of 192 problems by a method that ensured that each set would contain at least one valid and one invalid example of each basic problem type (e.g., would have at least one *modus ponens* argument with A or not-A as the antecedent of the conditional, and B or not-B as the consequent). Set 1 was used for the initial training period, which consisted of 3,000 epochs. An epoch consisted of 192 trials, during which each problem was presented once in random order. When tested on the training set (Set 1), the network answered all problems correctly. Its ability to generalize was then tested by presenting the 192 patterns of Set 2 in test mode. Since activations on output units could range from 0 to 1, an answer was judged to be correct if the value on all three output units was on the correct side of the neutral value 0.5.[6] On this test the network was correct on 139 patterns (that is, 76 percent of the test trials, where chance would be 12.5 percent). Thus, the network had generalized to a substantial extent, but there remained a good deal of room for improvement. We then trained the network for 5,000 epochs on the 384 problems produced by combining Set 1 and Set 2, after which it was correct on all but four of the training problems.[7] Finally, the network's ability to

6   When errors were made, they were usually large errors (e.g., when 0 was the target, the output would be 0.98). Conversely, correct answers were typically very close to the target (e.g., when 1 was the target, the output would be 0.98). Thus, the very relaxed criterion for correctness played only a small role in determining the overall level of correct answers.

7   The error that remained at this point could not be eliminated by further training with back-propagation. The reason has to do with a peculiarity of the back-propagation algorithm. If the network generates an answer that is completely reversed from the target (e.g., a 1 instead of a 0), the delta value becomes 0 since the equation for determining the delta value includes the product $a_u(1 - a_u)$. Since the weight change equation involves multiplying by delta, there will be no change to weights in such a situation and the network will continue to produce the error.

generalize was tested using Set 3. The network was correct on 161 patterns in Set 3 (84 percent of the trials).

The network did a credible job of learning to recognize argument forms and evaluate the validity of arguments. This is not a trivial accomplishment, since there were many features of the input that the network had to check in order to generate the correct answer on the output units. Without a detailed analysis of the activities of the hidden units (which we have not performed), we cannot determine exactly how the network solved this problem. But clearly the network exhibited one of the prominent characteristics of student performance: it required a good deal of practice and error correction before it could solve most of the problems. By the end of training, its overall performance was similar to that of our average students.

The second type of problem, enthymemes, presented a somewhat more difficult task and required a different network design. For these problems, both the argument itself (which required 14 units above) and the judgement of problem type and validity (which required three units above) were encoded on an identical set of 22 units on both the input and output layer. (The extra five units resulted from an unrelated change that we made to the network, in which we expanded the negation and validity encodings from one to two units each). Problems were posed to the network by providing informative input (values of 0 or 1) to only 18 of the 22 input units; the other four units were supplied with values of 0.5. The 0.5 values can be viewed as a query to the network concerning what values should be filled in to yield a correct, complete statement of the argument at the level of the output units. That is, the target output was a repetition of the input pattern but with the missing features filled in. The three queried units were always in the same problem constituent; in some problems the constituent was one of the atomic sentences along with its negation indicator (in Premise 2 or the Conclusion), and in other problems it was the argument type and validity judgement. For example, the previous problem, with the second premise missing so as to constitute an enthymeme, was encoded on the input layer as:

Premise 1					Premise 2		Conclusion	Judgement
((Neg1 Prop1)	Conn	(Neg2	Prop2))	(Neg3	Prop2)	(Neg4 Prop1)	(Argu	Val)
+ +	A	→	− −	C	? ?	? ?	+ +	A	MP	INV
0 0	0 1	1 1	1 1	1 1	0.5 0.5	0.5 0.5	0 0	0 1	1 1	0 0

The target output was then the same pattern of values, except that the network was to "infer" what sequence of values belonged in the queried units. In this example, the input values of (0.5 0.5 0.5 0.5) were to be replaced by (1 1 1 1).

For the enthymeme exercise, the same back-propagation learning procedure as for the judgement task was used, except that initial training was conducted on 384 problems (the previous Sets 1 and 2 combined). Because of the difficulty of this problem, extensive training was required. We trained the network for 30,000 epochs, at which point it was correct on 380 of the 384 problems in the training set. We then tested for generalization. It is worth examining the results on two types of generalization problems separately. On 128 of the problems the network was required to fill in the missing atomic sentence and its negation indicator. The network completed 125 correctly (97.6 percent correct). This is the task for which the network was explicitly designed, and the network performed extremely well on it. In contrast, on the remaining 64 problems the network was required to identify the form of the argument and determine its validity. Here the network, while still well above chance, made numerous errors: it misidentified the form 14 times, it misjudged the validity 18 times, and made both errors on two additional cases. Apparently, the way the network encoded the training problems was adequate for filling in form and validity judgements on those problems, but not for generalizing these judgements to new problems. But form and validity judgements were precisely what the first network *could* generalize. This suggests that there may be ways to revise the enthymeme network design that could provide it with this one capacity that it now lacks. Except for this, however, the enthymeme network performed quite well.

While the level of performance of these reasonably simple networks in noteworthy, there are obviously substantial differences between the way these networks perform and the way humans do. Clearly the large number of training cycles is a major difference, since even quite slow humans learn to identify argument forms correctly with only a few hundred practice trials, not the 576,000 trials which were used to train the first of these networks on Set 1, or the much greater number needed to train the second network. Why might this be? First, humans do not confront a problem like this as a *tabula rasa*. They already possess a great deal of information, such as the distinction between sentences and connectives, and some idea of what each connective means in ordinary speech. Moreover, it is likely that humans, especially as they are cultivating skill in recognizing the forms of arguments or completing enthymemes, do not treat the whole problem as a string of units to be recognized together. They presumably are able to use their prior knowledge to partition the input patterns into meaningful units (e.g., the conclusion); the network must discover these partitionings. However, the point of developing these simple models is not to attain a precise simulation of human performance. Rather, it is to show that logic problems, when viewed as pattern recognition tasks, can be solved by networks which, like humans, seem to be capable of learning from errors and tuning their performance.

The finding that networks can perform pattern recognition on logical argument forms, and thereby evaluate the validity of arguments and supply missing components, buttresses the suggestion that human competency in formal reasoning might be based on processes of pattern recognition and completion that are learned gradually as by a network. The ability to reason using logical principles may not need to be grounded on proposition-like rules, but rather reflect a kind of *knowing how* that is more dramatically distinguished from *knowing that*. This ability to apply pattern recognition to linguistic symbol strings may be an extremely useful capacity for organisms that encounter linguistic symbols in their environment and need to manipulate them in a truth-preserving manner. (This suggestion will be developed further in chapter 7.) The crucial suggestion that emanates from a connectionist perspective is that the ability to manipulate *external* symbols in accordance with the principles of logic need not depend upon a mental mechanism that itself manipulates *internal* symbols.

This suggestion gains further plausibility from considering the way in which students in a symbolic logic course learn to develop proofs in a natural deduction system. The task in constructing a proof is to proceed from initial premises to the conclusion, proceeding only by licensed steps. Valid argument forms such as those we have considered so far are rules of natural deduction (*external* symbol strings) that license adding new statements to a sequence of premises and already established statements. After teaching the rules, instructors typically do some model proofs to show students how proofs are constructed. Then students are sent off to construct proofs of their own. What students need to discover are the conditions under which it is useful to apply the various rules of natural deduction; that is, they must develop their pattern recognition capabilities. This generally requires practice.[8]

---

8   At a given step of the proof, there often are rules that are licensed (locally) but do not contribute to the proof (globally). To select an appropriate rule, the student must attend to the larger pattern that is formed by the premises, conclusion, and steps already taken. Although this larger pattern is produced by a serial process (e.g., working backwards from the conclusion), the whole pattern (or parts of it) must be available at each step. It takes a good deal of experience to become aware of these patterns and to become efficient at recognizing them.

Frequently, as students are trying to master this procedure, the instructor will continue to do model proofs in front of the students and explain why one step was taken rather than another. When the one of us who teaches symbolic logic (Bechtel) offers such explanations, however, he often has the uncomfortable feeling that he is confabulating. It is simply obvious, when one has done enough proofs, what steps are useful in which circumstances. The explanations seem to be developed after the fact. This is revealed most clearly when, after giving a reason that seems plausible in the context of a particular problem, one does another problem that presents a similar situation, but where another step seems more appropriate. A particularly attentive student may notice this fact and ask: *Why?* Again, one can usually come up with a reason, but it is not at all clear that these reasons capture what actually governed the behavior. What seems more plausible is that after much practice more complex pattern recognizing capacities have developed. Instead of simply recognizing the steps licensed by the basic argument forms, one recognizes situations in which application of particular rules of natural deduction should be useful.

A natural way of describing what happens when someone who knows logic constructs proofs is that he or she simply *recognizes* or *sees* what to do in particular situations. This way of describing the situation recalls the characterization of expertise offered by Dreyfus and Dreyfus. The expert solves a problem by recognizing what to do on the basis of extensive experience. If connectionists are able to provide accounts of how these patterns are recognized, as seems quite plausible, then we shall not have to try to formulate logical expertise in terms of a set of mental rules or procedures; rather, we can treat it as a quite different sort of knowledge. Since the procedures used in constructing logical proofs are a means of manipulating formal symbols, this raises the prospect that the very ability to engage in formal symbol manipulation may not be a basic cognitive capacity, but may be something we *learn how* to do by means of a very different sort of mental encoding.

Conclusion

Earlier in this chapter we introduced Ryle's (1949) interesting proposal that propositionally encoded knowledge might not be the most basic form of knowledge, but rather that what he called *knowing how* might be more basic. We have developed that idea by introducing the analysis of expertise put forward by Dreyfus and Dreyfus (1986). In their analysis, expert performance does not rely on propositionally encoded information, but rather on the ability to recognize situations as similar to previously encountered situations and to rely on what worked in those situations. Experts, that is, rely on *knowing how* rather than *knowing that*. As we discussed in chapter 4, this ability to recognize patterns is a strength of connectionist systems, suggesting that connectionism might provide detailed models of *knowing how*. We then further developed this approach by exploring how the knowledge required to perceive certain objects and events might be analyzed in terms of connectionist networks, in which the relevant knowledge is encoded in the weights on connections. We took this a step further by exploring how the knowledge required to do logic might similarly be encoded in connectionist networks. Since logic is a tool for manipulating linguistic propositions, this possibility lends further plausibility to Ryle's radical proposal.

6

Two Simulations of Higher Cognitive Processes

Most of the connectionist simulations we have discussed up to this point have been small-scale demonstrations, which were designed to show the potential of connectionist networks. Not infrequently, scholars presented with these demonstrations ask: "But what kinds of *interesting* things can these systems do?" In this chapter we shall describe two networks, which were advanced as possible models of higher cognitive processes, and which exhibit complexity in the way they encode input, in the number of units involved, or in the number of layers of units. The first of these is a model of past-tense formation in English, a model that, as we shall pursue in chapter 7, has proven extremely controversial. The second is a model of reasoning about kinship relations.

Rumelhart and McClelland's Model of Past-tense Acquisition

A central task of linguistics is to provide a systematic description of languages. Grammars generally include recursive rules in order to generate the infinite number of grammatical sentences in a natural language such as English (Chomsky, 1957). Some psyhologists have been attracted to the view that people produce and comprehend particular sentences from this infinite set by utilizing a mental representation of these rules. Within this psycholinguistic tradition, two assumptions are often made regarding how these rules could be acquired: (a) children possess an innate knowledge of the possible rules that can be employed in language; and (b) in learning a specific language children create hypotheses about how these rules apply to their language, and then test these hypotheses against their linguistic experiences. In contemporary versions, the set of possible rules is constrained by parameters that may be reset based on experience. What is important here is that the product is a system of rules that in some way is represented in the learner's mind. Often this is referred to as "tacit" knowledge, but it is always modeled by grammars composed of rules.

A Network for Modeling the Phenomena of Past-tense Acquisition

Rumelhart and McClelland's (1986) chapter in *PDP:18* on the acquisition of the past tense in English is a direct challenge to this approach. They proposed that

lawful behavior and judgments may be produced by a mechanism in which there is no explicit representation of the rule. Instead, we suggest that the mechanisms that process language and make judgments of grammaticality are constructed in such a way that their performance is characterizable by rules, but that the rules themselves are not written in explicit form anywhere in the mechanism. (1986, p. 217)

Their goal was to develop a simulation that can capture some of the details of linguistic capabilities and language acquisition which might otherwise be taken as evidence that a system of explicit rules is required. They chose to model the acquisition of the English past tense, a rather well-studied case for which considerable data are available. The data show that there are three (overlapping) stages of acquisition (summarized in Brown, 1973). In Stage 1 children learn the past tense of a few specific verbs; some of these are regular (e.g., *looked, needed*), but most are irregular (e.g., *came, got*, and *went*). In Stage 2 children learn to form the past tense of a much larger class of verbs, and here show evidence of acquiring a general rule for the regular past tense, that is, add *-ed* to the *stem* of the verb. In fact, they often overgeneralize this rule, incorrectly applying it to irregular verbs for which they had previously produced the correct irregular form. For example, they might produce either *comed* or *camed* instead of *came* (Ervin, 1964; Kuczaj, 1977). Moreover, if asked to produce the past tense of a nonsense verb, such as *rick*, they would produce *ricked* (Berko, 1958). Performance on irregular verbs is inconsistent during Stage 2, and there is a slow, gradual transition to Stage 3, in which children generally produce the correct forms for both regular and irregular verbs. This "U-shaped" developmental course for early irregular verbs (correct, then often overregularized, then correct again) suggests that Stage 2 children have acquired a rule, and that Stage 3 children have learned the exceptions to the rule. Note, however, that even the exceptional (irregular) verbs can be classified on the basis of phonological similarities,

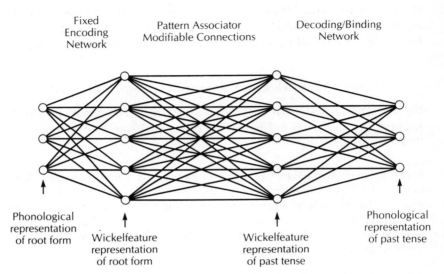

Figure 6.1 The basic structure of Rumelhart and McClelland's model for past-tense
formation. From D. E. Rumelhart and J. L. McClelland (1986a) On learning the past
tense of English verbs, in J. L. McClelland, D. E. Rumelhart, and the PDP Research
Group (1986) *Parallel Distributed Processing: Explorations in the microstructure of
cognition.* Volume 2: *Psychological and Biological Models*, Cambridge, MA: MIT
Press/Bradford, p. 222. Reprinted with permission.

and that verbs in the same class tend to form their past tense similarly.
Some of the errors that children make can be interpreted in terms of
these *subregularities*.

The primary goal of Rumelhart and McClelland's simulation was to
demonstrate that a connectionist network might exhibit many of the
same learning phenomena as children (especially the three learning
stages, the gradual transition between stages, and the error patterns
found for distinct classes of words). They did not attempt to show how
past-tense formation would be carried out as part of an overall language
production system, and they set limits on the extent to which they tried
to capture the many details in empirical data sets or in theoretical
linguistic accounts of the English past tense. Therefore, they were able
to substantially accomplish their goal using a model with a rather
simple structure, as shown in figure 6.1.

The heart of their model is a two-layer pattern associator network in
which the input units represent a verb stem in terms of context-sensitive phonological features called *Wickelfeatures* (defined below) and the
output units represent the past-tense form of the same verb, again

in terms of Wickelfeatures. Superficially it appears that these two Wickelfeature layers are the hidden layers in a four-layer network, but this is not the case. Figure 6.1 actually collapses the representation of three separate networks, each of which passes information from its input layer to its output layer in a different way. The encoding network at the front end uses a fixed (nonstatistical) procedure to translate a phonological representation of the stem into the Wickelfeature representation used by the pattern associator. The decoding/binding network at the back end, which translates the Wickelfeature outputs into a phonological representation of the past-tense form, is more complex. Roughly described, it is a dynamic network in which phonological representations on the output layer compete to account for incoming Wickelfeatures. When processing is terminated, each phonological representation has attained a different level of activation, and this is used to determine the model's response.

The pattern associator was the component emphasized by Rumelhart and McClelland. The units in both layers were binary, activations were propagated using the stochastic version of the logistic activation function (equation (9) in chapter 2), and it learned by using the delta rule to adjust its weights. The innovative part of the network's design was the way its units were defined to solve certain problems. The resulting encodings of the sound pattern of each verb stem (called the *base form* by Rumelhart and McClelland) and each past tense form appear unfamiliar, but they do their job impressively well and suggest new ways of thinking about representation. The traditional way of thinking about representation would lead one to represent each verb form using phonemes, and this works well for most purposes. Attempting to map the phonemic representation of the verb stem directly onto the phonemic representation for its past-tense form presents problems within a network architecture, however. The first problem is that the network cannot directly encode order information; but phonemic representations are composed of ordered sequences (*strings*) of phonemes. In the network a phoneme string can only be treated as though it were an unordered collection of phonemes. The phoneme string for the past-tense form *came*, /kAm/, is indistinguishable from /mAk/ or /Akm/, for example. (Rumelhart and McClelland use a nonstandard notation in which "long *a*" is written as /A/.) For this and other reasons, they initially adopted a phonological representation of a type invented by Wickelgren (1969), in which phoneme units are made context-sensitive by indicating the phonemes that precede and follow the phoneme of interest (which we shall call the *target phoneme*). Hence, each representational unit is sensitive to a target phoneme and its immediate context.

Using # to mark word boundaries, the verb *came* would be encoded using three units, which Rumelhart and McClelland call *Wickelphones*: $_\#k_A$, $_kA_m$, $_Am_\#$. It is generally possible to reconstruct the *sequence* of phonemes in a word from the unordered *collection* of Wickelphones; hence a distinctive representation of *came* can be obtained using three Wickelphones.

The next problem is a logistic one. To obtain this degree of precision with context-sensitive units, an enormous number of units are needed. Specifically, the number of Wickelphones is the cube of the number of phonemes (about 35) plus the number of units that include word boundary markers; Rumelhart and McClelland calculated that more than 42,000 units would be needed for their set of phonemes, only three of which would be active for a three-phoneme word (an uneconomical use of units). Also, this representation is so specific that special steps would be needed to obtain generalization to words with similar phonemes (e.g., from *sing/sang* to *sting/stang* and *ring/rang* and less so to *sink/ sank* and *drink/drank*). Rumelhart and McClelland's surprising solution was to obtain a *coarse coding* (a concept that we introduced in chapter 2) of the Wickelphones across the pattern associator layers by making each unit correspond to a *Wickelfeature*. Wickelfeatures were generated by analyzing the target and context phonemes in the Wickelphone according to four featural dimensions. (For example, /A/ is a *Low Long Vowel* that has a *Front* place of articulation.) Two dimensions were binary and two trinary, yielding ten different features plus an additional feature (#) to indicate word boundaries. A particular Wickelfeature consisted of an ordered triplet of features, one each from the preceding context phoneme, the target phoneme, and the following context phoneme. Altogether there is a pool of 1,210 different Wickelfeatures ($11 \times 10 \times 11$). A given Wickelphone for a target phoneme that is not at a word boundary corresponds to 64 different Wickelfeatures ($4 \times 4 \times 4$). By disregarding Wickelfeatures for which the two context features are from different dimensions, these figures can be reduced to a pool of 460 Wickelfeatures, with 16 different Wickelfeatures per Wickelphone. This makes the number of units quite manageable, and reduces unneeded redundancy.

By way of example, the Wickelphone $_kA_m$ (targeting the vowel in *came*) has the Wickelfeatures (Interrupted, Low, Interrupted), (Back, Low, Front), (Stop, Low, Nasal), (Unvoiced, Low, Voiced), plus 12 other Wickelfeatures obtained by substituting for Low, in turn, the three other features of the target phoneme: Long, Vowel, and Front. Only that particular Wickelphone has that particular set of 16 Wickelfeatures, but each individual Wickelfeature is associated with a number of different Wickelphones. For example, (Interrupted, Low, Interrupted) is a Wickelfeature for $_p e_t$, $_b I_k$, and a number of other Wickelphones. Generalization is enabled by this arrangement. To use an example from the preceding paragraph, the first Wickelphone for the verb *sing*, phonemically /siN/, is $_\# s_i$; that for *ring*, phonemically /riN/, is $_\# r_i$. Since the target phonemes /s/ and /r/ differ in two of their four features, and the context phonemes are identical, half of the Wickelfeatures for the first Wickelphone in each word are the same. Since the same phonemes are context phonemes for the second Wickelphone (and the other two phonemes are identical), half of the Wickelfeatures are identical for the second Wickelphone as well. Finally, the third Wickelphone is identical for the two words ($_i N_\#$), so all 16 Wickelfeatures are identical. Because the degree of overlap for each of the three Wickelphones is atypical, the network will show a relatively high degree of generalization across the verbs *sing* and *ring*.

The result of these choices concerning representation is that the input and output layers of the pattern associator part of the network each have identical sets of 460 units, one for each Wickelfeature. A verb stem is presented to the network by simultaneously activating all of the input units that correspond to its Wickelfeatures. To present the stem *come* (/kum/), for example, 16 Wickelfeatures would be activated for each its three phonemes, yielding a total of 48 activated Wickelfeatures. These would be propagated across the weighted connections, resulting in a somewhat different pattern of activation on the output units which, for a network at learning stage 3, should be translatable by the decoding/binding network into the past tense form *came* (/kAm/). Note that neither layer has any direct way of keeping track of which Wickelfeatures correspond to which target phonemes; also, in words that are longer than *come*, there typically would be some overlap in Wickelfeatures from different phonemes (to that extent, fewer units than 16 times the number of phonemes would be activated).

It turns out that this is just about the right state of affairs: the representations are distinctive enough that different words can be distinguished, but they overlap enough to support generalization on the basis of the similarity structure of the verb stems. Hence, the network can generate past tense forms for verbs on which it has not been trained by generalizing from the verbs on which it has been trained; this generalization is enabled by the overlap in Wickelfeature representations for phonologically similar verbs. Having learned that *sing* produces *sang*, for example, the network can be presented with *ring* and produce *rang* (retaining the distinctive first consonant and the shared final consonant, and appropriately changing the vowel). Knowing *sing* would not be as helpful for generalizing to a less similar new verb, such as *say*. (Of course, the network is not operating on the verb pairs as such, but rather on their distributed encoding across the Wickelfeature units.)

The same weight matrix that enables the network to form the past tense of regulars is also used to determine which verbs require a regular past tense. There are three variants of the regular past tense, based upon the phonological characteristics of the stem. Specifically, /əd/ is added to stems that end in alveolar stops /d/ or /t/; otherwise, /d/ is added to stems that end in a voiced obstruent, and /t/ is added to stems that end in a voiceless obstruent. By stage 3 the network does a good job of using a regular past-tense form where required and of using the correct variant. It can even generalize fairly well to untrained stems, as discussed later in this chapter.

To encourage generalization, Rumelhart and McClelland used an additional strategy for increasing the coarseness, or "blurring," of the representations across the Wickelfeature units. When a particular Wickelfeature was activated, they also activated a percentage (90 percent) of a randomly selected subset of similar Wickelfeatures (where a similar Wickelfeature is one that matches on the target feature and one of the context features).

The goal of the Wickelfeature encoding is thus to capture the phonological similarity among verbs for which a similar past tense is required so that the network could make the generalization. Rumelhart and McClelland made this point explicit in explaining their use of Wickelphones, from which Wickelfeatures are derived:

One nice property of Wickelphones is that they capture enough of the context in which a phoneme occurs to provide a sufficient basis for differentiating between the different cases of the past-tense rule and for characterizing the contextual variables that determine the subregularities among the irregular past-tense verbs. For example, [it is] the word-final phoneme that determines whether we should add /d/, /t/, or / ˆ d/ in forming the regular past. And it is the sequence ᵢN# which is transformed to ₐN# in the *ing* → *ang* pattern found in words like *sing*. (p. 234)

The encoding of inputs and outputs in terms of Wickelfeatures, however, has been one of the most criticized aspects of Rumelhart and McClelland's simulation. Most of the criticisms are fairly specific, and are discussed in the section on Pinker and Prince's (1988) critique in chapter 7. One criticism, however, exemplifies a generic objection that the performance of connectionist models is dependent upon particular ways of encoding inputs which are borrowed from other theories, usually symbolic theories. As applied here (see Lachter and Bever, 1988), the objection is that much of the model's work is actually accomplished by the Wickelfeature representation, which is a context-sensitive adaptation of standard linguistic featural analyses, leaving in doubt the contribution of the network's architecture as such. The usual connectionist response is that much processing remains to be done once an encoding scheme is decided upon, and the connectionist contribution is in offering a nonrule-based means of accounting for this processing.

To run the simulation, the Wickelfeature encoding of a verb stem is presented as an input pattern to the pattern associator (which is a two-layer feedforward network). The network computes the past tense form by applying the stochastic version of the logistic activation function (presented in the context of Boltzmann machines as equation (9) in chapter 2):

$$probability \ (a_u = 1) = \frac{1}{1 + e^{-(netinput_u - \theta_u)/T}}$$

The parameter θ_u is a threshold that is individualized for each unit during training. Input and output units are *binary* (active or inactive); whether or not a particular output unit is active on a particular trial is stochastically determined. As the equation shows, the probability of activation is a *continuous* function of the extent to which the net input from the input units exceeds the output unit's threshold. A stochastic function was chosen for two reasons: it enabled the network to give different responses on different occasions without change in the weights (the degree of variability being determined by the temperature parameter T), and it slowed the learning, allowing the effects of over-regularization to endure for some time.

Once a pattern of activation had been obtained on the output layer by means of the stochastic function, the network could learn by means of an error correction procedure. The obtained pattern was compared to the target output pattern (the correct Wickelfeature encoding of the past-tense form). For any output unit that had an activation of 0 when its target value was 1, the weights feeding into it were decreased and the threshold was increased by that amount. Note that this is the *perceptron convergence procedure* (Rosenblatt, 1962). Although Minsky and Papert (1969) demonstrated that there are serious limitations on what can be computed and learned by perceptrons, the particular input–output patterns used in this simulation were learned rather well.

Rumelhart and McClelland's pattern associator network was large by any standard, and the coarse coding scheme made it even more difficult to examine the detailed behavior of the network. These characteristics followed from their desire to show that past-tense formation could be substantially carried out by a network (rather than a rule system) utilizing distributed representations at the phonological level. Another objective, however, was to simulate the stage-like sequence by which children learn the past-tense forms of verbs. Regular (rule-describable) verbs show steady improvement, but irregular (exceptional) verbs exhibit a U-shaped learning function: the earliest irregulars are temporarily correct, but overregularization errors become common as more verbs are marked for tense, and there is a slow transition to the final stage of typically correct performance. Stage-like sequences like this can be obtained using much simpler networks, if the first objective is set aside. The advantage is that with a small number of weights, they can be inspected individually to see how the stage-like behavior emerged. Rumelhart and McClelland therefore carried out another simulation involving a simple, invented rule and exceptions to that rule. They used this simulation to clarify what was happening in the more complex domain of past-tense acquisition.

Overregularization in a Simpler Model: The Rule of 78

One of Rumelhart and McClelland's objectives was to simulate the stage-like sequence by which children learn the English past tense, wherein exceptional forms are correct, then overgeneralized, and finally correct again. They were able to illustrate this particular phenomenon in a much simpler network that had few enough weights to inspect them individually to see how the stage-like behavior emerged. This simulation could therefore be used to clarify what was happening in the more complex past tense simulation. Rumelhart and McClelland designed the *rule of 78* to operate on certain sequences of eight binary digits, producing modified sequences as its output. They used the rule to construct a set of exemplars which were presented as teaching patterns to a pattern associator network with eight units per layer. If the network learned to transform the input sequences into the appropriate output sequences, it could be said to have learned to behave in accordance with (but not by means of) the rule. In the more interesting condition, one of the exemplars was distorted by changing its transformation into one that violated the rule. To handle that condition, the network had to learn a rule with an exception.

Specifically, the rule applies to sequences in which one of the first three, one of the second three, and one of the last two digits must be "1" (one), and all other digits must be "0" (zero). Thus,

0 1 0 0 1 0 0 1

is a permissible input pattern, but

1 1 1 0 0 0 0 0

is not. It is easy to refer to these patterns by identifying the three positions in which a "1" appears. Thus, the first pattern above is (258). The rule then specifies a mapping from input patterns to output patterns according to which the first six units are identical, and the last two units reverse their values. Thus, the output for (258) is (257):

0 1 0 0 1 0 1 0

Any other output for this pattern would be an exception to the rule. The name of the rule comes from the fact that it requires the numbers in the seventh and eighth positions to exchange their values. There are 18 input–output pairs that satisfy this rule.

Rumelhart and McClelland taught the rule of 78 to the network using the same activation rule and learning rule as they used for the past tense simulation (however, θ_u was set at zero, and T had a lower value). The first thing to note is that the set of 18 input patterns is considerably larger than the number of linearly independent patterns for which the network could learn an arbitrary mapping to outputs (which is equal to the number of input units, here, eight). However, the fact that the input–output patterns exhibit considerable systematicity allowed the network to achieve perfect performance in learning these 18 cases.

McClelland and Rumelhart (1988) made this rule of 78 problem available as an exercise for the **pa** (pattern associator) program in their *Handbook* (pp. 114–19). We ran it with the 18 pairs of patterns that exemplify the rule of 78 for 30 epochs. At this point the network was making sporadic errors, generally attributable to the use of a stochastic activation function, which created a small probability of a unit firing even when it had a negative net input. An examination of the weight matrix for this network shows the exact mechanism by which the network behaves in accord with the rule of 78. The three outlined boxes in table 6.1 indicate the regions with the largest weights (recall that each weight specifies the strength of the connection between the two indicated units). The weights in the upper left box ensure that whichever input unit is active among the first three units (that is, the unit encoding the digit "1"), the corresponding output unit will get the greatest net input. Specifically, the corresponding units have positive

Table 6.1   Network weights for the rule of 78 with no exceptions

Input unit	1	2	3	Output unit 4	5	6	7	8
1	58	−36	−38	−4	−6	−10	−2	2
2	−34	62	−38	−2	−6	−8	4	−2
3	−40	−44	54	−6	−4	−4	0	−2
4	−6	−4	−4	62	−34	−44	2	6
5	0	−6	−6	−36	60	−36	4	−4
6	−10	−8	−12	−38	−42	58	−4	−4
7	−6	−16	−10	−10	−6	−14	−60	52
8	−10	−2	−12	−2	−10	−8	62	−54

weights whereas noncorresponding units have negative weights. Hence, whatever digit sequence is encoded on input units 1, 2 and 3 will be replicated on the corresponding output units. The weights in the central box do the same job for units 4, 5 and 6. The weights in the lower left box, however, are reversed in sign: if input unit 7 is active, the positive connection to output unit 8 will ensure that it becomes active as well, and the same holds for the connection from 8 to 7.[1] By means of its weights, the network has encoded information necessary to perform in accord with the rule of 78 without ever explicitly encoding it.

The important question is: what happens when some instances do not follow the general rule? Rumelhart and McClelland wished to see if they could simulate the three learning stages described for the past tense. To do this, they converted one of the 18 cases into an exception. The exceptional case was (147) → (147), in place of (147) → (148). Since, for children, a substantial percentage of the earliest learned verbs are irregular, Rumelhart and McClelland started the network with just the exceptional case and one regular case, (258) → (257). After 20 epochs of training, the network showed good but item-specific learning, since it had no way of extracting a rule from just two inputs (Stage 1). When the remaining 16 rule-generated cases were added, the network quickly exhibited rule-based learning with overregularization of the exception (Stage 2), and then slowly learned to incorporate the ex-

---

1   The alert reader might have noticed that learning to reverse the seventh and eighth digits is no more difficult for the network than keeping them in correspondence. Thinking of the units as unit 1, unit 2, etc., is a convenience for us in thinking about the inputs to the units, but to the network itself the units are not ordered or numbered in any way.

Table 6.2   Network weights for the rule of 78 with one exception

Input unit	Output unit 1	2	3	4	5	6	7	8
1	108	−66	−74	−08	−14	−14	**68**	−76
2	−72	112	−70	−10	−06	−08	−20	34
3	−66	−68	116	−12	−06	−08	−24	22
4	−14	−08	−08	116	−70	−74	**70**	−68
5	−10	−04	−08	−78	110	−72	−24	24
6	−06	−10	−12	−68	−66	116	−22	24
7	−08	−12	−10	−18	−16	−16	**−100**	108
8	−22	−10	−18	−12	−10	−14	**124**	**−128**

Note: Weights shown in bold face provide the mechanism for producing the correct output for the exceptional case 147. In that case, the net input to unit 7 is $68 + 70 + (−100) = 38$, giving unit 7 a probability of 0.926 of becoming active.

ception across hundreds of trials before achieving excellent performance (Stage 3).

To observe this ourselves, we again ran the rule of 78 exercise in the *Handbook*, this time using the version that included the exceptional case, $(147) \rightarrow (147)$. As expected, after 20 epochs of training on the first two cases, the network had learned these as separate cases. We then added the remaining 16 (rule-following) input–output cases. During the next ten epochs of training, the network essentially learned the regularity that is expressed in the rule of 78. In the process, though, it began to produce substantially more errors on the exceptional case. At this point the probability that input pattern (147) would result in activation of output unit 7 was only 0.28, while the probability of activating unit 8 was 0.60. Thus, there was a tendency to overregularize and produce (1 4 8). Forty epochs later this tendency was still in evidence. The probability of activating unit 7 was now 0.50 and of activating unit 8 was 0.53.[2] Across a great many more training epochs, however, the weights gradually adjusted to the point that the network almost always dealt correctly with the exceptional case. Table 6.2 shows the weights

2   Note that it was possible for both units 7 and 8 to be active as well as for neither or one to be active. There is also considerable variability in the specific probabilities over different runs of the simulation. What was common across the runs that we performed was that the probability of activation for units 7 and 8 varied around 0.50 for a considerable number of epochs and during this period the network overgeneralized about as often as it produced the correct, irregular answer.

after epoch 520. From this it can be calculated that the probability of activation was 0.92 for unit 7 and 0.08 for unit 8.[3]

Rumelhart and McClelland characterized this result as follows:

if there is a predominant regularity in a set of patterns, this can swamp exceptional patterns until the set of connections has been acquired that captures the predominant regularity. Then further, gradual tuning can occur that adjusts these connections to accommodate both the regular patterns and the exception. These basic properties of the pattern associator model lie at the heart of the three-stage acquisition process, and account for the gradualness of the transition from Stage 2 to Stage 3. (p. 233)

Simulation of Past-tense Acquisition

For the actual past tense learning simulation, Rumelhart and McClelland selected 506 English verbs, which they divided into sets of ten high-frequency verbs (eight of which were irregular), 410 medium-frequency verbs (76 irregular), and 86 low-frequency verbs (14 irregular). The verbs in the high-frequency set, for example, included the regular verbs *live* and *look* and the irregular verbs *come, get, give, make, take, go, have* and *feel*. The simulation began by training the network only on the ten high-frequency verbs, with each verb presented once per epoch. By epoch 10, the network had learned a good deal about how to produce the proper past tense forms from the stems for both regular and irregular verbs (between 80 and 85 percent of Wickelfeatures were correct). At this juncture the medium-frequency verbs were added to the training set and 190 more training epochs ensued. Figure 6.2 (from *PDP:18*) shows that early in this period the network exhibited the dip in performance on irregular verbs that is characteristic of children's Stage 2. Thus, immediately after the additional verbs were added on epoch 11 (referred to as trial 11 in this figure), the percentage of features correct on the high-frequency irregular verbs dropped approximately 10 percent, whereas progress on the high-frequency regular verbs was hardly affected. After the initial drop, however, the irregular verbs began to improve again by epoch 20, gradually increasing to approximately 95 percent of features correct by epoch 160. The drop in accuracy was due to interference from learning the regular pattern; once that pattern was established, the weights could be fine-tuned so

---

3   Note that the results we report are quite similar to those reported on p. 231 of *PDP: 18*, but not identical. This is because *PDP:18* used only an approximation to the logistic function that was used in the *Handbook* exercise, and because using any function stochastically yields slightly different results on every run.

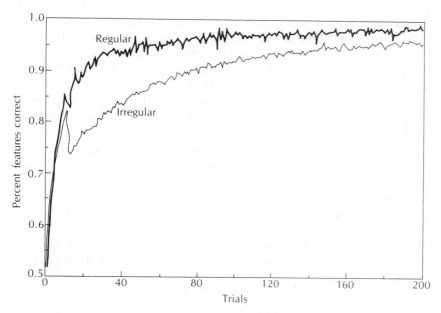

Figure 6.2   Performance of Rumelhart and McClelland's (1986) model for past-tense formation: percentage of features correct across trials (epochs) for regular and irregular high-frequency verbs. From D. E. Rumelhart and J. L. McClelland (1986a) On learning the past tense of English verbs, in J. L. McClelland, D. E. Rumelhart, and the PDP Research Group (1986), *Parallel Distributed Processing: Explorations in the microstructure of cognition*. Volume 2: *Psychological and Biological Models*, Cambridge, MA: MIT Press/Bradford Books, p. 242. Reprinted with permission.

that the irregular verbs could be relearned as exceptional cases, as in children's Stage 3. Finally, note that performance on the medium-frequency verbs became at least as good as performance on the original set of ten high-frequency verbs within a few epochs of their introduction on epoch 11 (not shown in figure 6.2); in fact, performance was a bit better for the new irregular verbs because on average they happened to involve easier transformations.

Through further analysis, Rumelhart and McClelland were able to show that during the period when the network was making errors on the irregular verbs, most errors were of the expected type; that is, in the direction of overregularization. For example, for the stem *come*, the correct (irregular) past tense form is *came*; errors that reflect over-regularization are the stem + ed (*comed*) and the past + ed (*camed*). Note that the past + ed error is actually a blend that combines the correct and incorrect way to form the past tense; it was counted as an over-regularization error since that is the only aspect of the form that is in error. (For most verbs, the past + ed form was relatively infrequent.) To examine the relative frequency of overregularization, Rumelhart and McClelland had to consider how the decoding/binding network would operate on the Wickelfeature representation of the past tense to generate a phonological representation. This would most easily be done by initially decoding the Wickelfeature representation into Wickelphones, from which context-free phoneme strings and hence words could be recovered. Even this would be a daunting task computationally, however, so what they actually did was to set up a competition between pre-defined alternative forms. In the case of *come*, the alternatives were the phoneme strings corresponding to *came*, *comed*, *camed*, and *come*. *Come* is the error of making no change to the stem, which was the only type of error explicitly considered in addition to overregularization. A response strength was calculated for each of these four alternatives by having them compete to account for the particular set of Wickelfeatures that were active; essentially, the response strength of an alternative reflected the proportion of Wickelfeatures that it could account for but the other alternatives could not. The response strength calculated in this way roughly captures the propensity to produce one form rather than the others. Adding the strengths of all four alternatives together, the maximum sum would be one. (The sum would be less than one to the extent that some features are not accounted for by any of the alternatives.) It should be noted that this procedure is sensitive to which alternatives are in competition. For example, if *camt* were added to the alternatives (as a phonologically impermissible way to regularize *come*), *camed* would presumably lose strength since the final phonemes share many features. Also, the sum of response strengths would be larger since those Wickelfeatures unique to /t/ would now be accounted for.

Figure 6.3 shows how the error of overregularization dominated during Stage 2 (approximately epoch 11, when the mid-frequency verbs were introduced, through epoch 30) and then declined during a gradual transition to the reliably correct performance of Stage 3. It does not, however, show what other forms might have had nontrivial response strengths had they been included; since the sum of the response strengths tended to fall into the 0.65 – 0.75 range during Stage 2 and the early transition, it would be of interest to know whether anything systematic was happening in the 0.25 – 0.35 gap. Nevertheless, the ability to simulate the overregularization of the past tense without positing rules is a striking result of this study.

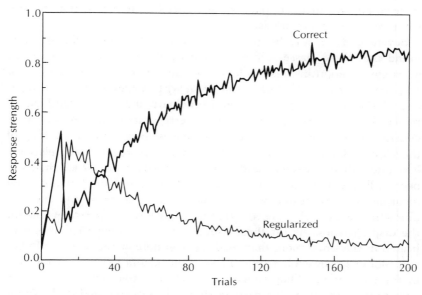

Figure 6.3   Performance of Rumelhart and McClelland's (1986) model for past-tense formation: response strengths across trials (epochs) for the high-frequency irregular verbs. The response strengths for the correct responses increase, while that for the regularized (incorrect) alternatives decrease. From D. E. Rumelhart and J.L. McClelland (1986a) On learning the past tense of English verbs, in J. L. McClelland, D. E. Rumelhart, and the PDP Research Group (1986), *Parallel Distributed Processing: Explorations in the microstructure of cognition*. Volume 2: *Psychological and Biological Models*, Cambridge, MA: MIT Press/Bradford Books, p. 243. Reprinted with permission.

Having simulated the stage-like aspect of children's acquisition data, Rumelhart and McClelland went on to consider more detailed aspects. In particular, the distinction between regular and irregular verbs is actually too coarse; there are subtypes within each of these classes that exhibit distinctive patterns of past tense formation. Bybee and Slobin (1982), for example, described the distinctive course of acquisition for each of nine different classes of irregular verbs. Rumelhart and McClelland found that many of these class differences showed up in the simulation results. For example, one class of irregular verbs ends in a final /t/ and is left unchanged in the past tense (e.g., *hit*). In human acquisition this irregular form tends to be overextended to certain verbs in other classes that also end in /t/ (or /d/). Also, children perform well on this class in a grammaticality judgement task (Kuczaj, 1978). As we shall see, the simulation results are consistent with these findings (and even go beyond them to make a more specific prediction that has not yet been tested on human data).

Seven of Bybee and Slobin's classes involved a vowel change; they found that these classes differed dramatically in their propensity for overregularization in preschoolers' spontaneous speech, from a low of 10 percent for class IV (e.g., *bring/brought*) to a high of 80 percent for class VIII (e.g., *fly/flew*). When Rumelhart and McClelland determined their network's propensity for overregularization errors in these classes, they found less dramatic differences, but a similar ranking of the classes. However, class VI verbs were overregularized relatively less often than expected, and class VII verbs more often than expected. Rumelhart and McClelland noted that their simulation did not incorporate more subtle word frequency differences within the medium-frequency verb class, and that this may have been responsible for the discrepancies. As for those aspects of the ranking that were replicated in the simulation, they made special note of the fact that Bybee and Slobin's own explanations focused on factors that were irrelevant in the simulation. They suggested that the actual explanations may have to do with other factors (ones that were incorporated in the simulation). For example, Bybee and Slobin had proposed that for certain classes of verbs (e.g., *fly/flew*) children have trouble matching up the present-tense form with its past-tense form. However, the two forms were always explicitly paired when presented to the network, and it made the same errors as the children. Rumelhart and McClelland focused their alternative explanation on the degree of similarity of the irregular past tense to the form *stem + ed* (the form obtained by overregularizing). Here is a case, then, in which the model suggests a hypothesis that conceivably would provide a superior account of the human data.

Finally, Rumelhart and McClelland considered the time-course of the two types of overregularization errors: *stem + ed* (e.g., *comed, singed*) and *past + ed* (e.g., *camed, sanged*). Kuczaj (1977) presented evidence that the latter error was most frequent in older children, and the model showed this effect as well. Early in Stage 2 (epoch 11 on), the response strength for *stem + ed* was much greater than for *past + ed*. The response strength for *stem + ed* showed the steepest decline, however, so that in later epochs the error *past + ed* became strongest. In examining their data in further detail, Rumelhart and McClelland also noted that the response strength for *past + ed* errors differed across the various classes of irregular verbs. Thus, they made a prediction, yet untested, that a similar result would be found in human learning of the past tense.

As their last experiment, Rumelhart and McClelland tested the model on 86 low-frequency verbs on which it had not been trained in order to assess its ability to generalize. Overall, presenting these items to the input units resulted in activation of 92 percent of the appropriate Wickelfeatures on the output units for regular verbs, and 84 percent for irregular verbs. Rumelhart and McClelland wondered to what extent this good performance on Wickelfeatures could be carried through to Wickelphone representations and thence to production of the correct word (phoneme string). Therefore, on these items they tried out a version of their decoding/binding network which would freely generate responses. Instead of a competition among designated words, there was a competition among all relevant Wickelphones. To encourage production of actual words, pairs of Wickelphones that could be pieced together into phoneme strings received extra excitation from one another. (This procedure consumes considerable processing time on a serial computer, and they cite this as the reason for not using it earlier. Wickelphones not needed for any of the verbs were excluded for the same reason.) Translating the Wickelphone representations into phoneme strings, it is then possible to calculate the response strength of each phoneme string that is generated. Rumelhart and McClelland adopted as a rule of thumb that only response strengths above 0.2 be regarded as relevant. Six of the 86 new low-frequency verbs generated no phoneme string that exceeded this level. The level was exceeded by exactly one string for 64 verbs, and by more than one string for an additional 13 verbs. Examining the 14 irregular verbs separately, in just one case the past tense was correctly produced and in two cases the correct form was one of two phoneme sequences achieving threshold. The rest of these verbs were either regularized or unchanged from the present tense. As for the 72 regular verbs, the correct response was generated to 48, and the correct response was one of two or three generated in 12 others. While this generalization is far from perfect, Rumelhart and McClelland took it as evidence that the basic principles for generating the past tense had been learned by the network. They noted that in a study with children, Berko found that they too were only correct in generating past tenses to novel verbs 51 percent of the time and commented: "Thus, we see little reason to believe that our model's 'deficiencies' are significantly greater than those of native speakers of comparable experience" (Berko, 1958, pp. 265–6).

On the basis of these experiments with their model, Rumelhart and McClelland contended that with a rather simple network and no explicit encoding of rules it is possible to simulate the important characteristics of the behavior of human children learning the English past tense. They also acknowledged certain respects in which their procedure departs from the actual process of verb acquisition in humans. First, the stem and the past-tense form are paired during training, whereas a child generally will hear just one form of the verb at a time. Second, the transition from Stage 1 to Stage 2 is somewhat artificially created by presenting the network first with a small number of verbs, mostly irregular, and then a much larger set of verbs, mostly regular. Rumelhart and McClelland tried to justify this last procedure by arguing that children learn the past tense of those verbs for which they have already mastered the present tense, and that the progression from a small set of verbs to a much larger set roughly corresponds to the explosion from a limited vocabulary to a much larger vocabulary in development. They commented that "the actual transition in a child's vocabulary of verbs would appear quite abrupt on a time-scale of years so that our assumptions about abruptness of onset may not be too far off the mark" (p. 241). Nevertheless, this aspect of Rumelhart and Mc-Clelland's simulation has generated a lively controversy, which we review in the next section.

The Role of Input in Producing Regularization

The role played by the input to the past-tense learning mechanism is not well understood either for humans or for network simulations of humans. In their critique of Rumelhart and McClelland's model, Pinker and Prince (1988) argued that the model's U-shaped acquisition curve for irregulars should be attributed to the discontinuity in its input, not to any intrinsic characteristic of learning in connectionist networks. The uncontested part of their argument is that the model's entry into Stage 2 (in which irregulars are often overregularized) was precipitated by the addition of the 410 medium-frequency verbs (82 percent of which were *regular*) to the original training set of ten high-frequency verbs (80 percent of which were *irregular*). The controversial part is what to make of this. Two separate issues are involved: (1) Are the input conditions under which children exhibit U-shaped learning so different as to undercut the usefulness of the existing simulation? (2) Under what range of input conditions can networks exhibit a U-shaped acquisition curve?

The role of input for children   Focusing on the first issue, Pinker and Prince (1986, pp. 139–42) compiled some useful, although incomplete, developmental data. One approach is to look at the percentage of verbs in a corpus that are regular versus irregular. Slobin (1971) made this count for adult speech to children (the initial input to the language-acquisition mechanism, which is then filtered according to what is salient to the child), and Pinker and Prince themselves made the count for the child's own speech (since this roughly indicates what part of the adult verb vocabulary has survived the child's filtering). In both cases, the data were from Roger Brown's (1973) studies of Adam, Eve, and Sarah prior to and during overregularization. If the count is made by verb *types* (i.e., number of different vocabulary items in a speech sample), the percentage of irregular verbs is very close to 50 percent throughout the period examined. Irregular verbs are used more frequently, however, so verb *tokens* are predominantly irregular (in parental speech, 75–80 percent).

Ullman, Pinker, Hollander, Prince, and Rosen (1989) pointed out that this discrepancy results in misestimates of type frequency from small samples, and applied the "capture–recapture" statistical technique to larger samples. With this correction, regular verb types outnumber irregular verb types even at the age of two, and the disparity increases through the preschool years. There is no sudden spurt in this percentage or in vocabulary size preceding the onset of overregularization, however. Ullman et al. concluded that these are not the factors that precipitate overregularization (McClelland and Rumelhart's stage 2), and that providing discontinuous input to the network model was an inappropriate way to achieve a U-shaped learning curve for irregulars.

What, then, triggers Stage 2? Kuczaj (1977) noted that children tend to produce the stem alone for most verbs during Stage 1, but for a few irregular verbs they also have an unanalyzed past-tense form that is sometimes used instead of the stem. They enter Stage 2 by becoming much more reliable at using a past-tense form in contexts that require it, and soon past-tense formation spreads to almost all of the child's verbs. However, for the irregular verbs about one-third of these past-tense forms are incorrect (typically overregularized). This is the change that traditionally has been cited as compelling evidence that rules are induced. Ullman et al. added to this the idea that the past-tense learning mechanism may have been off during Stage 1 and then turned on to precipitate Stage 2 (since there were no dramatic changes in the input to the mechanism).

Other interpretations are possible, and there are still crucial gaps in the data. In particular, little is known about early Stage 1 and the transition to Stage 2. (For example, how quickly does past-tense use become reliable?) Regarding early Stage 1, our own examination of published vocabularies indicates that irregular verb types outnumber regular verb types (a) for three of the four single-word speakers for whom Nelson (1973) reported 50-word vocabularies that included at least five verbs; and (b) for both of the early multiword speakers for whom Bloom (1970) listed vocabularies that included 15–58 verbs; mean length of utterance (MLU) was 1.12 to 1.42. In the latter study, the preponderance of irregulars was due primarily to those verbs that were used in multiword utterances (which presumably were older, more productive forms): 65 to 73 percent of such verbs were irregular (as were 60 to 88 percent of the tokens; the type-token discrepancy apparently arises later). Just a few of the verbs were used in a past-tense form (among the six children in the two studies, the total was one regular and eight irregular past tense verbs, all correct). These results were based on parental diaries (Nelson) or on two eight-hour speech samples per child (Bloom); hence, the effects of sampling were minimized. They contrast with the preponderance of regular verb types found by Pinker and his colleagues for the period after MLU 1.5 and with data from Bloom's third subject (whose unusually large vocabulary for MLU 1.32 included 93 verbs; one month later her MLU was 1.92).[4]

If the mechanism that learns stem-past tense mappings has been turned on already during Stage 1 (contrary to Ullman et al.'s suggestion), and if it attends primarily to pairs for which the child already produces the stem (or more rarely, just the past-tense form), then the data from Nelson and Bloom indicate that irregular verbs initially predominate in its input. The mechanism would not yet be involved in controlling the production of verbs; its learning would initially be receptive and perhaps Hebbian. That is, some other mechanism would control the child's production of verbs. Some of the child's verbs could then serve as input to the mechanism (as could parental utterances of those verbs) on just those occasions when they are paired with the outputs needed for Hebbian learning. For example, if a child says "Dog eat bone" and the parent responds "Oh, it ate the bone!" the child's past-tense network may accept the pair and adjust its weights without producing any observable past-tense form. (See Golinkoff, Hirsh-Pasek, Cauley, and Gordon (1987) for evidence that comprehension precedes production of syntactic forms.) Initially the receptive stem-past tense pairs would be learned as arbitrary mappings, but as larger numbers of regular verbs are included in the input during late Stage 1

4 Note that Pinker and Prince (1988) also reported a count of 53 percent regular verb types for one single-word speaker, a result that is inconsistent with our count on Nelson's and Bloom's data. Their subject was also reported to have a 53-verb vocabulary, which is very high for a single-word speaker.

the network may begin to generalize the regular mappings. During this period, the child's overt verb productions increasingly would include regular verb stems; because these would be uninflected forms, it would be clear that they were not yet under the control of the past-tense mechanism.

Again we meet the question of what pushes the child into Stage 2. Within our speculative account, the maturing past-tense mechanism must now become involved in controlling verb production. What might cause this shift? Several developmental theorists have recently emphasized the idea that certain developmental advances involve the coordination of competencies that had previously developed separately (e.g., Acredolo, in press; Bates, Bretherton, and Snyder, 1988). This insight is readily applied to our problem. Producing past-tense forms in appropriate contexts would seem to require at least: (1) a variety of mechanisms for planning and producing utterances more generally; among these may be mechanisms for recruiting knowledge that was gained receptively; (2) receptive knowledge of past-tense formation for some number of verbs; (3) ability to distinguish between past and present time; and (4) knowledge of the semantics and pragmatics of the past tense. All of these would be incomplete and imperfect at the onset of Stage 2.

The available data do not tell us whether Stage 2 awaits only the coordination of the imperfect parts, or whether the coordination itself is awaiting minimal attainment of one or more of those parts. The data do tell us, however, that the child's acquisition of additional verbs is rapidly progressing, and that regulars overtake irregulars before the onset of Stage 2 (Ullman et al., 1989). Hence, Rumelhart and McClelland's claim that changes in these two factors determine the forms used for the past tense at each stage remains quite plausible. The stronger claim that these changes (and their effects on a single network) are the primary *cause* of transition from Stage 1 to Stage 2 is harder to evaluate. Rumelhart and McClelland's training regimen may best be viewed as a convenient way to set up initially correct performance on a few irregular verbs, so that a reversal could then be observed in Stage 2. This simplification would be justified by our lack of knowledge about what really is happening, and by the inadvisability of building a more complete, speculative model at such an early stage of network research. More detailed analysis of child acquisition data is one avenue for assesssing the alternatives; exploring the behavior of networks under a variety of input conditions is another. In particular, Pinker and Prince's critique of the discontinuity (abrupt change) in Rumelhart and McClelland's input can be evaluated by providing networks with continu-

Table 6.3   Regular and exceptional patterns added after certain epochs

Subset	Epoch	Case [1]	Input Pattern	Desired Output [2]
A	0	*P147	10010010	100100<u>10</u>
		P258	01001001	01001010
B	20	*P357	00101010	0<u>1</u>001001
		P368	00100101	00100110
C	40	*P248	01010001	01001<u>1</u>10
		P148	10010001	10010010
D	60	*P158	10001001	10001<u>101</u>
		*P367	00100110	0011<u>0</u>0<u>0</u>1
		P347	00110010	00110001
		P157	10001010	10001001
E	100	*P167	10000110	<u>00</u>100101
		*P247	01010010	0100<u>1</u>001
		*P267	01000110	010001<u>10</u>
		*P348	00110001	10<u>0</u>10010
		P168	10000101	10000110
		P257	01001010	01001001
		P268	01000101	01000110
		P358	00101001	00101010

1   Irregular patterns noted with asterisk.
2   Irregularities are underlined.

ous input and observing the outcome. Two explorations of this type are described in the next section.

The Role of Input for Networks

The rule of 78 revisited   McClelland and Rumelhart (1988, p. 118) suggested that the rule of 78 simulation can be easily modified to provide an exploratory look at input conditions under which U-shaped learning curves can be obtained. They suggested using an incremental schedule for presenting cases (pairs of input–output patterns), which we carried out as follows. We began by training the network on just two cases (subset A), then added two more cases (subset B) so that training continued on four cases, and at intervals repeated this accretion of cases so that training continued using six, then ten, and finally all 18 patterns. For each subset, half of the cases were left unaltered (so that they followed the rule of 78) and half were transformed into exceptions by altering two or three of the eight binary digits. As is evident in table 6.3, the exceptions were quite varied.

Table 6.4   Rule of 78 network trained with exceptions

A.   Weights after 60 epochs

Input unit   *Output unit*

	1	2	3	4	5	6	7	8
1	32	−22	−24	22	−28	−8	2	−16
2	−20	26	4	−8	32	−14	2	8
3	−14	−20	10	−20	−24	20	−24	0
4	28	−26	−20	16	−26	−8	4	−22
5	−26	36	−10	−12	40	−28	−2	2
6	−24	−2	10	0	−34	18	−22	6
7	26	18	−12	26	−10	16	−2	34
8	−22	−26	16	−22	4	−14	8	−40

B.   Weights after 140 epochs

Input unit   *Output unit*

	1	2	3	4	5	6	7	8
1	64	−62	−28	28	−10	−44	−30	4
2	−58	72	−24	−14	24	−20	10	−20
3	−20	−52	42	−32	−26	28	−2	−28
4	2	−68	30	52	−66	−22	−8	−28
5	−26	34	−16	−12	80	−76	−4	−4
6	14	12	−44	−34	−30	46	−36	18
7	8	12	−8	28	−42	26	−36	48
8	−4	−14	8	−28	36	−18	32	−42

The weight matrices after learning subsets A–C (six cases) are shown in the top half of table 6.4. It can be seen that there was no systematic structure in the weights that would directly show that the regularities imposed by the rule had been extracted; yet the network performed quite well on all six cases. This illustrates that when there are few enough cases relative to the size of the network, each case can be learned separately as though it were an arbitrary mapping. The percentage of rule-following versus exceptional cases has no real impact, because the network is able to minimize error without extracting the regularities that the rule imposes. The behavior of the network at this point in training is comparable to that of the past tense network during Stage 1 (when it was learning to form the past tense for just eight irregular and two regular verbs). It is the small number of cases that matters, not the percentage that are exceptional.

After subset D had been learned as well (making a total of five regular and five irregular patterns), the weights began to show evidence of
systematic structure similar to that in the earlier simulation (cf. table
6.2). As can be seen by examining the weights, this structure became
even clearer after all 18 patterns had been made available for learning.
At this stage (epoch 140) the network also showed a strong tendency to
overregularize. Rather than examining actual outputs, which were determined by a stochastic function, we focused on the tendency of an
output unit to be active as indicated by the net input to the unit. We
classified as an error any case in which at least one output unit had a net
input that would result in a probability of error greater than 0.40. Of
the nine regular patterns, three had errors; just one had a probability
greater than 0.50. All nine of the irregular patterns, however, produced
errors; eight were overregularization errors. (Of these, the probability
of error was greater than 0.50 for five patterns.) Thus, the network's
tendency to extract and overgeneralize a rule to exceptional cases seems
to be robust, even when only half of the cases fully exhibit the rule.
This suggests that the past-tense network might have learned the regular past tense and overgeneralized it to irregulars in Stage 2 even with
a less abrupt change in its input. Conclusive evidence could be obtained
only by experimenting with the past tense network itself, of course.
The next study approximates this goal by experimenting with a
different past tense network.

The past tense revisited   Plunkett and Marchman (1989) carried out an
extensive series of simulations of past-tense formation in which they
presented the complete training set to their network on all 50 epochs of
training (rather than "priming" the network with a high proportion of
irregulars in the first few epochs). Hence, not only was there no abrupt
change in the input, there was no change at all, creating less favorable
input conditions for U-shaped learning than in fact are offered to children. Nevertheless, they obtained U-shaped learning curves for individual verbs (but not for all verbs averaged together).

All of Plunkett and Marchman's simulations used a back-propagation learning procedure in a three-layer network of 20 units per layer.
It was trained on artificial sets of "verb stems" that were three phonemes in length (two consonants and one vowel). All were phonologically
possible in English (e.g., /erk/ and /mEt/). Context-free phonological
features were used to encode the stem on the binary input units. Two
binary features required one unit, and two four-valued features required two units, for a total of six units per phoneme or 18 units per
three-phoneme stem. On the input layer, the two leftover units were

clamped off. The output layer was similarly arranged, except that units 19 and 20 were used for a nonphonological encoding of the three forms of the regular past-tense suffix. Hence, on units 1 through 18 there was a distributed encoding of the symbols (artificial verbs) across a localist encoding of subsymbols (phonological features). This encoding was considerably less distributed than the coarse coding across Wickelfeatures used by Rumelhart and McClelland, and so presumably provided less support for generalization. It required a much smaller network, however, enabling a large number of simulations to be run in order to compare the consequences of various input conditions.

In almost all of Plunkett and Marchman's simulations, four different kinds of cases were intermixed in training: regular past tense (appropriate suffix is added to stem, based on three classes of stem-final phonemes); arbitrary mapping (unrelated stem and past-tense form); identity mapping (past tense is identical to stem); and vowel change (vowel of stem is changed according to one of eleven patterns). All except the first class were designed to emulate common subclasses of irregular verbs.

What differentiated among the large number of simulations was the type and token frequency of each of the four classes of training cases. As a simplification, Rumelhart and McClelland had assumed a type-to-token ratio of one. This decision has been criticized, because irregular types (vocabulary items) are in fact used much more frequently than regular types. Bever (in press) speculated that the network would have learned only the irregulars if a more realistic type-to-token ratio had been used; Pinker and Prince wondered whether more extended training on the initial ten verbs would have "burned in the 8 irregulars so strongly that they would never be overregularized in Phase 2" (1988, p. 142).[5] Plunkett and Marchman (1989) sought to reply to these critics by providing their network with a steady diet of verbs, varying the type-to-token ratios in that diet across a large number of simulations but not within the same simulation. (Hence, no single simulation had realistic change in amount and composition of input across time, as would a child's past-tense network.)

Plunkett and Marchman's results are not easily summarized. In simulations for which 74 percent or more of the tokens were *irregular*, approximating stage 1 input, regulars were overwhelmed and not learned. (Performance on irregulars depended upon the type-to-token ratio that was used; few types with many tokens was best.) In simulations for which 74 percent or more of the tokens were *regular*, regulars were

5   Recall, however, that our own count from Bloom's data indicated a ratio close to one for verbs in multiword utterances in early Stage 1.

learned well; now irregulars were overwhelmed and not learned. Children are never exposed to this kind of input. However, the two sets of simulations together simply demonstrate that networks are sensitive to their training regimens. If dissimilar responses (e.g., vowel change versus suffixization) are required to rather similar input patterns (the stems), the network will minimize error by learning the more frequent response.

In several simulations (in what they called their *Parent* series), approximately 45 to 50 percent of the tokens (but only 18 percent of the types) were irregular, a situation that better approximates the input to children's past tense learning mechanisms during stage 2 (although the regulars were composed of 410 verbs, each with one token; a smaller number of regulars, each with a larger number of tokens, would be more realistic). In these simulations the arbitrary mapping class needed 15 or 20 tokens per type and the identity and vowel change classes needed five tokens per type to obtain learning outcomes of 75 percent correct or better. Regulars suffered somewhat but were always at least 50 percent correct. Errors included blends (vowel change plus regular suffix), no change to stem, and (for irregulars) overregularization; relative frequencies of error types varied according to verb class and type-to-token ratio. Learning curves that averaged together all items of a type were noisy but generally negatively accelerated (i.e., most improvement comes early in training). The lack of an overall U-shaped learning curve is not surprising, because input conditions that would produce good initial learning of a small number of items were not included. Plunkett and Marchman noted, however, that a number of individual items exhibited U-shaped learning curves.

A related series of simulations (the *Phone* series) incorporated phonological constraints in the identity and vowel change classes that helped to determine what mapping should be carried out (but did not reliably distinguish irregular from regular stems). For example, one vowel change subclass was defined by the subregularity /Em/ changing to /Om/, rather than /E/ changing to /O/. The Phone simulations, by making each class of stems more distinctive, exhibited somewhat better performance than the corresponding Parent simulations. However, the relative ordering of difficulty of the classes was generally similar.

Summary

Rumelhart and McClelland have offered a new proposal about the kind of mental mechanism that produces linguistic performance. On their view, the linkage between regular verb stems and their past tense forms is *described* using just a few general rules, but is *governed* by a mechanism that does not use explicit rules. Rather, it distributes knowledge of how to form the past tense across connection weights in a network. Furthermore, this mechanism is unified: the more complex linkages between irregular verb stems and their exceptional past-tense forms are encoded in the same set of connection weights. (In a rule-based account, by contrast, exceptions must be listed separately.) In moving towards this end-state, the network exhibited learning stages that were similar in important respects to those of human children.

Perhaps because this model was so explicitly set forth as a direct challenge to rule-based accounts, it has become a prime target of critics of connectionism. We have considered two issues here. First, to what extent did the input to the network approximate the input to children's past-tense learning mechanism? We pointed to data which, combined with certain assumptions about when and how past-tense learning occurs, suggest that the network's input indeed is predominantly irregular early in the learning process. Second, under what range of input conditions can stages like those of children be obtained in networks? Plunkett and Marchman's simulations indicate that regularization, overregularization, blends, and other Stage 2 phenomena can be exhibited by networks even when the higher token frequency of irregular verbs is taken into account. Furthermore, the transition to Stage 3 is partly captured in the improvements in performance across training epochs. Their simulations have more limited applicability to Stage 1 and the transition to Stage 2, in that they showed that individual items can exhibit U-shaped learning under constant input conditions involving a large number of items. The final rule of 78 simulation which we carried out indicates, however, that general stages of U-shaped learning can be observed in a very simple network if it is fed a small (but increasingly large) training set in which exceptions are kept at a constant percentage of 50 percent. Hence, abrupt changes in the input are not the only way to attain U-shaped learning curves.

Rumelhart and McClelland's past-tense model was an early feasibility study that made innovative use of a relatively primitive kind of network (the pattern associator). It is certainly appropriate to probe at its limitations in pursuit of improved models, and the methodological points raised by critics can be a useful part of this process. Critics have also raised other arguments, however, that go to the core of our understanding of what it is to do cognitive modeling. We shall consider these arguments at some length in chapter 7. First, however, we shall briefly describe a second connectionist model of human language processing. Like Plunkett and Marchman's (1989) model, it was designed recently

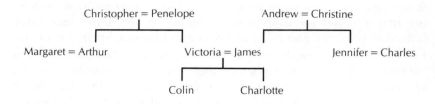

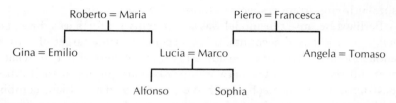

Figure 6.4 The two isomorphic family trees for which Hinton's (1986) network learned
to infer pairwise kin relations. The top tree represents an English family, and the bottom
tree an Italian family. The symbol "=" means "married to." From G. E. Hinton (1986)
Learning distributed representations of concepts, *Proceedings of the Eighth Annual
Conference of the Cognitive Science Society*, Hillsdale, NJ: Lawrence Erlbaum. Reprinted
with permission.

enough to take advantage of the generalized delta rule, which implements gradient-descent learning in multi-layered networks.

Hinton's Model of Kinship Knowledge and Reasoning

In many cognitive domains, the information given in the input must be
combined and recombined before it can appropriately generate output
patterns; hidden units are the means of carrying out this processing.
Hinton (1986) designed a multi-layered network to carry out a reasoning task involving the kinship relations between 24 individuals. The
ability to handle kinship relations is a traditional test case for assessing
general theories in linguistics and psycholinguistics, so this is a particularly salient connectionist model of higher-level cognition.

Figure 6.4 shows that the 24 individuals in Hinton's simulation are
equally divided between two families, one Italian and one English,
which have isomorphic family trees. All the information about the kin
relations shown in these trees can be represented in a set of triplets
of the form < **person1, relationship, person2** >. There are 12 relationships (*mother, daughter, sister, wife, aunt, niece*, and their male coun-
terparts), which generate such triplets as *Colin has-mother Victoria.*

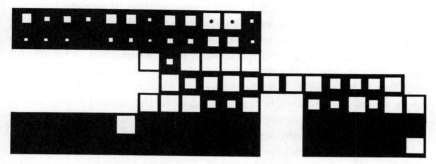

Figure 6.5   The activity levels of units in Hinton's (1986) family tree network after training when presented with the problem "Colin has-aunt" on the input layer. The input layer has two groups of units. First, the 24 units for representing **person1** are shown as two rows of twelve units each at the bottom left (the bottom row is used for members of the Italian family, and the row above it is used for members of the English family). The unit representing Colin is fully activated (as indicated by the white square); the 23 units representing other family members are inactive (as indicated by the 23 black squares). Second, the 12 units for representing a **relationship** are shown in two rows of six units each at the bottom right. The unit for "has-aunt" is activated. The next three rows represent the three sets of hidden units. The first hidden layer consists of 12 units, six of which receive inputs from the **person1** units, and six of which receive inputs from the **relationship** units. The next hidden layer also consists of 12 units, each of which receives inputs from all 12 units in the first hidden layer. The last hidden layer consists of six units, each of which receives input from all 12 units on the second hidden layer. The degree of activation of each of these units is indicated by the size of the white square (a smaller square indicating less activation). Finally, the 24 output units for encoding **person2** (the network's response to the problem) are shown in two rows at the upper left. Different units have different degrees of activation, but the units for Penelope and Christine are most active (indicated by the black dot in the center of their white squares). These are both correct responses. From G. E. Hinton (1986) Learning distributed representations of concepts, *Proceedings of the Eighth Annual Conference of the Cognitive Science Society*, Hillsdale, NJ: Lawrence Erlbaum. Reprinted with permission.

There are 104 such triplets, but as we shall see, not all of them need be explicit; the information encoded in some triplets can be inferred from others. Input to the network consists of an encoding of **person1** and the **relationship** on the input layer. The target output for the network is an encoding of **person2** on the output layer.

Hinton's network design is shown in figure 6.5, using a format in which each unit is represented by a box, and white boxes are most active for the problem illustrated. The network has five layers of units. The input units (lower two rows) use a localist encoding for **person1** (24 units, one for each person) and the **relationship** (12 units, one for each possible relationship). The output layer (upper two rows) similarly has 24 units which permit a localist representation of **person2**. In between are three hidden layers. The first layer of hidden units consists of 12 units, six of which receive inputs from the 24 **person1** units, and six of which receive inputs from the 12 **relationship** units. The second layer also consists of 12 units, which receive inputs from all 12 units in the first hidden layer. The final layer of hidden units consists of six units which receive inputs from all units in the second layer, and it provides input to the output layer (indicating the identity of **person2**). The fact that the 24 units coding for **person1** must feed their activity pattern through a bottleneck of six units forces the network to find a distributed representation of the different individuals that extracts the relevant features for inferring **person2**. The same principle operates with respect to the six hidden units receiving input from the 12 **relationship** units. It also applies in reverse to the six hidden units that feed into the 24 output units: those hidden units must employ a relevant distributed representation of **person2**.

A back-propagation learning procedure was used to train the network on 100 of the 104 triplets across 1,500 epochs. It was then tested on its ability to infer the correct **person2** for the remaining four triplets. This procedure was repeated a second time using different initial weights. In one run the network was correct on all four inferences, and in the other run it was correct on three out of four inferences. While this represents a fairly limited inference capacity, the network nevertheless was able to infer answers to new questions based on already acquired information. Moreover, it did so without propositional representations and without traditional sorts of inference rules.

What is significant is the way in which the network accomplished this task. Hinton showed that the first set of hidden units adopted quite distinct representational functions. This can be appreciated by examining the weights from the input units to the first layer of hidden units. Figure 6.6 displays the six hidden units which received inputs from the 24 **person1** units. White boxes indicate positive weights on the connection, and black boxes indicate negative weights. The size of the boxes represents the strengths of these connections. One thing that is clear is that the hidden units for **person1** drew heavily on the symmetry of the two families, despite the fact that this information was never explicitly provided to the network. Thus, the connections to unit 1 ensure that it becomes active whenever **person1** is British, whereas unit 5 becomes active whenever **person1** is Italian. Unit 2 becomes most active when **person1** is of the senior generation, while unit 3 becomes active when **person1** is of the younger generation. Units 4 and 6 seem to be representing the two branches in each family tree (unit 4 favoring the

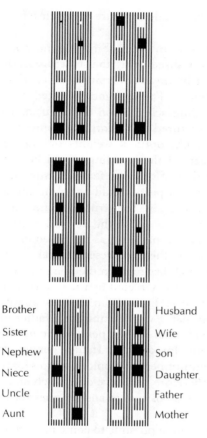

Figure 6.6 Some of the weights acquired by Hinton's (1986) family tree network. The weights for the connections from the 12 input units representing **relationship** to the six units in the first hidden layer are indicated. Specifically, the weights for each of the six hidden units are grouped together within one of the six rectangles. Within a rectangle, each of the twelve small boxes represents the weight from an input unit to that hidden unit. A white box represents a positive connection, and a black box a negative connection. The size of the box represents the strength of the connection. From G. E. Hinton (1986) Learning distributed representations of concepts, *Proceedings of the Eighth Annual Conference of the Cognitive Science Society*, Hillsdale, NJ: Lawrence Erlbaum. Reprinted with permission.

kin shown on the right side in figure 6.4, unit 6 favoring the kin on the left).

Three comments are in order. First, the network itself did much of the work involved in discovering the structure in the environment that was presented to it by means of training cases. (Here the environment was the family trees.) The designer selected the training cases and designed the encoding schemes on the input and output layers. The network then restructured this information into new encodings on hidden layers and sought optimal weights on the connections between layers. Some aspects of the recoding would be anticipated by the designer (the extraction of obvious features, such as familial branch or generation), but other aspects would be subtle and unanticipated. All of these aspects are caused by the structure implicit in the input; hence there is a strong sense in which the derived representations are intentional, or *about* the input patterns, as discussed in chapter 4.

Second, developing these representational capacities provided the key to the network's ability to learn the relationships in the families. On the basis of the features extracted by the hidden units, the network was able to make (at least limited) inferences about relationships. For example, knowing that it was looking for a father of a *middle-aged person*, and for a father of an *Italian* person, the network could determine that it was looking for an old, Italian person, thus specifying the features that the output person would have to satisfy. Once the network was trained and therefore had developed such an internal featural representation, it was in a position to answer questions on which it had not been trained.

Third, while it is often possible to come up with labels for the hidden units after examining their behavior, these labels are *very approximate*. For example, if activation of unit 1 does indeed represent being English and unit 5 being Italian, they do not treat all members of the respective families equally. Thus, Penelope is treated by unit 1 as more of an English person than Charles, and unit 5 actually treats Arthur and Christine as being a little bit Italian. Presumably the reason that these units do not learn to give an equal response to all members of the set is that they are also capturing other information for which we may not have a simple label. In this respect, the network is not simply an implementation of a symbolic system that might have solved the problem by employing precise dimensions of difference such as nationality, sex, and generation.

The internal encoding that Hinton's network has achieved is clearly very impressive. We must recall that the network never encountered figure 6.4 as such, but only specific relationships. The network's success raises questions, however: how commonly are hidden units so readily interpreted? What difference does it make whether or not they are? What if more triples had been left untrained and then used as tests of inference? These are the kinds of question that can be pursued within the connectionist research program. As in the case of the past tense model, it is also possible to raise questions at a different level, questions that would challenge this approach to cognitive modeling at its foundations. We have not approached this particular model in this way, but many of the points of discussion in chapter 7 are germane.

Summary

In this chapter we examined two networks that were designed as models of higher cognitive tasks. Rumelhart and McClelland's model simulated the learning of the past tense of English verbs, and Hinton's model learned and inferred kinship relations. Although neither model provides a completely satisfactory account of human performance, the results are intriguing. They have led proponents of connectionism to claim that at least some tasks that seem to require knowledge of rules and complex information processing can be accomplished by other means. Critics have characterized these means, however, as inadequate and (merely) associationist. The result has been a lively, sometimes acrimonious, controversy, to which we shall now turn.

7

Are Rules and Symbols Needed? Critiques and Defenses of Connectionism

Up to this stage we have been focusing on the characteristics of connectionist systems and the ways in which they offer new perspectives on cognitive phenomena. However, we have also made reference to the competing symbolic tradition which, until recently, has been the dominant approach to cognitive modeling. Not surprisingly, many advocates of the symbolic approach have presented arguments purporting to show the inadequacy of connectionism. In the first section of this chapter we shall examine two of the most potent critiques that have been raised by representatives of the symbolic tradition. Each argues that certain crucial aspects of cognition require a symbolic approach and thus indicate intrinsic limitations of the connectionist approach. In the remainder of the chapter we shall consider connectionist responses.

Two Critiques of Connectionism

Fodor and Pylyshyn's Arguments for Symbolic Representations with Constituent Structure

Fodor and Pylyshyn (1988) begin their critique of connectionism by distinguishing between *representationalist* and *eliminativist* approaches to theorizing about cognition. Representationalists claim that the internal states of the cognitive system are "representational (or 'intentional' or 'semantic') states" that "encode states of the world"; eliminativists "dispense with such semantic notions as representation" (Fodor and Pylyshyn, 1988, p. 7).[1] After offering the distinction, Fodor

1 It is unclear who actually qualifies as an eliminativist so defined. Fodor and Pylyshyn cite John Watson's (1930) behaviorism, Patricia Churchland's (1986) neuroscience elimi-

and Pylyshyn place connectionism on the representationalist side, citing both textual evidence from connectionist publications and the fact that connectionists typically provide semantic interpretations of the activities of either single units or ensembles of units. This assignment is the foundation of Fodor and Pylyshyn's argument against connectionism, because it is structured to show that connectionist systems are inadequate *as representationalist systems*. Without the resources of a *symbolic* representational system, they maintain, one does not have an adequate representational system for modeling cognitive processes.

What is critical, for Fodor and Pylyshyn, is the linguistic character of symbolic representations. (For more than a decade, Fodor has been advocating the *language of thought* hypothesis, according to which cognitive activities require a language-like representational medium. See Fodor, 1975.) In particular, symbolic representations have a *combinatorial syntax and semantics* so that molecular representations can be formed out of constituents (atomic representations, or already composed molecular ones). Rules of composition, as well as other rules that operate on symbols, are syntactic and can be applied without regard to the semantics of the symbols; but when the time comes to provide a semantic interpretation, it is compositional in a way that mirrors the syntax. The semantics of the whole depends upon that of the parts. In chapter 1 we noted that proof procedures that are complete provide an interface between proof theory (which derives propositions from other propositions syntactically) and model theory (which focuses on whether the propositions are true, that is, on their semantics). In Dennett's terminology, the *syntactic engine* mimics a *semantic engine*. Fodor and Pylyshyn charge that connectionist systems lack a combinatorial syntax and semantics. Although individual units or coalitions of units in a connectionist system may be interpreted semantically, they cannot be built into linguistic expressions and manipulated in accord with syntactic rules. The units are not symbols, and the system is inadequate for its task of representation.

The crux of Fodor and Pylyshyn's argument, then, is that only a system with symbolic representations possessing constituent structure can adequately model cognitive processes. More specifically, they maintain that this system is a language of thought, and exhibits three features

---

nativism, and Stephen Stich's (1983) syntactic eliminativism. However, Churchland, while indeed a strong proponent of eliminativism, accepts the idea that neural states may serve a representational role; her quarrel is with the sentential or propositional approach to representation. Similarly, most connectionists regard networks as representational, but emphasize their distinctness from traditional symbolic representations.

(exhibited by conventional human languages as well) that require a combinatorial syntax and semantics.

1   The *productivity* of thought refers to the capacity to understand and produce propositions from an infinite set. Since this capacity is achieved using finite resources, recursive operations are needed; this entails a combinatorial syntax of thought.

2   The *systematicity* of thought results from an intrinsic connection between the ability to comprehend or think one thought and the ability to comprehend or think others. It is claimed, for example,[2] that anyone who can think *Joan loves the florist* can also think *the florist loves Joan*. For this to be so, "the two mental representations, like the two sentences, *must be made of the same parts*" (p. 39).

3   The *coherence* of inference involves the ability to make syntactically and semantically plausible inferences. For example, one can infer from *x is a brown cow* that *x is a cow*, or from a true conjunction (A & B) that both conjuncts are true (A is true and B is true).

Fodor and Pylyshyn contend that connectionist systems have no way of composing simple representations into more complex representations, and therefore lack these essential features. Part of their argument goes as follows. First, consider connectionist networks that have a *localist* semantic interpretation. Each representational unit is atomic, and there is just one way the units relate to one another: by means of pairwise causal connections. Thus, if **A & B** and **A** are two nodes in a network, the weight of the connection from **A & B** to **A** can be set such that activating **A & B** results in (causes) the activation of **A**. This could be viewed as a kind of inference, but the representation of *A* is not in any way part of the representation *A & B*. Any two nodes could be wired to have the same pattern of influence, for example, node **A & B** might excite node **Z**. Clearly, then, the connection is not compositional in nature, and the inference does not go through in virtue of the syntactic relation between the nodes. One unpleasant outcome, they claim, is that the inference must be built in separately for each instance of conjunction rather than by means of a rule that utilizes variables to specify the syntactic relation of inclusion. For example, the unit **B & C** must be specifically linked to unit **B** if the inference from *B & C* to *B* is to be made, just as **A & B** had to be linked to unit **A**. On this basis, Fodor and

---

2   As our small contribution to reducing the gender-typing prevalent in linguistic examples, we have adapted their actual base example, *John loves the girl*, to one with a female grammatical subject and gender-neutral grammatical object.

Pylyshyn conclude that localist connectionist systems lack the requisite resources for cognition.

Might *distributed* systems be more suitable as cognitive systems? In certain networks of this type, the units that are active in a particular representation encode features or microfeatures of the entity that is being represented. Smolensky (1987) has specifically criticized Fodor and Pylyshyn's A & B analysis as too simplistic and not relevant to distributed networks. By way of illustration, he suggests a set of *ad hoc* features for *cup of coffee* which fall into three subsets with respect to questions of combinatorial structure: a set that apply to *cup* alone (e.g., **porcelain curved surface**); a set that apply to *coffee* alone (e.g., **brown liquid**); and (importantly) a set that applies only to *cup* and *coffee* as they interact, such as **brown liquid contacting porcelain**. In Smolensky's view, the inclusion of the subsets for *cup* and *coffee* in the set for *cup of coffee* achieves the property of compositionality; but furthermore, the subset for the interaction provides additional, relevant information that would be harder to represent within the symbolic approach.

Fodor and Pylyshyn (1988, p. 19ff.) respond that this is not the right kind of composition for the purpose they have in mind. The way in which a microfeature is part of a representation of an object is not the same as the way in which one syntactic unit (e.g., an adjective) is part of a larger syntactic unit (e.g., a noun phrase). Thus, in a symbolic representation of the proposition *Joan loves the florist*, the representation of *florist* stands in a particular syntactic relationship to the rest of the proposition, such that the proposition is not confused with *the florist loves Joan*. This is not true of a distributed representation. For example, a (minimally) distributed representation of the proposition *Joan loves the florist* could be achieved in a network whose units corresponded to such concepts as *Joan*, *loves*, and *florist*; activating these three units would provide a distributed representation of the proposition. However, Fodor and Pylyshyn argue, it would be indistinguishable from the representation of *the florist loves Joan*. It would not help to add units for relationships, such as a unit for subject, for there is no straightforward way to capture the fact that it is Joan who is the subject and not the florist (that is, to compose the units hierarchically). The units are just bundled together in a relation of co-occurrence, without the structure that a syntax would provide. Fodor and Pylyshyn conclude that connectionist networks, whether localist or distributed, forfeit the benefits offered by a combinatorial syntax and semantics.

According to Fodor and Pylyshyn, the symbolic theories which they favor specify how *Joan loves the florist* and *the florist loves Joan* are constructed out of the same parts using two different applications of the same rules of composition; such a theory

> will have to go out of its way to explain a linguistic competence which embraces one sentence but not the other. And similarly, if a theory says that the mental representation that corresponds to the thought that P&Q&R has the same (conjunctive) syntax as the mental representation that corresponds to the thought that P&Q and that mental processes of drawing inference subsume mental representations in virtue of their syntax, it will have to go out of its way to explain inferential capacities which embrace the one thought but not the other. Such a competence would be, at best, an embarrassment for the theory, and at worst a refutation.
>
> By contrast, since the Connectionist architecture recognizes no combinatorial structure in mental representations, gaps in cognitive competence should proliferate arbitrarily. It's not just that you'd expect to get them from time to time; it's that, on the 'no-structure' story, *gaps are the unmarked case*. It's the *systematic* competence that the theory is required to treat as an embarrassment. But, as a matter of fact, inferential competencies are *blatantly* systematic. So there must be something deeply wrong with Connectionist architecture. (p. 49)

Following these and other arguments that an adequate representational system must be symbolic rather than connectionist, Fodor and Pylyshyn do acknowledge that the nervous system in which our symbolic representations are implemented may be a connectionist system. This might seem to be an admission that connectionism has a role to play in modeling cognition. But Fodor and Pylyshyn maintain that only the analysis at the level of symbolic processing is relevant to cognitive theorizing, and that this level is nonconnectionist. Connectionism is *merely* an account of the implementation of the symbolic representational system, and as such is not pertinent to theorizing about cognition itself. This aspect of their critique is grounded on an account of levels of organization in nature. Like most theorists, they assume that nature is comprised of entities of different sizes; smaller entities are components of larger ones. There is a causal story to be told about interactions *within* each level (e.g., about interactions among molecules, about interactions among stones and rivers, and about interactions among galaxies). But unlike many theorists, Fodor and Pylyshyn maintain that these stories are quite independent: "the story that scientists tell about the causal structure that the world has at any one of these levels may be quite different from the story that they tell about its causal structure at the next level up or down" (p. 9). Moreover, since, as Fodor has argued elsewhere (Fodor, 1974), there are many lower-level mechanisms that can perform the same higher-level function, and the same lower-level components can figure in many higher-level functions, the scientific accounts at different levels only minimally constrain each other. Thus there is no causal story to be told *between* levels. The causal story that is relevant to cognitive science, for Fodor and Pylyshyn, is a story about actions performed on symbolic representations. Since connectionism *per se* cannot provide an adequate story about actions performed on representations, but the symbolic account does, then connectionism is not a candidate theory of cognition. At best, it is a story about another level, but as such it is no more relevant to theories of cognition than are stories about molecular processes in the brain.

Fodor and Pylyshyn's views about implementation are made particularly clear in the way in which they respond to many of the arguments commonly given on behalf of connectionism (such as those discussed in chapter 2). They maintain that most of the advantages connectionist systems seem to have over symbolic systems are due entirely to the fact that symbolic systems are currently implemented on von Neumann computers. When symbolic systems are implemented in more neural-like hardware, they will exhibit the same virtues as connectionist systems. Moreover, the fact that these characteristics stem from the mode of implementation shows that they are not cognitive characteristics at all, but merely features of the implementation. For example, Fodor and Pylyshyn maintain that the time consumed by a particular cognitive process is a matter of implementation, and does not inform us as to the nature of the architecture itself:

the absolute speed of a process is a property *par excellence* of its implementation.... Thus, the fact that individual neurons require tens of miliseconds [sic] to fire can have no bearing on the predicted speed at which an algorithm will run *unless there is at least a partial, independently motivated, theory of how the operations of the functional architecture are implemented in neurons*. Since, in the case of the brain, it is not even certain that the firing of neurons is invariably the relevant implementation property (at least for higher level cognitive processes like learning and memory) the 100 step "constraint" excludes nothing. (1988, p. 55)

In particular, Fodor and Pylyshyn point out that nothing prohibits operations on symbols from being implemented in a parallel architecture and hence being performed much more rapidly than in a von Neumann computer. They apply similar arguments to other purported virtues of connectionist systems (e.g., resistance to noise and damage and use of soft constraints).

It should be noted that Fodor and Pylyshyn's *mere implementation* argument relies on some very particular assumptions about how levels of nature, and the disciplines that study them, relate to one another. Specifically, they place information-processing accounts of cognition and language at the same level as abstract accounts, such as those provided in logic or linguistic theory. The gap we left in the quote above was the following parenthetical comment: "(By contrast, the *relative* speed with which a system responds to different inputs is often diagnostic of distinct processes; but this has always been a prime empirical basis for deciding among alternative algorithms in information processing psychology)" (p. 55). Information processing accounts are not a matter of mere implementation for Fodor and Pylyshyn, but rather are aspects of the symbolic theory itself. We would point out that this exemplifies the desire on the part of Chomskian linguistics to cover the traditional territory of cognitive psychology as well as linguistics (see Abrahamsen, 1987). In contrast, many psychologists (e.g., McNeill, 1975; Marr, 1982; Rumelhart and McClelland, 1985) distinguish between abstract accounts of language as a static product (which make no reference to the real time processes that produce it) and processing accounts of behavior.

In our own interpretation of this distinction (see chapter 8), abstract accounts are the tasks of disciplines such as linguistics and logic. Both information processing and connectionist models occupy a lower level of analysis and are the tasks of such processing-oriented disciplines as cognitive psychology and artificial intelligence.[3] Neural modeling is at a third, yet lower level of biological inquiry. The neural account might be regarded as implementing the processing account, and the processing account as implementing the abstract (linguistic) account. In a multi-level account such as this, one can envisage different levels causally constraining each other without endorsing a strong reductionism (Bechtel, 1986, chapter 6); in this way the gap between abstract and neural accounts can be bridged. In contrast, Fodor and Pylyshyn have just two levels of analysis to work with. Connectionist models can, for them, be assigned only to the neural level. The processing accounts that they find acceptable are at the same level as abstract accounts (the symbolic level), and must achieve their combinatorial syntax and semantics by means of operations on symbol strings.

---

3 Although connectionist models use smaller-size units (*subsymbols*) to account for a given phenomenon than do most information processing models, this is irrelevant to determining whether they occupy the abstract or processing level of analysis. The size and nature of the units reflect choices made within that level, e.g., how deeply one must go into that level's part-whole hierarchy in order to achieve the best account of the phenomenon. As discussed in chapter 8, each level has its own part–whole hierarchy of units of analysis appropriate to that level.

The connectionist gambit is to develop processing accounts using means other than operations on symbol strings. Connectionists generally agree that their alternative means must be adequate to account for data that are suggestive of combinatorial structure in language. Furthermore, connectionists themselves have recognized a closely related problem known as the *variable binding problem*. Symbolic representations usually employ variables so that rules can be applied to various individuals in a class. In a given application, all occurrences of the same variable must be instantiated by the same individual. The challenge for connectionists is to make networks do the work that in symbolic theories is performed by means of combinatorial structures of symbol strings which include variables. Unlike Fodor and Pylyshyn, connectionists do not assume that symbolic representations are the only adequate means for doing this work; they are just the most obvious means. Nor do they agree that success at the difficult task of finding alternative means can only be regarded as "mere implementation" of the symbolic account. The connectionist goal is to achieve models that give an account of the phenomena that are handled rather well by rules but also, without additional mechanisms, give an elegant account of other phenomena as well (e.g., learning and variation). If connectionist accounts did nothing more than implement what traditional rules already do well, they probably would not be worth the effort involved in constructing them.

For connectionist replies to Fodor and Pylyshyn's critique, see Chater and Oaksford (1989), Clark (in press), Kaplan, Weaver and French (1990), and Smolensky (1987). In the following section we summarize another critique.

Pinker and Prince's Arguments for Rules

Steven Pinker and Alan Prince (1988) focus their critique not on the language of thought, but rather on children's acquisition of competence in a conventional language.[4] The traditional view, which they endorse,

---

4 Pinker and Prince remark: "Language has been the domain most demanding of articulated symbol structures governed by rules and principles and it is also the domain where such structures have been explored in the greatest depth and sophistication, within a range of theoretical frameworks and architectures, attaining a wide variety of significant empirical results. Any alternative model that either eschews symbolic mechanisms altogether, or that is strongly shaped by the restrictive nature of available elementary information processes and unresponsive to the demands of high-level functions being computed, starts off at a seeming disadvantage. Many observers thus feel that connectionism, as a radical restructuring of cognitive theory, will stand or fall depending on its ability to account for human language" (1988, p. 78).

is that rules are necessary to obtain an adequate account of the phenomena of language; 20 years ago the arguments for this position were convincing enough to turn many psychologists away from behaviorism and
into cognitive psychology. Connectionists are not generally behavio-
rists, but they have reopened the debate by seeking to model these same
phenomena of language acquisition and use by means of networks rather than rules. If these attempts are successful, the plausibility of connectionism is enhanced, and the choice between the traditional and
connectionist approaches would need to be made on other grounds.
Rumelhart and McClelland's (1986) simulation of the acquisition of the
English past tense, which we described in chapter 6, is specifically targeted at this issue:

We have, we believe, provided a distinct alternative to the view that children
learn the rules of English past-tense formation in any explicit sense. We have
shown that a reasonable account of the acquisition of past tense can be provided
without recourse to the notion of a "rule" as anything more than a *description* of
the language. We have shown that, for this case, there is no *induction problem*.
The child need not figure out what the rules are, nor even that there are rules.
The child need not decide whether a verb is regular or irregular. There is no
question as to whether the inflected form should be stored directly in the lexi-
con or derived from more general principles. There isn't even a question (as far
as generating the past-tense form is concerned) as to whether a verb form is one
encountered many times or one that is being generated for the first time. A uniform procedure is applied for producing the past-tense form in every case. The
base form is supplied as input to the past-tense network and the resulting pattern of activation is interpreted as a phonological representation of the past
form of that verb. This is the procedure whether the verb is regular or irregular, familiar or novel. (1986, p. 267)

Pinker and Prince have mounted an extensive critique of Rumelhart
and McClelland's claims. They analyze the model in detail "to determine whether the RM [Rumelhart and McClelland] model is viable as a
theory of human language acquisition – there is no question that it is a
valuable demonstration of some of the surprising things that PDP
models are capable of, but our concern is whether it is an accurate
model of children" (1988, p. 81). Their conclusion is that it is not.

Pinker and Prince's critique is long and multifaceted. We do not
agree with many of their specific claims or their overall stance, but the
paper well exemplifies its genre (that is, defense of the symbolic approach against the challenge of connectionism) and it deserves to be
read in its entirety. Perhaps the most enduring contribution will be the
broad array of linguistic analyses and acquisition data on past-tense for-

mation that were marshalled and organized by Pinker and Prince to provide a framework for criticism of the Rumelhart and McClelland model. Their own summary of their objections is as follows:

- Rumelhart and McClelland's actual explanation of children's stages of regularization of the past tense morpheme is demonstrably incorrect.
- Their explanation for one striking type of childhood speech error is also incorrect.
- Their other apparent successes in accounting for developmental phenomena either have nothing to do with the model's parallel distributed processing architecture, and can easily be duplicated by symbolic models, or involve major confounds and hence do not provide clear support for the model.
- The model is incapable of representing certain kinds of words.
- It is incapable of explaining patterns of psychological similarity among words.
- It easily models many kinds of rules that are not found in any human language.
- It fails to capture central generalizations about English sound patterns.
- It makes false predictions about derivational morphology, compounding, and novel words.
- It cannot handle the elementary problem of homophony.
- It makes errors in computing the past tense forms of a large percentage of the words it is tested on.
- It fails to generate any past tense form at all for certain words.
- It makes incorrect predictions about the reality of the distinction between regular rules and exceptions in children and in languages. (1988, p. 81)

It should be clear from the contents of this list that Pinker and Prince held the past-tense model to a higher standard of performance than it was ever intended to meet (and that no other implemented language acquisition model has met). Rumelhart and McClelland's model was not advanced as a definitive model of past-tense acquisition, but rather as a demonstration that connectionist networks can perform tasks that are usually assumed to require explicit rules. To get the demonstration underway, Rumelhart and McClelland made certain simplifications and heuristic decisions which, while reasonable, are not immutable. Most important, when they designed the model, effective learning algorithms existed only for two-layer networks. The number of developmental phenomena that they squeezed out of this architecture is impressive, but Pinker and Prince focus on what was missed instead.

We cannot discuss all of Pinker and Prince's objections here. Instead, we provide a brief portrayal of three dimensions of their argument and suggest some avenues of connectionist response. We focus first on their

argument that Rumelhart and McClelland fail to do justice to important linguistic facts, and second on their argument that the network's
behavior fails to adequately simulate human behavior. Third, we consider their claim that the shortcomings of the past tense network are not
fixable, but rather are generic failures that reflect intrinsic limitations of
parallel distributed processing networks. (Particularly at the end of the
paper, they clarify that this gloomy assessment is limited to two-layer
networks, which removes much of the punch from this third part of
their argument.)

Putative linguistic inadequacies of Rumelhart and McClelland's model   In developing their contention that Rumelhart and McClelland fail to do justice to important aspects of linguistic analysis, Pinker and Prince echo
one of Fodor and Pylyshyn's major points:

> rules are generally invoked in linguistic explanations in order to *factor* a com-
> plex phenomenon into simpler components that feed representations into one
> another. Different types of rules apply to these intermediate representations,
> forming a cascade of structures and rule components. Rules are individuated
> not only because they *compete* and mandate different transformations of the
> same input structure (such as *break-breaked/broke*), but because they apply to
> different *kinds* of structures, and thus impose a factoring of a phenomenon into
> distinct components, rather than generating the phenomena in a single step
> mapping inputs to outputs. (1988, p. 84)

We should point out that the strategy of factoring complex phenomena
into their components is not limited to linguistic theory or to rule-
based theories in general. Many advances in science, for example, have
involved working out a particular decomposition, separately analyzing
each component, and then figuring out how the components are assembled together into a functioning system. (Bechtel and Richardson, in
preparation, provide an extensive discussion of mechanistic models of
biological systems that have been obtained in this way.) Within the domain of language, both linguistic theories and connectionist theories
specify a decomposition but, by design, these decompositions are quite
different. (For example, the connectionist decomposition is intended to
be mechanistic in the sense just described, whereas a linguistic decomposition is abstract.) The fundamental question is not whether to
decompose, but rather what sort of decomposition is needed for particular purposes.

Many of Pinker and Prince's criticisms can be interpreted as arguments that Rumelhart and McClelland have invoked the wrong de-

composition. To begin with, Rumelhart and McClelland have treated past-tense formation as though it were autonomous, whereas the same principles governing past-tense formation also figure in formation of the perfect passive participle and the verbal adjective. Although there are different exceptions in each case, the similarities are sufficient to warrant a unified account. Moreover, there is a strong parallel between the three regular ways of forming the past tense (/əd/ after stems ending in alveolar stops /d/ or /t/, and elsewhere /d/ after a voiced obstruent, and /t/ after a voiceless one) and the three regular ways of forming plurals, third person singulars, possessives, etc. (/əz/ after stems ending in sibilants like /s/ and /z/, elsewhere /z/ after voiced obstruents and /s/ after voiceless ones). Pinker and Prince maintain that the similarity is due to general phonetic factors, a consideration that is lost when one develops a separate network to handle past-tense formation. Hence, in their view Rumelhart and McCllelland made the wrong sort of decomposition of linguistic knowledge.

Pinker and Prince contend that further linguistic injustice is perpetrated by the use of Wickelphones and Wickelfeatures. The first problem is that they work imperfectly; specifically, they fail to give an unambiguous encoding of all phoneme sequences, they miss generalizations such as the similarity of *slit* and *silt*, and they do not exclude phonological rules that are alien to human languages (e.g., inverting the order of the phonemes in the verb). Pinker and Prince acknowledge that Rumelhart and McClelland had themselves noted that their coding scheme was adequate to their purpose, but imperfect; however, Pinker and Prince find this research strategy somewhat alien from their own, more linguistic perspective.[5]

The Wickelfeature structure is not some kind of approximation that can easily be sharpened and refined; it is categorically the wrong kind of thing for the jobs assigned to it. At the same time, the Wickelphone or something similar is demanded by the most radically distributed forms of distributed representations, which resolve order relations (like concatenation) into unordered sets of features. Without the Wickelphone, Rumelhart and McClelland have no account about how phonological strings are to be analyzed for significant patterning. (Pinker and Prince, 1988, p. 101)

---

5 Generally, linguists strive to account for *all* of the relevant *linguistic* facts, and a single counterexample can lead to rejection of a theory. Psychologists, in contrast, are accustomed to accounting for only a *portion* of the variability in a *psychological* data set; it is the failure to predict the central tendency or pattern of results that leads to rejection of a theory. This "cultural difference" stems from differences in goals, and colors most linguistic (and even psycholinguistic) critiques of connectionism.

Pinker and Prince also point out a second problem with Wickel-phones: these units are limited to encoding phonemic information, whereas the past tense system must utilize syntactic, semantic, and morphological informaton as well. One particularly interesting example involves verbs that are derived from the nominalization of an existing verb. For example, the verb *fly out* as used in baseball is derived from the noun *fly ball* which in turn is derived from the irregular verb *fly*. Because of the intermediate nominal form, *fly out* functions like other verbs derived from nouns in that it takes a regular past tense. Thus, just as we say *he righted the boat*, we say *he flied out*, not *he flew out* (although in performance errors do occur). Pinker and Prince maintain that this is a regular feature of English grammar and thus that forma-tion of the proper past tense requires knowledge of the lexical item, not just a phonemic representation. Moreover, the regularity itself must be expressed by a rule; they claim that only via rules can we keep different bodies of information separate, and yet bring them to bear on one another when required. Rumelhart and McClelland's connectionist model is limited to encoding patterns of association between input and output representations, and therefore cannot utilize and coordinate the various kinds of abstract information that are necessary to account for linguistic competence.

There is yet another respect in which Pinker and Prince claim that the Rumelhart and McClelland model fails to respect linguistic facts: the same network learns variations within both the regular and the irregular past-tense forms, but linguistically these are quite different. The choice among the three forms of the regular past tense is based upon phonological principles, is predictable, and therefore can be expressed in general rules. The varieties of irregular stems, in contrast, at best exhibit a family resemblance structure. Their mappings onto past-tense forms are not sufficiently predictable, and must be memor-ized. The Rumelhart and McClelland model, however, makes no such principled distinction; it applies a single method to both regular and irregular verbs, extracting whatever regularities it can find.

To these specific linguistic objections, a connectionist might respond as follows. (1) The past tense was isolated because it was premature to include related phenomena in the same model. (Also, it is not obvious which linguistic generalizations should, or should not, be accounted for in terms of the same psychological mechanism or component.) (2) The decision to focus on phonological representations (at the levels of Wick-elfeatures and Wickelphones) exemplified the subsymbolic approach to modeling: phenomena at one level (e.g., acquisition of past-tense mor-phology) are best understood in terms of mechanistic models at a lower level (here, phonological features). The addition of lexical, syntactic, and other higher-level constraints might improve accuracy somewhat in a later model but is of secondary importance. (3) The particular kind of phonological representation that was chosen (context-sensitive Wickel-features) was a clever solution to the problem of representing order in a network, but more general solutions will need to be found if the connectionist program is to advance. Coarse-coding across those features worked impressively well for achieving generalization. (4) The fact that regular and irregular past-tense formation were carried out by a single mechanism is at the heart of Rumelhart and McClelland's project. Linguistic-level accounts impose a different decomposition, isolating irregulars as exceptions, but that does not determine what is appropriate in a mechanistic (processing) account. The connectionist model must be judged on such grounds as whether it generates behavior that is sufficiently similar to human data on acquisition or processing. We now turn to Pinker and Prince's second line of criticism, which addresses that question.

Putative behavioral inadequacies of Rumelhart and McClelland's model Pinker and Prince's second line of criticism involves examining in detail the operation of the Rumelhart and McClelland model and arguing that at just those crucial points where the model is thought to capture important elements of human behavior, it either fails or it succeeds for the wrong reason. First, Rumelhart and McClelland succeeded in simulating a U-shaped acquisition function, in which correct past-tense forms during Stage 1 were sometimes supplanted by overregularizations during Stage 2. Pinker and Prince attribute this result to characteristics of the input (in particular, discontinuities between Stages 1 and 2) rather than the connectionist architecture. We considered this point in some detail in chapter 6, and described recent simulations that were directed at exploring the role of type and token input frequencies. We shall not repeat that discussion here; the conclusions were that Pinker and Prince's claims are too strong (U-shaped functions can be obtained without dramatic input discontinuities), but additional simulations and child data are needed.

Pinker and Prince also consider the ability of the model to generalize to new cases, that is, the 72 test verbs that Rumelhart and McClelland presented to the model after it completed training on the initial set of 420 verbs. They interpret the poor performance on some of these test cases as indicating the basic inadequacy of connectionist models. First, they focus on the fact that the network offered no above-threshold response to six verbs (*jump, pump, soak, warm, trail,* and *glare*) and they attribute this to the fact that the network had not been trained on any sufficiently similar verbs from which it could generalize. They argue that to generalize to any new verb, not just ones similar to the training set, requires a system of rules. Roughly, morphological rules would add the past tense morpheme /d/ to the verb stem, and phonological rules would then determine which of the three phonetic variants was appropriate to the context. Second, they examine cases in which the network offered the incorrect past tense (although 91 percent of the verbs with at least one above-threshold response had the correct past-tense form as one response or the only response). They note how bizarre a few of the errors were (e.g., *tour/toureder*, *mail/membled*, and *brown/brawned*). Pinker and Prince contend that a human, treating irregulars as specially learned exceptions; would initially form regular past tenses for all new cases, regular or irregular, and thus would not make these errors. But the Rumelhart and McClelland network seems to be trying to use some of the regularities discovered in the already learned exceptions to handle new cases as well. Thus, Pinker and Prince comment,

Well before it has mastered the richly exemplified regular rule, the pattern-associator appears to have gained considerable confidence in certain incorrectly-grasped, sparsely exemplified patterns of feature-change among the vowels. This implies that a major "induction problem" – latching onto the productive patterns and bypassing the spurious ones – is not being solved successfully....

What we have here is not a model of the mature system. (1988, p. 125)

Returning to their task of contrasting the model's behavior to that of children, Pinker and Prince also work through the model's performance on subregularities (such as different classes of irregular verbs) and its simulation of children's blends (erroneous past-tense forms that include both a vowel change and suffixization, e.g., *come/camed*). The discussion is too detailed to summarize here, but the general theme is the same: rather than focusing on the considerable extent to which the model reproduces phenomena observed in children, they focus on the discrepancies that were duly reported by Rumelhart and McClelland as points to consider if an improved version of the model were to be designed.

Do the inadequacies reflect inherent limitations of PDP networks? Pinker and Prince argue that, although some of the specific discrepancies between predicted and observed performance might be eliminated by tinkering with the existing past-tense network, for the most part they are due to inherent limitations of PDP networks (by which they mean, it turns out, two-layer networks). Connectionists would agree that the work Pinker and Prince wanted the model to do (e.g., incorporating lexical constraints) would require a more elaborate architecture than the one that was available to Rumelhart and McClelland.

Advances in connectionist modeling during the last decade have yielded a variety of elaborations that might be incorporated in an improved model. Hidden layers now provide additional computational power (and can learn using the back-propagation technique proposed by Rumelhart, Hinton, and Williams, 1986a, 1986b). These additional layers can be viewed as imposing particular factorings (decompositions) of the information in the input layer. (This is clearly illustrated by Hinton's (1986) kinship network. As discussed in chapter 6, different hidden units took on specialized tasks such as representing the generation of a particular family member.) Also, structured networks provide ways to utilize and interconnect multiple subnetworks (e.g., Hummel, Biederman, Gerhardstein, and Hilton, 1988; and Touretzky and Hinton, 1988; the latter model is discussed later in this chapter).[6] Using them in an improved model would facilitate the incorporation of nonphonological sources of constraint. However, new network architectures will not help with certain other desired improvements. For example, it is important to know the actual input to the child's system, taking into account possible roles for comprehension and filtering mechanisms, but no one knows how to do this (including Pinker and Prince, who rely solely on observed frequencies of production in their claims concerning appropriate input to the past-tense system).

In the end, Pinker and Prince acknowledge that more powerful connectionist architectures might be adequate to produce a model that meets all of their criteria; but then they dismiss this important concession in two ways. First, they note that no one has yet built such a model, so its success is hypothetical. Second, they echo Fodor and Pylyshyn in asserting that if someone did build the model, it "may be nothing more than an implementation of a symbolic rule-based account" (1988, p. 182). They express doubt that the model would diverge enough from mere implementation of standard grammars to "call for a revised understanding of language" (1988, p. 183), and exhibit little curiosity as to whether they are correct in this negative assessment. Therein lies a difference that may count for more than the arguments advanced from each camp: for connectionists, but not for

6 These subnetworks can be regarded as modules in a weak sense of that term; cf. the modules of Fodor (1984), which function independently.

their critics, the properties of networks elicit the curiosity and excite-
ment that prompt entry into unknown territory. In the case of the
past-tense network, much of the appeal was in the potential for a unified account of rule-like and exceptional cases that would provide a
mechanistic explanation for abstract linguistic phenomena. Pinker and
Prince's criticisms accurately target some specific deficiencies of the
model, but do not diminish this appeal.

Connectionist Responses

In the remainder of this chapter, we consider three kinds of global
responses that connectionists can give to critiques that insist on the
need for symbolic representations and rules. We refer to them as the
approximationist, compatibilist, and *externalist* approaches.[7]

The Approximationist Approach

Description of the approach   The first, most radical approach is to view
connectionist models as providing the most detailed, accurate account
of cognitive performance. On this view, symbolic models are more abstract (perhaps idealized) accounts that lose some of the detail, but provide an efficient means of stating the regularities that remain. That is, a
symbolic model *approximates* a connectionist model and provides a less
detailed account of performance than does the connectionist model.
This approach has been most explicitly formulated by Smolensky
(1988), in the part of his "Proper Treatment of Connectionism" in
which he contrasts *symbolic* (i.e., rule-based) and *subsymbolic* (i.e., PDP)
models of what he refers to as the *subconceptual* level of analysis. His entire argument is considerably more complex than this, and is worth
reading in its entirety. For example, he distinguishes between intuitive
processing, which he emphasizes and assigns to the subconceptual
level, and conscious application of rules, which he assigns to the *conceptual* level. Symbolic models can give an exact account of conscious rule
application but, he contends, a subsymbolic account is required to
obtain an exact account of intuitive processing (which is akin to the
nonpropositional approach to knowledge, emphasizing pattern recognition, presented in chapter 5). The levels can be crossed in either direction, but if so, only an approximation will be achieved. Hence,

---

7   Distinctions related to our approximationist/compatibalist distinction have been advanced by others. See Derthick and Plaut (1986) and Barnden (1988).

Smolensky allows for the idea that conscious rule processing does exist, and is only approximated by a subsymbolic model; however, he does not put language processing at this level. For language, he would say that it is symbolic theorists who are doing the approximating, and connectionists who will, someday, provide the exact account. This is consistent with the idea that language is not *exactly* compositional, recursive, productive, systematic, or coherent and that therefore one would not want a model that *exactly* exhibits these properties. We return to Smolensky's treatment of conscious rule processing in the last section of this chapter.

The approximationist approach is also advocated by Rumelhart and McClelland. One of the considerations that led Rumelhart and his colleagues to distributed connectionist models in the first place was a recognition that the cognitive system displays variability, flexibility, and subtlety in its behavior which was not being adequately captured in traditional rule-based systems (see the first section of Rumelhart, Smolensky, McClelland, and Hinton, 1986, in *PDP:14*). Traditional rule systems are *brittle*, and can be made to capture these detailed phenomena only awkwardly (e.g., by having a separate rule for each "exception") or by introducing numerical parameters (e.g., strength parameters on rules that can produce certain kinds of variability). Rules and symbols have their most obvious use in building higher-level models that abstract away from many of the detailed phenomena exhibited in behavioral data. When the details are not needed these are the models of choice (at least for description); but to model the actual mechanisms of cognition, more detailed, less brittle models are needed. Connectionism provides one avenue of approach, which is to use devices other than explicit rules to build the mechanistic account. In Rumelhart and McClelland's terminology, the behavior of the cognitive system is not *rule-governed*, but rather is only (approximately) *rule-described*. The behavior is actually governed by a unified mechanism that operates at a somewhat lower level than traditional rules (Smolensky's subconceptual level; Rumelhart and McClelland's microstructure level). As expressed by Rumelhart (1984):

It has seemed to me for some years now that the "explicit rule" account of language and thought was *wrong*. It has seemed that there must be a *unified* account in which the so-called *rule-governed* and *exceptional* cases were dealt with by a unified underlying process – a process which produces rule-like and rule exception behavior through the application of a single process ... both the rule-like and non-rule-like behavior is a product of the interaction of a very large number of "sub-symbolic" processes. (1984, p. 60)

Rumelhart and McClelland (1986) in *PDP:18* elaborate:

> An illustration of this view, which we owe to Bates (1979), is provided by the honeycomb. The regular structure of the honeycomb arises from the interaction of forces that wax balls exert on each other when compressed. The honeycomb can be described by a rule, but the mechanism which produces it does not contain any statement of this rule. (1986, p. 217)

It should be noted that some rule-based theorists have chosen an alternative avenue of approach to building more detailed mechanistic models (e.g., Holland et al., 1986). They have retained rules, but reduced their brittleness by introducing numerical parameters, equations that govern the activation of rules, and soft constraints among rules. Often the rules are made more detailed as well (one might call them micro-rules). These low-level mechanistic rules systems bear about the same relation to traditional rule-based accounts as do connectionist systems; that is, the traditional rules are more abstract, approximate statements of regularities in the mechanistic system.

Preliminary evidence   The plausibility of the approximationist approach is supported by connectionist simulations, which can accomplish tasks that would seem to require the use of rules and symbolic representations. We have already encountered some exemplars of this research strategy. First, the word recognition model in chapter 4 (McClelland and Rumelhart, 1981; Rumelhart and McClelland, 1982) exhibited emergent behavior that seemed to follow rules that were not explicitly encoded in the system. For example, the system behaved differently with nonwords that met orthographic constraints of English than with those that did not, even though it had no explicit rules encoding those constraints. Second, the past-tense acquisition model discussed in chapter 6 (Rumelhart and McClelland, 1986, in *PDP:18*) was directly targeted at the goal of obtaining rule-like behavior without the use of rules. The most convincing evidence, however, would come from a network that could carry out syntactic processing. The sentences of a natural language clearly exhibit constituent structure and a combinatorial syntax; a nonrule-based system that could generate this structure by some means would be adjudged to at least equal the capacities of a rule-based system. In what sense the system would thereby exhibit Fodor and Pylyshyn's features of productivity, systematicity, and inferential coherence is a less straightforward question, which we shall not pursue here.

We are not aware of any connectionist system that can process a sub-

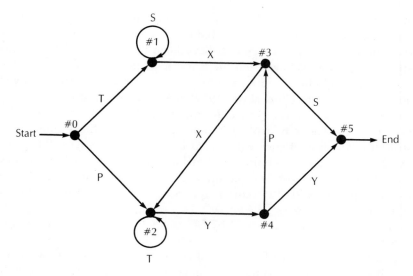

Figure 7.1   Reber's (1967) finite state grammar. States are labeled by numerals, and transition arcs by letters. A grammatical sentence can be generated by traversing a path from "Start" to "End". Each transition produces a letter, such that a string is sequentially generated. From D. Servan-Schreiber, A. Cleeremans, and J. L. McClelland (1988) Encoding sequential structure in simple recurrent networks, Technical Report CMU-CS-88-183, Carnegie Mellon University, p. 6. Reprinted with permission.

stantial subset of a natural language such as English. This is a major undertaking, and it is too early in the development of connectionism to accomplish it. There are, however, attempts to deal with more limited, tractable language-processing tasks. We shall consider one of these in some detail: Servan-Schreiber, Cleeremans, and McClelland's (1988) network for processing strings generated by a finite state grammer. What is noteworthy about this network is that it performs a task that is economically described in terms of (finite state) rules, but the network does not explicitly use rules to achieve its performance.

A recurrent network for a finite state grammar The grammar that Servan-Schreiber et al. used for most of their experiments was developed by Reber (1967) and is shown in figure 7.1. It can be seen that the grammar specifies eight different states (the six numbered nodes as well as **Start** and **End**). A transition is made from one state to another by traversing one of the arcs that leads away from the current state; in the initial version, each transition was assigned a probability of 0.5. A series of such choices specifies a path from **Start** to **End**. Grammatical strings, such as *TSSXS* or *PVPS*, are generated by recording the sequence of labels that are encountered in traversing an entire path. Note that the labels could just as well have been words, in which case the string *PVPS* might have been the English sentence *Children have children nowadays*. The limitations of finite state grammars are well known, due in good part to Chomsky's (1957) evaluation of different classes of automata as devices for generating different classes of languages. For example, they do not explicitly capture the hierarchical constituent structure which is of such concern to Fodor and Pylyshyn.[8] They do, however, generate an infinite set of strings (if loops are included); they are rule-governed; and they exhibit a property that presents a challenge for recognition tasks: the same letter can be generated from different states of the network.

In the recognition task used by Servan-Schreiber et al., the system was presented with a string letter by letter; for each current (test) letter it had to predict which letter would come next in the string (actually, which *two* letters could come next, since there were always two equally probable possibilities which were randomly sampled). To make an accurate prediction, the system must use more information than it is currently given; that is, it needs to know not only what letter has been presented as the test letter, but also what node in the path has been reached. If the test letter is *S*, that node could be either node **#1** or node **#5**. One way to distinguish indirectly between these nodes is to examine the preceding context in the string. Suppose the system is being presented with *TSSXS* and the current test letter is the second *S*; we shall indicate this by the notation *TSSXS*, and refer to it as the third pass on trial *TSSXS*. Given that the preceding context is *TS*, the finite state device must have been at node **#1** when it generated that *S*. But two passes later, when the test letter is once again *S* but now at *TSSXS*, the preceding context is *TSSX*; the node could only be **#5**. The prediction regarding the next letter will be quite different in these two cases (*S* or *X* versus *End*). What Servan-Schreiber et al. did was to build a connectionist network that was able to carry out the prediction task by making use of preceding context as a proxy for the node itself. As we shall see, a network with this capability can, to some extent, deal with contingencies between nonadjacent elements of the string. Parsing natural language sentences requires this ability; for example, the sub-

---

8   More elaborate finite state grammars have been suggested, however, that have devices such as memory buffers; these *augmented transition network grammars* not only build a constituent structure, but are as powerful as transformational grammars. See Kaplan, (1975) for an introduction.

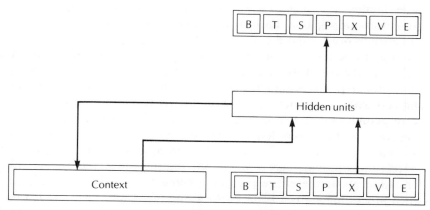

Figure 7.2   Servan-Schreiber et al.'s (1988) recurrent network for predicting
successive letters in a string generated by Reber's (1967) finite state grammar. From D.
Servan-Schreiber, A. Cleeremans, and J. L. McClelland (1988) Encoding sequential
structure in simple recurrent networks, Technical Report CMU-CS-88–183, Carnegie
Mellon University, p. 7. Reprinted with permission.

ject and verb must agree even if there is an intervening relative clause.
Nevertheless, Servan-Schreiber et al.'s investigation must be recognized as a preliminary endeavor to produce just one of the many capabilities needed to process natural language.

The main challenge they faced was designing the network in such a
way that it would bring preceding inputs to bear on the way a current
input is processed. Most connectionist network architectures cannot do
this; to overcome this limitation Servan-Schreiber et al. experimented
with a specialized architecture, the *recurrent network*. This architecture
was suggested by Elman (1988, 1989), and is a variation on Jordan's
(1986b) sequential network. The specific network used by Servan-
Schreiber et al. is shown in figure 7.2. In part it is an ordinary three-
layer feedforward network, in which the input and output layers are set
up with an identical localist encoding of the letters and of the special
symbols *Start/Begin* (unit **B**) and *End* (unit **E**). The novel part is a
special subset of input units (the *context units*). These do not receive
external input; rather, each hidden unit sends its activation to one
context unit as well as sending activation forward to the output units.
The result is that the hidden layer's construal of the input presented
at time t is available to it as part of the input at time $t + 1$. Exactly
what is encoded in the hidden units depends to some extent on their
number; most of the experiments used either 3 or 15 hidden units.

The network's global task is to figure out what is systematic in the large number of strings to which it is exposed during a learning phase using back-propagation. Each string is presented one letter at a time, in left-to-right order from the *Start/Begin* symbol to the last letter. Thus, a string of *n* letters is presented as a series of *n* + *1* training steps. At each step, the specific task is to predict what can come next. A typical successful step will begin with the activation of exactly one input unit and end with substantial activation of exactly two output units – those corresponding to the two letters that the network judges to be possible successors to the current letter. (The only other type of successful step involves predicting the *End* symbol when appropriate.) Because the context units provide part of the input, and they do so recursively, information about the entire preceding context is potentially available when processing a given letter in the string (although it is degraded to some degree).

To explore the behavior of this type of network, Servan-Schreiber et al. carried out several studies, which differed in procedural details and particularly in the nature of the training set: (1) 200,000 strings that were randomly generated from the grammar in figure 7.1 with *no restrictions* on length; (2) 21 of the 43 strings that could be generated from that grammar with *length restricted* to 3–8 letters; (3) a subset of the strings from (1) which could be generated from a simplified grammar that lacked node **#0** and its two arcs, with the purpose of examining the hidden units at different points in the *learning process*; (4) strings for which information needed to be preserved across an *embedded sequence*. Fifteen hidden units were standard, but the effects of varying this factor were examined in studies (1) and (4).

Studies (1)–(3) yielded the following picture:

(a) Early in training the network learns to focus on *letters* and makes its predictions on that basis (ignoring position in the sequence). For example, after 100 epochs the network in study (3) has almost identical patterns of hidden unit activation when the current letter is *S*, regardless of whether the arc was the one leading back to node **#1** or to node **#5**. The predictions on the output units regarding the next letter are a composite of the arcs leading from these two nodes; that is, the most active output units are those that predict *S* and *X* (appropriate for node **#1**) and *End* (appropriate for node **#5**); there is also one inappropriate prediction (*V*). The context units have unstable weights during this period and are more or less ignored.

(b) After considerably more training (e.g., 700 epochs in study (3)), arcs are distinguished. For example, the *S* leading to node **#1** produces a different hidden layer pattern from the S leading to node #5. Thus, the context units are now being utilized systematically; however, the network is still working at improving its predictions and does not always see the connection between different arcs leading to the same node.

(c) Finally, the network makes the appropriate predictions on the output layer, as though it now knows what node of the finite state grammar has been reached and what arcs lead from it. The number of epochs required was not reported for study (3). For study (1), which used the complete version of the grammar, there were 200, 000 training trials. However, the best run with 15 hidden units required only 20,000 trials to meet a rather weak criterion of success; the best run with three hidden units required 60,000 trials to meet the same criterion. In both cases the network continued to make useful changes during the additional training, such as sharpening the activation patterns on the output units.

It is useful to characterize this final phase of learning in more detail. Servan-Schreiber et al. used the method of cluster analysis to get a close look at what information was being encoded in the hidden units. This method extracts regularities in the activation patterns across the hidden units that occur for different letter sequences, and uses them to construct a tree structure representation that clusters together those sequences with similar hidden unit patterns. In study (1), just three hidden units were sufficient to achieve a separate cluster of letter sequences for each of the nodes #1 through #5. That is, from the seven input letter units and three context units the hidden units condensed the most economical possible encoding of the 20,000 training patterns for carrying out the task of prediction: they abstracted out a close approximation to the nodes of the grammar. From a symbolic perspective, this network did just the right thing (although it took a painfully long time to do it).

Given that a network with three hidden units could learn to emulate the grammar closely, Servan-Schreiber et al. wondered what a network with excess resources would do. They ran the same study on a network with 15 hidden units, and obtained a much more complex cluster analysis. There were more levels of clustering, more clusters at a given level, and the only nodes of the grammar that corresponded to distinct clusters were those for nodes #4 and #5. The other nodes had been divided according to the arcs leading into them (that is, the identity of the current letter), even though that information was not needed to make an accurate prediction once it had been used to help identify the current node. For example, the cluster for arc T leading to node **#1** was in a completely different part of the tree than the cluster for arc S leading to node **#1**. Lower levels of clustering captured even more detailed information about the path that had led to the current test letter. For example, sequences ending in $SSXXV\underline{V}$ were in one small cluster, those ending in $VPXV\underline{V}$ were in another, and those two clusters were combined into a slightly larger cluster; at the next level these were combined with a cluster ending in $TV\underline{V}$, and at a higher level this was part of the large cluster corresponding to node **#5**. Similarly detailed results were obtained with the restricted-length sequences in study (2); fairly high-level clusters in that network were based not only on the node and the current letter but also on whether the letter had occurred early or late in the sequence. This permitted the network to cut back its prediction to a single next letter when length restrictions ruled out the other letter from that node. For example, if node **#3** were reached by the sequence $TSXXYP$, only the choice of S would yield a complete sequence within the limit of eight characters, but if it had been reached by the sequence $TXXYP$, the choice of X would also be legitimate.

What we learn from this is that feedback about the accuracy of prediction, delivered by means of back-propagation, is only one influence on the development of the network. The hidden units will tend to encode as much detail as possible about the patterns that are fed to it through the input units, even though the weights are not being tuned to enhance this activity. It will also make moderate abstractions that are adequate to the task for which it is being trained. Only when resources are scarce will it make the most parsimonious (highest-level) abstractions, and exhibit behavior that is similar to that of the most obvious rule-based system that would perform the same task. When there are more hidden units than necessary, they will be used to produce behavior that is more elaborate than that of a traditional rule system; in this event, the rule system only approximates the network. The outputs themselves may be identical for the two types of systems, but the network will carry out more extensive processing to arrive at the output. (In fact, even the network with three hidden units weakly encoded limited information about the preceding context in subclusters within four of its five node-equivalent clusters.)

Since we are attempting to model human cognitive systems, this makes the following questions quite salient: how detailed are the memory traces of particular acts of processing that we retain? To what extent are regularities extracted in addition to, or instead of, the most detailed traces? How parsimoniously is this done (i.e., do the regularities tend to be computed at the highest possible level of abstraction)?

Are the regularities encoded as separate abstractions (the rules approach) or integrally with more detailed information (the network approach)? How much exposure to what range of exemplars is needed to achieve a reasonably well-functioning system? Traditional models tend to emphasize the extraction of regularities, but there is a class of nontraditional models that retain a maximum of detail instead (the exemplar models of Medin and Schaffer, 1978) which receive some support in human data. The results of Servan-Schreiber et al. make it clear that networks "prefer" detail, but can also be pushed to generalize. They generate *rule-describable* (not *rule-governed*) outputs by means of hidden-layer representations that, depending upon the input and the number of units, can range from extremely detailed to quite parsimonious (approximating rule systems). To the extent that human systems utilize more detail than seems necessary, the plausibility of models that can do likewise is enhanced.

This leads to the broader issue of the extent to which the "mental grammar" is like the symbolic grammars proposed within Chomskian linguistics. Possibly, a grammar is best regarded as a very economical way for a linguist to describe certain (nonquantitative) regularities in the sentences that people produce and understand. The mechanisms that produce and comprehend sentences might have a very different architecture, and utilize detail that would be excessive in a grammar. We like to think of *linguistic competence* as one of many possible levels of description of linguistic functioning, in which most aspects of the functioning itself have been abstracted out; the products of that functioning remain, and have regularities that the grammar describes (see Abrahamsen, 1987 and in press).[9] In this context, it is better for a psychological model to be approximated by a grammar than to incorporate a grammar, and for the approximation to be a close one only at a general level of description. In fact, even Fodor and Pylyshyn's features of productivity, systematicity, and inferential coherence may overstate the properties of the mechanisms that process language. For example, they profess surprise at the idea that a person could understand the sentence *Joan loves the florist* but not *The florist loves Joan* (a failure of systematicity). Yet, children exhibit a variety of asymmetries that indicate incomplete systematicity; they are most evident when there are differences in plausibility or in ease of mapping onto a visible state of affairs (Huttenlocher and Strauss, 1968; and Strohner and Nelson, 1974). Adults will not reject the less favored sentences, but often show

9   This idea was developed in conversation with S.-Y. Kuroda, who would not necessarily endorse this precise version.

processing time differences that correspond to developmental differences (e.g., H. Clark, 1972). As we have already stated above, much of
the problem comes from placing insufficient distance between the
linguistic and processing accounts.

If the connectionist approach is viewed as promising, certain challenges must be faced. First, although the network with 15 hidden units
is very sensitive to details about the preceding part of the sequence, it is
sensitive in a fuzzy way. There is no explicit encoding of what each
subcluster has in common; there are no separate representations that
can be accessed and operated upon with precision. What the network
knows can only be discovered indirectly, by devising tests and observing its patterns of activation. It may be that humans are fuzzy in the
same way; if so, fuzziness is a virtue for accuracy of simulation (but a
disadvantage for ease of simulation). Second, the network requires a
huge number of training trials. We do not really know how much exposure, and what kind of exposure, humans require in a domain in
order to master it. It seems likely, however, that humans would have
required substantially less training than the network. Reber's (1967)
subjects, asked to learn 20 strings from the finite state grammar, did so
within a single experimental session and could then generalize to new
strings with 73.5 percent accuracy. The network, in contrast, required
2,000 epochs to learn 21 strings in study 3. Possibly humans have some
advantage which, if better understood, could be applied to design of
more realistic network models. For example, the fact that the subjects
already knew English may be relevant. This difference between network and human performance would be a more immediate problem if
the studies were less exploratory. Third, Servan-Schreiber et al. limited their explorations to a very simple finite-state grammar. Few
connectionists would wish to argue that an unaugmented finite-state
grammar provides a realistic model of human language, and a good deal
of development work remains to be done on connectionist modeling of
language processing.

A key point about Servan-Schreiber et al.'s investigation is that the
recurrent network architecture permitted the network to use information about already processed parts of a sequence to influence the
processing of current input. Without the use of stacks or registers as
memory devices, which the traditional symbolic system would utilize
for this task, the network retains nonlocal information about preceding
context in a sequence. The representation is fuzzy, as noted above, but
is good enough to support very closely drawn distinctions. Dealing
with sequence (whether spatial or temporal) has been one of the more
difficult problems in connectionist modeling; for example, Rumelhart

and McClelland's past-tense simulation (chapter 6) used Wickelfeatures in part as a means of getting around this problem. The results of Servan-Schreiber et al. are intriguing as an alternative strategy for dealing with sequences.

These investigators carried out a final study to push the recurrent network approach even further with respect to the issue of representing sequences. For study (4) they designed a more complex network, in which the entire network in figure 7.1 served the role of an embedded clause. The grammar had two major paths. In one, the first arc was T, followed by the embedded clause, and finally by another T (contingent on the first T). The other was similar, except that the first and last arcs were P. To carry out the prediction task properly for the last letter, the network had to retain some encoding of the first letter by means of the context units. As it turned out, this task was difficult but not impossible. If the transition probabilities on the arcs were set somewhat *differently* for the T-embedded clause (0.6) than for the P-embedded clause (0.4), the network could perform fairly well on embedded strings of 3–4 letters. For strings of seven or more letters (combined), however, there were almost as many wrong choices as correct choices (as well as a number of no-choice responses). If the transition probabilities were *identical* in the two clauses, moreover, the network could generate only no-choice responses even after 2,400,000 training trials. Servan-Schreiber et al. argue that language in fact exhibits enough statistical asymmetry that the case of identical probabilities may not be true to life and therefore humans need not be able to handle embedding in the case of symmetric probabilities.

This network's limited ability to deal with constituent structure (including embedding) is far from sufficient to satisfy Fodor and Pylyshyn, it is safe to surmise. Connectionists are still discovering what their models can and cannot do, and Servan-Schreiber et al.'s application of Elman's (1988) architecture is an informative contribution to this preliminary phase of investigation. The general strategy of these and other approximationists is clear. They seek to emulate the performance of symbolic systems using patterns of connectivity rather than symbolic rules and representations. The network approach facilitates capturing subtle distinctions that can be made only awkwardly in a traditional symbolic model. The connectionist's goal is to obtain a model which, by capturing these distinctions, provides a more accurate model of actual human performance than traditional symbolic models. We have suggested that it is the discrepancies that provide the best argument for pursuing connectionist models; if the approximation were too close there would be too little to gain.

The Compatibilist Approach

In contrast to Rumelhart and McClelland's approximationist position, some connectionists maintain that humans do carry out explicit symbolic processing for some purposes. On this view, complex reasoning and problem-solving seem inexplicable except by positing symbols that are systematically manipulated by rules. David Touretzky is one of the strongest advocates of this approach. Touretzky and Hinton (1988) wrote that, while accepting the relevance of network models that do not use explicit rules,

we do not believe that this removes the need for a more explicit representation of rules in tasks that more closely resemble serial, deliberate reasoning. A person can be told an explicit rule such as "i before e except after c" and can then apply this rule to the relevant cases. (pp. 423–4)

Unlike traditional symbolic theorists, however, these investigators seek to implement the explicit rules in a connectionist network and maintain that crucial benefits accrue as a result of the connectionist implementation. We will call this the *compatibilist approach*. Dyer (in press, p. 11) well describes the appeal of pursuing this approach (although he is not a "pure" compatibilist as is Touretzky):

What we currently appear to have is a situation in which subsymbolic, distributed processing models exhibit massive parallelism, graceful error degradation, robust fault tolerance, and general adaptive learning capabilities, while symbol/rule based systems exhibit powerful reasoning, structural and inferential capabilities. If we could embed symbol representations and structure-manipulating operations within a distributed, subsymbolic architecture, then very powerful, massively parallel, fault tolerant high-level reasoning/planning systems could be created.

Perhaps the clearest way to differentiate the approximationist and compatibilist approaches is that the approximationist works from the bottom up. The usual strategy is to present a series of training patterns to the network and to observe the regularities that the network extracts. Any attempt to build explicit rule processing into the system is avoided. In contrast, the compatibilist works from the top down, beginning with a rule processing account and designing a network that will implement those rules. To date compatibilists have tended to engineer their own networks to insure that the desired rules are implemented rather than allowing the network to construct its own solutions.

One type of system that uses symbols and explicit rules is the *pro-*

duction system (*PS*), which we have already introduced in several chapters. In a PS, symbolic expressions are manipulated by production rules (often referred to as *productions*). Each rule has the form *If A then B* where A is a condition and B is an action. The condition side specifies what expressions must be in *working memory* (*WM*) in order for the rule to fire. The action side specifies which expressions should be moved in (or out) of WM when the rule does fire. Consider, for example:

$$\textbf{(FAB) (FCD)} \longrightarrow \; + \textbf{(GAB)} + \textbf{(PDQ)} - \textbf{(FCD)} \qquad \text{Rule 1}$$

This specifies that if **(FAB)** and **(FCD)** are both in working memory, **(GAB)** and **(PDQ)** should be added and **(FCD)** should be deleted. In a realistic PS, the symbolic expressions are meaningful: some of them are goals and subgoals, which direct the activity of the system towards accomplishing a task, and others are more directly task-related (e.g., numerals if the task is multiplication). The basic operations of the system are the same even for meaningless expressions like those in Rule 1, however: finding a rule that matches some of the current contents of WM (on its condition side), and executing the rule by making the changes to WM that are specified on its action side. Hence, the basic components of a PS are (1) a list of production rules of the form condition-action; and (2) a working memory that serves as a "blackboard," driving the selection of rules and recording the results of executing them.

Touretzky and Hinton (1988) wished to show that they could achieve a connectionist implementation of a PS. As compatibilists, their goal was to build a system that could actually use rules to manipulate symbols, in contrast to the approximationist goal of building a system that generates appropriate behavior without using symbols or rules. Given their goal of demonstration, it was adequate to their purposes to implement a system that was formally a PS but did not simulate any human task. In chapter 2 we introduced their symbolic expressions: meaningless triples such as **(GAB)** formed from a symbol vocabulary of 25 letters. We also described how they achieved a distributed representation of the triples by means of the ingenious method of coarse coding, and will not repeat that discussion here. The first version of their system, DCPS1 (Distributed Connectionist Production System 1) manipulated triples like **(GAB)** by means of rules like Rule 1. The actual implementation, however, has a very different character than a traditional PS. It is quite complex (they state that it is one of the largest connectionist systems yet constructed), and the unfamiliarity of its

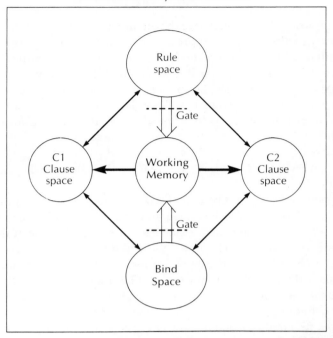

Figure 7.3 The five components of the complete version of Touretzky and Hinton's (1988) Distributed Connectionist Production System (DCPS2). From D. S. Touretzky and G. E. Hinton (1988) A distributed connectionist production system, *Cognitive Science*, 12, page 427. Reprinted with permission.

architecture makes it difficult to characterize. While we offer an overview of their system, we encourage readers to consult the paper to get a more direct and detailed sense of Touretzky and Hinton's impressive engineering.

DCPS has five major components, as sketched in figure 7.3. The internal structure and functioning of each component, as well as the inter-component relationships, are quite unlike a traditional PS. As will become apparent, even the components that have familiar names (*rule space* and *working memory*) serve somewhat different functions here. For the most part, DCPS operates as a Boltzmann machine (a type of interactive network that asymmetrically iterates its computations until an energy minimum is reached; see chapter 2). Another unfamiliar feature is that, except for the *rule space*, each component has a large number of units that provide a fully distributed representation of symbolic expressions by means of coarse coding. For example, in this connectionist version of working memory (WM), there are 2,000 binary "receptor" units (units that take activations of 0 or 1) that coarse-code triples such as (**GAB**). At a given time, dozens of WM units are active; with an average of 28 units in the receptive field of a given triple, several triples will thereby be active in this coarse-coded fashion. Which triples are active constrains which rule can next be selected for execution.

The representation of the rules themselves involves all five components (although *bind space* is needed only in DCPS2 and will therefore be ignored at present.) *Rule space* is essentially a switching station that puts together appropriate sets of connections to other components to implement each rule. Each rule is assigned to its own "clique" of 40 units in rule space. The units within a clique differ somewhat in their individual patterns of connection with units in other components; therefore, they encode the rule collectively rather than redundantly. This "semidistributed" encoding lies somewhere between fully distributed (like the coarse coded representations in WM) and fully symbolic (like the list of rules in a traditional PS).[11] If most of the units in a clique are active when the system has stabilized, that rule will fire. Inhibitory connections are used to assure that only one rule will win the competition (a "winner-take-all" scheme; see Feldman and Ballard, 1982).

The "clique" of units in rule space can be thought of as simply naming or indexing the rule. Figure 7.4 shows how just one of the various rules (Rule 1) is parceled out among the spaces. Each of the condition-side triples is represented in one of two *clause spaces*, and the rule's actions are carried out in WM. At the beginning of processing, the entire contents of working memory are copied into each clause space by means of excitatory one-way connections from each of the 2,000 units in WM to the corresponding units in C1 and C2. This ensures that all of the contents of WM are available for comparison to all of the rules when computation ensues. The rule that comes closest to finding both its first and second triple (in C1 and C2 respectively) wins. Like the rule space (but unlike WM), the clause spaces have inhibitory connections among their units; these are carefully calibrated to assure that only about 28 units will end up active by the end of processing (i.e., the number needed to pick out one triple). Hence, computation between the rule and clause spaces narrows attention to just two triples in clause space without disturbing WM, and these serve to activate the appropriate rule.

11 On p. 462 Touretzky and Hinton explain why they use semidistributed representations in this version of DCPS, and discuss prospects for fully distributed representations in a future version. The difficulty has to do with the fact that rules can be very similar on the condition side but very dissimilar on the action side.

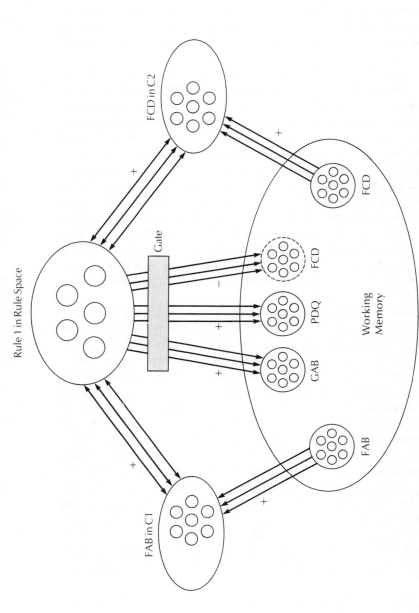

Figure 7.4 The representation of Rule 1 across four spaces of units in Touretzky and Hinton's (1988)DCPS1. Only a few of the 2,000 different units in working memory are shown; these are used to coarse code the triples specified in the rule. Each rule is semidistributed across a clique of 40 units in rule space. The figure illustrates that FAB and FCD are activated in working memory at the beginning of processing. By the end of processing, FAB is active in clause space 1(C1), FCD is active in clause space 2 (C2), and Rule 1 is active in rule space. When the gate is opened, the triples on the left side of Rule 1 become excited (GAB and PDQ) or inhibited (FCD) in working memory.

To explain this processing in a bit more detail: excitatory connections between rule space and each clause space are wired such that as units representing a triple in a clause space become active, they activate a rule with that triple in its antecedent. These connections are bidirectional, so that as rule units become active, they send additional activations to the units in clause space that satisfy their antecedents. The effect is that the system acts as a constraint satisfaction device, where the constraints are the pattern of activation in WM (as copied into the clause spaces), the triples that are on the condition side of the various rules, and the inhibitory activity in the rule and clause spaces. By the time the system settles, there should be one active rule; the first triple in that rule should be active (coarse-coded) in C1, and the second triple should be active in C2. None of these has priority; the run is initiated by the contents of WM, and the rule that best matches WM should emerge (in rule space) along with the separate encodings of its clauses (in clause space). The gate from rule space to WM is then opened and the system carries out the actions specified in the winning rule. This will alter the contents of WM, setting the stage for a different rule to become active on the next round.[12] (The gates in figure 7.3 regulate these phases, and are a non-Boltzmann-like addition to an otherwise parallel processing system. The authors argue that gated connections are, however, biologically realistic.) The performance of this system appears at least promising; one sequence of 1,000 rule firings was carried out without error (using a six-rule loop). However, detailed data were not provided.

We have not yet mentioned the *bind space* in figure 7.3. Variable binding (see above, p. 217) has been a troublesome problem for connectionism; either it must be directly solved, or mechanisms of equivalent effect must be developed. It is encountered when rules include variables, such as:[13]

$$(\mathbf{xAB})\,(\mathbf{xCD}) \longrightarrow\; +\,(\mathbf{GxP})\, -\,(\mathbf{xRx}) \qquad \text{Rule 2}$$

The binding problem is that the same letter must appear at each **x**. So far Touretzky and Hinton have limited their attention to rules like Rule

12 Note that the alterations are to the units that coarse code the triples, since the triples have no other encoding in the system. Because the same units also code for a variety of other triples, other triples would gain (or lose) a bit of their support in WM if they had one or a few units in common with **(GAB)** or **(PDQ)** (or **(FCD)**); that is, the coarse coding scheme implements generalization and memory decay "for free."

13 Tourezky and Hinton precede each instance of the variable with an equal sign as a notational device indicating that a variable follows, e.g., (= **x A B**); we have suppressed these.

2: there is one variable, and it appears in the initial position in each of the condition triples and anywhere in the action triples. For these rules, they devised a solution to the binding problem that appears to work rather well (DCPS2). First, the clique of 40 units for a rule like Rule 2 are wired to a broader array of clause units. There are excitatory connections to C1, for example, for triples such as (**MAB**) and (**SAB**) as well as (**FAB**). To narrow down this broader range of possibilities in a way that properly binds the variable **x**, the *bind space* is introduced. This is the only space that focuses on the 25 letters that compose the triads, and it coarse codes these letters by using units that are sensitive to three letters each. Two-way excitatory connections between units in the bind space and appropriate units in each clause space ensure that the two clause spaces both employ the same substitution for the variable in the triples selected. That is, the bind space is used to implement an additional constraint on the network, and the solution into which it settles should satisfy this constraint in addition to the others already discussed for the no-variables case. Thus, when (**FAB**) is excited in C1, the units coding for F as the first letter are excited in the bind space, and they in turn excite units in C2 that begin with F. Although a great deal of detail is provided on the design of this version of the network, and Touretzky and Hinton discuss it as a functioning system, they report no quantitative performance data. (Instead, they discuss how the system deals, not always successfully, with the most difficult cases.)

The network developed by Touretzky and Hinton does appear to exhibit many of the features of rule-based processing, and of production systems in particular, even though it implements rules by means of a coarse coding scheme rather than ordered strings of symbols.[14] Rules get selected on the basis of WM contents and fire; iterating the process generates a sequence of actions on WM. Also, to the extent that DCPS can deal with variable binding, the systematicity feature demanded by Fodor and Pylyshyn seems to have been provided. For example, the condition side of Rule 2 can be satisfied by (**FAB**) and (**FCD**), by (**GAB**) and (**GCD**), and so forth. A number of questions are salient in evaluating the system, however, in addition to the question of whether it exhibits the features of rule systems. We shall mention a few of them.

First, DCPS is undoubtedly an impressive job of engineering; but is it also impressive as a model of human cognition? One way that DCPS falls short (at least in its 1988 version) is that it is limited to rules with

14   For other examples of networks that implement rule systems, see Barnden (1989), Lange and Dyer (in press), Shastri (1988), Shastri and Ajjanagadde (1989), and Touretzky (1986; in press).

just one variable, whereas human cognition clearly is not. Monadic systems are much less powerful than dyadic systems (in the predicate calculus, for example). Another concern is whether humans carry out variable binding in anything like the way DCPS does. We do not mean to suggest that the answer is no; we do suggest that the answer, and the grounds it would be based upon, are not obvious. As computer scientists, Touretzky and Hinton do not themselves make this issue primary; one advantage of the interdisciplinary character of connectionism is that both engineering and psychological modeling questions will tend to get asked of each system.

Second, if DCPS is simply an implementation of a rule system, what advantages have been gained by doing a *distributed, connectionist* implementation? One advantage that is especially salient to production systems is that it adds the capacity to do "best-fit" matches rapidly without having to specify in advance all the parameters on which fit might be evaluated. In addition, the usual advantages that are generally cited for connectionist models should obtain (e.g., damage-resistance, support for generalization). Adding a learning capability to a connectionist PS would be an especially noteworthy achievement, but this was not attempted in DCPS and could well present difficulties. Some, but not all, of these advantages could be obtained using a localist rather than distributed encoding, and some localists who share the compatibilist objectives have criticized this aspect of the work. Feldman (1986), for example, has objected that distributed implementations of symbols, which involve extreme parallelism at the *subsymbolic* level, make *symbolic* processing overly sequential and slow. McDermott has dubbed this the *Touretzky tarpit* problem (reported in Dyer, in press).

Third, the introduction of a gating mechanism to separate condition-matching from rule-firing touches on an issue of strategy. Investigators differ in the degree to which they are willing to produce hybrid systems that interface connectionist design and mechanisms with nonconnectionist design and mechanism. Touretzky and Hinton's system is connectionist in general, with only the gating mechanism making it somewhat of a hybrid (only somewhat, because the gating mechanism is not a *symbolic* device). At the other end, there are systems that are basically symbolic but gain some of the connectionist advantages by incorporating certain features. Examples of production systems that hybridize to some extent are Thibadeau, Just, and Carpenter's (1982) CAPS system and J. R. Anderson's (1983) ACT* system. It is possible that some (preferably elegant) hybrid will turn out to offer the best framework in five or ten years. The hybrids being produced now are intriguing and worthy of consideration as early sketches, and there is room for a variety of strategies. For the present, however, some prefer the strategy of pushing connectionist models at the subsymbolic level as far as they can go (e.g., Rumelhart and McClelland's various models) or at least limiting additional mechanisms to nonsymbolic ones (e.g., Touretzky and Hinton's gating mechanism). To do this well, investigators need to keep an eye on the regularities that have been noted by symbolic researchers, while eschewing use of their approaches to modeling these regularities (as recommended by Smolensky, 1988). This strategy would provide the clearest answers concerning exactly what the limitations of connectionist models might be, and therefore exactly what kinds of additional mechanisms need to be added if any. It also sets the stage for later theoretical work on the relationship between subsymbolic and symbolic models.

Fourth, even though compatibilist and approximationist research strategies are different, they share the assumption that the distinctive contributions of the network architecture yield a superior model for satisfying certain goals, and that traditional symbolic models can at best only approximate certain aspects of the network's behavior. Even Touretzky and Hinton sound somewhat approximationist when they write:

We view DCPS as only the first step in the development of connectionist symbol manipulation architectures. Future advances should lead to models which make better use of the powerful constraint satisfaction and generalization abilities of connectionist networks. Such models would be more than mere implementations of conventional symbol processing ideas because the connectionist substrate would provide important computational properties that are not available in standard implementations. (pp. 462–3)

Critics like Fodor and Pylyshyn tend to minimize the importance of any such advantages of connectionist models, regarding them as "mere" implementation. To counter them, connectionists may need to adopt a more aggressive posture by arguing that the characteristics ascribed to symbolic systems by Fodor and Pylyshyn, combinatorial syntax and semantics, are important but not sufficient. Touretzky and Derthick (1987) began to develop such an argument by identifying five features that cognitive symbols ought to exhibit:

Mobile: ability to appear in multiple locations, perhaps simultaneously.
Meaningful: composed of meaningful units in such a manner that similar objects are represented by similar symbols.
Memorable: posses a static representation that can be recalled.
Malleable: flexible capacity to match symbol structures.
Modifiable: can be constructed and altered easily.

An implementation of symbols in a von Neumann system provides for mobility (the same symbol can be used in different composed structures) and modifiability (rules can direct symbol manipulations), and to a lesser degree, memorability (symbols can be recovered from memory via their address). It does not provide either meaningfulness (since atomic symbols are arbitrary, and not composed of meaningful units) or malleability (since symbols are rigid entities). These are two features which can be procured by implementing symbols in a connectionist framework. In a distributed representation, the units are subsymbols that can represent microfeatures; the "symbol" is encoded indirectly by activating any relevant set of subsymbols. This provides the network with a way of recognizing the similarity when two symbols refer to similar objects, and of generalizing from target objects to similar objects. This overlap of microfeatures also provides for malleability, in that conditions which only partially match those required for the symbol to be satisfied may nevertheless activate the symbol. Connectionist networks also provide for recall from memory through content, not just by knowing an address. Mobility and modifiability, however, are more difficult to obtain in most connectionist systems, but these are the features that Touretzky and his colleagues have sought to obtain by building hybrid systems. Thus, Touretzky contends that the compatibilist strategy can not only provide those features of a symbolic system that Fodor and Pylyshyn claim are important, but additional features which are needed for symbols to constitute adequate tools for cognitive modeling.

Dyer (in press) develops a different compatibilist strategy. He suggests thinking in terms of a hierarchy of levels of research as shown in table 7.1:

Table 7.1 Dyer's proposed levels of research between mind and brain

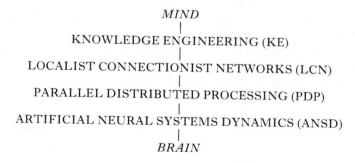

MIND
|
KNOWLEDGE ENGINEERING (KE)
|
LOCALIST CONNECTIONIST NETWORKS (LCN)
|
PARALLEL DISTRIBUTED PROCESSING (PDP)
|
ARTIFICIAL NEURAL SYSTEMS DYNAMICS (ANSD)
|
BRAIN

Different levels occupy "distinct 'niches' in what might be termed an abstract processing 'ecology'. That is, what subsymbolic/PDP models do well, purely symbolic models do poorly *and vice versa*'' (p. 4). In part, these differences keep the levels apart. But the goal, as Dyer sees it, is to allow resources at different levels to complement each other. Discussing the mappings between models at different levels is a crucial step towards achieving a synthesis. For example, the knowledge engineering level is the level of symbolic AI; it is well suited to stating the content and structure of a domain and supporting such tasks as goal/plan analysis. By going down to the next level, localist networks, dynamics such as spreading activation can be considered. Having such multiple levels available can enable choices that may produce better models. For example, in their work on analogical problem-solving, Holyoak and Thagard (1989) faced the task of identifying the best analog to the problem situation, where there are many dimensions on which situations can be matched, and no perfect matches. To handle this task, they invoked a localist connectionist program which was well suited to identify best matches with multiple constraints. For other tasks, they did traditional AI programming. Dyer (in press) has suggested particular techniques for bridging levels, for example, using conjunctive codings to implement role bindings and forming hybrid systems with spreading activation, thresholds and markers to propagate bindings. Note also Miikullainen and Dyer's (1989) paper on a system that uses recurrent networks and modularization to carry out a story paraphrasing task.

Using External Symbols to Provide Exact Symbolic Processing

So far we have examined two views of how the key types of models relate: (a) that symbolic models *approximate* connectionist models; and (b) that symbolic models are *implemented* by connectionist models. In this section we shall consider a final alternative, proposed by Rumelhart, Smolensky, McClelland, and Hinton (1986) in *PDP:14*, and elaborated upon by Smolensky (1988) and A. Clark (1989). The basic idea is that networks may develop the capacity to interpret and produce symbols that are *external* to the network. Consider language as the quintessential symbol system. Part of its interest lies in its dual role as an internal tool (e.g., for mental problem-solving) and as an external tool (e.g., for written or verbal problem-solving and for communication). This duality is emphasized in Vygotsky's (1962) characterization of problem-solving as carried out externally early in development (by means of *egocentric speech*) and internally later on (by means of *inner speech*). It is in the external mode that we can actually observe symbols being manipulated, somewhat as they might be manipulated in a formal symbol system. In the externalist approach to symbol processing, the focus is turned from symbols in their mental roles to symbols in their external roles. (For development of a related approach to religious symbols and religious systems see Lawson and McCauley, 1990.)

Smolensky (1988) discusses the cultural practice of formulating knowledge in external symbols that can be used to communicate that knowledge (e.g., in a textbook or lecture). He views these external symbolic formulations as being internalized and utilized by a *conscious rule interpreter* that is distinct from the inherently subconceptual *intuitive processor*. Although his interest is directed primarily towards the latter processor, which is the one that requires a connectionist account, he notes three properties of the linguistic encoding of knowledge that are important, for example, to the advancement of science:

a. *Public access*:   The knowledge is accessible to many people.
b. *Reliability*:   Different people (or the same person at different times) can reliably check whether conclusions have been validly reached.
c. *Formality, bootstrapping, universality*:   The inferential operations require very little experience with the domain to which the symbols refer. (1988, p. 4)

The pre-connectionist assumption has been that in order for people to operate as conscious rule interpreters it is necessary that they function internally as rule processing systems. It may be fruitful to approach this from another angle, however. Each human is born into a community which makes extensive use of external symbols, and these symbols and the regularities in their relation to one another and in their relation to the world are part of the environment of the developing infant and child. The novice human acquires the ability to interact with the external symbols by lower-level processes (such as connectionist pattern recognition) that do not themselves involve a direct internalization of these symbols. That is, the infant *learns how* to use external symbols. Although an individual's ability to think and reason appears to be aided by eventually internalizing the use of symbols in some sense, this internalization comes later and is incomplete. Even in mature individuals, difficult problems elicit the use of external symbols. And, it is quite unclear *in what sense* symbols are internalized. The connectionist program includes the goal of uncovering the causal mechanisms that occur at the subsymbolic level in carrying out what is identified at a higher level as "symbolic processing." Until the program has been actualized to a much greater extent, there is no way of knowing whether additional causal mechanisms at the higher, symbolic level will also be needed to *account for* those regularities that are most efficiently *described at* that level. Alternatively, connectionist processes such as pattern recognition may suffice to account for the ability to use symbols. Hence, if a connectionist wishes to examine symbol processing at this time, networks' use of external symbols may be the most appropriate focus of research.

The suggestion we are developing here is rather different from the compatibilist approach of directly designing networks to perform symbolic processing. Rather than trying to implement a rule system, we are proposing to teach a network to *use* a system (language) in which information, including rules, can be encoded symbolically. In using these symbols, however, the network behaves in the same basic manner as it always does: it recognizes patterns and responds to them as it has been trained (for a relatively simple simulation of how a network might learn to use language, see Allen, 1988). If the external symbols are in an enduring modality (e.g., handwriting), the external storage will enable the network to perform tasks that it cannot solve on the basis of a single act of pattern recognition. Rumelhart, Smolensky, McClelland, and Hinton (1986) in *PDP:14* illustrate this by constructing a scenario for solving a three-digit multiplication problem:

We are good at "perceiving" answers to problems.... However, ... few (if any) of us can look at a three-digit multiplication problem (such as 343 times 822) and see the answer. Solving such problems cannot be done by our pattern-matching apparatus, parallel processing alone will not do the trick; we need a kind of serial processing mechanism to solve such a problem. Here is where our ability to manipulate our environment becomes critical. We can, quite readily, learn to write down the two numbers in a certain format when given such a problem.

$$\begin{array}{r} 343 \\ \underline{822} \end{array}$$

Moreover, we can learn to see the first step of such a multiplication problem. (Namely, we can see that we should enter a 6 below the 3 and 2.)

$$\begin{array}{r} 343 \\ \underline{822} \\ 6 \end{array}$$

We can then use our ability to pattern match again to see what to do next. Each cycle of this operation involves first creating a representation through manipulation of the environment, then a processing of this (actual physical) representation by means of our well-tuned perceptual apparatus leading to a further modification of this representation. (Rumelhart, Smolensky, McClelland, and Hinton, 1986, p. 45)[15]

They go on to suggest that this kind of iterative operation using external symbols is what allows difficult problems, as in logic and science, to be solved:

These dual skills of manipulating the environment and processing the environment we have created allow us to reduce very complex problems to a series of very simple ones.... This is *real* symbol processing and, we are beginning to think, the primary symbol processing that we are able to do. (p. 46)

Our discussion of formal logical abilities (chapter 5) can be viewed from this perspective. A person or a network that confronts external symbols that are configured in accord with rules of logic might learn to process those symbols in the appropriate logical manner.

Rumelhart et al. take the additional step of considering how this use of external symbols might to some extent be internalized. Their basic idea is that a mental model of the external symbolic environment is constructed, and the procedures that would ordinarily operate on external symbols operate instead on the mental model. By using the output of the mental model as the input to the next mental operation of pattern-matching, and the output of that operation as an input to the mental model, a loop is obtained that can sustain a series of mental operations. A mental operation itself is viewed as the network's process of settling or "relaxing" into an interpretation of a symbolic expression. They suggest that the resulting stable state endures long enough (approximately half a second) to be conscious, but that the rapid cycles of computation involved in settling are not conscious. (Cf. Dennett's (1978) analysis of one aspect of consciousness in terms of a specialized speech module that provides a means of reporting the results of cognitive processing.) Rumelhart et al.'s speculative, but intriguing, development of this idea can be consulted on pp. 38–48 of *PDP:14*. Although they do not specifically discuss the status of the internalized symbols, it is clear from their discussion that the symbols are simply patterns in a network. Stable states of the network are the "symbols;" but this is achieved by a subsymbolic, dynamic encoding that is quite distinct from the construal of symbols in the symbolic tradition.

15   More recently, Cottrell and Tsung (1989) have developed simulations of addition of two multi-digit numbers that use versions of Jordan's (1986b) sequential network and of Elman's (1988) recurrent network to store partial results for later stages of processing.

Processing loops of the type used in the multiplication example would be one way to support recursion computationally, providing a connectionist means of obtaining Fodor and Pylyshyn's properties of productivity, systematicity, and inferential coherence. Fodor and Pylyshyn would not be satisfied by this, because the connectionist means is not one that *guarantees* the systematicity that they attribute to all thought. They may be wrong, however, to insist on the ubiquity of systematicity. The capacity for recursion arises rather late in development, and therefore should not be a part of a model of nascent cognition. That is, children do not initially construct models and use them to produce the processing loops that may support recursion. This may partly account for the fact that young children's language does not fully exhibit Fodor and Pylyshyn's properties of productivity, systematicity, and inferential coherence. Children's language (and thought) is particularly dependent upon the eliciting conditions and feedback provided by the external environment (symbolic or otherwise). A close analysis of the development of language from a connectionist perspective would pay high dividends as a way of grappling with questions concerning the properties of language and how the cognitive system functions so as to exhibit them.

Smolensky's (1988) distinction between a *conscious rule interpreter* and *intuitive processor* pursues a somewhat different approach to the internalization question. Here, Smolensky is willing to accept symbolic models as providing an adequate account of the internal encoding and use of linguistically communicated rules. A chess novice would rely heavily on rules, for example, before she had developed sufficient experience to build a good intuitive processor that could often "see" which move to make (see above, p. 156). Smolensky does suggest that there are advantages to performing a subsymbolic encoding even of rules (in particular, this would simplify interaction with the intuitive processor, which is a nontrivial problem for his approach); but still Smolensky presses hardest on the idea that two distinct levels are involved at least with respect to explanatory adequacy.

Although we find most of Smolensky's ideas in this paper quite attractive, we are uncomfortable with the sharpness of this distinction. A somewhat different way of thinking about rules (which he touches on but does not apply to this issue) is to regard them as encodings that are unusually isolated from other encodings, and in particular are relatively context-invariant. (Either the rule is elicited in only one context, such as a preceding rule, or is accessible in the same form from any relevant context.) This approach would predict a fair degree of continuity in the process of acquiring expert knowledge, and would view rule-like versus nonrule-like knowledge representation more as a continuum than as a dichotomy. At all points on this continuum, the same subsymbolic network approach to encoding would be used. Higher levels would simply be more abstract levels of description of certain regularities displayed in the network.

Leaving behind the issue of levels, we shall note one last idea in Smolensky (1988): his vision of what could be achieved by coordination between a *rule interpreter* and *intuitive processor*. He writes:

An integrated subsymbolic rule interpreter/intuitive processor in principle offers the advantages of both kinds of processing. Imagine such a system creating a mathematical proof. The intuitive processor would generate goals and steps, and the rule interpreter would verify their validity. The serial search through the space of possible steps, which is necessary in a purely symbolic approach, is replaced by the intuitive generation of possibilities. Yet the precise adherence to strict inference rules that is demanded by the task can be enforced by the rule interpreter; the creativity of intuition can be exploited while its unreliability can be controlled. (Smolensky, 1988, p. 13)

It is interestng to note that in many cases of actual mathematical proofs, the rule-checking function is only incompletely performed. The mathematician will say, following Laplace, "It is easily seen that . . .", when in fact many steps remain to be filled in and sometimes it turns out that the steps cannot be filled in since the move is invalid (Cipra, 1989).

The proposals summarized in this section represent the most speculative of the three connectionist perspectives on symbols that we have considered. They treat symbol manipulation as a learned capacity that is initially carried out on symbols in the external environment. On this view, symbols are primarily human artifacts such as linguistic and mathematic expressions, but they may eventually be internalized in the same format as nonsymbolic information.

Conclusion

We began this chapter by reviewing two of the most compelling recent arguments that connectionist networks are inadequate to model cognition because symbolic systems are required for cognition. We have considered three responses connectionists are pursuing: (1) the approximationist approach, which claims that network models provide a more accurate account of actual cognition than symbolic models; (2) the compatibilist approach, which tries to build explicit symbol processing capacities directly into networks; and (3) an approach that emphasizes symbols as external entities. All of these approaches have something to offer, but the combination of the first and third is perhaps most promising. Together they suggest a radical reconceptualization of cognition from the way it has been viewed in the symbol processing tradition, and yet provide a means for explaining how it is that we are able to perform, at least on occasion, as real symbol processors.

While connectionists and symbolic theorists have devoted considerable effort to arguing for their position and against the alternative, these debates are not likely to settle the dispute. Although these debates have brought up serious issues, it is our impression that they do not address the reasons a reseacher might adopt connectionism or symbol processing. In large measure, whether investigators have been attracted to connectionism has depended on how dissatisfied they have been with symbolic models. If a researcher had found symbolic models sufficiently adequate for present purposes, he or she has not seen any advantage in adopting a connectionist perspective. On the other hand, if a researcher has found symbolic models to be inadequate, he or she is much more likely to have explored the connectionist alternative. This in part explains the quite varied group of researchers, who do not seem to share common objectives, that have turned to connectionism. In part, whether one is satisfied or dissatisfied depends on what one takes as the data to be explained. Those who are most impressed with the abstract regularities in behavior, as captured, for example, in linguisitc competence theories, have tended to be quite satisfied with symbolic theories. Many of those who are concerned with variations in actual performance, on the other hand, have found traditional symbolic theories to be too rigid and have either pursued connectionist alternatives or have developed less traditional symbolic theories. In a strong sense, this initial difference in basic objectives leads the theorists for the two sides to talk past one another.

8

Connectionism and the Disciplines of Cognitive Science

Connectionism is not a discipline. In part it is an integration of the symbolic approach and the behaviorism that preceded it; but these are not disciplines either. All three of these can be regarded as intellectual traditions. Each provides a different scientific framework, which, viewed most broadly, spans a variety of related disciplines including psychology, linguistics, anthropology, philosophy, and (more recently) computer science and neuroscience. As applied more specifically within disciplines, each tradition provides a paradigm: a set of assumptions, constructs, techniques, and goals that guide research (Kuhn, 1962/ 1970). At times, the commonalities among the different disciplinary interpretations of a single intellectual tradition has spawned a great deal of interdisciplinary activity. Most particularly, the rise of the symbolic approach resulted first in interdisciplinary activity in the 1960s, and then in a more highly organized interdisciplinary cluster, *cognitive science*, in the 1970s. While cognitive science has been a highly successful enterprise, and has enjoyed a certain unity grounded in the shared symbolic tradition, there has also been a degree of tension due to differences among its constituent disciplines.

Now connectionism, the most recent of the three intellectual traditions mentioned above, has introduced a new source of tension as it seeks to displace the symbolic tradition. The character of cognitive science itself is placed in question by the rise of connectionism, and so is the character of some of its constituent disciplines. In the previous chapters of this book we have discussed how connectionism relates to various issues and topics within cognitive science. In this final chapter, we look more specifically at the constituent disciplines themselves (or those of their subdisciplines that are most relevant to cognitive science), and consider what impact connectionism might have upon them individually. First, though, we shall orient the discussion by considering how the various cognitive science disciplines are related to one another.

Overview of the Structure of Disciplines

It is commonly assumed that disciplines are hierarchically organized in correspondence to levels of organization in nature, where these levels are understood in terms of part–whole relations. For example, atoms are parts of molecules, which are parts of cells, which are parts of human beings, which are parts of social systems. Thus, one has a hierarchy with physics at the bottom, followed by chemistry, biology, psychology, and sociology. This approach is too simple, however. Note that there are other part–whole hierarchies which remain entirely within the domain of the physical sciences. For example, atoms are parts of molecules, which are parts of rocks, which are parts of planets, which are parts of solar systems. While there are separate disciplines associated with these different levels of organization, all of them are physical sciences.

An alternative conceptual framework for considering how disciplines relate to one another was developed by Abrahamsen (1987; in press). This framework makes a primary four-way distinction among the physical sciences, the biological sciences, the behavioral sciences, and those arts and sciences that focus on the products of behavior (shown as four levels in figure 8.1). What differentiates disciplines at one level from those at an adjacent level is not a part–whole relation, but rather a specialization of focus. All phenomena in nature can be construed as part of the domain of the *physical sciences*, but some of these phenomena have been of special interest to the humans who investigate nature. In particular, phenomena that are limited to living organisms have become the focus of the *biological sciences*. In turn, the behavior of such organisms, including social interactions, have become the specialized focus of the *behavioral sciences* (whereas nonbehavioral phenomena exhibited by living organisms are studied solely within the less specialized level of the biological sciences). Finally, the most specialized disciplines, the *cultural products arts and sciences*, examine products of the behavior of organisms, especially humans (e.g., rules of logical inference, languages, economic systems, and physical products such as buildings).

Within each of these four levels of the specialization hierarchy, we find portions of the part–whole hierarchies that have been emphasized in more traditional analyses of scientific disciplines. For example, within biology we have subdisciplines dealing with cells and their parts (e.g., genetics, molecular biology, cell biology), with organs (e.g., anatomy and physiology), and with whole organisms (e.g., botany and zo-

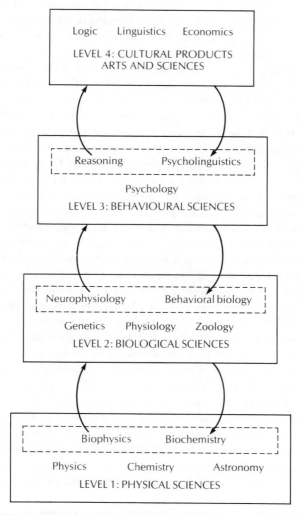

Figure 8.1 The specialization hierarchy of disciplines. For each of the four levels, examples are provided of disciplines at that level (in the main box) and of subdisciplines that can be coordinated with work at the next higher level (in the inner box). The arrows pointing upwards indicate that each lower-level subdiscipline obtains specialized descriptions of the domain of concern from a higher-level discipline. The arrows pointing downwards indicate that each upper-level discipline may look to a lower-level subdiscipline as a source of explanation, constraint, and ancillary evidence.

ology). Within the behavioral sciences, we have subdisciplines focusing on particular mental/behavioral systems and subsystems (e.g., cognitive psychology), on the behavior of whole organisms (e.g., experimental analysis of behavior and comparative psychology), and on social interactions of organisms (e.g., social psychology and parts of sociology and anthropology). So we have at least two kinds of hierarchy in terms of which we can situate disciplines. The specialization hierarchy forms the primary (vertical) axis which distinguishes different levels of disciplines. Within each level, there is at least one part–whole hierarchy on its own (horizontal) axis which is distinctive to that level of analysis.[1]

Much of the interest in this analysis lies in the fact that the distinctive constructs of each of the four different levels can be applied to the same events or domains and that interdisciplinary interactions can be helpful, if not essential, in doing so. Consider the event in which a child utters the sentence *Kitty-cat comed home*. In understanding this event at *level 4*, the linguist contributes an abstract analysis involving constructs of syntax, morphology, phonology, etc., which reflect linguistic part-whole hierarchies (e.g., morphemes are composed of phonemes). At *level 3*, the psycholinguist focuses instead on the real-time mental activities, learning mechanisms, and behaviors involved in producing the utterance; here the part-whole hierarchies involve mental states and the processes by which they change. Linguistic constructs, if applied to a mechanistic account of how the utterance is produced, may be altered to obtain constructs that are appropriate to that level of analysis. For example, phonemes may be reinterpreted as Wickelphones if the mechanism does not explicitly utilize ordered strings. At *level 2* the neurolinguist is most directly concerned with neurons and the systems into which they are organized, and attempts to describe how functioning at this level undergirds production of the sentence at the behavioral level. Finally, even at *level 1* physical scientists may contribute analyses of the speech waveform as a kind of acoustic event, of the eardrum as a kind of membrane, and so forth.

Thus, lower-level disciplines include subdisciplines (e.g., psycholinguistics) that focus on the same events or domains as higher-level disciplines (e.g., linguistics). This is emphasized in figure 8.1 by including examples of these subdisciplines in boxes within each level. The up-

---

1   One way to define a part-whole hierarchy is in terms of systems and their subsystems. Systems are typically described in terms of structure and function (process), however, and separate part-whole hierarchies might therefore be proposed. For example, within generative grammar there is a structural hierarchy that includes the composition of lexical items into phrases, and there are also rule hierarchies that compose individual rules into derivations.

wards arrows indicate that a lower-level subdiscipline may obtain specialized descriptions of the domain from a higher-level discipline; the downwards arrows indicate that the higher-level discipline may use the lower level discipline as a source of explanation, constraint, and ancillary evidence. These interdisciplinary relations are often fruitful, and suggest that it is advantageous to retain multiple levels of analysis rather than engage in a reductionist program.

Where do connectionist networks fit into this framework? One possibility is to speculate that they occupy a new level that is intermediate between levels 2 and 3; alternatively, reductionists regard connectionist networks as level 2 accounts that will eventually replace level 3 accounts. We believe that both of these approaches are misguided. Rather, those networks that are constructed to simulate aspects of human perception and cognition clearly are level 3 accounts; they are the concern of cognitive, developmental, and other psychologists, and of those computer scientists who focus on simulating human mentation. In contrast, other networks are constructed as explicit models of neural elements and systems. They are situated at level 2, and are utilized by neurobiologists as well as certain computer scientists who construe their networks as artificial or ideal neural systems. Just as in the case of nonconnectionist research, some investigators will have a special interest in interdisciplinary questions; for example, how activity in neural circuits undergirds certain aspects of mental functioning. Their inquiries should be understood to involve coordination of work at different levels, not the creation of new levels or the reduction of one level to another.[2]

Is there a role for connectionism at level 4? In the final section of this chapter we shall argue against the idea that connectionist networks should be directly incorporated in theoretical accounts of human products (e.g., linguistic theories), on the grounds that mechanistic accounts belong at level 3. They might, however, be of interest to linguists and other level 4 theorists as part of an interdisciplinary endeavor that does consider the relation between mechanism and product. Connectionist networks also can themselves be regarded as

2   In comparison, Dyer (in press) proposed a single hierarchy, which we displayed in figure 7.5. His hierarchy emphasizes research approaches from our level 3, but the top of his hierarchy apparently includes some level 4 accounts as well, and we would assign the bottom of his hierarchy to our level 2. His emphasis on the importance of working at multiple levels is consistent with our own analysis of interdisciplinary relations. Also, note that Marr's (1982) distinction among computational theory, algorithm, and implementation closely corresponds to our levels 4, 3, and 2 (although these accounts were independently arrived at with somewhat different goals in mind).

artifacts of human activity (cultural products), and designing such networks would be a level 4 activity just as designing buildings is a level 4 activity. That part of computer science that is oriented to the engineering aspects of networks rather than their status as mental or neural models would therefore be classified as a level 4 profession.

If connectionist simulations do not occupy a new, intermediate level of inquiry, what is to be made of the idea that they model the *microstructure* of cognition? In our view, microstructure is best regarded as a relative rather than absolute notion, and has to do with part–whole hierarchies within level 3 rather than different levels of the specialization hierarchy. The connectionist claim is that (level 3) mechanistic models of phenomena at a particular location in a part–whole hierarchy require the use of units that encode a lower level in that hierarchy. Thus, traditional symbolic accounts of past-tense formation include rules that apply to words such as *come* and *look*. In contrast, Rumelhart and McClelland (1986, in *PDP:18*) built a mechanism for past-tense formation exclusively from units that encoded phonemes and phonemic features (using a context-sensitive scheme in lieu of ordered strings). The ability to form the past tense of a stem was attributed to statistical regularities in the behavior of these finer-grained units rather than the application of rules to ordered strings of coarser-grained units. Another way to say this is that stems were given a distributed coding across phonological units, rather than an explicit representation as morphemic units.[3] If Rumelhart and McClelland had aimed to account for phenomena of clause embedding rather than past tense formation, a microstructural account may have involved units corresponding to words rather than phonological features. The key idea is that the units would be selected from a lower (finer-grained) portion of the part–whole hierarchy than would ordinarily be regarded as appropriate for the phenomenon to be modeled.[4]

3 Note further that Rumelhart and McClelland's units had a correspondence to linguistic elements at level 4, and in fact their design was informed by linguistic analysis. However, the elements of the level 3 mechanistic account were not identical to the level 4 elements; i.e., they were context-sensitive and were used in a statistical manner. Abrahamsen (1987) argued that this is the ordinary, cooperative way in which psycholinguists make use of linguistic theory (borrowing linguistic analyses, but adapting them to the needs of a mechanistic account). In this respect the connectionist model is similar to other psycholinguistic models.

4 In Smolensky's (1988) language, the past-tense model accounts for a symbolic process by means of a network of subsymbols. His analysis appears to be anchored to a particular portion of the part–whole hierarchy, however. (That is, symbols correspond to semantically nonprimitive concepts such as *come* or *table*, and subsymbols correspond to components of those concepts.) Therefore, his analysis is not as readily applied to the clause-embedding example as to the past-tense example.

In this context, we shall now consider several of the disciplines and subdisciplines on which connectionism might have some impact. We shall begin with disciplines that work primarily at level 3 (artificial intelligence, cognitive psychology, ecological psychology, and developmental psychology). Then we shall drop down to neuroscience (level 2, with interdisciplinary connections to level 3), and finally move up to philosophy (level 4 and meta-level analyses) and linguistics (level 4, with interdisciplinary connections to level 3). We shall have little to say about networks as products of design and engineering, because we have restricted our focus to networks as models of human systems.

Artificial Intelligence and Cognitive Psychology

Artificial intelligence and cognitive psychology are the central subdisciplines of cognitive science, and they have served as the port of entry through which network models have become a part of contemporary cognitive science. Recall the historical context, as sketched in chapter 1. Neural network modeling originated mid-century and was thriving by the 1960s, but the symbolic tradition was thriving as well. By the end of the 1960s the symbolic approach dominated the small field of artificial intelligence, and had begun to replace behaviorism within psychology. By the end of the 1970s, symbolic modeling within these disciplines had become the core of a well-established cognitive science. Neural network modeling had become unfashionable, but survived at the periphery of such fields as neurobiology.

The symbolic approach, in its purest form, had limitations that became harder to accept by the end of the 1970s. A serial system composed solely of symbolic representations and rules that operate upon them tends to be "brittle" and inflexible, and it provides a poor medium for modeling learning or pattern recognition. Two avenues were open to cognitive scientists who were concerned by these limitations. First, they could improve the design of rule systems (e.g., by adding strength parameters to rules and selecting them by a parallel process of constraint satisfaction, or by adding procedures for knowledge compilation or learning). A number of investigators chose that avenue, and by the end of 1980s had developed nontraditional symbolic systems that were far more flexible than earlier systems. The second avenue was to make a more definite break with symbolic systems by returning to networks. Where symbolic models would use coarse-grained symbols, network models would use finer-grained microsymbols. Where symbolic models would operate upon ordered strings, network models would rely upon the statistical behavior of large networks of units.

Investigators who chose this avenue utilized techniques from the surviving neural network tradition in building nonlinear dynamical systems, but combined these with ideas from within artificial intelligence and psychology, such as probabilistic feature models of categorization, semantic networks with spreading activation, and schema theory. The emphasis was placed upon distributed representation and statistical explanation.

By the end of the 1980s, both nontraditional symbolic systems and network systems could exhibit some degree of flexibility, subtlety, ability to learn from experience, and resilience to damage. However, they differed in whether they relied upon ordered strings of symbols or statistical regularities in the dynamics of large networks of interconnected units. Furthermore, traditional symbolic models remained a force to be reckoned with. The result has been considerable controversy within cognitive psychology and artificial intelligence regarding the future direction of these subdisciplines.

A number of questions are involved in this controversy, and these will need to be answered during the next decade: How deeply and broadly will the connectionist approach become incorporated into cognitive psychology and artificial intelligence? How rapidly? And how permanently? Will the gap between symbolic systems and connectionist networks widen, or will harmony be found in some way? (Harmony could be obtained if one approach clearly "wins;" if satisfying hybrids emerge; if a peaceful pluralism comes to prevail; or if there is a gradual process of co-option and evolution.) How will the effects of connectionism within these subdisciplines relate to the effects in cognitive science more generally? For example, will it become more important whether one is a connectionist, or whether one is a cognitive psychologist? Finally, what effect will connectionism have on other areas of psychology and computer science? The answers to these questions will depend upon which of two extreme characterizations holds (or which middle ground). At one extreme (Schneider, 1987), connectionism may represent as much a scientific revolution as did behaviorism and the symbolic approach earlier. (It has been a matter of debate whether either of these actually qualifies as a revolution; like Baars (1986) we shall assume they do.) At the other extreme, it may become just one tool in an extensive toolkit, in which case it would have no far-reaching effect on the way each discipline construes its domain and its task.

We can suggest some factors that will help determine the overall outcome and the answers to some of the specific questions above. If connectionism is to take hold, either as a revolution or as part of a hybrid or pluralistic framework, at least the following events must occur. First, connectionism will have to provide the framework for the development of a number of specific models that are judged successful. Current models are exploratory, and a very large promissory note remains due. Second, in the competition for the loyalties of established investigators, connectionism will have to compete successfully with nontraditional rule models that exhibit some of the same capabilities as networks. The competition will be based only partly on the success of specific models; the attractiveness of connectionism as an *idea* about the nature of the mind should play an important role as well. Third, a large number of researchers will need to go beyond attraction to connectionism to put in the hard work of retooling (both in techniques and in their construal of their discipline). Fourth, a critical mass of graduate students will need to "vote with their feet" in favor of connectionism by seeking that training. Fifth, institutional supports and grant funds will need to increase (a process that is already well underway). Finally, additional factors would need to be involved in order to move toward some kind of hybrid framework or pluralism. For example, for a hybrid framework to become predominant, the belief that there is an explanatory role that can only (or best) be filled by rule systems would need to become widespread among connectionists. Currently this is the subject of debate (and modeling attempts). For example, Holyoak and Thagard (1989) suggest that it may prove useful to employ connectionist designs in memory modules so as to be able to utilize content addressable memory, but to perform various computations upon the contents retrieved from memory in a symbolic manner (cf. J. R. Anderson, 1983).

The degree of interest in changing or modifying one's research framework, as well as the criteria for the success of models, depend to a great extent on factors that differ for the two subdisciplines, such as the goal of the modeling. In artificial intelligence (AI), for example, researchers universally desire to write programs that behave intelligently, but differ in their interest in the question of whether the programs are artificial or qualify as simulations of human cognition; when computer modeling techniques are used in cognitive psychology, in contrast, simulation is a fundamental goal. Moreover, not all research in either subdiscipline is directly committed to building models. In AI some research is directed toward more theoretical issues such as exploring different schemes of knowledge representation, search techniques, and control structures; many AI researchers are motivated more by technical or theoretical challenges than by questions of modeling. In cognitive psychology, modeling is only one technique for arriving at a characterization of the cognitive system. Other techniques include experiments that are directed at evaluating hypotheses about the cognitive system, and multiple regression analysis of nonexperimental data to determine factors that influence the operation of the cognitive system.

Artificial intelligence   Within artificial intelligence, a number of very useful programs have been constructed using a symbolic approach. MYCIN, for example, is a program that encodes extensive knowledge about bacterial infections and is quite successful at diagnosing and recommending drug therapies for problems involving bacterial infection (see Buchanan and Shortliffe, 1984). In domains such as this, where symbolic knowledge representation has proven fairly satisfactory, there may little motivation to pursue a connectionist alternative (particularly if one is focusing on immediate performance rather than exploring the foundations of computation or issues of simulation). The utility of continued pursuit of symbolic models is further enhanced by the fact that many AI programs are designed to perform tasks requiring fairly high-level reasoning capabilities, tasks at which connectionist models are not yet very adept.

There are other considerations that are more favorable to connectionism. Even successful AI programs have limitations that could be regarded as serious. For example, they tend to be domain-specific, brittle, and insensitive to context. They also are expensive; in the absence of practical learning mechanisms, each system must be built by knowledge engineers. Also, there are other domains in which traditional AI has been relatively unsuccessful. For example, it has been difficult to develop systems (such as robots) with sophisticated capabilities for recognizing objects in their environment. It is too early to say whether these limitations will be addressed predominantly by nontraditional symbolic models, connectionist networks, hybrid systems, or a pluralistic approach. It would be surprising, however, if connectionism did not find at least a few stable niches in AI.

Cognitive psychology   Cognitive psychology presents a somewhat different picture. The goal of psychological modeling is to account for empirical data about behavior and to provide some understanding of how that behavior is produced. For connectionist modeling to satisfy this goal, specific models must be developed that can provide a superior account of a variety of data sets. They also should suggest fruitful new approaches to unsolved problems, and point the way to new questions and new experiments to perform. Rumelhart and McClelland's past tense model (summarized in chapter 6), was a major early effort of this kind. Like other such models, it performed in a manner that is qualitatively like human performance in some important respects, but is incomplete in certain other respects. Rumelhart and McClelland, for example, readily acknowledged that they modeled past-tense formation in isolation from other linguistic functions, and that the actual mechanisms used to form the past tense are likely to be closely integrated with these other functions. Are the limitations of current connectionist models all of this superficial nature, or does connectionism exhibit fundamental inadequacies that bring its viability into doubt more generally? Massaro (1988) has argued that interactive networks fail to make the correct predictions for certain empirical results, and that multi-layered networks, because they predict a variety of mutually inconsistent results, are too powerful. More recently, Ratcliff (1990) has evaluated the ability of connectionist models to account for recognition memory phenomena; he reports disappointing results to date. For committed connectionists, results like these are either challenged, or are used as an impetus to build better models. The process of testing and then stretching the limits can continue for some time.

One of the major objections that cognitive psychologists have raised against connectionist models is that the important work is not accomplished by the network architecture as such, but rather by the way information is encoded on the input and output layers; see Lachter and Bever (1988) and Pinker and Prince (1988). Thus, the results may be attributable not to the architecture, but rather to insights borrowed from rule-based theories. Connectionists must acknowledge that, almost always, the encoding schemes are adapted from analyses previously worked out by traditional symbolic researchers. For example, in the past-tense model the coarse coding in terms of Wickelfeatures was adapted from linguistic analyses (level 4); the charge is that all that remained for the network to do was to find the mapping between these pre-defined inputs and outputs. There are two responses to this criticism. First, in the case of multi-layered networks that learn, the network constructs its own encodings for the hidden layers (as we saw for Hinton's kinship network, for example); the behavior of the network is then due in part to these encodings, not simply to the pre-defined encodings on the input layer. So part of the objection might be answered with more sophisticated connectionist models. But second, there is a part of the objection that is well founded. Connectionist models need to be backed by principled accounts of why the input patterns and output patterns were constructed as they were. Currently, and presumably in the future as well, this part of the connectionist program involves cooperation with disciplines that describe the structure of a domain. Several of these disciplines have been fairly successful at using symbols to capture and efficiently state generalizations about the structure of items in a domain, and there is nothing wrong with taking advantage of this expertise in constructing connectionist encoding schemes. In the case of connectionist models of language processing, for example, the appropriate donor discipline is linguistics. The reason for placing the adapted encodings into a connectionist network is that the network can generate subtle, interesting, and important kinds of behavior that are difficult to incorporate in a traditional symbolic system.

We shall stop short of forecasting the future course of connectionism in these crucial subdisciplines. Whatever the outcome, it will be of some interest to observe the changes between as well as within these subdisciplines across the next decade. In the following sections, we consider disciplines that have been only minimally influenced by connectionism to date, but that have the potential to be influenced. For these cases, we shall focus on pointing out some of the kinds of influence that seem either appropriate or likely. Furthermore, the influence need not be unidirectional; some of these disciplines can themselves contribute in certain ways to the development of connectionism.

Ecological Psychology

Connectonism is not the only intellectual movement that has posed a challenge to traditional cognitive psychology. Around the same time that investigators such as Rosenblatt were exploring perceptrons, J. J. Gibson (1966) was developing an ecological approach to perception (particularly vision). Gibson contended that there is abundant information about the real world and its invariants in the light that reaches the retina; the ambient optic array specifies not merely what objects are in our surround, but also what actions they *afford* to us. The perceiver's role is to *pick up* that information and use it to control action in dynamic interaction with the environment. The emerging information-processing approach to cognition also emphasized structured information, but situated it in the perceiver's mind. The environment's role was simply to provide a static stimulus, which would produce information on the retina (or other sensory organ); that information would then be serially processed to obtain a series of mental representations culminating in some sort of semantic construal of the stimulus.[5]

5 In a critique of Gibson's theory, Fodor and Pylyshyn (1981) further insisted that the human mind was the primary source of structure, not the environment. In this vein, per-

In a remarkably prescient book, *Cognition and Reality*, Neisser (1976) argued for an integration of these approaches that would give due regard to structure in both the environment and in the mind. He suggested that mental schemata continuously predict and accommodate to events in the environment in a dynamic, interactive manner. Neisser criticized cognitive psychology for attempting to reduce the environment to a static moment that was retinally encoded and then sequentially processed with no further reference to the flow of events in the environment. (In particular, he cast a jaded eye on psychologists' faithful attachment to their tachistoscopes, which were used to present isolated visual events for durations well under one second.) He argued for a change in emphasis to dynamic perception of spatio-temporal patterns.

There was little reason in the 1960s to make a connection between Rosenblatt's simple perceptrons and Gibson's purely ecological psychology. No explicit connection of this kind was made by Neisser (1976) in his book either. (It may be relevant to note, however, that Neisser had an early interest in parallel pattern recognition models such as Selfridge's Pandemonium, which was a feedforward network for recognizing letters on the basis of letter features; see Selfridge and Neisser, 1960.) Within the next dozen years, however, network research received a new lease on life from (a) mathematical advances that characterize nonlinear dynamical processing in complex, many-layered networks as well as learning algorithms for such networks; and (b) design innovations that structure the flow of information in useful ways (e.g., recurrent networks). In the context of this new connectionism, Neisser's (1976) book can be read retrospectively as urging attention to a task that networks could be made to perform, that is, modeling the functioning of the mental system in dynamic articulation with the environment. (The book was written, and most often has been read, however, without making this connection.) Our claim is that as cognitive psychology becomes increasingly connectionist, it may become increasingly ecological as well.

There is a large promissory note attached to this prediction, because the habits of the past have carried over to connectionist modeling: typically an input pattern is presented to a network, and then the network processes it. Even if the network is interactive, a single input pattern is presented once, or is "clamped" on throughout processing. Hence, the network is dynamic but the input is not. There is nothing inevitable about this arrangement, however; network processing of dynamic input patterns is an area that is ripe for exploration. This

ceptual psychologists such as Rock (1983) emphasized the use of ambiguous stimuli such as visual illusions to learn how the mind imposed structure upon sensory arrays.

would pose logistical challenges (preparation of training patterns can already be a complex undertaking), but would also accelerate the trend towards increased attention to the structure of the environment that connectionism has already fostered within cognitive psychology. Because the emphasis would then be placed on the dynamics of the environment, connectionists within cognitive psychology would gain a route to rapprochement with ecological psychology. Some ecological psychologists might themselves adopt (and adapt) connectionism's tools for dynamic modeling of cognitive networks in articulation with environments. Hence, connectionist models that incorporate dynamic input could help to realize Neisser's dream of a cognitive psychology that explores the mind in its environment.

In Neisser's own most recent contribution to an integrated theory (Neisser, 1989), he argues for distinguishing between two different perceptual systems on the basis of a careful analysis of the tasks which organisms must perform in their ecological situation. He cites supporting evidence from neurological disorders, infant and adult perception, prism experiments, and animal research. One system is specialized for *direct perception*. It locates the organism in its surround, attends to the positions and shapes of nearby objects with respect to the possibilities for action which they afford, and obtains information from and about movement (e.g., it uses the structure of optical flow to track the perceiver's own motion, and can anticipate the time of collision with an approaching object). The other system is actually a cluster of systems, each of which carries out some aspect of *recognition*. These systems identify and categorize stimuli, individual objects and persons, linguistic entities, and so forth, on the basis of their fit to a mental representation. Recognition works differently from direct perception, by accumulating evidence rather than resonating to invariants. Movement is not an important source of that evidence. Because current network models work on static input patterns, they are most suitable as models of the recognition system. In a more mature connectionism, however, static input may be regarded as a special case of dynamic input. Interactive networks operating on dynamically changing input could be used to model the direct perception system; indeed, the connectionist concept of relaxing or settling into a stable state is reminiscent of the ecological concept of resonating to an invariant.

Finally, at the same time that connectionists come to view the environment as more dynamic, they might also come to view the mind as more biologically constrained. That is, as Shepard (1989) and Rumelhart and McClelland (1986, *PDP:4*) have explored, networks need not be the *tabula rasa* that was assumed by the ancestral tradition of associationism. Evolution has granted our species a particular array of biological constraints, including innate mechanisms and maturational programs, and ultimately these will have to be incorporated in connectionist models of cognition. An expansion of connectionist research in this direction would provide yet other opportunities for rapprochement, not only with ecological psychology's tendency to assume biological constraint, but possibly reaching as far as Chomsky's construal of language as an innate cognitive system. The disciplines that could become most directly involved in this facet of connectionist research are developmental biology (at level 2 of the specialization hierarchy described earlier), and developmental psychology (at level 3, along with cognitive and ecological psychology). We shall not discuss developmental biology, but turn now to considering the possible impact of connectionism on issues and approaches in developmental psychology, including but not limited to the nature/nurture question.

Developmental Psychology

Developmental psychology is the part of psychology that addresses questions of change (and stability) in the developing organism. It intersects with cognitive psychology in certain areas of inquiry, specifically, cognitive and linguistic development. Hence, developmental psychology stands to benefit from all of the properties of connectionism that already have been considered throughout this book. A few of these are: (1) an alternative approach to rules and representations that is less brittle than the traditional symbolic approach; (2) adaptive feature extraction by means of hidden units; (3) the implementation of multiple soft constraints; and (4) resistance to damage and similar features related to neural plausibility. In addition to these, there are specifically developmental implications of connectionism that could substantially reinvigorate developmental psychology as a discipline, particularly in the areas of developmental theory, cognitive development, and linguistic development. We shall discuss several of these implications, all of which are variations on the theme that connectionism suggests (1) new interpretations of traditional constructs; and (2) a means of exploring an area of concern by means of connectionist modeling of developmental data. The areas of concern for which we shall develop these themes are mechanisms of development, context effects, stage-like changes, and developmental (and acquired) disabilities.

Mechanisms of Development

Understanding the mechanisms of development is a central task for developmental psychology, but progress has been disappointingly slow.

Some of the proposed mechanisms are intuitively appealing, but uncomfortably vague or difficult to substantiate or investigate. Consider the traditional distinction between two mechanisms at the highest level of generality: maturation and learning. Maturation is a biological growth process by which sequences of developmental changes (especially neurological changes such as myelination) emerge under genetic control. Learning, by contrast, is the means by which experience serves as a source of change in how an individual construes the environment. The fact that there is a complex interplay between these two mechanisms has made it quite difficult to conceptualize or study them except in situations of reduced complexity, such as neurobiological studies in infrahuman species.

Now consider how the distinction could receive fruitful new interpretations in the context of connectionist networks. *Maturation* (both pre- and post-natal) might be interpreted in terms of network characteristics such as (a) the maximum number of layers of units that can be achieved within each subnetwork or module; (b) the number of functional connections in the fan-out of an average unit (i.e., those connections with weights not too close to zero); (c) the equation(s) available for calculating new activation levels, and the values of their parameter(s); (d) the equation(s) available to govern learning, and the value of the learning rate parameter. (For example, Hebbian learning might antedate ability to use the delta rule.) Hence, maturation would determine the basic architecture of the system. *Learning*, in contrast, would involve relatively enduring changes in a system of a given architecture that result from its interaction with the environment. The most obvious form of learning is adjustment in the weights of connections, but additional forms will need to be pursued as well. For example, there should be ways of recruiting the knowledge in existing networks in learning a new task, perhaps by copying the existing network (or combining two such networks) and then adapting the copy. (This kind of proposal would presumably apply at the level of psychological modeling, and would need to be implemented in some other way at the neural level.)

As noted above, there is an interplay between maturation and learning in the developing organism, and so these two sources of change cannot be considered solely in isolation. To consider one example, developmental changes in the basic architecture of the system may be affected by experience as well as the innate biological program for maturation. Organisms of identical genetic endowment differ in their rate of maturation as a function of the richness of the environment. The rapid pace of learning that is afforded by a rich environment may mediate this effect. As a second example, one could study the interaction between very early learning and the phenomenon of neurological development in which overproduction of synapses is followed by pruning after relevant experience (see Greenough, Black, and Wallace, 1987). Connectionist networks could be used as a medium for modeling these sorts of interaction (although we are not aware of anyone who has done so). At the very least, it would be worthwhile to use network models as a tool for characterizing changes in learning capabilities that accompany maturation.

Connectionism might also provide a means to augment, reinterpret or replace certain constructs in Piagetian theory (Piaget, 1952). In particular, two strengths of Piaget's theory are (1) the integration of learning with ongoing processing (by means of a process of *accommodation* that carries out both functions in conjunction with a process of *assimilation*), and (2) the postulation of systems that achieve qualitatively distinct stable states (stages) by means of small, gradual changes over time. Connectionism could be viewed as a modern mechanism for achieving stage-like states by means of the heretofore somewhat mysterious processes of accommodation and assimilation. Specifically, assimilation can be interpreted in terms of the tendency of an interactive network to settle into the most appropriate of its stable (attractor) states (see Hinton and Shallice, 1989) when input is presented to it; in Piaget's language, this is the schema to which the experience has been assimilated. Accommodation can be interpreted as the changes in activations as well as weights that occur in order to assimilate the experience. (That is, transient state changes and learning are highly interrelated both in connectionist networks and in Piaget's notion of accommodation. The assimilation of any experience involves both of these aspects of accommodation.) The advantage is that the connectionist interpretation of these processes can actually be designed into networks and observed under a variety of scenarios.

Context Effects

Tasks effects and other types of context effects have been a major frustration for developmental theory. There has been a number of convincing demonstrations that context can influence developmental data to the point that the feasibility of assessing what a child knows is brought into question, and the concept of knowledge itself seems threatened. An extreme case is the difficulty that children with severe retardation have with tests of what they have learned if the test is carried out in a different room or by a different examiner (Garcia and DeHaven, 1974).

However, context can exert a strong influence even for children of normal intelligence. In particular, seemingly minor differences in how a task is designed can determine whether or not preschoolers can perform it (for a review, see Gelman, 1978). Also, some developmental changes have been shown to be quite domain-dependent in their time of occurrence (e.g., Keil's (1989) characterizing-to-defining features shift in semantic development; see also Gardner, 1983). Unfortunately, no *interesting* way to incorporate most context effects into developmental theory has been found.

The one partial exception is the *decontextualization* hypothesis that has been proposed to characterize development, especially during the first few years of life; see Bates (1979) and also Wertsch's (1985) presentation of Vygotsky's theory. The claim is that the child's sensory-motor or cognitive schemata initially are rigidly bound to one or a few contexts, and gradually become more flexible and accessible in a variety of contexts. In symbolic play, for example, a child will pretend to drink from a cup, but not from a cup-like object. Nor will the child initially make a doll or other person drink from the cup (Nicholich, 1977; Bates, 1979). In language comprehension, Reich (1976) noted the highly restricted interpretation his eight-month-old had for "Where's the shoe?" He crawled (past a shoe on the floor if necessary) into his mother's (not his father's) closet and played with the shoes that were in that particular location. In language production, it has been claimed that a particular word initially is limited to a single communicative function (such as naming or requesting), or shows other contextual restrictions. Some of the initial claims of this kind have been shown to be too strong (Huttenlocher and Smiley, 1987). Nevertheless, the notion of decontextualization clearly has some role to play in characterizing development in this early period. What has been lacking is a mechanism.

We suggest that connectionism has considerable potential for providing an explanatory framework for context effects. In fact, this could be the single most important contribution that connectionism would be able to offer to developmental psychology in the next decade. Connectionist research has not emphasized context effects to date; perhaps the entry of developmental psychologists into the field, which has begun, will make this more of a priority. If so, attention may also turn to the likelihood that substantial context effects characterize *adult* performance as well as children's performance, and that their importance has been underrated in cognitive psychology. (For an excellent argument for the importance of context in adult performance, see Jacoby and Brooks, 1987.)

Already there has been some attention to *beneficial* effects of context. Recall McClelland and Rumelhart's (1981; also Rumelhart and

McClelland, 1982) model of context effects in letter perception which we discussed in chapter 4. It suggested a mechanism by which letter recognition can be enhanced by the presence of relevant context, specifically, the rest of a word in which the letter appears. That model relied on effects of top-down activation, but it is possible to obtain certain context effects even in a simple, two-layer feedforward network (which, however, are primarily *disadvantageous*). As a demonstration, we designated two input units in such a network as unchanging *context* units and the other eight units as *content* units. The system learned two arbitrary patterns for each context – that is, given a pattern of binary values ($+1$ and -1) across the input units, the system learned to respond with a designated pattern of binary values across the output units. If a neutral value (0) was placed on the context units on test trials, performance was degraded somewhat, illustrating that the learning had been somewhat context-dependent. This is advantageous if testing is carried out in the same context, but not otherwise. In further illustration, when the same patterns were tested but now with the contexts reversed, performance was degraded even further. Finally, as we increased the number of patterns and the number of units that were context rather than content units, performance was degraded to the point that some output patterns were actually reversed (depending upon which context was used in the test).

Of course, this particular network architecture is too simple to serve as a realistic model of context effects in humans. Such a network has no way to distinguish relevant from irrelevant context, nor even to clearly distinguish context from target information. It does, however, provide a starting point for considering how to simulate (a) disadvantageous effects of irrelevant context, as are often exhibited by children with severe retardation; (b) advantageous effects of relevant context; (c) the kinds of changes needed to support decontextualization. A very simple example of (c) would involve changes in training, such as assuring that irrelevant aspects of context are varied across trials. A genuine account of decontextualization, however, would presumably require changes in the way the network itself is built. Being able to experiment with context effects in network models would provide an entirely new avenue of approach that could lift the study of context effects out of the doldrums, and show them to reflect fundamental mechanisms of development.

Stage-like Transitions

It has been a puzzle that, observed on a large timescale, development seems to involve a succession of discontinuous stages that are qualitatively distinct, internally well-integrated, and to some extent general across domains; but observed on a small timescale, development seems to exhibit considerable continuity across a succession of small changes. Drawing boundaries between stages is difficult enough that many developmental psychologists argue against doing so; a less drastic response is to use the term *stage-like* to characterize the general sequence. Similarly, a particular stage-like achievement can be broadly characterized by rules, but the exceptions and variations in performance are difficult to characterize or account for.

We have already discussed at some length (in chapter 6) a connectionist simulation which sought to address both of these puzzles. Rumelhart and McClelland's (1986) past-tense acquisition model exhibited stage-like learning, including a stage of over-regularization that is characteristic of children, but also exhibited an impressive degree of detail with respect to the mechanisms producing the stages. Exceptional forms were produced by the same mechanism as rule-like forms, and variability was prominent during the transition between stages. Although the model is an initial demonstration, not a mature account, the fact that it suggests a mechanistic explanation for pervasive phenomena of development merits attention. It invites developmental psychologists to develop improved connectionist models, and to use them to explore the mechanisms of development.

Plunkett and Marchman (1989) were among the first developmental psychologists to accept this invitation, and performed an extensive series of past-tense learning simulations, which were discussed in chapter 6. Using rather restrictive assumptions about input to their network (in response to criticisms that had been made of Rumelhart and McClelland's assumptions), they nevertheless were able to obtain (a) a learning stage in which overregularization and other typical errors were made, and (b) at least part of the transition to a final stage of correct past-tense formation. Within individual items, but not as global stages, they also obtained U-shaped learning functions in which good initial performance preceded a period of over-regularization and then correct performance. Plunkett and Marchman further demonstrated that network performance was highly sensitive to the design of training regimens (e.g., type/token ratios). Only some of their training regimens yielded a stage of overregularization, for example.

As a final example, Taraban, McDonald, and MacWhinney (1989) designed a connectionist simulation of German children's acquisition of definite articles, instantiating MacWhinney and Bates's (1989) Competition Model. They were roughly as successful as McClelland and Rumelhart (1986), achieving 98 percent correct production of articles for nouns in the training set, and substantial generalization to new forms. The network's course of acquisition was similar to that of children in several respects; for example, the article for feminine nouns was overextended, and some of the cues were picked up early in learning. Available cues were (a) auditory, lexical, case, and semantic features of the noun, which were presented to the network's input units; and (b) microfeatures, which were extracted by the hidden units, capturing interactions among these explicit cues. These results provide a degree of increased confidence that Rumelhart and McClelland's (1986) past tense results were not a fluke, nor highly dependent on one particular network architecture or training regimen.

Taken together, these simulations underscore something we already know, but may overlook. Like other theoretical approaches, connectionism provides a perspective on development and a tool for investigating developmental issues, but it does not provide many general answers to questions about development. Hence, the conditions under which networks can model global stages of learning can be examined, and we can fruitfully compare different studies that are targeted to that goal. No overall answer can be given, however, to a question such as "Do networks exhibit global stages of learning?".

Developmental and Acquired Disabilities

Given the complexity of human cognition, it is not surprising that there are numerous ways in which the mechanism can fail to develop as expected (developmental disabilities) or in which it can be damaged (acquired disabilities). The performance of a mechanism when it is not intact is a very useful source of information about its components and how they function. Many developmental disabilities (including learning disabilities, autism, language delay, and some varieties of mental retardation) are associated with particular ability profiles that are suggestive of what components are assembled together in the overall cognitive/linguistic system. Information like this can contribute to the design of explicit models of unimpaired performance, and in turn, these models can be altered to simulate particular impairments.

We are not yet aware of any investigations that have applied connectionist modeling techniques to developmental disabilities; however, acquired disabilities can be investigated in a similar fashion and some initial reports are available. *Acquired dyslexia* is a family of reading impairments that may occur when adults suffer lesions in certain brain areas (e.g., due to head injury or stroke). There are several types of acquired dyslexia, and their characteristic symptoms have provided important evidence regarding the components of the language system and how they are interconnected to function cooperatively. For example, individuals with one form of *surface dyslexia* (sometimes called *semantic dyslexia*) can access the pronunciation, but not the meaning, of written words. They also tend to overregularize the pronunciation of words with atypical pronunciations, suggesting that they are processing written words only as letter strings (not as lexical items that have predetermined pronunciations as well as meanings). In contrast, individuals with *deep dyslexia* can access the meaning of a written word, but can pronounce the word only by using an indirect route through the meaning (hence, they cannot read nonwords such as *zat*). The semantic route itself shows some impairment, resulting in semantic errors (e.g., reading *peach* as "apricot"). Somewhat more puzzling is the fact that such individuals also make visual errors (reading *cat* as "mat") and mixed errors (reading *cat* as "rat").

Hinton and Shallice (1989) reported a connectionist simulation of deep dyslexia that provided a non-obvious, but elegant, explanation for the co-occurrence of these three types of error. It well illustrates the use of connectionist simulation of impairment to gain insight into the system that is impaired. The results are rather tentative, as Hinton and Shallice pointed out, because they limited their training set to 40 words that were all three or four letters in length and belonged to one of five semantic categories. They modeled the first half of the semantic route (spelling to meaning) by means of a three-layer feedforward network of units taking continuous activations between 0 and 1. Each of 28 grapheme units encoded a particular letter in a particular position within the word. Using the logistic function, activation was propagated through 40 hidden units to a layer of 68 sememe units (e.g., *green, sweet, does-fly*). The network was trained by back-propagation for approximately 1,000 epochs. (There were certain innovations that need not concern us, including the use of a specialized error measure, an iterative training procedure, and an additional set of interactive "clean-up" units connected to the sememe units; the effect these units was to make actual word meanings more powerful "attractors" than other combinations of sememes.)

Hinton and Shallice then lesioned each part of the network in turn, by removing a proportion of connections (or units) or by adding noise to the connections. After each lesion they tested the network on the 40 words, and interpreted the resulting sememe patterns in terms of the best-fitting word responses. Almost every lesion condition yielded the three characteristic types of error, in varying proportion. They suggested that this outcome is the mark of a cascaded/distributed network: "Such a mixture of error-types may be as much a sign of the operation of a layered connectionist system as dissociations are of modular systems" (1989, p. 34). This is a rather sweeping claim, but appears justified and important at least for the particular case before us: it is the first model that has produced a mechanistic explanation for the combination of error types that are diagnostic of this particular disability. Hinton and Shallice also reported results on other tasks (e.g., they were successful in obtaining good below-threshold forced-choice performance, but not in simulating lexical decision).

Finally, Hinton and Shallice made the important point that the network does not treat the spelling of the word as an arbitrary pointer to the meaning, because networks prefer to learn similar outputs for similar inputs.[6] If words are neighbors in orthographic space (i.e., have similar spellings and hence have similar encodings on the grapheme units), the network tries to set up "basins of attraction" in semantic space that are distinct but adjacent. (The basin is an area around the point corresponding to the exact sememe encoding that is being trained; the clean-up units enable that point to capture activation patterns from throughout its basin.) The network cannot satisfy this preference completely, given the semi-arbitrary structure of the language, but it will do so to the extent possible.

Patterson, Seidenberg, and McClelland (1989) reported a connectionist simulation of dyslexia that focused on the direct (non-semantic) route linking orthography to phonology. They "lesioned" Seidenberg and McClelland's (1989) word-reading network with the aim of producing symptoms of at least one form of surface dyslexia. They were partly successful in this preliminary simulation, but plan further studies to clarify certain unexpected results. It is not yet known whether they will satisfy their more ambitious goal of showing that a single three-layer network is adequate to encode the non-semantic route. Dyslexia provides a challenging test of the Seidenberg and McClelland model, because the existence of different clusters of symptoms has been used to argue for a system with two non-semantic routes rather than one. Their claim of a single route is reminiscent of Rumelhart and McClelland's (1986) treatment of past-tense formation in *PDP:18*, and in fact the same Wickelfeature representation is used for the phonological component in both models. In the present case they are using impairment data rather than developmental data to test the limits of a one-network model in accounting for regular as well as exceptional linguistic mappings.

---

6 Note the relation of this point to our discussion of intentionality in chapter 4. We argued that connectionist representations are nonarbitrary, whereas traditional symbolic theories commonly make the opposite assumption.

We have briefly shown how connectionist networks can be used as models of an unimpaired system, and how alterations in those networks can be used to model impairments and their effects. These are not separate enterprises, because a network that can simulate impaired as well as intact performance is a better-supported model of the human mechanism than a network that can only simulate intact performance. Hence, modeling the impairments in this way is basic research. The basic research can lead to some important applied research, however. A precise understanding of the mechanism, and of how specific types of impairment translate into symptoms, can help to guide the design of interventions. For example, Hinton and Shallice's model suggests (indirectly) that it might be advantageous to re-train the reading system using distinctive orthographic styles for words that tend to be confused semantically. Or if it is graphemes themselves that matter, and not the print style of the grapheme, further simulations (guided by the locations of words in orthographic and semantic space) may suggest optimal ways to select sets of items for training or to sequence those sets. Interventions suggested by the model would be handled the same way as ideas from any other source: they would be tested for efficacy, and incorporated into clinical practice if warranted by the results. What is encouraging is the likelihood that some of the interventions suggested by connectionist modeling may be both non-obvious and highly successful. We have focused our discussion on acquired dyslexia, but this optimistic assessment applies to developmental disabilities and to other acquired disabilities as well.

Concluding Comments

We have focused upon connectionism's potential impact on developmental psychology as well as the fields of developmental and acquired disabilities. It is worth emphasizing that research in these fields can contribute to the connectionist program as well; the influence need not occur in only one direction. As one illustration, there are large data sets in these fields that can be used to suggest and evaluate particular simulations. Intervention, in particular, is a context that can generate detailed longitudinal learning data. As a second illustration, development is in part a process of building more complex systems from simpler ones. The particular simple and complex systems of the developing child are ones that will be highly relevant to model, and the characterizations of those systems that already exist in developmental psychology should provide at least some clues as to how to proceed. Third, developmental neurobiology can suggest directions to pursue in biologically-oriented neural networks. (Eventually, pursuit of networks at both the lower, neural level and the higher, cognitive level might result in better potential for integrating accounts across levels.)

Our final comment is one that applies to a number of subdisciplines in addition to developmental psychology: connectionism carries difficulties as well as promises, and the difficulties will affect how and whether the promises are kept. Connectionism does not offer many answers at this time, but rather the potential to obtain answers as connectionist modeling itself is altered and enhanced. Hard work, not just ardent belief, is needed to actualize the potential, and there is no way of knowing how many developmental psychologists will sign on for this job. Considering how few have pursued the previously most promising approach to modeling, production systems, the number could be smaller than the advantages would suggest. Also, there is no reason to think that connectionism will be any less controversial in developmental psychology than in cognitive psychology. Hence, while connectionism will almost certainly enliven developmental theorization in the 1990s, it may fail to penetrate deeply or broadly enough to become a dominant theoretical force.

Neuroscience

Although our own focus has been on connectionism as practised in artificial intelligence and psychology, its oldest and most prominent roots are in neuroscience. Networks in neuroscience are regarded more or less literally as *neural networks* that model neural structures and events. That is, the units are taken to be neurons, and the connections to represent synapses (correspondences that are now understood to involve a greater degree of idealization than was evident initially). Some of these models have involved specific neural areas (e.g., Grossberg, 1976; Bienenstock, Cooper, and Munro, 1982); others have targeted a particular function such as concept formation (e.g., Amari, 1977) or memory (e.g., J. A. Anderson, 1972; Little and Shaw, 1975); and others have been quite general proposals (e.g., Edelman, 1987; Reeke and Edelman, 1988; Grossberg, 1982, 1988; McCulloch and Pitts, 1943; Rosenblatt, 1958). When neural network modeling began to influence some key cognitive scientists in the late 1970s (particularly through the influence of J. A. Anderson), networks were used to obtain a more abstract kind of model that could be applied to the cognitive, rather than neural, level of description. Yet these investigators adopted, as a starting point, essentially the same network architectures that had been developed for the neural level. (Innovations soon followed, including the discovery of the back-propagation learning algorithm for training hidden units.)

Within cognitive science, which is the perspective we have adopted throughout this book, it is common to speak of connectionist models as *neurally inspired* and of their units as *neuron-like*. Investigators who use this language are conveying that they do not consider their models to be models of neural systems as such. This is justified by the observation that there are many well-described features of neural systems that are not embodied in connectionist models, and a number of connectionist features (such as back-propagation) that do not have a straightforward neural interpretation. Instead, units are taken to correspond to symbols (in localist models) or to subsymbols or microfeatures (in distributed models). Yet, certain similarities are intriguing. For example, connectionist units and neurons are both elementary processing units that combine inputs from some units and send outputs to yet other units. In both connectionist networks and nervous systems it is the pattern of connectivity that seems to be a principal determinant of behavior. These and other similarities lend plausibility to the assumption that whatever processing can be done in connectionist architectures could be performed in the nervous system.

This history has made for a rather tangled set of claims about how connectionist models of the abstract, cognitive variety relate to the neural level of organisms, to neuroscience, and to connectionist models of the explicitly neural variety. One view is that the distinction itself is misguided; connectionism should be viewed as a type of neural research, which facilitates the reduction of cognitive investigations to neural theorizing. A second view is that connectionism (within cognitive science) should be focused at a more abstract level of analysis, related to but not identified with neural research. In the following sections we shall explore both of these alternatives. (For more extensive discussion from an interdisciplinary conference on this topic, see Nadel, Cooper, Culicover and Harnish, 1989.)

Connectionism as a Neural Model

A major point of controversy in the philosophy of cognitive science has been the proper relation between cognitive theories and neuroscience theories. The model of theory reduction has provided one standard view of how theories from different disciplines are to be related. For one theory to be reduced to another, two requirements must be satisfied: (1) translation principles must be established equating the basic terms of the theory to be reduced to terms in the reducing theory; and (2) the laws of the reduced theory must then be derived from laws of the reducing theory (Nagel, 1960). Among the virtues often cited for the reduction of one set of theories to another are ontological economy (achieved by showing that the terminology of the reduced theory does not refer to entities not already identified in the reducing theory) and explanatory unification (achieved by showing that the explanatory laws of the reduced theory can be derived from and thus explained in terms of the laws of the reducing theory). (For a more detailed presentation and critical discussion of the theory reduction model, see Bechtel, 1988a.)

Advocates of the reduction of cognitive theories to neuroscience theories argue that from neuroscience to the most basic disciplines of physics, theories either have been, or are in the process of being, reduced to those of more basic disciplines. To oppose the reduction of cognitive theories to neuroscience ones would create an unnatural rift between cognitive science and the rest of science and cut the cognitive sciences off from the benefits to be procured by integration with the rest of science. The basic entities of cognitive science would not be related to the more basic entities of science, and so we could not use what we know about more basic phenomena to understand the entities posited in cognitive theories. Likewise, the basic laws of cognitive science would lack any justification in terms of more basic phenomena, and we could never understand why they should hold.

Advocates of the theory reduction model for the cognitive sciences, such as Patricia and Paul Churchland, have criticized cognitive theories developed within the symbolic tradition for not being reducible to neuroscience theories. The basic entities of symbolic theories, symbols and rules for manipulating symbols, have not been identified with more basic physical entities (in the brain). The laws postulated to describe symbolic information processing have not been reduced, and are not viewed as reducible, to more basic physical laws. On first encounter, this charge appears implausible. As we have noted, one of the models for the development of symbolic cognitive science was the development of a physical device, the digital computer, which can be interpreted as a symbol processing machine. The ways in which symbols are implemented in a (physical) computer at least suggest that they might also be implemented in a (physical) brain.

The construal of cognitive theories as not reducible to neuroscience theories, however, did not originate with reductionists. It is due, in fact, to certain advocates of the symbolic tradition and to the perspective they have taken on the mind–body problem. Philosophers such as Hillary Putnam (1975b) opposed the reductionistic mind–brain identity theory. Using the model of a programmed computer, he noted that programs (symbolic structures) can be implemented on many different computers. Similarly, he argued, mental states could in fact be realized in many different kinds of physical systems. Hence, he concluded it was incorrect to identify symbolic states or mental states with their physical instantiations. This argument gave rise to what is commonly called the *functionalist* theory of mind according to which mental states are characterized and to be understood in terms of their interactions with other mental states, not in terms of their physical embodiment (see Bechtel, 1988b). Symbolic theories are functionalist theories *par excellence*, and thus are construed as not reducible to neuroscience theories. (Multiple realizability of mental states is, in fact, not sufficient to show that mentalistic theories cannot be reduced to neuroscience ones. See Richardson (1979). Below we shall outline a somewhat more compelling argument.)

For reductionists like the Churchlands, the failure of a theory to reduce to more basic theories is evidence of the vacuousness and misguidedness of the unreduced theory. If a theory does not reduce, it should be abandoned. Thus, the Churchlands are prepared to abandon symbolic approaches to cognitive science (as well as propositional attitude or folk psychological theories of mind, which we shall discuss in the next section). They recommend that cognitive science should seek to develop theories of information processing that are not just compatible with, but actually modeled upon, neural information-processing theories so as to insure reduction. Because connectionism is modeled on aspects of neural processing, they see it as facilitating a reduction of cognitive theorizing to neuroscience theorizing, and thus as integrating cognitive science into the main fabric of science (P. S. Churchland, 1986; P. M. Churchland, 1989).

Not surprisingly, one of the major advocates of the symbolic approach, Jerry Fodor, has addressed the issue of theory reduction, and argues that the theory reduction model is inappropriate for what he calls the *special sciences*, of which psychology is one (Fodor, 1974). The core of his argument is the claim that there are law-like regularities in nature that are not reducible to the laws of the more basic sciences. The reason they are not reducible is that the concepts used to state these regularities cannot be translated into the concepts of the more basic sciences. For example, one cannot specify in the terms of the more basic sciences what conditions must be met for something to count as money, and yet there are law-like regularities in economics that refer to money. Hence, economics might not be reducible to more basic sciences. Fodor maintains that it nevertheless is a legitimate science, and contends that the same applies to cognitive disciplines such as psychology. There are regularities in the behavior of organisms that might be stateable in terms of psychology but not in the vocabulary of the more basic sciences.

While Fodor's arguments for the nonreducibility of special sciences may allow for what many practitioners of those sciences may judge to be a healthy sort of autonomy, there are drawbacks to this approach. The strong autonomy position seems to entail that there can be no fruitful direct interactions between the special sciences and more basic sciences. Since the categories employed in cognitive science and neuroscience are incompatible with each other, we cannot learn about cognitive processes by studying how they are instantiated in the brain. The history of science, however, suggests that studies at different levels do contribute to each other. For example, understanding biochemical processes helped researchers better understand physiological processes, and vice versa (Bechtel, 1984, 1986b). Within psychology itself fruitful interactions with neuroscience have already been realized for peripheral processes (e.g., the study of color vision) and in a more general way for cognitive processes (e.g., neurolinguistic research). These examples lend plausibility to the idea that we can learn more about how our cognitive systems operate by learning about neural substrates in which they are realized, and that characterizations of cognitive processes would be a useful guide in developing an understanding of neural processes.

The difficulty here may lie in employing theory reduction as the model for relating different scientific investigations. Evidence from basic sciences suggests that the most fruitful interactions may occur without the reduction of theories in one discipline to those in another. In some instances interaction is facilitated by what Darden and Maull (1977) term *interfield theories*, theories which relate phenomena which are primarily studied in different disciplines. For example, the chromosomal theory of inheritance related Mendelian factors (which were understood functionally in terms of the traits for which they were responsible) with chromosomes, and suggested that Mendelian factors (i.e., genes) might be located on chromosomes. Making this connection led to fruitful developments in work on the nature of chromosomes in cytology, as well as work on the role of genes in studies of heritability of traits. This example illustrates one common kind of interfield theory, which connects entities whose function might be examined in one discipline with entities whose structure is primarily the focus of another discipline. (It is important to bear in mind that an entity that is viewed as a structure from the point of view of one discipline might itself be viewed as a functional product of other structures in another discipline. Hence, the structure/function distinction is relative.) If we do not need reduction to relate disciplines, fruitful interaction might be possible between cognitive science and neuroscience even if we cannot define cognitive entities in neuroscience terms. We can examine constraints on what kinds of neural structures and functions could underlie cognitive processes and what kinds of cognitive processes might be achieved in a system of neurons.

One of the factors that drives people to construe connectionist models as neural models is the desire to employ connectionist models in a reduction of cognitive theories to neuroscience ones. Such a treatment of connectionist theories might also be useful if all we are trying to do is develop interfield connections. We might, for example, construe connectionist theories as attempts to give functional accounts of the processing that occurs in neural structures. But if we are not engaged in constructing reductions, we are not forced to treat connectionist models as neural models, and we can consider whether a looser connection might be more satisfactory.

Connectionism as More Abstract than Neural Models

In neuroscience, the units of a connectionist model are generally taken to correspond, at least roughly, to neurons. Most cognitive science investigators, while appreciating the advantages of "brain-style" modeling, prefer to maintain some distinction between the cognitive and neural levels, and some use the term *connectionist* as though it refers only (or principally) to the cognitive level (a practice we follow in this section for convenience). Smolensky, for example, argues that

it is better *not* to construe the principles of cognition being explored in the connectionist approach as the principles of the neural level. . . . To be sure, the level of analysis adopted by PTC [the proper treatment of connectionism] is lower than that of the traditional, symbolic paradigm; but, at least for the present, the level of PTC is more explicitly related to the level of the symbolic paradigm than it is to the neural level (1988, p. 3).

What are the reasons for differentiating between connectionist and neural models? First, it is critical for cognitive theorizing that connectionist networks carry a semantic interpretation. Very little is known at present about how to do this at the neural level, leaving a lacuna on the neural side in an area which is critical to connectionist research. Second, while connectionist models are inspired by the general character of the nervous system, there are many features of the brain which are not replicated in connectionist systems. An example is the role played by neurotransmitters in the brain, and the differences in function among these transmitters. Another difference is the manner in which inputs are integrated. In connectionist networks net input is computed by means of a linear function, whereas neurons seem to use a more intricate mechanism. Third, conversely, the connectionist program in cognitive science incorporates mathematical, behavioral, computational, and other concerns that might be dealt with quite differently, if at all, at the level of neural modeling. For example, as Smolensky points out (1988, p. 9), "In the drive for more computational power, architectural decisions seem to be driven more and more by mathematical considerations and less and less by neural ones." That is, the equations of dynamical nonlinear modeling need not be thought of as applying to neurons. Neural network modelers have contributed a great deal to the mathematical characterization of networks, but the properties of neurons have guided this work only very broadly.

If it were a goal of connectionist research to facilitate a reduction of cognitive theorizing to neuroscience, these would seem to be serious difficulties that should be addressed immediately. However, as the just-cited comment by Smolensky made evident, many connectionist theorists currently place little priority on making their models more neurally realistic. Furthermore, models are often explored because they seem to be capable of performing interesting cognitive tasks; it is not even clear how one might find a neural implementation of some of the techniques (e.g., back-propagation). (See McCauley (1987b) for an argument that disciplines sometimes need to pursue internal development before developing linkages to adjoining fields.)

If we do not treat connectionist models as modeling activity in the nervous system *per se*, how are we to understand these models? What are they models of? One possibility is to treat connectionist models as relatively abstract models of the processing that occurs in the nervous system. While not constrained to account for specific features of the nervous system at any particular level, they model the sort of information processing which the nervous system is capable of performing. The hope is that by abstracting away from specific features of the brain we may be able to understand the general factors that are involved in performing cognitive operations. Such an account may be useful as a guide to what sorts of activity in the brain are relevant to information processing and help in the identification of actual brain mechanisms involved in cognitive performance.

In discussions of reduction, theories are central and disciplines are identified in terms of their theories. If one theory is reduced to another, then the corresponding discipline is thought to be reduced. But this may result in a misunderstanding of the character of disciplines, which are principally comprised of individuals committed to certain approaches to inquiry (Bechtel, 1987). Thus, we may gain a better perspective on disciplines by considering the kinds of investigation that disciplines are likely to pursue. As we noted in the introduction to this chapter, Abrahamsen (1987) made a distinction between those scientists who are primarily interested in understanding biological systems (biologists) and those who focus on the behavior of organisms (behavioral scientists). Some biologists, however, specialize in those biological systems that underlie behavior, while some behavioral scientists are particularly interested in the biological underpinnings of behavior. This can generate useful interactions in which theories at the two levels are brought to bear on one another, bridging the boundary between disciplines. One perspective to take on connectionism is that it may provide a common formalism that eases the task of bridging this boundary. Investigators from neuroscience may find the abstract characterization of neural events that connectionism offers to be useful in determining how biological systems can constrain or contribute to the behavior of organisms. Behavioral scientists can use connectionism to explore cognitive performance in a way that is at least somewhat sensitive to the nature of the biological system that underlies that performance. Thus, even without facilitating a reduction, connectionism can contribute to fruitful integration of cognitive science and neuroscience.

Philosophy

In many respects symbolic cognitive science is a product of ways of thinking that originated in philosophy. Philosophy has long given primacy to symbolic, especially propositional, modes of representing information. In epistemology and philosophy of science, for example, the information a person might claim to know is assumed to be represented propositionally. Logic is devoted to the study of inference relations between propositions. Such areas of philosophy as ethics and aesthetics are principally concerned with ethical or aesthetic *judgements*, with the contents of judgements being represented propositionally. Perhaps central to all of these uses of propositions is the philosophical way of characterizing mental life in terms of what are known as *propositional attitudes*. Propositional attitudes are attitudes that people are thought to take toward propositions. A person may *believe* that a proposition is true, *wish* that it were true, or *doubt* that it is true. We use sentences ascribing propositional attitudes regularly in characterizing people. For example, we might characterize Churchland as believing that connectionism offers a correct theory of the mind. This idiom is extremely useful since with it we can easily present the differences between people (e.g., by noting that Fodor doubts the same proposition which Churchland believes). Philosophers have coined the term *folk psychology* to refer to people's naive theories of how various propositional attitudes interact, which enable them to predict and explain other people's behavior. In addition to describing folk psychology, philosophers recently have become extremely interested in its scientific status. Philosophers have been taking stands on the claim that folk psychology is likely to go the way of other folk knowledge, for example, folk physics, and be replaced by a more credible scientific account of people.

The importance of connectionism to philosophy emerges first with respect to the question of whether folk psychology remains viable or must be replaced. If it needs to be replaced, then the reliance on propositional representations of knowledge in other areas of philosophy may also be at risk. Even if folk psychology turns out to be compatible with connectionism, connectionism may still have consequences for areas of philosophy such as epistemology and philosophy of science. Thus, we shall first examine the question of whether connectionism contributes to the replacement of folk psychology, then consider its implications for other areas of philosophy.

Folk Psychology

The question of reduction, which emerged as central in our discussion of the relation of connectionism to neuroscience, also figures prominently in discussions about folk psychology. Some advocates of the symbolic approach to cognition have construed it as offering a natural explication of folk psychology since it allows for the possibility that the propositions toward which people hold attitudes might be actually represented in the head. Such a view might treat reasoning as involving the performance of operations on these propositions. For theorists who adopt this perspective the claims of folk psychology will be vindicated if symbolic accounts of mental operations are true, since they will be reducible to true scientific theories (Fodor, 1975, 1987). Other philosophers, however, have anticipated that folk psychology will face a quite different fate. Rorty (1965) and Feyerabend (1963) predicted that folk psychology will go the way of other folk theories – it will be dismissed once we develop an adequate theory of the operation of the mind/brain. This view is known as *eliminative materialism*. Both Patricia and Paul Churchland have recently defended eliminative materialism by maintaining that if a theory fails to reduce to our best scientific theories at lower levels, it must be dismissed as false. They contend that reduction fails in the case of folk psychology because there is nothing in the head with which to identify the propositions it posits. With the re-emergence of connectionism, the Churchlands have deployed it as further support for the nonreducibility of propositions and hence of folk psychology. Their contention again is that network accounts do not provide a place for propositions in our accounts of mental life (P. S. Churchland, 1986; P. M. Churchland, 1988).

We have already raised questions about whether higher-level sciences must reduce to more basic sciences. But the status of folk psychology can be addressed independently of that concern. If connectionism should provide a correct account of mental processing, and if it does not turn out merely to implement symbolic systems, then the account of mental life as actually involving the manipulation of propositions would appear to be false. That is, mental states involving propositions will not figure in the causal genesis of behavior. For the Churchlands, this conclusion entails the further conclusion that folk psychology is false. In making this entailment, they are assuming that folk psychological theories are theories about processes occurring inside people's minds.[7] A number of investigators have argued against collapsing these notions, however (Bechtel, 1985; A. Clark, 1988; Garfield, 1988). Folk psychology refers to people's attributions of propositional attitudes to other people and uses these to predict and explain their behavior. These attributions are made to whole persons; folk psychology does not itself offer an account of the finer-grained internal operations that may produce propositional attitudes or lead to action. If we attribute to a person a particular belief about his or her environment, the internal activities within that person must explain how the person could have such a belief, but the belief itself need not be a discrete internal state. The states inside the person that enable the person to have a belief could have a quite different character.

An example from another discipline may help to clarify this. Certain cells, such as yeast cells, perform fermentation. That is an activity the

---

7 This assumption was promoted by Fodor, who attempted to legitimize folk psychology by showing that the internal activities of the mind involve the same sort of operations as figure in folk psychological accounts. The Churchlands accepted the assumption, but because they characterized the mind differently, it led them to reject rather than accept folk psychology.

cell carries out when in an appropriate environment (e.g., one with adequate sugar and appropriate temperature). But, despite the temptations of early biochemists to explain the fermentation of sugar as itself due to a series of internal fermentation reactions, we now know that it is most useful to characterize the internal operations of the cell in a quite different manner. The activities inside the cell consist of oxidations, reductions, phosphorylations, etc. The complex Embden–Meyerhof pathway inside the cell makes it possible for the cell to carry out fermentation (Bechtel, 1986b).

Applying this point to the case of cognition, the activities inside the head may make it possible for a person to have beliefs and desires, but we do not need to assume that they have internal states that directly correspond to these propositional attitudes. It may be that the internal activities are best described in connectionist vocabulary. That, however, does not show that folk psychology is false. On the one hand, folk psychology might still correctly describe the mental states of persons. Thus, the fate of folk psychology need not be tied to the fate of symbolic theories of cognition. On the other hand, folk psychology could be false, but if it is false, it will be because it does not give a correct characterization of the cognitive states of persons and must be replaced by a better theory at the same level. (McCauley (1986) maintains that, historically, replacements occur when better theories are developed at the same level as the original theory, and not directly as a result of new theories at lower levels.) Neither connectionism nor any other frameworks developed to model internal cognitive processes will disprove folk psychology (see Bechtel, 1985, 1988b).

Epistemology

Even if the rise of connectionism does not suffice to discredit folk psychology or propositional attitude discourse as a tool for describing people, it may still have profound implications for other domains of philosophy, especially epistemology and philosophy of science. The reason for this is that these areas of philosophy have generally taken the proposition to be the basic unit of analysis. Knowledge is taken to be represented in propositions and so most of the major questions have been construed as questions about the relations between these propositions. For example, in epistemology a central issue has been to define what constitutes knowledge. The most widely discussed candidate has been the proposal that knowledge involves *justified true belief*. This is recognized to be inadequate (Gettier, 1963), and much attention has been directed toward finding additional criteria that will adequately distinguish knowledge from mere belief. For our purposes, though, what is most salient in this approach is that all of the defining conditions are limited to a propositional conception of knowledge. Only propositions are generally assigned truth values, and belief is generally analyzed as a propositional attitude. Accordingly, the analysis of justification has focused on identifying the sorts of relation between propositions (logical relations) or between external evidence and propositions (causal relations) that are sufficient to turn a belief into knowledge.

For the most part, epistemologists have not tried to relate their analyses of knowledge to psychological findings about cognition. One reason for this is that epistemology is generally thought to have a major normative dimension; its goal has been to specify what *should* constitute knowledge and not merely describe what is taken to be knowledge. But increasingly epistemologists have become interested in fitting normative accounts to psychological accounts of the knowledge acquisition process. For example, one approach to analyzing justification treats a proposition as known if it is the product of a reliable belief-making mechanism (Goldman, 1986). This invites collaboration with empirical psychology in order to determine what belief making processes are reliable. As long as the psychological accounts are symbolic, then this sort of collaboration between epistemologists and psychologists is at least possible. But connectionism raises the prospect that belief-making processes should not be understood as logical operations upon propositions, and that even the states of believing or knowing should not be understood in terms of propositionally encoded information. For example, connectionists do speak of a network recognizing an object presented to it, which in folk psychological terms we might gloss as forming a belief as to what is presented, and relying on knowledge to do so. The belief that a particular object is presented to the network is not encoded propositionally, but in terms of activations of units. The knowledge that is required to arrive at this belief is also not encoded propositionally, but in the weights of the various connections in the network. The propositional attitude statement provides a gloss on the system's state, but not a description of its internal structure.

If connectionism should provide an adequate account of the processes occurring in us when we believe or know certain things, then the question arises as to whether understanding network mechanisms can be of any use to epistemologists seeking to understand, for example, when a belief should count as knowledge. It is clear that since networks do not work by logically manipulating propositions (at least directly), any account of justification that would draw on connectionist principles would not be able to limit itself to principles of logical inference in describing how the belief state was arrived at. Rather, we would rely on something like the notion of maximal satisfaction of soft constraints to describe how the network behaved, and in evaluating its performance we would presumably consider whether the constraints it satisfied in arriving at its output state were the appropriate constraints. This would lead us into an evaluation of how a network had been trained, specifically, whether its training had resulted in weights that enabled it to respond to inputs in a manner that was most likely to meet its needs in the environment. For example, a network that has not been trained so as to recognize predators reliably, and which sometimes mistook them for allies, would be judged to have an unreliable belief generator.

What this suggests is that if connectionist accounts are correct, epistemologists who want to understand how humans arrive at belief states might benefit from interfacing with connectionist-level accounts. At an extreme, some epistemologists might even decide to work directly at the connectionist level. If such epistemologists were interested in normative questions, they would have to develop standards for assessing how such networks ought to behave in particular situations. For example, they might explore what weight settings would best enable a network to deal with a particular context and what alternative settings might only provide an illusion of competence in a particular domain. This would constitute a major change, since epistemology has generally been pursued through conceptual analysis, not empirical inquiry. Such a recasting of epistemology would be one way of answering Quine's (1969b) call for epistemology to become a part of empirical science.

There is a distinction within epistemology, however, that might enable something like the more traditional approaches to epistemology to continue even if connectionism is generally accepted as an account of mental mechanisms. Epistemologists distinguish between whether persons arrive at beliefs in a manner that is justified and whether they can in fact produce justifications for their beliefs subsequently, no matter how they arrived at them. If an individual asserts a proposition, then the question might arise as to whether she could produce in support of it a set of propositions that would meet the canons of argumentation. Inquiry into what types of propositions would be needed to provide justification might provide a domain for more traditional epistemology.

Even this more traditional sort of epistemology might be broadened, however, in response to interdisciplinary considerations. In particular, connectionist researchers within cognitive psychology may convincingly demonstrate that pattern recognition processes are a primary means by which we formulate propositions and move from accepting one proposition to accepting another. If so, if would raise a question of whether these pattern-based movements from proposition to proposition, which might deviate from the inference rules of deductive logic, are nevertheless rational. If so, epistemologists would need to add alternative canons of rationality to those of deductive logic, and include them within the scope of epistemological inquiry. Presumably, they would seek to do this in a way that allowed them to continue working at the propositional level, leaving to psychologists the task of constructing network models of the underlying mechanisms. Nevertheless, this sort of shift in the scope of epistemology could substantially contribute to bringing epistemologists further into the cognitive science research cluster.

Philosophy of Science

Turning briefly to philosophy of science, where the goal is to specify what scientific explanations consist in and to identify the proper criteria for evaluating proposed explanations, we find that many of the same concerns arise. For example, scientists do rely upon linguistic expressions to announce their results and to defend them. For these aspects of science some of the traditional analyses might suffice. For example, explanation is often thought to involve arguments that show that what was to be explained was the expected result of a general law. This law is viewed as being tested by determining whether its predicted consequences are true or false. To some degree, this is what appears to happen in the linguistic discourse and publications of scientists. But there is also the question of what happens in the head of a scientist as he or she seeks explanations and evaluates whether proposed ones are true. Here connectionism may provide a quite different picture of what is involved in science. Paul Churchland (1989) argues that explaining a phenomenon is very similar to the process of recognizing it. He proposes that explanation involves activating a prototype (explanans) that enables the organism to deal with a situation (explanandum) for which understanding is needed:

Explanatory understanding consists in the activation of a specific prototype vector in a well-trained network. It consists in the apprehension of the problematic case as an instance of a general type, *a type for which the creature has a detailed and well-informed representation*. Such a representation allows the creature to anticipate aspects of the case so far unperceived, and to deploy practical techniques appropriate to the case at hand. (1989, p. 210)

This proposal offers a variety of benefits. It accounts for the observation that explanation often seems to have much in common with pattern recognition and is sometimes arrived at instantaneously: one simply sees that a puzzling phenomenon fits a well-established pattern. It also seems to accommodate the fact that scientists sometimes arrive at an explanation before they are fully able to verbalize it. Finally, it provides a new perspective on the relation between discovery and justification. Following Reichenbach (1966), it became popular to construe these two activities as totally distinct, with discovery being a non-logical process to be analyzed by psychologists, while justification was a matter of logic to be analyzed by philosophers. Recently some philosophers of science (e.g., Nickles, 1980) have rejected the distinction, arguing that the reasoning involved in discovery is not totally dissimilar to that employed in justification, and that both should be analyzed together since in fact they are not clearly distinguished in scientific practice. In Churchland's proposal, these two processes are closely linked; both involve determining which prototype best fits the situation.

There remains, however, much to be done to develop this proposal. There appear to be differences as well as similarities between perception and explanation. Perception is almost always immediate, whereas the quest for an explanation is often prolonged. A connectionist account is needed of what is entailed in the search for explanations and why finding an explanation often is difficult. One possibility is that explaining a phenomenon not previously explained requires more than activating a prototype; it may require modifying the network so that a prototype, or an altered prototype, will now apply to the new situation. (A new prototype will only count as an explanation, presumably, if it facilitates appropriately dealing with the new phenomenon in ways that relate it to previously known phenomena.) Such alteration may take time and constitute a kind of change quite unlike that envisioned in current connectionist learning rules (which rely principally on error correction). There is also the difference that in perception, once an object is recognized, a response may simply ensue. Once an explanation is suggested, however, there is usually a process of testing the adequacy of that explanation. What kind of processing this would require in a network must be examined.

Although it has been possible only to sketch them here, the network model does suggest new fruitful ways of exploring old topics in philosophy of science as well as epistemology, and so offers great potential for modifying and expanding philosophical inquiries in these areas. Its impact may also go beyond these domains to other areas in philosophy. If we take seriously the idea that recognizing a pattern and responding to it is a basic cognitive activity, that may suggest different ways of thinking about ethical reasoning, for example. Instead of construing ethical reasoning as a matter of evaluating actions by rules (deontological or utilitarian), we may think of it as a matter of developing and employing prototypes. So far connectionism's influence has been limited to philosophy of mind, but clearly it has potential for shaping many other areas of philosophy.

Linguistics

In light of the forays that connectionists have made into modeling language processing, it is not surprising that a number of linguists and psycholinguists have given connectionism some notice. There have been three quite distinct responses, which reflect different assumptions about what levels of description are germane to language, and who should carry out the work at each level. First, some linguists within the Chomskian tradition of generative grammar have regarded connectionism as a challenger. Second, adherents of what has recently become known as *cognitive linguistics* have welcomed connectionism as an ally in their construction of a psychologically-oriented alternative to Chomskian linguistics. Third, other linguists have chosen a middle ground. They emphasize that linguistic theory and connectionism involve different levels of inquiry, and can peacefully coexist in carrying out their respective missions.

Connectionism as a Challenger

Virtually every linguistic theory uses symbols and rules of some kind to describe the regularities that characterize human languages. In a generative grammar the rules are constructed to *operate* on symbols so as to generate all of the grammatical sentences of the language. One of Chomsky's most notable claims is that a grammar is a model of the speaker/hearer's tacit knowledge of language (linguistic *competence*). That knowledge is mentally represented, and hence linguistics is (or should be) a part of cognitive psychology. The study of linguistic *performance*, in which the tacit knowledge is actually used, is assigned to a different set of investigators in this expanded cognitive psychology – those who call themselves psychologists or psycholinguists. Within this framework, it is possible (although not inevitable) to view as a challenge the approximationist claim that explicit rules need not be mentally represented, and that rules merely approximate the more detailed account of data that is provided by connectionist models. The approximationists would seem to be claiming that there is no rule-based competence for the performance theory to consult and use. Linguistic rules therefore lose their causal role in cognition, an unacceptable outcome. The conclusion is that the connectionist program is misguided and must be rejected. In those critiques that have appeared in print a variety of much more specific arguments have been marshalled, but the fundamental objection is to the loss of rules as an explanatory device. It is worth noting that most of the authors of these critiques have been psycholinguists who work within a broadly Chomskian framework, in particular, Jerry Fodor, Tom Bever, and Steven Pinker. Chomskian linguists have perhaps seen the threat as more distant, since the connectionist theories are psycholinguistic in nature and have not directly challenged linguistics as a discipline; among them only Alan Prince has offered a published critique (with Pinker). Nevertheless if one interprets the Chomskian notion of competence as providing the model of how language is represented in the mind, connectionists would seem to be offering a counter-proposal that would deny this role to linguistic theory. (For two alternative interpretations of competence, see the third section of this chapter and Lawson and McCauley, 1990.)

If one assumes that linguistic analyses ought to conform to psychological processing, then connectionism, if successful, would have dramatic consequences for linguistic analyses in the Chomskian tradition. In place of analyses that used formal rules to account for the grammatical structures in a language, linguistics would need to develop analyses that rely on the satisfaction of soft constraints that are accomplished by networks.

Connectionism as an Ally: Cognitive Linguistics

Chomsky, while making claims about the mind on the basis of linguistic analysis, has little interest in incorporating traditionally psychological data or constructs in forming his linguistic theory. While claiming that competence is mental, he sharply distinguishes competence from performance. This framework has been challenged by a number of theorists (e.g., Fouconnier, 1985; Lakoff, 1987; Langacker, 1987a), who deny that we can understand either the syntax or semantics of language without understanding the psychological processing that underlies it. They refer to their program as *cognitive linguistics*. Langacker (1987a), a principal advocate, characterizes some of the core commitments of cognitive linguists as follows. First, they deny the autonomy (and primacy) of syntactic analysis advocated by the Chomskian tradition; instead, semantics is regarded as fundamental and pervasive. Furthermore, they reject the sort of *objectivist* semantic analysis that starts with propositions and seeks to explicate meaning in terms of truth conditions. Rather, they advocate a *subjectivist* or *conceptualist* analysis of language which tries to show how both the grammar and meaning of linguistic idioms is grounded in such factors as the body of knowledge that speakers possess, the mental models they build, and the mappings they make between domains of knowledge. Proponents of this view emphasize the role of metaphor in shaping language and the manner in which the meanings of terms might be extended by decisions to include conceptually related entities, resulting in what Lakoff (1987) refers to as *radial categories.*

Logical reasoning and rule application are not the sort of cognitive activities that cognitive linguists view as central to understanding language. Rather, they emphasize such functions as the extraction of prototypes and the identification of metaphors and analogies, and often regard linguistic expressions as solutions to multiple, soft constraints, many of which are directly cognitive in nature. Therefore it is not surprising that cognitive linguists have embraced connectionism as quite relevant to their program. Langacker, for example, draws the linkage as follows:

cognitive grammar (at least my own formulation of it) is basically compatible with the connectionist philosophy. First, cognitive grammar makes no qualitative distinction between rules and their instantiations-rules are simply schematized expressions; moreover, the "schemas" in question are thought of as being "immanent" to their instantiations, not as separate or discrete structures. Second, only elements with semantic and/or phonological content are permitted, and they are characterized directly in terms of such content, not in a propositional format. Third, analyses are based on the overt form of expressions; derivation from abstract, "underlying" representations is precluded, as is any sort of algorithmic computation. Finally, a linguistic system is viewed as simply an inventory of "cognitive routines", which are interpretable as recurrent patterns of activation that are easily elicited by virtue of connection weights; the construction of complex expression reduces to the coactivation of appropriate routines and "relaxation" into a pattern of activation that simultaneously satisfies all constraints. (Langacker, 1987b, pp. 9–10)

To date there have been only limited attempts to directly implement the analyses of cognitive linguistics in a connectionist framework (see Harris, 1989, in press). Hence, it is premature to judge how fruitful the link will be. If a connectionist cognitive linguistics does emerge, we would welcome the insights it might offer, but would also question the status of the theory. Specifically, we would be inclined to regard it as a psycholinguistic rather than linguistic theory, leaving a gap at the most abstract level of analysis that would need to be filled by another theory that is clearly linguistic in nature (and might, for example, reintroduce an autonomous syntax). For arguments that this abstract level is in fact necessary, we turn now to the third position that has been adopted by some linguists.

A Middle Ground

Finally, a middle ground is possible in which connectionist modeling is clearly distinguished from linguistic theory, and therefore need not be viewed as either a challenger or a close ally. From this perspective, linguistic theories are abstract analyses that specify the well-formed utterances of the language, and bear only indirectly on the design of theories that specify how language is mentally processed by a mechanism operating in real time. The psycholinguistic (mechanistic) account should not generate sentences that violate a correct grammar, but the grammar does not determine *the means by which* this should be accomplished. A connectionist network is one means of modeling the embodiment of linguistic knowledge in a psycholinguistic mechanism. There are other possible means as well, and the linguist may choose to remain aloof from the disagreements among psycholinguists regarding the choice of means. This is the stance that we endorse. Kuroda (1987) develops it so clearly in a reply to Langacker (1987b) that we shall use his words to convey this stance here. We enter Kuroda's argument at the point where he takes issue with Langacker's apparent assumption that Chomsky's transformational grammar and its descendants presuppose von Neumann architecture. This architecture, which is utilized in virtually all digital computers, specifies serial processing; all retrieved symbols are funneled through a single central processing unit (CPU), creating a bottleneck that constrains the speed of processing. The parallel processing of connectionist networks is intended to break that bottleneck, permitting more processing to occur per unit of time. But, Kuroda asks:

Where is Chomsky's bottleneck?

   Chomsky's bottleneck does not exist in transformational grammar ... because transformational grammar (or, to put it in a more general form, the concept of grammar presupposed by transformational grammar) is not an information processing device, either of the von Neumann architecture or of the connectionist architecture. Chomsky's bottleneck cannot exist, simply because the notion of such a bottleneck implies a category mistake. (p. 5)

Language behavior implies information processing, but transformational grammar is not a model of an information processing mechanism. Instead, it is a theory (of knowledge) that characterizes (or, at least, partially, determines) the type of information that is to be processed in language behavior.... Grammar itself does not say anything about how the processing of information is done... (p. 5)

Kuroda notes that there is no such category mistake if the claims are limited to cognitive grammar, which does not make this distinction between levels; however, Kuroda himself prefers the Chomskian assumption that grammars should be abstract rather than absorbed into a processing (performance) theory.

It may be tempting to think that, if the grammar characterizes knowledge, it specifies the representations upon which processes act. A complete performance theory includes both representations and processes, however. In an informative discussion of Paul Churchland's (1986) postulation of the neural circuitry of a hypothetical animal (the chchl), Kuroda makes it clear that one role of the theory of knowledge is to provide an abstract framework within which one can make sense of the processing theory. This is a rather subtle point that is native to linguistics rather than psychology, and most psychologists outside of Chomskian psycholinguistics do not explicitly make use of competence theories (if Kuroda is correct, however, they do so implicitly). He writes (quoting Langacker in part):

Whether we attribute "knowledge" ... to the chchl is a terminological question that should not concern us here. The point is that we do not understand what the massive system of connections is about unless we understand the structural characteristic of the information, i.e., the cognitive objects, the chchl's cognitive process deals with.... If "all of the systems' 'knowledge'" that we are to find "lies distributed in connection weights," if all we understand is massive connections and connection weights, understanding a cognitive process would be like trying to disentangle connections of branches and roots of a banyan tree. (p. 9)

Even if studies at a neurological or connectionist level did help to determine the nature of cognitive structures, however:

that does not mean that the study of cognitive faculties is reduced to the study of networks of weighted connections. One has to understand what is reduced... The processing mechanism for linguistic performance ... may well look like a connectionist model; it would be most unlikely to look like a digital computer with the von Neumann architecture. The real issue is whether or not the information it is built to deal with is so structured as to lend itself to human rational comprehension, at least to a substantial degree. (pp. 8–9)

If the information is so structured, on this view, grammars should be consulted in constructing a performance theory:

According to Chomsky's conception of linguistics, linguistic theory is a study that endeavors to determine the form of knowledge that is put to use in linguistic behavior. The study of grammar, in this view, in some methodological sense precedes that of linguistic performance; the latter is crucially dependent on the former. (p. 7)

Kuroda's argument emphasizes the irreducible role that the grammar plays as (a) a competence theory for the linguist, and (b) a guide to constructing a performance (processing) theory for the psycholinguist. He does not focus on the question of in what sense the grammar is a part of the cognitive capacities of the individual. Chomsky's conception of grammar as abstract, yet mentally real, has produced such a variety of interpretations that Kuroda can conclude that connectionism is a different kind of theory than a linguistic theory, while Prince and Langacker view it as quite relevant (at which point their agreement ends, however).

Kuroda's perspective is consistent with the analysis of interdisciplinary relations proposed by Abrahamsen (1987), which we have previously summarized. Her analysis more clearly demarcates the major boundary between biology (neural modeling) and psychology (cognitive modeling, including higher-level connectionist models), but is in agreement with Kuroda in placing yet another major boundary between psychology and linguistics. To understand language, inquiries must be carried out at all of these levels; each makes its own contribution. Cooperation among disciplines in bridging these boundaries makes yet another contribution, and is highly recommended. Attempting to collapse levels, however, results in the loss of distinctive perspectives and the loss of interdisciplinary work. Hence, we endorse connectionist modeling as a promising approach in cognitive science; we resist collapsing these models with the equally promising neural network models; and we resist any inference that disciplines like linguistics have been superseded by the successes of connectionist models.

Concluding Remarks

In encountering the claims of connectionists and counter-claims of traditional symbol theorists, we have often experienced a sense of *déjà vu*. When one of us (Abrahamsen) was a graduate student in the late 1960s, there were vigorous arguments over the adequacy of stimulus-response models versus the newer cognitive models. Suppes (1969), for example, offered a proof that for any finite automaton there is a stimulus-response model that converges to the automaton. Hence, any model involving rules, plans, or other higher-order entities could be reduced to a computationally equivalent stimulus-response model. Our reaction at the time was to note the proof, but not to act on it. Rosenblatt notwithstanding, no one had any idea of how to build a stimulus-response device that could carry out complex cognitive tasks; if it were somehow to be built, we had no means of understanding the behavior of its huge number of stimulus-response pairs. And as Arbib (1969) pointed out, the time required to learn all of the necessary stimulus-response pairings would exceed the lifespan of the organism. It seemed to us that theory should be pushed in the direction that will bring interesting results and deeper understanding. In the late 1960s, that meant pushing towards the cognitive approach. The stimulus-response approach had enjoyed a great deal of success, but its very success was its downfall; there was too little left to learn by pushing it further at that time.

In the late 1980s the situation is similar, but now it is rule models that may be victims of their own success, and a finer-grained approach that offers new insights. The competing claims cannot be settled by abstract proofs of adequacy, however, any more than they could in the earlier era. We now know more about building fine-grained models and understanding their behavior, and we have the computational resources to do so. The only way to find out what we can learn from such models is to build them and learn it. Where they fail, they can be patched; and by the time there are too many patches a new approach should appear from the wings in time to rescue us from frustration and boredom.

In the earlier era, the primary units of fine-grained models were stimulus-response pairs, and there was little idea of how these might organize themselves to exhibit emergent properties. In the connectionist models which are the focus of this book, the primary units are weighted connections between features or other semantically interpreted pairs of units, and there is an abundance of ideas about the macro-architecture of systems of such units. In the nontraditional symbolic models which are contemporaneous with connectionist models, the primary units include microrules, feature probabilities, and the like. Connectionist and nontraditional symbolic modelers have an advantage over stimulus-response psychologists: cognitive science has learned a great deal about cognition at a coarse grain of description, and contemporary modelers can use this knowledge to help guide accounts of cognition at a fine grain. If so, connectionism is not merely a swing back on the pendulum towards associationism, but rather offers a cumulative advance in our knowledge. Connectionism has the potential to coexist peacefully and cooperatively with traditional symbolic models by means of appropriate division of labor; it is less clear how connectionism and nontraditional symbolic models will resolve their desire for the same territory.

Appendix A: Notation

The following diagram compares three notations for frequently used equations. They are shown with respect to input unit i and output unit u in a two-layer network that is being trained using the delta rule for changing weights and the logistic function for computing activation.

Notation used in this book (index for time or input–output pattern is suppressed)	PDP:2 (t indexes time)	PDP:8 (p indexes input-output pattern)
$a_u = \dfrac{1}{1 + e^{-netinput_u}}$	$a_i(t+1) = \dfrac{1}{1 + e^{-net_i(t)}}$	$o_{pj} = \dfrac{1}{1 + e^{+net_{bj}}}$
FAN-IN FROM ALL INPUT UNITS $\quad netinput_u = \sum_i weight_{ui}\, output_i + bias_u$ $\quad input_{ui} = weight_{ui}\, output_i$	$net_i(t) = \sum_j w_{ij}\, o_j(t) - \theta_i$	$net_{bj} = \sum_i w_{ji}\, i_{pi} + \theta_j$
$\boxed{weight_{ui}}$ $\quad \Delta weight_{ui} = lrate\,(d_u - a_u)\, a_i$	$\Delta w_{ij} = \eta\,(t_i(t) - a_i(t))\, o_j(t)$	$\Delta w_{ji} = \eta\,(t_{pj} - o_{pj})\, i_{pi}$
FAN-OUT TO ALL OUTPUT UNITS $\quad output_i = a_i$	$o_j(t) = a_j(t)$	i_{pi} (or o_{pi} in a more general version of the notation)
PROVIDED: a_i (input) and d_u (desired output)	PROVIDED: a_j (input) and t_i (target output)	PROVIDED: i_{pi} (input) and t_{pj} (target output)

Appendix B: Glossary

Note: Terms appearing in definitions which are defined elsewhere in this glossary are indicated in SMALL CAPITAL LETTERS.

activation, activation function, activation rule: The activation of a UNIT is a value that indicates its current level of activity. It is calculated by an activation function (activation rule) from the NET INPUT to the unit, and for some functions, also from the DECAY RATE, previous activation, and/or other factors. Typically nonlinear functions are used, e.g., a threshold or logistic function, and activations are binary (0 or 1) or continuous. Activations are calculated once for each presentation of an INPUT PATTERN in a FEEDFORWARD NETWORK, or once per CYCLE in an INTERACTIVE NETWORK (i.e., many times per input pattern). They are calculated regardless of whether the network is in TRAINING MODE or TEST MODE (in contrast to WEIGHTS, which are changed only in training mode). The pattern of activations across the HIDDEN and OUTPUT UNITS indicates the network's construal of the input pattern. (See pp. 24, 39–47.)

back-propagation, generalized delta rule: A LEARNING RULE that can be applied to MULTI-LAYERED NETWORKS by utilizing a generalization of the DELTA RULE. The ERROR measure, which is calculated at the output units, is propagated back through the network layer by layer. At each layer, WEIGHTS are adjusted according to the equation: $\Delta weight_{jk} = lrate\ delta_j\ a_k$. The $delta_j$ itself is calculated recursively by a function that utilizes the delta values and weights on the next-higher layer as well as the activation of unit j. (See pp. 85–97.)

bias: A constant input to a unit which is provided regardless of the amount of activation propagated from other units. It is sometimes simulated by introducing an additional unit with a constant activation of 1.0 that has a CONNECTION only to the biased unit. Optionally, the WEIGHT of this connection can be adjusted during learning. The negation of bias can be used as a threshold which the input to a binary unit must exceed in order for it to become active.

Boltzmann machine: A type of INTERACTIVE NETWORK proposed by Hinton and Sejnowski (1983, 1986). It has (a) UNITS that take binary ACTIVATION values; (b) an asynchronous update procedure; (c) a stochastic ACTIVATION RULE which is a probabilistic version of the logistic function; (d) a TEMPERATURE parameter that is typically lowered across time by a procedure called *simulated annealing*, by analogy with cooling schedules used to avoid faults in the formation of crystals. Characteristics (c) and (d) help to avoid the local minima to which Hopfield nets are subject. Harmony theory (Smolensky, 1986) specifies a similar type of interactive network. (See pp. 44–5, 97–9.)

case: The term we have used to refer to a particular pairing of an INPUT PATTERN with an OUTPUT PATTERN (which may be a DESIRED OUTPUT pattern); for clarity, we often use the term *input–output* case. A network is trained by presenting it with a series of cases, usually with many trials for each case (one per EPOCH). Its performance can be tested using the same cases, or its ability to generalize can be tested using a new set of cases from the same universe of cases.

cluster analysis: A method of analysis that is increasingly being used to characterize globally what information the HIDDEN UNITS have become sensitive to in a learning paradigm; it is often more tractable than trying to characterize each hidden unit separately. The method extracts regularities in the ACTIVATION patterns across the hidden units across various input–output CASES, and uses them to construct a tree structure representation that clusters together those cases with similar hidden unit patterns. (See pp. 233–4.)

coarse coding: An innovative means of achieving DISTRIBUTED REPRESENTATIONS. Each individual UNIT (called a *receptor* in this context) is designed to have many different INPUTS in its receptive field, and each input is in the receptive field of many different units. The coding scheme can be set up such that no two units have exactly the same receptive field. The presence of a particular input is inferred if there is a high level of activity across many of the units that are receptive to it. (See pp. 54–6.)

competitive learning: An UNSUPERVISED LEARNING PROCEDURE in which a network is presented with a series of INPUT PATTERNS and must discover regularities in those patterns that can be used to divide them into clusters of similar patterns. In the simplest case, there is a set of input units and a set of what we refer to as *detector units* (which combine some of the properties of HIDDEN UNITS and of OUTPUT UNITS); there are INHIBITORY CONNECTIONS among the detector units to assure that just one unit will "win" the competition for a particular input pattern. The effect is to classify the inputs into *n* categories when there are *n* detector units. In more complex systems there may be multiple sets of detector units, or intermediate layers of units. (See pp. 99–100.)

connection: The UNITS in a network are linked by connections, which may be either unidirectional or bidirectional and either EXCITATORY or INHIBITORY. Each connection has a WEIGHT which indicates its importance and modulates the propagation of ACTIVATION along that connection. (See pp. 24–5, 34–8.)

connectionism: An approach to cognitive modeling that has rather deep historical roots, but that in contemporary usage refers to particular classes of computer-implemented models of human or artificial intelligence. Most narrowly, it refers to LOCALIST NETWORKS such as those of Feldman and his colleagues at the University of Rochester. More broadly, it also refers to PARALLEL DISTRIBUTED PROCESSING networks such as those of Rumelhart, McClelland, and their colleagues at University of California, San Diego; Stanford University; and Carnegie-Mellon University. SPREADING ACTIVATION models such as those of Anderson at Carnegie-Mellon University could also be regarded as connectionist, but the term is not typically used in that context (primarily for reasons of sociology of science). Similarly, connectionist-style models by individuals with a neuroscience focus, such as Grossberg, are often referred to by such terms as *neural networks*. Usage is not consistent; for example, some cognitive modelers prefer the term *neural networks*. We have limited our use of the term *connectionism* to refer to localist networks in the Rochester tradition and to PDP networks, distinguishing between these when relevant. Most of our general material also applies to neural networks in neuroscience, but we do not specify those links.

cycle: The updating loop in a synchronous INTERACTIVE NETWORK. One presentation of an INPUT PATTERN results in multiple cycles of processing during which the ACTIVATIONS dynamically interact until the network relaxes into a stable state (a state in which the INPUT to any unit does not change the probability of ACTIVATION of the unit). The complete set of cycles is needed to yield a response (solution, stable state) to a single input pattern; in contrast, in a FEEDFORWARD NETWORK a single pass of activation updates yields the network's response to the input. Cycles (which involve computation of activations) should not be confused with training EPOCHS (which involve computation of WEIGHTS). (See pp. 25, 41, 97.)

decay: A decrease in ACTIVATION that occurs as a function of time or number of events. For example, in an INTERACTIVE NETWORK with a synchronous update procedure, each UNIT can be set to decay once per timing CYCLE by including a decay term in the equation that is used to calculate change in activation (Δa). (Feedforward networks typically do not include a decay term, since activations are computed in a single forward sweep across the layers of units.) Often the decay term is obtained by multiplying a decay rate (a constant between 0 and 1) by some other value. For example, in equations 3 and 4 of chapter 2, the decay rate of 0.1 is multiplied by the difference between the current activation and the resting activation. (See pp. 27–8, 46.)

delta rule: A LEARNING RULE that utilizes the discrepancy between the DESIRED and actual OUTPUT of each OUTPUT UNIT to change the WEIGHTS feeding into it. Specifically, $\Delta weight_{ui} = lrate\ (d_u - a_u)\ a_i$. The delta rule's incorporation of an error correction procedure makes it a prototypical example of SUPERVISED LEARNING. The delta rule is guaranteed to find a solution if the input patterns form a linearly independent set and the input–output mappings are linearly separable, but it also works well at detecting regularities in input–output mappings for nonindependent inputs. It is also known as the Widrow–Hoff rule and as the least mean squares (LMS) rule. (See pp. 74–85.)

desired output: The ACTIVATION value for an OUTPUT UNIT that has been designated as correct in certain SUPERVISED LEARNING procedures, such as those utilizing the DELTA RULE or the GENERALIZED DELTA RULE. The pattern of designated values across all output units is the desired output pattern. Often the terms *target output* and *target output pattern* are used instead.

distributed network, distributed representation: A distributed network is one in which each item of interest is encoded across multiple UNITS in the network (cf. a LOCALIST NETWORK, in which each item of interest is encoded by a single unit in the network). There are a variety of ways to obtain a distributed encoding. The least extreme approach is to distribute the representation across meaningful, context-free units at a lower level of analysis (e.g., phonemic distinctive features if recognition of spoken words is the task). Two ways of further distributing the encoding are (a) to make units like these context-sensitive (e.g., Wickelfeatures) or (b) to use a learning paradigm to obtain HIDDEN

UNITS whose behavior is not defined by the designer. Finally, COARSE CODING is an innovative means of obtaining highly distributed representations. (See pp. 51–6.)

enthymeme: A logic problem in which some parts of a complete pattern or string representing an argument are left unspecified; when the incomplete pattern is presented on the INPUT UNITS of a network, the task is to respond with the complete pattern on the OUTPUT UNITS.

epoch: The training loop, usually with regard to FEEDFORWARD NETWORKS. When a network is in learning or TRAINING MODE, one way to schedule training is to present repeatedly the same set of training cases (input–output patterns) to the network. One run through the set of training patterns is one epoch of training; that is, the epoch includes one trial per training case. WEIGHTS may be altered either after each case within the epoch, or just one time at the end of the epoch (with almost equivalent results). Generally, a large number of epochs is needed to arrive at weights that cannot be further improved. Note that an alternative way to schedule training is to present a large number of cases that are randomly selected from the universe of cases of interest; weights are changed after each case has been processed, and there is no organization of training trials into epochs. Variations on either method may be used in training INTERACTIVE NETWORKS, but if the TEMPERATURE parameter is altered (by simulated annealing) this additional factor yields a more complex training schedule in which the unit relevant to weight-changes is sometimes called a *sweep*.

error: The discrepancy between the DESIRED OUTPUT and ACTUAL OUTPUT of a UNIT in a SUPERVISED LEARNING paradigm. In McClelland and Rumelhart's (1988) exposition of error correction procedures, the errors are squared and summed across all output units to obtain the *pattern sum of squares* (*pss*). Further, the *pss* values are summed across all input–output cases to obtain the *total sum of squares* (*tss*). The *tss* value is a measure of the network's current performance; alternative versions of *pss* and *tss* are obtained by dividing them by 2 (see Boxes 1 and 2, chapter 3). The goal is to drive error as low as possible (to a global, rather than local, minimum). (See pp. 74–5.)

excitatory connection: A CONNECTION that tends to increase the activity of the UNIT into which it feeds INPUT, typically by means of a positive WEIGHT. Excitatory connections are the means by which activation is propagated through a network. Many connectionist networks have INHIBITORY CONNECTIONS as well as excitatory connections.

feedforward network: A network in which the UNITS are organized into separate layers, including at least an input layer and output layer and optionally one or more intermediate layers of HIDDEN UNITS, and activations feed forward from the input to the output layer. In the most typical version, each unit of a given layer has a unidirectional CONNEC-TION to each unit of the next (adjacent) layer. When an INPUT PATTERN is presented, units in one layer feed their ACTIVATION forward to the units in the next layer until the output layer is reached; there are no iterative cycles of change in activation as in an INTERACTIVE NETWORK. Variations include: the addition of INHIBITORY CONNECTIONS within a layer; the addition of connections between nonadjacent layers; sequential networks; recurrent networks; and networks with downwards connections in order to achieve top-down constraints on activation. Note that the number of layers in a feedforward network can be expressed either in terms of the number of layers of connections (the most usual practice) or units (the practice in this book). (See pp. 35–8.)

generalized delta rule: See BACK-PROPAGATION.

graceful degradation: The property of gradual decline of function when a system is overloaded or damaged. Nervous systems exhibit this property, and so do connectionist networks (particularly those using DISTRIBUTED REPRESENTATIONS). (See pp. 60–2.)

harmony theory: See BOLTZMANN MACHINE.

Hebbian learning rule: A LEARNING RULE that specifies how much the WEIGHT of the CONNECTION between two UNITS should be increased or decreased in proportion to the products of their ACTIVATIONS: $weight_{ui}$ = $lrate\ a_u\ a_i$. It builds on Donald Hebb's suggestion that the connection between two neurons might be strengthened whenever they fire at the same time. The Hebbian rule works well if the INPUT PATTERNS are uncorrelated (orthogonal), but this and other limitations are so severe that contemporary connectionist models use different rules, or additional rules. One of the Hebbian rule's most important roles is as an ancestor of the DELTA RULE. (See pp. 48–50, 72–4.)

hidden units: The UNITS in a network which cannot be accessed externally; their operations are "hidden" from the environment. There are no hidden units in the simplest networks, such as a typical PERCEPTRON. In a multi-layered FEEDFORWARD NETWORK, the units in all layers except the INPUT and OUTPUT layers are the hidden units; in an INTERACTIVE

NETWORK, units that do not function to receive input and deliver output are the hidden units. Units that are not hidden units are called VISIBLE UNITS. (See pp. 85–6.)

Hopfield net: A type of INTERACTIVE NETWORK developed by physicist John Hopfield by analogy with a physical system known as a *spin glass*. It has (a) UNITS that take binary ACTIVATION values (0 or 1); (b) an asynchronous update procedure; (c) an ACTIVATION RULE that yields an activation of 1 if the net input is greater than zero. Hopfield showed that such networks can reach a stable state by tending towards an energy minimum. (pp. 42–4.)

inhibitory connection: A CONNECTION that tends to reduce the activity of the UNIT into which it feeds INPUT, typically by means of a negative WEIGHT. Inhibitory connections are often used to assure that just one unit of a set or layer of units will achieve a high degree of activation, as in COMPETITIVE LEARNING. They are inspired by the phenomenon of lateral inhibition in the nervous system. Many connectionist networks have EXCITATORY CONNECTIONS but no inhibitory connections.

input: The $input_{ui}$ to a UNIT u is the product of the $output_i$ of unit i and the WEIGHT of the CONNECTION from i to u. That is, it is the propagated ACTIVATION from i to u, as scaled by the strength of the connection. All of the inputs to u are summed to obtain the *net input* to u. Inputs can be fed *from* INPUT UNITS or HIDDEN UNITS, and are fed *to* hidden units or OUTPUT UNITS.

input units, input layer, input pattern: Input units are those UNITS that can receive ACTIVATION from the external environment (or from another part of the network), initiating the propagation of activation to other units. In a FEEDFORWARD NETWORK, units are organized into layers; the first layer is the input layer (which may itself be subdivided into sets of units that receive specialized types of input). In an INTERACTIVE NETWORK, the input units may perform double-duty as OUTPUT UNITS and may simply be referred to as *visible units*. The input pattern is the pattern of activation across the n input units (which can be treated mathematically as a vector in n-dimensional space). Note that the term *input* alone is sometimes a short form for *input pattern*, but it properly (and distinctively) refers to the value being fed to a unit u along each incoming CONNECTION.

input–output case: See CASE.

interactive network: A network in which UNITS are bidirectionally connected to one another, and ACTIVATIONS change dynamically across a large number of CYCLES. A distinction is made between VISIBLE UNITS and HIDDEN UNITS. INPUT PATTERNS are typically presented to the visible units (or a subset of those units); OUTPUT PATTERNS are the activation pattern across the visible units after processing. Sometimes the input pattern is "clamped" onto a subset of visible units, and the output of interest is the pattern attained across the remaining visible units (i.e., pattern completion). Exemplars include HOPFIELD NETS, BOLTZMANN MACHINES, and HARMONY THEORY; also, the Jets and Sharks simulations in chapter 2 involve a LOCALIST interactive network. (See pp. 38, 41–7.)

language of thought: Jerry Fodor's (1975) term for the innate language-like medium in which, he claims, thought is carried out. Like external language or any other means of symbolic representation, the language of thought has a compositional syntax and semantics. Connectionists typically would deny these claims. (See p. 13.)

learning rule: An algorithm or equation which governs changes in the WEIGHTS of the CONNECTIONS in a network. A good learning rule is adaptive; that is, it increases the appropriateness of the network's responses to a class of INPUTS. Many learning rules incorporate an error-reduction procedure, by which the weight changes tend to minimize the difference between the actual and DESIRED OUTPUT pattern across a set of training inputs. A learning rule is typically applied repeatedly to the same set of training inputs across a large number of training EPOCHS; error is gradually reduced across epochs as the weights are fine-tuned. (See pp. 47–50, 70–101.)

linear associator: A learning device obtained by applying the HEBBIAN LEARNING RULE in a two-layer FEEDFORWARD NETWORK with a linear ACTIVATION RULE.

linear threshold unit: A UNIT that takes binary ACTIVATION values; if its NET INPUT exceeds a threshold (usually 0) the activation is set to 1; otherwise its activation is set to 0.

localist network: A network in which each item of interest is encoded by assigning it to one UNIT in the network (cf. a DISTRIBUTED NETWORK, in which each item of interest is encoded across multiple units in the network). Generally, each individual unit of a localist network can be semantically interpreted. (See pp. 50–1.)

microfeature, microstructure: See SUBSYMBOL.

multi-layered network: A FEEDFORWARD NETWORK that has three or more layers of UNITS (and hence, two or more layers of CONNECTIONS). We describe networks in terms of the number of layers of units; more frequently, networks are described in terms of the number of layers of connections.

net input: The sum of all of the inputs to a UNIT u: The sum may be scaled by a constant, and separate sums and constants may be used if the same unit receives external inputs as well as internal inputs (from other units). Most simply: $\sum_i input_{ui}$. There is one internal input for each CONNECTION from another unit i. In the simplest case $activation_i = output_i$. In all cases $weight_{ui}$ multiplied by $output_{ui}$ yields $input_{ui}$. By combining these inputs from all units i feeding into unit u, ACTIVATIONS propagate through the network. In some (*interactive*) networks, the net input to u is the major (sometimes the only) value that determines the activation of u (in accord with the ACTIVATION FUNCTION). Calculating net input is analogous to a neuron pooling the influences of all the dendrites from other neurons that contact that neuron. (See pp. 27, 39–40.)

nodes: See UNITS

output: The $output_i$ of a unit i is a function of the $activation_i$ of UNIT i. In the simplest case it is the identity function: $output_i = activation_i$. One alternative is to set a threshold at zero so that outputs will never be negative. Unit i sends the same output value to every unit u to which it is connected, but the outputs are modified by WEIGHTS before they reach the units u; hence, some units well be more affected by the activity of i than others. The CONNECTIONS feeding out of i are sometimes called the *fan-out* of i. Each output is analogous to the activity sent along one dendrite leading out of a neuron. (See p. 26.)

output units, output layer, output pattern: Ouput units are those UNITS that deliver the network's response to an INPUT PATTERN, culminating the propagation of activation through the network. In a FEEDFORWARD NETWORK, units are organized into layers; the final (highest) layer is the output layer. In an INTERACTIVE NETWORK, the output units may perform double-duty as input units and may simply be referred to as *visible units*. The output pattern is the pattern of activation across the n output units (which can be treated mathematically as a vector in n-dimensional space). Note that the term *output* alone is sometimes a short form for *output pattern*, but it properly (and distinctively) refers to the value being fed from a unit i along each outgoing connection.

overregularization: See REGULARIZATION.

parallel distributed processing (PDP): See PARALLEL PROCESSING.

parallel processing: An approach to cognitive or computer system design in which computations are carried out in parallel, rather than serially as in the von Neumann architecture that characterizes contemporary digital computers. Although early advances are being made in parallel hardware, most cognitive models that specify parallel processing are actually implemented on serial computers presently (at considerable cost in processing speed). All connectionist models, including LOCALIST models, specify that processing is carried out in parallel. The parallel distributed processing (PDP) type of connectionist model achieves extreme parallelism by combining parallel processing with DISTRIBUTED REPRESENTATIONS. It has been pointed out that certain rule models can also exhibit some degree of parallel processing (e.g., parallel matching of the conditions of production rules).

pattern associator: A FEEDFORWARD NETWORK that has just two layers of UNITS: INPUT UNITS and OUTPUT UNITS. When its WEIGHTS are properly set, this type of network can respond to each of a variety of input patterns with its own distinctive output pattern; therefore it is sometimes referred to as a *pattern associator*. The best-known variety of pattern associator is the *perceptron*. (See pp. 35–7.)

perceptron: In its narrowest sense, a two-layer network for which both the INPUT and OUTPUT UNITS take binary ACTIVATIONS, and the output units act as linear threshold units. Rosenblatt (1962) did much of the early research on these devices, and contributed the important *perceptron covergence theorem*. (See pp. 4–6.)

recurrent network: A variation on the FEEDFORWARD NETWORK architecture, in which the pattern obtained on a HIDDEN layer is copied onto special units in a lower layer which feed back into the hidden layer. Typically the input is a string that is presented sequentially rather than as a simultaneous pattern, and the OUTPUT UNITS are used to predict the next element in the sequence. For example, after processing the first element, the network has copied the pattern on the hidden units onto the special units. When the network then processes the second element, the hidden units will receive INPUT both from the regular INPUT UNITS and the special units. Hence, this kind of network is able to gather and utilize information about a sequence. (See pp. 37–8, 231.)

regularization, overregularization: The application of a general rule to a variety of items. When the scope of application is appropriate, the items have been regularized (e.g., forming a regular past tense for the set of regular verbs). When the scope of application is overly broad, the items have been overregularized (e.g., forming a regular past tense for irregular as well as regular verbs). (See pp. 184–203.)

relaxation, settling: Terms for the process by which an INTERACTIVE NETWORK approaches a stable state that maximizes constraint satisfaction and minimizes ERROR. A network has fully relaxed, or settled, when it reaches a global energy minimum. (See pp. 41–5.)

soft constraints: Refers to a situation in which multiple constraints compete, and the best overall solution is found by satisfying as many of them as possible. Connectionist networks are well suited to this task. A set of hard constraints, in contrast, must be completely satisfied; for example, in a traditional production system if no rule has all of its conditions met, no rule will fire. (See pp. 58–60.)

spreading activation: A term that, in its most narrow usage, designates the theory of activation embodied in a class of LOCALIST NETWORKS derived from semantic networks beginning in the 1970s. The most prominent examples are found in John Anderson's (1976, 1983) ACT and ACT* theories. The ACTIVATION RULE in ACT* achieves nonlinearity by incorporating a negative exponential function, and shows other similarities to the propagation of activation within some connectionist networks. The activation functions differ in several respects, however, and ACT* is further distinguished by its hybrid architecture (a production system utilizes the network) and by its localist (rather than distributed) approach to encoding. In its broadest usage, the term *spreading activation* is used interchangeably with the connectionist term *propagation of activation*. The terminology and theory of spreading activation are antecedent to the modern (1980s) era of connectionist models, and can be regarded as an early subclass of the localist variety of connectionist modeling. (See pp. 46–7.)

subsymbol, subsymbolic paradigm: One way of characterizing PDP (PARALLEL DISTRIBUTED PROCESSING) models is to point out that they are subsymbolic rather than symbolic, and that PDP research adheres to a subsymbolic paradigm rather than the symbolic paradigm of the traditional rules and representations approach to cognition. Smolensky (1987) distinguishes between *conceptual* and *subconceptual* levels of analysis, and argues that subsymbolic models can capture either level exactly, whereas symbolic models can capture only the conceptual level exactly. Further, a number of competencies traditionally regarded as conceptual are claimed to require a subconceptual level of analysis. Subsymbols are also called *microfeatures* (see Rumelhart and McClelland, 1986), and refer to encodings that are small-grained rather than large-grained; often they are designed to be context-sensitive as well. For example, Rumelhart and McClelland's (1986) Wickelfeatures are context-sensitive adaptations of phonological distinctive features (the smallest grain of traditional linguistic analysis). Subsymbols need not be derived from theories, however; some COARSE CODING schemes for INPUT UNITS have rather arbitrary receptive fields (e.g., Touretzky and Hinton, 1988), and individual HIDDEN UNITS in trained networks are often difficult to interpret or label. Also, note that one way of thinking about subsymbols would use grain size as a relative notion; whether the UNITS are subsymbols would depend upon whether they are at a smaller grain than usual for modeling performance on the task. (See p. 226.)

supervised learning: The class of LEARNING procedures in which the network is provided with explicit feedback as to what OUTPUT PATTERN was desired for a particular INPUT PATTERN (and must compare that to its actual output); the DELTA RULE is one example. UNSUPERVISED LEARNING, in contrast, refers to the class of learning procedures in which the network gradually achieves, without feedback, a weight matrix that allows it to classify a set of inputs (by discovering the regularities exhibited by subsets of the input patterns). COMPETITIVE LEARNING is one example.

target output: See DESIRED OUTPUT.

temperature (T): A parameter in certain ACTIVATION RULES for INTERACTIVE NETWORKS (e.g., BOLTZMANN MACHINES); lower values of T generally make activation patterns change more slowly. When a *simulated annealing* schedule is used, temperature is slowly reduced to avoid settling into local minima.

test mode, test trial: Relevant to a network in a LEARNING paradigm. When the network is in test mode, typically following a period in training mode, it is presented with a series of INPUT PATTERNS in order to observe its response to those patterns. They can be the same input patterns used in training, or may be a new set from the universe of input patterns in order to assess generalization. The purpose of test trials is limited to assessment of the performance achievable with the current WEIGHTS; no changes are made in the weights. (See p. 71.)

training mode, training trial: Relevant to a network in a LEARNING paradigm. When the network is in training mode, it is presented with a series of training trials. Each trial consists of one presentation of one INPUT–OUTPUT CASE; at the end of the trial (or at the end of the set of training trials constituting an EPOCH), the WEIGHTS of the CONNECTIONS in the network are altered in accord with a LEARNING RULE. (See p. 71.)

units, nodes: The elements of a network. Units receive INPUTS from other units (or from the environment) and compute a function that determines what OUTPUT they send to other units. In some models they are intended to function as a simplified neuron; in other models they are regarded as higher-level elements that do not correspond to neurons but are neuron-like or neurally-inspired. (See pp. 23–4.)

unsupervised learning: See SUPERVISED LEARNING.

variable binding: A capacity of certain systems of symbolic representation that is challenging to achieve in connectionist networks. When a rule (or other symbolic expression) includes variables, in order to apply the rule each variable must be bound to (linked to, or replaced by) a constant. If there are multiple instances of the same variable, each instance must be bound to the same constant. (See pp. 217, 243–4.)

visible units: The UNITS in a network which can be accessed externally (e.g., from the environment). In a FEEDFORWARD NETWORK, the units of the INPUT and OUTPUT LAYERS are the visible units; in an INTERACTIVE NETWORK, the same units may function both to receive input and to deliver output. Units that are not visible are called *HIDDEN UNITS*.

weight: Weight is a variable that indicates the strength (importance) of the CONNECTION between two UNITS. The OUTPUT of unit i ($output_i$) is multiplied by the weight of its connection to unit u ($weight_{ui}$) to obtain the input to unit u ($input_u$). Typically weights range between -1 and $+1$, or between 0 and 1, but they may also be unbounded. The weights between two layers can be displayed in a weight matrix using rows for the units in one layer and columns for the units in the other layer. Weights can either be set by the network designer and left unchanged, or can be changed in TRAINING MODE according to a function that is computed each EPOCH. The weights (and optionally, the BIASES) are the means by which knowledge about a domain is retained in a network. Along with the more transitory activation values, they determine the network's responses (OUTPUT PATTERNS) to a variety of INPUT PATTERNS. (See pp. 24–5.)

Wickelphones, Wickelfeatures: Elements of a system for phonological representation. Wickelphones, proposed by Wickelgren (1969), are phonemic segments that have been made context-sensitive by indicating the immediately preceding and immediately following phoneme as well as the phoneme of interest, e.g., $_k A_m$. Wickelfeatures, an extension proposed by Rumelhart and McClelland (1986) in *PDP: 18*, provide a lower level of representation. A Wickelfeature includes just one distinctive feature for each of the three phonemes comprising a Wickelphone. For example, (Back, Low, Front) is one Wickelfeature for the Wickelphone $_k A_m$. Wickelfeatures are used to provide a DISTRIBUTED REPRESENTATION of the segmental phonology of a word. Their context sensitivity is a device for constraining the order of phonemic segments, since connectionist networks do not straightforwardly encode serial order. (See pp. 178–81.)

XOR, exclusive or: A logical operation (propositional connective) of disjunction, meaning "one or the other but not both." That is, *A XOR B* is true if *A* is true and *B* is false, or if *B* is true and *A* is false; it is false if *A* and *B* are both true, or if *A* and *B* are both false. These truth conditions are distinct from those for *inclusive or* (often written v), which means "one or the other and possibly both" and therefore is false only if both A and B are false. *Inclusive or* is the connective commonly used in propositional logic (along with *and, not, if . . . then*, and *if and only if*). *Exclusive or* has been of particular interest to connectionists because it cannot be computed by a two-layer network; this was one of the limitations of PERCEPTRONS that were pointed out in the critique by Minsky and Papert (1969). The problem is that both-true and both-false are maximally dissimilar but must yield the same output (i.e., false). Inclusion of a HIDDEN layer solves this problem by permitting intermediate computations that produce a pattern with a more tractable similarity structure for use by the OUTPUT LAYER. (See pp. 83–4.)

Bibliography

Abrahamsen, A. A. (1987) Bridging boundaries versus breaking boundaries: Psycholinguistics in perspective, *Synthese*, 72, 355–88.

Abrahamsen, A. A. (in press) Bridging interdisciplinary boundaries: The case of kin terms, in C. Georgopoulos and R. Ishihara (eds) *Interdisciplinary Approaches to Language: Essays in Honor of S.-Y. Kuroda*, Dordrecht: Kluwer.

Ackley, D. H., Hinton, G. E., and Sejnowski, T. J. (1985) A learning algorithm for Boltzmann machines, *Cognitive Science*, 9, 147–69.

Acredolo, L. and Goodwyn, S. (in press) Sign language in babies: the significance of symbolic gesturing for understanding language development, in R. Vasta (ed.) *Annals of Child Development*, vol. 7, Greenwich, CT: JAB Press, Inc.

Allen, R. B. (1988) Sequential connectionist networks for answering simple questions about a microworld, *Proceedings of the Tenth Annual Conference of the Cognitive Science Society*, pp. 489–95.

Amari, S. I. (1977) Neural theory of association and concept-formation, *Biological Cybernetics*, 26, 175–85.

Amari, S. I. (1983) Field theory of self-organizing neural nets, *IEEE Transactions on Electronic Computers*, EC-16, 741–8.

Anderson, J. A. (1972) A simple neural network generating an interactive memory, *Mathematical Biosciences*, 14, 197–220. Reprinted in Anderson and Rosenfeld (1988), pp. 181–92.

Anderson, J. A. and Rosenfeld, E. (eds) (1988) *Neurocomputing: Foundations of Research*, Cambridge, MA: MIT Press.

Anderson, J. R. (1974) Retrieval of propositional information from long-term memory, *Cognitive Psychology*, 6, 451–74.

Anderson, J. R. (1976) *Language, Memory, and Thought*, Hillsdale, NJ: Lawrence Erlbaum.

Anderson, J. R. (1978) Arguments concerning representations for mental imagery, *Psychological Review*, 85, 249–77.

Anderson, J. R. (ed.) (1981) *Cognitive Skills and their Acquisition*, Hillsdale, NJ: Lawrence Erlbaum.

Anderson, J. R. (1983) *The Architecture of Cognition*, Cambridge, MA: Harvard University Press.

Anderson, J. R. (1987) Skill acquisition: Compilation of weak-method problem solutions, *Psychological Review*, 94, 192–210.

Anderson, J. R. (1989) A theory of the origins of human knowledge, *Artificial Intelligence*, 40, 313–51.

Anderson, J. R. and Bower, G. (1973) *Human Associative Memory*, Washington, DC: V. H. Winston.

Anderson, J. R. and Thompson, R. (1989). Use of analogy in a production system architecture, in S. Vosniadou and A. Ortony (eds) *Similarity and Analogical Reasoning*, Cambridge: Cambridge University Press.

Arbib, M. A. (1969) Memory limitations of stimulus–response models, *Psychological Review*, 76, 507–10.

Armstrong, S. L., Gleitman, L., and Gleitman, H. (1983) What some concepts might not be, *Cognition*, 13, 263–308.

Baars, B. J. (1986) *The Cognitive Revolution in Psychology*, New York: Guilford Press.

Barnden, J. A. (1988) Conposit, a neural net system for high-level symbolic processing: Overview of research and description of register-machine level. MCCS-88-145. Memoranda in Computer and Cognitive Science, Computing Research Laboratory, New Mexico State University Las Cruces, NM.

Barnden, J. A. (1989) Neural-net implementation of complex symbol-processing in a mental model approach to syllogistic reasoning, *Proceedings of the International Joint Conference on Artificial Intelligence – 1989*, San Mateo, CA: Morgan Kaufmann.

Barsalou, L. W. (1983) Ad hoc categories, *Memory and Cognition*, 11, 211–27.

Barsalou, L. W. (1987) The instability of graded structure: Implications for the nature of concepts, in U. Neisser (ed.) *Concepts and Conceptual Development: Ecological and Intellectual Factors in Categorization*, Cambridge: Cambridge University Press, pp. 101–40.

Barsalou, L. W. (1990) On the indistinguishability of exemplar memory and abstraction in category representation, in T. K. Srull and R. S. Wyer, Jr. (eds) *Advances in Social Cognition*. vol. 3: *Content and Process Specificity in the Effects of Prior Experiences*, Hillsdale, NJ: Lawrence Erlbaum, pp. 61–88.

Barsalou, L. W. and Billman, D. (1989) Systematicity and semantic ambiguity, in D. S. Gorfein (ed.) *Resolving Semantic Ambiguity*, New York: Springer-Verlag, pp. 146–203.

Bartlett, F. C. (1932) *Remembering*, Cambridge: Cambridge University Press.

Barto, A. G. and Anandan, P. (1985) Pattern recognizing stochastic learning automata, *IEEE Transactions on Systems, Man, and Cybernetics*, 15, 360–75.

Bates, E. (1979) *The Emergence of Symbols: Cognition and Communication in Infancy*, New York: Academic Press.

Bates, E., Bretherton, I., and Snyder, L. (1988) *From First Words to Grammar: Individual Differences and Dissociable Mechanisms*. Cambridge, Cambridge University Press.

Bechtel, W. (1984) Reconceptualizations and interfield connections: The discovery of the link between vitamins and coenzymes, *Philosophy of Science*, 51, 265–92.

Bechtel, W. (1985) Realism, instrumentalism, and the intentional stance, *Cognitive Science*, 9, 473–97.

Bechtel, W. (1986a) The nature of scientific integration, in W. Bechtel (ed.) *Integrating Scientific Disciplines*, Dordrecht: Martinus Nijhoff.

Bechtel, W. (1986b) Building interlevel pathways: The discovery of the Embden–Meyerhof pathway and the phosphate cycle, in J. Dorn and P. Weingartner (eds) *Foundations of Biology*, Vienna: Holder-Pichler-Tempsky, pp. 65–97.

Bechtel, W. (1987) Psycholinguistics as a case of cross-disciplinary research: Symposium introduction, *Synthese*, 72, 293–311.

Bechtel, W. (1988a) *Philosophy of Science. An Overview for Cognitive Science*, Hillsdale, NJ: Lawrence Erlbaum.

Bechtel, W. (1988b) *Philosophy of Mind: An Overview for Cognitive Science*, Hillsdale, NJ: Lawrence Erlbaum.

Bechtel, W. (1989) Connectionism and intentionality, *Proceedings of the Eleventh Annual Meeting of the Cognitive Science Society*, Hillsdale, NJ: Lawrence Erlbaum, pp. 553–600.

Bechtel, W. and Abrahamsen, A. A. (1990, in press) Beyond the exclusively propositional era, *Synthese*, 82.

Bechtel, W. and Richardson, R. C. (in preparation) *A Model of Theory Development: Decomposition and Localization as Scientific Research Strategies*.

Berko, J. (1958) The child's learning of English morphology, *Word*, 14, 150–77.

Bever, T. G. (in press) The demons and the beast – Modular and nodular kinds of knowledge, in C. Georgopoulos and R. Ishihara (eds) *Interdisciplinary Approaches to Language: Essays in Honor of S.-Y. Kuroda*, Dordrecht: Kluwer.

Bienenstock, E. L., Cooper, L. N., and Munro, P. W. (1982) Theory for development of neuron selectivity: orientation specificity and binocular interaction in visual cortex, *Journal of Neuroscience*, 2, 32–48. Reprinted in Anderson and Rosenfeld (1988), pp. 439–55.

Block, H. D. (1962) The perceptron: A model for brain functioning. I, *Reviews of Modern Physics*, 43, 123–35.

Bloom, L. (1970) *Language Development: Form and Function in Emerging Grammars*, Cambridge, MA: MIT Press.

Bobrow, D. G. and Winograd, T. (1977) An overview of KRL, a knowledge representation language, *Cognitive Science*, 1, 3–46.

Bower, G. and Trabasso, T. (1968) *Attention in Learning: Theory and Research*, New York: John Wiley & Sons.

Brentano, F. (1874/1973) *Psychology from an Empirical Standpoint* (A. C. Pancurello, D. B. Terrell, and L. L. McAlister, trans.), New York: Humanities Press.

Brown, R. (1973) *A First Language*, Cambridge, MA: Harvard University Press.

Buchanan, B. G. and Shortliffe, E. H. (1984) *Rule-based Expert Systems: The MYCIN Experiments of the Stanford Heuristic Programming Project*, Reading, MA: Addison-Wesley.

Bybee, J. L. and Slobin, D. I. (1982) Rules and schemas in the development and use of the English past tense, *Language*, 58, 265–89.

Carey, S. (1985) *Conceptual Change in Children*, Cambridge, MA: MIT Press/Bradford Books.

Carson, M. T. and Abrahamsen, A. A. (1976) Some members are more equal than others: The effect of semantic typicality on class-inclusion performance, *Child Development*, 47, 1186–90.

Chater, N. and Oaksford, M. (1989) Autonomy, implementation, and cognitive architecture: A reply to Fodor and Pylyshyn, Research Paper EUCCS/ RP – 27, Centre for Cognitive Science, University of Edinburgh.

Chisholm, R. M. (1958) Sentences about believing, in H. Feigl, M. Scriven, and G. Maxwell (eds) *Minnesota Studies in the Philosophy of Science*, vol. 2, Minneapolis: University of Minnesota Press, pp. 510–20.

Chomsky, N. (1957) *Syntactic Structures*. The Hague: Mouton.

Chomsky, N. (1959) Review of Skinner's *Verbal Behavior*, *Language*, 35, 26–58.

Chomsky, N. (1968) *Language and Mind*, New York: Harcourt, Brace, & World.

Churchland, P. M. (1986) Some reductive strategies in cognitive neurobiology, *Mind*, 95, 279–309.

Churchland, P. M. (1988) *Matter and Consciousness: A Contemporary Introduction to the Philosophy of Mind*, revised edition, Cambridge, MA: MIT Press.

Churchland, P. M. (1989) On the nature of explanation: A PDP approach, in P. M. Churchland (ed.) *A Neurocomputational Perspective. The Nature of Mind and the Structure of Science*, Cambridge, MA: MIT Press Bradford Books.

Churchland, P. S. (1986) *Neurophilosophy: Toward a unified science of the mind–brain*, Cambridge, MA: MIT Press/Bradford Books.

Churchland, P. S. and Churchland, P. M. (1983) Stalking the wild epistemic engine, *Nous*, 17, 44–52.

Cipra, B. A. (1989) Do mathematicians still do math? *Science*, 244, 769.

Clark, A. (1988) Thoughts, sentences, and cognitive science, *Philosophical Psychology*, 1, 263–78.

Clark, A. (1989) *Microcognition: Philosophy, Cognitive Science, and Parallel Distributed Processing*, Cambridge, MA: MIT Press/Bradford Books.

Clark, A. (in press) Systematicity, structured representations, and cognitive architecture, in T. Horgan and J. Tienson (eds) *Connectionism and the Philosophy of Mind*, Dordrecht: Kluwer.

Clark, H. H. (1969) Linguistic processes in deductive reasoning, *Psychological Review*, 76, 387–404.

Clark, H. H. (1972) Difficulties people have in answering the question "Where is it?" *Journal of Verbal Learning and Verbal Behavior*, 11, 265–77.

Colby, K. M. (1975) *Artificial Paranoia*, New York: Pergamon.

Collins, A. M. and Loftus, E. F. (1975) A spreading activation theory of semantic processing, *Psychological Review*, 82, 407–28.

Collins, A. M. and Quillian, M. R. (1969) Retrieval time from semantic memory, *Journal of Verbal Learning and Verbal Behavior*, 8, 240–7.

Cooper, L. A. and Shepard, R. N. (1973) Chronometric studies of the rotation of mental images, in Chase, W. G. (ed.) *Visual Information Processing*, New York: Academic Press.

Cottrell, G. W. and Tsung, F.-S. (1989) Learning simple arithmetic procedures, *Proceedings of the Eleventh Annual Conference of the Cognitive Science Society*, Hillsdale, NJ: Lawrence Erlbaum, pp. 58–65.

Cottrell, G. W., Munro, P., and Zipser, D. (1987) Learning internal representations from gray-scale images: An example of extensional programming, *Proceedings of the Ninth Annual Conference of the Cognitive Science Society*, Hillsdale, NJ: Lawrence Erlbaum, pp. 461–73.

Cowan, J. D. and Sharp, D. H. (1988) Neural nets and artificial intelligence, *Daedalus*, 117, 85–121.

Darden, L. and Maull, N. (1977) Interfield theories, *Philosophy of Science*, 43, 44–64.

Dennett, D. C. (1971) Intentional systems, *Journal of Philosophy*, 68, 87–106. Reprinted in D. C. Dennett (ed.) *Brainstorms*, Montgomery, VT: Bradford Books, 1978, pp. 3–22.

Dennett, D. C. (1978) Toward a cognitive theory of consciousness, in C. W. Savage (ed.) *Perception and Cognition: Issues in the Foundations of Psychology. Minnesota Studies in the Philosophy of Science*, vol. 9, Minneapolis, MN: University of Minnesota Press. Reprinted in D. C. Dennett (ed.) *Brainstorms*, Montgomery, VT: Bradford Books, 1978, pp. 149–73.

Derthick, M. and Plaut, D. C. (1986) Is distributed connectionism compatible with the physical symbol system hypothesis? *Proceedings of the Eighth Annual Conference of the Cognitive Science Society*, London: Lawrence Erlbaum, pp. 639–44.

Dretske, F. I. (1983) *Knowledge and the Flow of Information*, Cambridge, MA: MIT Press/Bradford Books.

Dreyfus, H. L. (1979) *What Computers Can't Do: The Limits of Artificial Intelligence*, 2nd edition, New York: Harper & Row.

Dreyfus, H. L. and Dreyfus, S. E. (1986) *Mind over Machine: The power of human intuition and expertise in the era of the computer*, New York: The Free Press.

Dreyfus, H. L. and Dreyfus, S. E. (1988) Making a mind versus modeling the brain. Artificial intelligence back at the branch point, *Daedalus*, 117, 15–43.

Durbin, R. and Willshaw, D. J. (1987) An analogue approach to the travelling salesman problem using an elastic net method, *Nature*, 326, 689–91.

Dyer, M. G. (in press) Symbolic NeuroEngineering for natural language processing, A multilevel research approach, in J. Barnden and J. Pollack (eds) *Advances in Connectionist and Neural Computation Theory*, Norwood, NJ: Ablex.

Edelman, G. (1987), *Neural Darwinism. The Theory of Neuronal Group Selection*, New York: Basic Books.

Elman, J. L. (1988) Finding structure in time, *Cognitive Science*, 14, 179–211.

Elman, J. L. (1989) Structured representations and connectionist networks, *Proceedings of the Eleventh Annual Conference of the Cognitive Science Society*, Hillsdale, NJ: Lawrence Erlbaum, pp. 17–25.

Ervin, S. (1964) Imitation and structural change in children's language, in E. Lenneberg (ed.) *New Directions in the Study of Language*, Cambridge, MA: MIT Press.

Farah, M. J. (1988) Is visual imagery really visual? Overlooked evidence from neurophysiology, *Psychological Review*, 95, 307–17.

Feldman, J. A. and Ballard, D. H. (1982) Connectionist models and their properties, *Cognitive Science* 6, 205–54. Reprinted in Anderson and Rosenfeld (1988), pp. 484–507.

Feyerabend, P. K. (1963) Materialism and the mind–body problem, *The Review of Metaphysics*, 17, 49–67.

Fodor, J. A. (1974) Special sciences (Or: Disunity of science as a working hypothesis), *Synthese*, 28, 97–115.

Fodor, J. A. (1975) *The Language of Thought*, New York: Crowell.

Fodor, J. A. (1980) Methodological solipsism considered as a research strategy in cognitive psychology. *The Behavioral and Brain Sciences*, 3, 63–109.

Fodor, J. A. (1983) *Modularity of Mind*, Cambridge: MIT Press/Bradford Books.

Fodor, J. A. (1984) Semantics, Wisconsin style, *Synthese*, 59, 231–50.

Fodor, J. A. (1987) *Psychosemantics: The Problem of Meaning in the Philosophy of Mind*, Cambridge, MA: MIT Press.

Fodor, J. A. and Pylyshyn, Z. W. (1981) How direct is visual perception? Some reflections on Gibson's "ecological approach," *Cognition*, 9, 136-96.

Fodor, J. A. and Pylyshyn, Z. W. (1988) Connectionism and cognitive architecture: A critical analysis, *Cognition*, 28, 3–71.

Fouconnier, G. (1985) *Mental Spaces*, Cambridge, MA: MIT Press.

Frege, G. (1892) Über Sinn und Bedeutung [On Sense and Reference], *Zeitschrift für Philosophie und philosophische Kritik*, 100, 25–50.

Fukushima, K. (1980) Neocognitron: A self-organizing multilayered neural network model for a mechanism of pattern recognition unaffected by shift in position, *Biological Cybernetics*, 36, 193–202.

Garcia, E. E. and DeHaven, E. D. (1974) Use of operant techniques in the establishment and generalization of language: A review and analysis, *American Journal of Mental Deficiency*, 79, 169–78.

Gardner, H. (1983) *Frames of Mind: The Theory of Multiple Intelligences*, New York: Basic Books.

Garfield, J. L. (1988) *Belief in Psychology*, Cambridge, MA: MIT Press/Bradford Books.

Gelman, R. (1978) Cognitive development, *Annual Review of Psychology*, 29, 297–332.

Gettier, E. L. (1963) Is justified true belief knowledge? *Analysis*, 25, 121–3.

Gibson, J. J. (1966) *The Senses Considered as Conceptual Systems*, Boston, MA: Houghton Mifflin.

Gluck, M. A. and Bower, G. H. (1988a) From conditioning to category learning: An adaptive network model, *Journal of Experimental Psychology: General*, 117, 227–47.

Gluck, M. A. and Bower, G. H. (1988b) Evaluating an adaptive network model of human learning, *Journal of Memory and Language*, 27, 166–95.

Gluck, M. A., Bower, G. H., and Hee, M. R. (1989) A configural-cue network model of animal and human associative learning, *Proceedings of the Eleventh Annual Conference of the Cognitive Science Society*, Hillsdale, NJ: Lawrence Erlbaum, pp. 323–32.

Goldman, A. (1986) *Epistemology and Cognition*, Cambridge, MA: Harvard University Press.

Golinkoff, R. M., Hirsh-Pasek, K., Cauley, K., and Gordon, L. (1987) The eyes have it: Lexical and syntactic comprehension in a new paradigm, *Journal of Child Language*, 14, 23–46.

Goodman, N. (1955) *Fact, Fiction, and Forecast*, Cambridge, MA: Harvard University Press.

Gorman R. P. and Sejnowski, T. J. (1988) Learned classification of sonar targets using a massively-parallel network, *IEEE Transactions: Acoustics, Speech, and Signal Processing*.

Greenough, W. T., Block, J. E., and Wallace, C. S. (1987) Experience and brain development, *Child Development*, 58, 539–59.

Grossberg, S. (1976) Adaptive pattern classification and universal recoding: I. Parallel development and coding of neural feature detectors, *Biological Cybernetics*, 23, 121–34. Reprinted in Anderson and Rosenfeld (1988), pp. 245–58.

Grossberg, S. (1982) *Studies of Mind and Belief*, Dordrecht: Reidel.

Grossberg, S. (ed.) (1988) *Neural Networks and Natural Intelligence*. Cambridge, MA: MIT Press/Bradford Books.

Hampshire, J. B. and Waibel, A. H. (1989) A novel objective function for improved phoneme recognition using time-delay neural networks, Technical Report CMU-CS-89-118, Computer Science Department, Carnegie Mellon University, Pittsburgh, PA.

Hanson, N. R. (1958) *Patterns of Discovery*, Cambridge: Cambridge University Press.

Harnad, S. (1990) The symbol grounding problem. *Physica D*.

Harris, C. L. (1989) A connectionist approach to the story of "over," *Proceedings of the Annual Meeting of the Berkeley Linguistics Society*, 15.

Harris, C. L. (in press) Connectionism, and cognitive linguistics, *Connection Science*.

Haugeland, J. (1981) Semantic engines: An introduction to mind design, in J. Haugeland (ed.) *Mind Design*, Cambridge, MA: MIT Press/Bradford Books.

Haugeland, J. (1985) *Artificial Intelligence: The Very Idea*, Cambridge, MA: MIT Press/Bradford Books.

Hebb, D. O. (1949) *The Organization of Behavior*, New York: John Wiley & Sons.

Henley, N. M. (1969) A psychological study of the semantics of animal terms, *Journal of Verbal Learning and Verbal Behavior*, 8, 176–84.

Hetherington, P. A. and Seidenberg, M. S. (1989) Is there "catastrophic" interference in connectionist networks?, *Proceedings of the Eleventh Annual Conference of the Cognitive Science Society*, Hillsdale, NJ: Lawrence Erlbaum, pp. 26–33.

Hinton, G. E. (1986) Learning distributed representations of concepts, *Proceedings of the Eighth Annual Conference of the Cognitive Science Society*, Hillsdale, NJ: Lawrence Erlbaum, pp. 1–12.

Hinton, G. E. (1987) Learning translation invariant recognition in a massively parallel network, in *PARLE Parallel Architectures and Languages Europe*, vol. 1, Berlin: Springer-Verlag, pp. 1–14.

Hinton, G. E. (1989) Connectionist learning systems, *Artificial Intelligence*, 40, 185–234.

Hinton, G. E. and Anderson, J. A. (eds) (1981) *Parallel Models of Associative Memory*, Hillsdale, NJ: Lawrence Erlbaum.

Hinton, G. E. and Sejnowski, T. J. (1983) Optimal perceptual inference, in *Proceedings of the Institute of Electronic and Electrical Engineers Computer Society Conference on Computer Vision and Pattern Recognition*, Washington, DC, IEEE, pp. 448–53.

Hinton, G. E. and Sejnowski, T. J. (1986) Learning and relearning in Boltzmann machines, in Rumelhart, McClelland, and the PDP Research Group (1986), chapter 7.

Hinton, G. E. and Shallice, T. (1989) Lesioning a connectionist network: Investigations of acquired dyslexia, Technical Report CRG-TR-89-3, University of Toronto, Toronto, Ontario, Canada.

Hinton, G. E., McClelland, J. L., and Rumelhart, D. E. (1986) Distributed representations, in Rumelhart, McClelland, and the PDP Research Group (1986), chapter 3.

Hobbes, T. (1651/1962) *Leviathan: Or the Matter, Forme and Power of a Commonwealth Ecclesiasticall and Civil*, London: Collier Books.

Holland, J. H. (1975) *Adaptation in Natural and Artificial Systems*, Ann Arbor, MI: University of Michigan Press.

Holland, J. H., Holyoak, K. J., Nisbett, R. E., and Thagard, P. R. (1986) *Induction: Processes of Inference, Learning, and Discovery*, Cambridge, MA: MIT Press.

Holyoak, K. J. and Thagard, P. R. (1989) Analogical mapping by constraint satisfaction, *Cognitive Science* 13, 295–355.

Honavar, V. and Uhr, L. (1988) A network of neuron-like units that learns to perceive by generation as well as reweighing of its links, in D. Touretzky, G. Hinton, and T. Sejnowski (eds) *The Proceedings of the 1988 Connectionist Models Summer School*, San Mateo, CA: Morgan Kaufmann, pp. 472–84.

Hopfield, J. J. (1982) Neural networks and physical systems with emergent collective computational abilities, *Proceedings of the National Academy of Sciences*, 79, 2554-8. Reprinted in Anderson and Rosenfeld (1988), pp. 460–4.

Hopfield, J. J. (1984) Neurons with graded response have collective computational properties like those of two state-neurons, *Proceedings of the National Academy of Sciences*, 81, 3088-92. Reprinted in Anderson and Rosenfeld (1988), pp. 579–83.

Hopfield, J. J. and Tank, D. W. (1985) "Neural" computation and constraint satisfaction and the travelling salesman, *Biological Cybernetics*, 55, 141–52.

Hummel, J. E., Biederman, I., Gerhardstein, P. C., and Hilton, H. J. (1988) From image edge to geons: A connectionist approach, in D. Touretzky, G. Hinton, and T. Sejnowski (eds.) *The Proceedings of the 1988 Connectionist Models Summer School*. San Mateo, CA: Morgan Kaufmann, pp. 462–71.

Huttenlocher, J. and Higgins, E. T. (1971) Adjectives, comparatives and syllogisms, *Psychological Review*, 78, 487–504.

Huttenlocher, J. and Smiley, P. (1987) Early word meanings: The case of object names, *Cognitive Psychology*, 19, 63–89.

Huttenlocher, J. and Strauss, S. (1968) Comprehension and a statement's relation to the situation that it describes, *Journal of Verbal Learning and Verbal Behavior*, 7, 300–4.

Hyams, N. (1986) *Language Acquisition and the Theory of Parameters*. Dordrecht: Reidel.

Jacoby, L. L. and Brooks, L. R. (1984) Nonanalytic cognition: Memory, perception, and concept learning. In G. H. Bower (ed.) *The Psychology of Learning and Motivation*, vol. 18, New York: Academic Press, pp. 1–47.

Johnson-Laird, P. (1983) *Mental Models*, Cambridge, MA: Harvard University Press.

Jordan, M. I. (1986a) An introduction to linear algebra in parallel distributed processing, in Rumelhart, McClelland, and the PDP Research Group (1986), chapter 9.

Jordan, M. I. (1986b) Attractor dynamics and parallelism in a connectionist sequential machine, in *Proceedings of the Eighth Annual Conference of the Cognitive Science Society*, Hillsdale, NJ: Lawrence Erlbaum, pp. 10–17.

Kahneman, D. and Miller, D. T. (1986) Norm theory: Comparing reality to its alternatives, *Psychological Review*, 93, 136–53.

Kaplan, R. (1975) On process models for sentence analysis, in D. A. Norman and D. E. Rumelhart (eds) *Explorations in Cognition*, San Francisco: Freeman, pp. 117–35.

Kaplan, S., Weaver, M., and French, R. M. (1990) Active symbols and internal models: Towards a cognitive connectionism, *AI and Society*.

Katz, J. J. and Fodor, J. A. (1963) The structure of a semantic theory, *Language*, 39, 170–210.

Keil, F. C. (1989) *Concepts, Kinds, and Cognitive Development*, Cambridge, MA: MIT Press/Bradford Books.

Kintsch, W. (1974) *The Representation of Meaning in Memory*, Hillsdale, NJ: Lawrence Erlbaum.

Knapp, A. G., and Anderson, J. A. (1984) Theory of categorization based on distributed memory storage, *Journal of Experimental Psychology: Learning, Memory, and Cognition*, 10, 616–37. Reprinted in Anderson and Rosenfeld (1988), pp. 588–609.

Kohonen, T. (1972) Correlation matrix memories, *IEEE Transactions on Computers C-21, 353–9*. Reprinted in Anderson and Rosenfeld (1988), pp. 174–80.

Kohonen, T. (1982) Clustering, taxonomy, and topological maps of patterns. In M. Land (ed.) *Proceedings of the Sixth International Conference on Pattern Recognition*, Silver Spring, MD: IEEE Computer Society Press, pp. 114–25.

Kohonen, T. (1988) *Self-Organization and Associative Memory*, Berlin: Springer-Verlag.

Kosslyn, S. M. (1980) *Image and Mind*, Cambridge, MA: Harvard University Press.

Kosslyn, S. M., Ball, T. M., and Reiser, B. J. (1978) Visual images preserve metric spatial information: Evidence from studies of image scanning, *Journal of Experimental Psychology: Human Perception and Performance*, 4, 47–60.

Kuczaj, S. A. (1977) The acquisition of regular and irregular past tense forms, *Journal of Verbal Learning and Verbal Behavior*, 16, 589–600.

Kuczaj, S. A. (1978) Children's judgments of grammatical and ungrammatical irregular past tense verbs, *Child Development*, 49, 319–26.

Kuhn, T. S. (1962/1970) *Structure of Scientific Revolutions*. Chicago: University of Chicago Press.

Kuroda, S.-Y. (1987) Where is Chomsky's bottleneck?, *Center for Research in Language Newsletter* (University of California, San Diego), 1 (7), 4–11.

Lachter, J. and Bever, T. G. (1988) The relation between linguistic structure and associative theories of language learning – A constructive critique of some connectionist learning models, *Cognition*, 28, 195–247.

Laird, J. E., Newell, A., Rosenbloom, P. S. (1987) SOAR: An architecture for general intelligence, *Artificial Intelligence*, 33, 1–64.

Lakoff, G. (1970) *Irregularity in Syntax*, New York: Holt, Rinehart, & Winston.

Lakoff, G. (1987) *Women, Fire, and Dangerous Things. What Categories Reveal About the Mind*, Chicago: University of Chicago Press.

Langacker, R. W. (1987a) *Foundations of Cognitive Grammar*, Stanford, CA: Stanford University Press.

Langacker, R. W. (1987b) The Chomskian perspective, *Center for Research in Language Newsletter* (University of California, San Diego), 1 (3): 3–15.

Lange, T. E. and Dyer, M. G. (in press) High-level inferencing in a connectionist network, *Connection Science*, 2.

Lawson, E. T. and McCauley, R. N. (1990) *Rethinking Religion: Connecting Cognition and Culture*, Cambridge: Cambridge University Press.

Le Cun, Y. (1986) Learning processes in an asymmetric threshold network, in

Bienenstock, E., Fogelman-Soulie, F., and Weisbuch, G. (eds) *Disordered Systems and Biological Organization*, Berlin: Springer.

Lin, S. and Kernighan, B. W. (1973) An algorithm for the TSP problem, *Operations Research*, 21, 498.

Lindsay, P. H. and Norman, D. A. (1972) *Human Information Processing: An Introduction to Psychology*, New York: Academic Press.

Little, W. A. and Shaw, G. L. (1975) A statistical theory of short and long term memory, *Behavioral Biology*, 14, 115–33. Reprinted in Anderson and Rosenfeld (1988), pp. 231–41.

MacWhinney, B. and Bates, E. (eds) (1989) *The Crosslinguistic Study of Sentence Processing*. Cambridge: Cambridge University Press.

Marchman, V. and Plunkett, K. (1989) Token frequency and phonological predictability in a pattern association network: Implications for child language acquisition, *Proceedings of the Eleventh Annual Conference of the Cognitive Science Society*, Hillsdale, NJ: Lawrence Erlbaum, pp. 179–87.

Margolis, H. (1987) *Patterns, Thinking, and Cognition. A Theory of Judgment*, Chicago: University of Chicago Press.

Marr, D. (1969) A theory of cerebellar cortex, *Journal of Physiology of London*, 202, 437–70.

Marr, D. (1970) A theory for cerebellar neo cortex, *Proceedings of the Royal Society of London B*, 176, 161–234.

Marr, D. (1971) Simple memory: A theory for archicortex, *Philosophical Transactions of the Royal Society of London, B* 262, 23–90.

Marr, D. (1982) *Vision*, San Francisco: Freeman.

Massaro, D. W. (1988) Some criticisms of connectionist models of human performance. Journal of Memory and Language, 27, 213–34.

Masterman, M. (1970) The nature of a paradigm, in I. Lakatos and A. Musgrave (eds) *Criticism and the Growth of Knowledge*, Cambridge: Cambridge University Press.

McCauley, R. N. (1986) Intertheoretic relations and the future of psychology, *Philosophy of Science*, 53, 179–199.

McCauley, R. N. (1987a) The role of theories in a theory of concepts, in U. Neisser (ed.) *Concepts Reconsidered: The Ecological and Intellectual Bases of Categories*, Cambridge: Cambridge University Press, pp. 288–309.

McCauley, R. N. (1987b) The not so happy story of the marriage of linguistics and psychology or why linguistics has discouraged psychology's recent advances, *Synthese*, 72, 341–53.

McClelland, J. L. (1979). On the time-relations of mental processes: An examination of systems of processes in cascade, *Psychological Review*, 86, 287–330.

McClelland, J. L. (1981) Retrieving general and specific information from stored knowledge of specifics, *Proceedings of the Third Annual Conference of the Cognitive Science Society*, 170–2.

McClelland, J. L. and Rumelhart, D. E. (1981) An interactive activation model of context effects in letter perception: Part 1. An account of basic findings, *Psychological Review*, 88, 375–407.

McClelland, J. L. and Rumelhart, D. E. (1988) *Explorations in Parallel Distributed Processing: A Handbook of Models, Programs, and Exercises*, Cambridge, MA: MIT Press/Bradford Books.

McClelland, J. L., Rumelhart, D. E., and the PDP Research Group (1986) *Parallel Distributed Processing: Explorations in the Microstructure of Cognition*, vol. 2: *Psychological and Biological Models*, Cambridge, MA: MIT Press/Bradford Books.

McCloskey, M. and Cohen, N. J. (1989) Catastrophic interference in connectionist networks: The sequential learning problem, in G. H. Bower (ed.) *The Psychology of Learning and Motivation*, vol. 24, New York: Academic Press, pp. 109–65.

McCulloch, W. S. and Pitts, W. (1943) A logical calculus of the ideas immanent in nervous activity, *Bulletin of Mathematical Biophysics*, 5, 115–33. Reprinted in Anderson and Rosenfeld (1988), pp. 18–27.

McKoon, G. and Ratcliff, R. (1979) Priming in episodic and semantic memory, *Journal of Verbal Learning and Verbal Behavior*, 18, 463–80.

McNeill, D. (1975) Semiotic extension, in R. L. Solso (ed.), *Information Processing and Cognition: the Loyola Symposium*, Hillsdale, NJ: Lawrence Erlbaum.

Medin, D. L. (1989) Concepts and conceptual structure, *American Psychologist*, 44, 1469–81.

Medin, D. L. and Schaffer, M. M. (1978) A context theory of classification learning, *Psychological Review*, 85, 207–38.

Medin, D. L. and Wattenmaker, W. D. (1987) Category cohesiveness, theories, and cognitive architecture, in U. Neisser (ed.), *Concepts and Conceptual Development: Ecological and Intellectual Factors in Categorization*, Cambridge: Cambridge University Press, pp. 25–62.

Miikkulainen, R. and Dyer, M. G. A modular neural network architecture for sequential paraphrasing of script-based stories, *Proceedings of the International Joint Conference on Neural Networks (IJCNN-89)*, Washington, DC.

Minsky, M. A. (1975) A framework for representing knowledge, in P. H. Winston (ed.) *The Psychology of Computer Vision*, New York: McGraw-Hill, pp. 211–77.

Minsky, M. A. and Papert, S. (1969) *Perceptrons*, Cambridge, MA: MIT Press.

Moyer, R. S. (1973) Comparing objects in memory: Evidence suggesting an internal psychophysics, *Perception and Psychophysics*, 13, 180–4.

Nadel, L., Cooper, L. A., Culicover, P., and Harnish, R. M. (eds) (1989) *Neural Connections, Mental Computation*, Cambridge, MA: MIT Press/Bradford Books.

Nagel, E. (1961) *The Structure of Science*, New York: Harcourt, Brace.

Neisser, U. (1967) *Cognitive Psychology*, New York: Appleton-Century-Crofts.

Neisser, U. (1976) *Cognition and Reality: Principles and Implications of Cognitive Psychology*, San Francisco: W. H. Freeman.

Neisser, U. (1983) Toward a skillful psychology, in D. R. Rogers and J. A. Sloboda (eds) *The Acquisition of Symbolic Skills*, New York: Plenum.

Neisser, U. (1987) From direct perception to conceptual structure, in U. Neisser (ed.) *Concepts and Conceptual Development: Ecological and intellectual factors in categorization*, Cambridge: Cambridge University Press, pp. 11–24.

Neisser, U. (1989, August) *Direct perception and recognition as distinct perceptual systems*, Address presented at the Eleventh Annual Meeting of the Cognitive Science Society, Ann Arbor, MI.

Nelson, K. (1973) Structure and strategy in learning to talk, *Monographs of the Society for Research in Child Development*, 38 (1–2, Serial No. 149).

Nelson, K. E. and Bonvillian, J. D. (1978) Early language development: Conceptual growth and related processes between 2 and 4½ years of age, in K. E. Nelson (ed.) *Children's Language*, vol. 1, New York: Wiley/Halsted/Gardner Press, pp. 467–556.

Newell, A. (1989) *Unified Theories of Cognition*, Cambridge, MA: Harvard University Press.

Newell, A. and Simon, H. A. (1972) *Human Problem Solving*, Englewood Cliffs, NJ: Prentice Hall.

Newell, A. and Simon, H. (1981) Computer science as empirical inquiry, in J. Haugeland (ed.) *Mind Design*, Montgomery, VT: Bradford Books, pp. 35–66.

Nicholich, L. M. (1977) Beyond sensorimotor intelligence: Assessment of symbolic maturity through analysis of pretend play, *Merrill-Palmer Quarterly*, 23, 89–99.

Nickles, T. (1980) Introductory essay: Scientific discovery and the future of philosophy of science, in T. Nickles (ed.) *Scientific Discovery: Logic and Rationality*, Dordrecht: Reidel, pp. 1–59.

Norman, D. A., Rumelhart, D. E., and the LNR Research Group (1975) *Explorations in Cognition*, San Francisco: Freeman.

Nosofsky, R. M. (1988) Exemplar-based accounts of relations between classification, recognition, and typicality, *Journal of Experimental Psychology: Learning, Memory, and Cognition*, 14, 700–8.

Paivio, A. (1971) *Imagery and Verbal Processes*, New York: Holt, Rinehart, & Winston.

Palmer, S. E. (1978) Fundamental Aspects of Cognitive Representation, in E. Rosch and B. B. Lloyd (eds) *Cognition and Categorization*, Hillsdale, NJ: Lawrence Erlbaum, pp. 259–303.

Parker, D. B. (1985) Learning logic, Technical Report TR-87, Center for Computational Research in Economics and Management Science, MIT, Cambridge, MA.

Papert, S. (1988) One AI or many?, *Daedalus*, 117, 1–14.

Patterson, K. E., Seidenberg, M. S., and McClelland, J. L. (1989) Connections and disconnections: Acquired dyslexia in a computational model of reading processes, in R. G. M. Morris (ed.) *Parallel Distributed Processing: Implications for Psychology and Neurobiology*. Oxford: Oxford University Press, pp. 131–81.

Pavel, M., Gluck, M. A., and Henkle, V. (1988) Generalization by humans and multi-layer adaptive networks, *Proceedings of the Tenth Annual Conference of the Cognitive Science Society*, Hillsdale, NJ: Lawrence Erlbaum, pp. 680–7.

Pazzani, M. J. and Dyer, M. G. (1987) A comparison of concept identification in human learning and network learning with the generalized delta rule, *Proceedings of the 10th International Joint Conference on Artificial Intelligence* (IJCAI-87).

Peters, S., Shapiro, S. C., and Rapaport, W. J. (1988) Flexible natural language processing and Roschian category theory, *Proceedings of the Tenth Annual Conference of the Cognitive Science Society*, Hillsdale, NJ: Lawrence Erlbaum, pp. 125–31.

Piaget, J. (1952) *The Origins of Intelligence in Children*, New York: International Universities Press.

Pinker, S. and Prince, A. (1988) On language and connectionism: Analysis of a parallel distributed processing model of language acquisition, *Cognition*, 28, 73–193.

Pitts, W. and McCulloch, W. S. (1947) How we know universals: the perception of auditory and visual forms, *Bulletin of Mathematical Biophysics*, 9, 127–47. Reprinted in Anderson and Rosenfeld (1988), pp. 32–41.

Plunkett, K. and Marchman, V. (1989) Pattern association in a back propagation network: Implications for child language acquisition, Technical Report No. 8902, Center for Research in Language, University of California, San Diego, La Jolla, CA.

Posner, M. I. and Keele, S. W. (1968) On the genesis of abstract ideas, *Journal of Experimental Psychology*, 77, 353–63.

Putnam, H. (1975a) Philosophy and our mental life, in H. Putnam, (ed.) *Language, Mind, and Reality. Philosophical Papers of Hilary Putnam*, vol. 2, Cambridge: Cambridge University Press, pp. 291–303.

Putnam, H. (1975b) The meaning of "meaning," in H. Putnam (ed.) *Mind, Language, and Reality: Philosophical Papers of Hilary Putnam*, vol. 2, Cambridge: Cambridge University Press, pp. 215–71.

Pylyshyn, Z. W. (1981) The imagery debate: Analogue media versus tacit knowledge, *Psychological Review*, 88, 16–45.

Pylyshyn, Z. W. (1984) *Computation and Cognition: Toward a Foundation for Cognitive Science*, Cambridge, MA: MIT Press/Bradford Books.

Quillian, M. R. (1968) Semantic memory, in M. Minsky (ed.) *Semantic Information Processing*, Cambridge, MA: MIT Press, pp. 227–70.

Quine, W. V. (1969a) Natural kinds, in W. V. Quine, *Ontological Relativity and Other Essays*, New York: Columbia University Press, pp. 114–38.

Quine, W. V. (1969b) Epistemology naturalized, in W. V. Quine, *Ontological Relativity and Other Essays*, New York: Columbia University Press, pp. 69–90.

Raphael, B. (1968) SIR: A computer program for semantic information retrieval, in M. Minsky (ed.) *Semantic Information Processing*, Cambridge, MA: MIT Press, pp. 33–145.

Ratcliff, R. (1990) Connectionist models of recognition memory: Constraints imposed by learning and forgetting functions, *Psychological Review*, 97, 285–308.

Ratcliff, R. and McKoon, G. (1988) A retrieval theory of priming in memory, *Psychological Review*, 95, 385–408.

Reber, A. S. (1967) Implicit learning of artificial grammars, *Journal of Verbal Learning and Verbal Behavior*, 6, 855–63.

Reeke, G. N. and Edelman, G. M. (1988) Real brains and artificial intelligence, *Daedalus*, 117, 142–73.

Reich, P. A. (1976) The early acquisition of word meaning, *Journal of Child Language*, 3, 117–23.

Reichenbach, H. (1966) *The Rise of Scientific Philosophy*, Berkeley: University of California Press.

Reicher, G. M. (1969) Perceptual recognition as a function of meaningfulness of stimulus material, *Journal of Experimental Psychology*, 81, 274–80.

Richardson, R. C. (1979) Functionalism and reductionism, *Philosophy of Science*, 46, 533–58.

Rips, L. J., Shoben, E. J., and Smith, E. E. (1973) Semantic distance and the verification of semantic relations, *Journal of Verbal Learning and Verbal Behavior*, 12, 1–20.

Rock, I. (1983) *The Logic of Perception*, Cambridge, MA: MIT Press/Bradford Books.

Rorty, R. (1965) Mind–body identity, privacy, and categories, *The Review of Metaphysics*, 19, 24–54.

Rosch, E. (1973) Natural categories, *Cognitive Psychology*, 7, 328–50.

Rosch, E. (1975) Cognitive representations of semantic categories, *Journal of Experimental Psychology: General*, 104, 192–233.

Rosch, E. (1978) Principles of categorization, in E. Rosch and B. B. Lloyd (eds) *Cognition and Categorization*, Hillsdale, NJ: Lawrence Erlbaum, pp. 27–48.

Rosch, E. H. and Mervis, C. B. (1975) Family resemblances: Studies in the internal structure of categories, *Cognitive Psychology*, 7, 573–605.

Rosenblatt, F. (1958) The perceptron: A probabilistic model for information storage and organization in the brain, *Psychological Review*, 65, 368–408. Reprinted in Anderson and Rosenfeld (1988), pp. 92–114.

Rosenblatt, F. (1959) Two theorems of separability in the perceptron, in *Mechanisation of Thought Processes: Proceedings of a Symposium Held at th. National Physical Laboratory, November, 1958*, vol. 1, London: HMSO, pp. 421–56.

Rosenblatt, F. (1962) *The Principles of Neurodynamics*, New York: Spartan.

Rumelhart, D. E. (1975) Notes on a schema for stories, in D. G. Bobrow and A. M. Collins (eds) *Representation and Understanding*, New York: Academic Press.

Rumelhart, D. E. and Abrahamsen, A. A. (1973) A model for analogical reasoning, *Cognitive Psychology*, 5, 1–28.

Rumelhart, D. E. and McClelland, J. L. (1982) An interactive activation model of context effects in letter perception: Part 2. The contextual enhancement effect and some tests and extensions of the model, *Psychological Review*, 89, 60–94.

Rumelhart, D. E. and McClelland, J. L. (1985) Levels indeed! A response to Broadbent, *Journal of Experimental Psychology: General*, 114, 193–7.

Rumelhart, D. E. and McClelland, J. L. (1986a) On learning the past tense of English verbs, in McClelland, Rumelhart, and the PDP Research Group (1986), chapter 18.

Rumelhart, D. E. and McClelland, J. L. (1986b) PDP models and general issues in cognitive science, in Rumelhart, McClelland, and the PDP Research Group (1986), chapter 4.

Rumelhart, D. E. and Siple, P. (1974) Process of recognizing tachistoscopically presented words, *Psychological Review*, 81, 99–118.

Rumelhart, D. E. and Zipser, D. (1985) Feature discovery by competitive learning, *Cognitive Science*, 9, 75–112. Reprinted in Rumelhart and McClelland (1986), chapter 5.

Rumelhart, D. E., Hinton, G. E., and McClelland, J. L. (1986) A general framework for parallel distributed processing, in Rumelhart, McClelland, and the PDP Research Group (1986), chapter 2.

Rumelhart, D. E., Hinton, G. E., and Williams, R. J. (1986a) Learning internal representations by error propagation, in Rumelhart, McClelland, and the PDP Research Group (1986), chapter 8.

Rumelhart, D. E., Hinton, G. E., and Williams, R. J. (1986b) Learning representations by back-propagating errors, *Nature*, 323, 533–6.

Rumelhart, D. E., McClelland, J. L., and the PDP Research Group (1986) *Parallel Distributed Processing: Explorations in the Microstructure of Cognition*, vol. 1: *Foundations*, Cambridge, MA: MIT Press/Bradford Books.

Rumelhart, D. E., Smolensky, P., McClelland, J. L., and Hinton, G. E. (1986) Schemata and sequential thought processes in PDP models, in McClelland, Rumelhart, and the PDP Research Group (1986), chapter 14.

Ryle, G. (1949) *The Concept of Mind*, New York: Barnes & Noble.

Schank, R. C. (1982) *Dynamic Memory: A Theory of Reminding and Learning in Computers and People*, Cambridge: Cambridge University Press.

Schank, R. C. and Abelson, R. (1977) *Scripts, Plans, Goals, and Understanding*, Hillsdale, NJ: Lawrence Erlbaum.

Schneider, W. (1987) Connectionism: Is it a paradigm shift for psychology?, *Behavior Research Methods, Instruments, and Computers*, 19, 73–83.

Seidenberg, M. S. and McClelland, J. L. (1989) A distributed, developmental model of word recognition and naming, *Psychological Review*, 96, 523–68.

Sejnowski, T. J. and Rosenberg, C. R. (1986) NETtalk: a parallel network that learns to read aloud, Electrical Engineering and Computer Science Technical Report JHU/EECS-86/01, The Johns Hopkins University, Baltimore, MD. Reprinted in Anderson and Rosenfeld (1988), pp. 663–72.

Sejnowski, T. J. and Rosenberg, C. R. (1987) Parallel networks that learn to pronounce English text, *Complex Systems*, 1, 145–68.

Selfridge, O. G. (1959) Pandemonium: A paradigm for learning, in *Symposium on the Mechanization of Thought Processes*, London: HMSO.

Selfridge, O. G. and Neisser, U. (1960) Pattern recognition by machine, *Scientific American*, 203, 60–8.

Servan-Schreiber, D., Cleeremans, A., and McClelland, J. L. (1988) Encoding sequential structure in simple recurrent networks, Technical Report CMU-CS-88-183, Computer Science Department, Carnegie Mellon University, Pittsburgh, PA.

Shapere, D. (1964) The structure of scientific revolutions, *Philosophical Review*, 73, 383–94.

Shastri, L. (1988) A connectionist approach to knowledge representation and limited inference, *Cognitive Science*, 12, 331–92.

Shastri, L. and Ajjanagadde, V. (1989) A connectionist system for rule based reasoning with multi-placed predicates and variables, Technical Report MS-CIS-89-06, Linc Lab 141, Department of Computer and Information Science, University of Pennsylvania, Philadelphia, PA.

Shepard, R. N. (1989) Internal representation of universal regularities: A challenge for connectionism, in L. Nadel, L. A. Cooper, P. Culicover, and R. M. Harnish (eds) *Neural Connections, Mental Computation*, Cambridge, MA: MIT Press/Bradford Books, pp. 104–34.

Shepard, R. N., Hovland, C. I., and Jenkins, H. M. (1961) Learning and memorization of classifications, *Psychological Monographs*, 75, 1–42.

Shipley, E. F. (1988, June) Two types of hierarchies: Class inclusion hierarchies and kind hierarchies, Paper presented at the annual meeting of the Jean Piaget Society, Philadelphia, PA.

Siegler, R. S. (1976) Three aspects of cognitive development, *Cognitive Psychology*, 8, 481–520.

Simon, H. A. (1967) The logic of heuristic decision making, in N. Rescher (ed.) *The Logic of Decision and Action*, Pittsburgh, PA: University of Pittsburgh Press, pp. 1–20.

Skrzypek, J. and Hoffman, J. (1989) Visual recognition of script characters: Neural network architectures, Technical Report UCLA-MPL-TR-89-10, Machine Perception Laboratory, University of California, Los Angeles.

Slobin, D. I. (1971) On the learning of morphological rules. A reply to Palermo and Eberhart, in D. I. Slobin (ed.) *The Ontogenesis of Grammar: A Theoretical Symposium*, New York: Academic Press.

Smith, E. E. (1988) Concepts and thought, in R. J. Sternberg and E. E. Smith (eds) *The Psychology of Human Thought*, Cambridge: Cambridge University Press, pp. 19–49.

Smith, E. E. and Medin, D. L. (1981) *Categories and Concepts*, Cambridge, MA: Harvard University Press.

Smith, E. E., Shoben, E. J., and Rips, L. J. (1974). Structure and process in semantic memory: A featural model for semantic decision, *Psychological Review*, 81, 214–41.

Smolensky, P. (1986) Information processing in dynamic systems: Foundations of harmony theory, in Rumelhart, McClelland, and the PDP Research Group (1986), chapter 6.

Smolensky, P. (1987) The constituent structure of connectionist mental states:

A reply to Fodor and Pylyshyn, *The Southern Journal of Philosophy, Supplement*, 26, 137–61.

Smolensky, P. (1988) On the proper treatment of connectionism, *Behavioral and Brain Sciences*, 11, 1–74.

Stich, S. (1983) *From Folk Psychology to Cognitive Science*, Cambridge, MA: MIT Press.

Strohner, H. and Nelson, K. (1974) The young child's development of sentence comprehension: Influence of event probability, nonverbal context, syntactic form, and strategies, *Child Development*, 45, 564–76.

Suppes, P. (1969) Stimulus-response theory of finite automata, *Journal of Mathematical Psychology*, 6, 327–55.

Suppes, P. (1970) Probabilistic grammars for natural languages, *Synthese*, 22, 95–116. Reprinted in D. Davidson and G. Harman (eds) *Semantics of Natural Languages*, Dordrecht: Reidel.

Taraban, R. M., McDonald, J. L., and MacWhinney, B. (1989) Category learning in a connectionist model: Learning to decline the German definite article. In R. Corrigan (ed.) *Milwaukee Conference on Categorization*, Philadelphia: John Benjamins.

Taylor, W. (1956) Electrical simulation of some nervous system functional activities, in E. C. Cherry (ed.) *Information Theory*, London: Butterworths.

Thagard, P. (1988) *Computational Philosophy of Science*, Cambridge, MA: MIT Press/Bradford Books.

Thibadeau, R., Just, M. A., and Carpenter, P. A. (1982) A model of the time course and content of reading, *Cognitive Science*, 6, 157–204.

Touretzky, D. S. (1986) BoltzCONS: Reconciling connectionism with the recursive nature of stacks and trees. *Proceedings of the Eighth Annual Conference of the Cognitive Science Society*, London: Lawrence Erlbaum, pp. 522–30.

Touretzky, D. S. (in press) BoltzCONS: Dynamic symbol structures in a connectionist network: *Artificial Intelligence*.

Touretzky, D. S. and Derthick, M. A. (1987, Spring) Symbol structures in connectionist networks: Five properties and two architectures, Digest of papers: COMPCON Spring 87, Thirty-second IEEE Computer Society International Conference, February 23–27, Cathedral Hill Hotel, San Francisco, pp. 30–4.

Touretzky, D. S. and Hinton, G. E. (1988) A distributed connectionist production system, *Cognitive Science*, 12, 423–66.

Tversky, A. and Kahneman, D. (1982) Judgments of and by representativeness, in D. Kahneman, P. Slovic, and A. Tversky (eds) *Judgment under Uncertainty: Heuristics and Biases*, Cambridge: Cambridge University Press, pp. 84–98.

Ullman, M., Pinker, S., Hollander, M., Prince, A., and Rosen, T. J. (1989) Growth of regular and irregular vocabulary and the onset of overregularization, Paper presented at the 14th Annual Boston University Conference on Language Development, Boston, MA.

von der Malsburg, C. (1973) Self-organizing of orientation sensitive cells in the striate cortex, *Kybernetik*, 14, 85–100.

von Neumann, J. (1956) Probabilistic logics and the synthesis of reliable organisms from unreliable components, in C. E. Shannon and J. McCarthy (eds) *Automata Studies*, Princeton, NJ: Princeton University Press.

Vygotsky, L. S. (1962) *Thought and Language*, Cambridge, MA: MIT Press. (Originally published in Russian, 1934.)

Wasserman, P. D. (1989) *Neural Computing: Theory and Practice*. New York: Van Nostrand Reinhold.

Watson, J. B. (1930) *Behaviorism*, Chicago: University of Chicago Press.

Wertsch, J. V. (1985) *Vygotsky and the Social Formation of Mind*, Cambridge, MA: Harvard University Press.

Wheeler, D. D. (1970) Processes in word recognition, *Cognitive Psychology*, 1, 59–85.

Widrow, B. and Hoff, M. E. (1960) Adaptive switching circuits, *1960 IRE WESCON Convention Record*. New York: IRE, pp. 96–104. Reprinted in Anderson and Rosenfeld (1988), pp. 126–34.

Wimsatt, W. C. (1986) Developmental constraints, generative entrenchment, and the innate-acquired distinction, in W. Bechtel (ed.) *Integrating Scientific Disciplines*, Dordrecht: Martinus Nijhoff, pp. 105–208.

Winograd, S. and Cowan, J. (1963) *Reliable Computation in the Presence of Noise*, Cambridge, MA: MIT Press.

Wittgenstein, L. (1953) *Philosophical Investigations*, New York: Macmillan.

Zadeh, L.A. (1965) Fuzzy sets, *Information and Control*, 8, 338–53.

Zemel, R. S., Mozer, M. C., and Hinton, G. E. (1988) Traffic: A model of object recognition based on transformations of feature instances, in D. S. Touretzky, G. E. Hinton, and T. J. Sejnowski (eds) *Proceedings of the 1988 Connectionist Models Summer School*. San Mateo: Morgan Kaufmann.

Index

Note: Page reference in italics indicate tables and figures.

Index by Meg Davies

WITHDRAWN

KELLY LIBRARY
Emory & Henry College
Emory, VA 24327

3 1836 0021